Special Education Programs

Publication Number 711
AMERICAN LECTURE SERIES®

A Monograph in
The BANNERSTONE DIVISION *of*
AMERICAN LECTURES IN SPECIAL EDUCATION

Edited by
MORRIS VAL JONES, Ph.D.
Speech and Hearing Center
Sacramento State College
Sacramento, California

Special Education Programs

WITHIN THE UNITED STATES

Edited by

MORRIS VAL JONES, Ph.D.

Speech and Hearing Center
Sacramento State College
Sacramento, California

Foreword by

Edith Green

Congresswoman from Oregon
United States House of Representatives

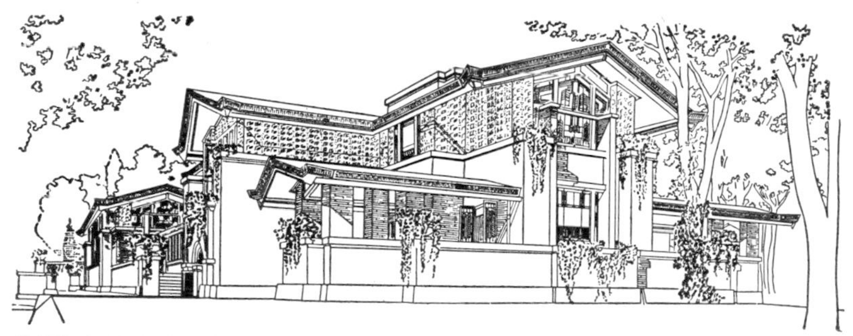

CHARLES C THOMAS · PUBLISHER
Springfield · Illinois · U.S.A.

Published and Distributed Throughout the World by
CHARLES C THOMAS • PUBLISHER
BANNERSTONE HOUSE
301-327 East Lawrence Avenue, Springfield, Illinois, U.S.A.
NATCHEZ PLANTATION HOUSE
735 North Atlantic Boulevard, Fort Lauderdale, Florida, U.S.A.

Library of Congress Catalog Card Number: 68-13763

Printed in the United States of America
C-1

CONTRIBUTORS

MRS. ELLA T. ALLAN, M.A. (San Francisco State College) has worked for twenty years in special education in the areas of the physically handicapped and the mentally retarded, serving as a speech therapist, teacher and administrator. She is now principal of two county office operated schools for orthopedically handicapped, including the cerebral palsied, in San Mateo County, California. She is active in several organizations including the California State Federation of the Council for Exceptional Children, the California Administrators of Special Education, and the National Rehabilitation Association.

ALBERT W. ATWOOD, L.H.D. (Amherst College) graduated from Fredonia New York State University in 1899 and from Amherst College in 1903. He received honorary M.A. degrees from Amherst and Princeton, an L.L.D. Degree from Gallaudet College and an L.H.D. Degree from Amherst. He has written hundreds of articles for the *Saturday Evening Post,* the *National Geographic Magazine* and has published ten books. He has been president of the Board of Trustees for the District of Columbia Public Library for more than thirty years, and Chairman of the Board at Gallaudet College for more than twenty years.

RUTH E. BENDER, Ph.D. (Western Reserve University) also received a diploma from Pestalozzi-Froebel Teachers College and special training at the Western Pennsylvania School for the Deaf and at the National College of Education. She is now Assistant Clinical Professor at Western Reserve University and Director in charge of the Preschool Auditory Program at the Cleveland Hearing and Speech Center. She has published many articles and has helped to pioneer the binaural hearing aid techniques for children.

CLAYTON L. BENNETT, Ph.D. (University of Southern California) is presently Special Education Coordinator, Department of Education, at San Diego County, California. He was formerly Associate Professor and Director, Speech and Hearing Clinic, Auburn University and Associate Director, Superior Student Project, North Central Association of Colleges and Secondary Schools. Dr. Bennett is currently writing and lecturing in Special Education, Speech Pathology and Psychology, and conducting teacher workshops concerned with reading disability.

RICHARD G. BRILL, Ed.D. (Rutgers University) has been Superintendent of the California School for the Deaf, Riverside, since it opened in 1951. Before that he was Principal of the Virginia School for the Deaf in Staunton, Principal of the Day School for the Deaf in Newark, New Jersey, and Assistant Professor of Education at the University of Illinois. He has served as President of the American Instructors of the Deaf and the Council on Education of the Deaf, and he has been a member of several advisory committees for the United States Department of Health, Education and Welfare.

RICHARD G. CANNICOTT, Ph.D. (University of Iowa) is currently Director of Associated Clinics and Associate Professor of Psychology at the California State College at Los Angeles. He formerly held a joint appointment as Director, Department of Psychology at Central State Griffin Memorial Hospital and Assistant Professor of Psychology at the University of Oklahoma. He has also served as Psychological Consultant and Acting Director of Psychological Services in the Oklahoma State Department of Mental Health.

FRANCIS W. DOYLE, Ph.D. (College of the Pacific) is Deputy Superintendent and Chief of the Division of Special Schools and Services of the California State Department of Education. He has taught exceptional children in private, state residential and public day schools. He has served as Director of Special Education for the Oakland public schools. Dr. Doyle is a former President of the Council for Exceptional Children and has played a prominent role in the development of California's special education legislation.

JON EISENSON, Ph.D. (Columbia University) is Professor of Speech Pathology and Audiology and Director of the Institute for Childhood Aphasia, Speech and Hearing Sciences Section of the Division of Otolaryngology of the Department of Surgery, Stanford University. He is a Fellow in the American Speech and Hearing Association, the American Psychological Association, and the American Association for the Advancement of Science. He is a Consultant in Speech Pathology, Central Office of the Veterans Administration, and in Clinical Psychology, Regional Office of the Veterans Administration. He is a member of the subcommittee on Human Communication and Its Disorders, National Institute of Neurological Disorders and Blindness. He is also chairman, Special Education Advisory Committee and a member of the Medical and Scientific Committee of the United Cerebral Palsy Association.

EDWARD L. FRENCH, Ph.D. (Ursinus College, University of Pennsylvania) is President and Director of the Devereux Foundation, headquartered in Devon, Pennsylvania. He is also President of the Clinical Biochemistry and Behavioral Research Institute, a trustee of the National Association of Private Psychiatric Hospitals, a member of the Executive Committee of the American Psychological Association's Division of School Psychologists, a member of the Council of Representatives of the American Psychological Association, and a Fellow of numerous professional societies. He is a frequent contributor to professional books and journals.

MARIANNE FROSTIG, Ph.D. (University of Southern California) is founder and Executive Director of the Marianne Frostig Center of Educational Therapy in Los Angeles, and Clinical Professor of Education at the University of Southern California. Her research interests include the evaluation of developmental abilities; the relationship of various psychological functions to school learning and adjustment; the nature and evaluation of therapeutic processes with emotionally disturbed children; and the construction and assessment of special training methods based on developmental evaluation.

EDITH GREEN, B.S. (University of Oregon) pursued graduate work at Stanford University and became a teacher in the elementary and secondary schools of Oregon. She also served as Director of Public Relations for the Oregon Education Association. In 1954 she was elected to the 84th Congress of the United States and has been reelected to each succeeding Congress. She is chairman of the Special Subcommittee on Education and Labor of the United States House of Representatives. Congresswoman Green has received eighteen honorary doctorate degrees for her contributions to education, including Yale University, Georgetown University, Linfield College (Oregon), Gonzaga College, Oberlin College, Seattle University, Boston College, Reed College and Goucher College.

LEROY F. GREENE, A.B. (Purdue University), a graduate in civil engineering, is serving his third term as representative of the Third Assembly District, the eastern half of

Sacramento County. He is Chairman of the Assembly Education Committee, a member of the Assembly Committees on Ways and Means and Governmental Efficiency and Economy. He is also one of four members on the State Allocation Board which apportions millions annually to impoverished school districts. In 1964-1966 he served as Chairman of the Assembly Special Education Subcommittee which did an in-depth analysis of education programs for handicapped and exceptional children from which a number of proposed improvements resulted.

NORRIS G. HARING, E.D. (Syracuse University) is currently Professor of Education, Lecturer in Pediatrics, and Director of the Experimental Education Unit of Mental Retardation and Child Development Center at the University of Washington. He has been Coordinator of Special Education in Arlington County, Virginia, and Educational Director of the Children's Rehabilitation Unit of the University of Kansas Medical Center. Currently he is an associate editor of *Exceptional Children,* a consultant to the United States Bureau of Handicapped Children and Youth, and chairman of the Educational Services Committee of the National Project for Children with Minimal Brain Dysfunction.

ALICE H. HAYDEN, Ph.D. (Purdue University) is Professor of Education and Associate Director of the Experimental Education Unit of the Mental Retardation and Child Development Center at the University of Washington. She has served the university on various committees, as Director of Graduate Studies in Education and Director of the Pilot School for Neurologically Impaired Children. She has served on the governor's Inter-Agency Subcommittee on Mental Retardation and was Co-chairman of the state Task Force on Manpower Training, Mental Retardation for the Mental Retardation Planning Committee.

WILLIAM S. HERBIG, A.B. (University of California) has been working in the area of special education for nineteen years and is currently administrator of county office operated programs for physically handicapped, trainable mentally retarded, dysphasic children and juvenile facilities in San Mateo County, California. He has done graduate work at the University of California and at San Francisco State College. He is active in many organizations including the California Administrators of Special Education, the California State Federation of the Council for Exceptional Children and others.

EDMUND M. HORAN, Ed.D. (Teachers College, Columbia University) is a Supervisor for the Bureau for Children with Retarded Mental Development in the New York City Public School System. He has written several educational television scripts for the Office of Special Education and Pupil Personnel Services. He also teaches courses in the area of mental retardation at Hunter College and the College of the City of New York.

DAVID HORNE, B.A. (University of California at Los Angeles) has been a member of the staff of the Frostig Center since graduating from UCLA. He was trained at the center as a research therapist with emotionally disturbed children. He has helped in the preparation of many of the center's publications, and has been responsible for the production of two films at the center—*The World Outside,* a longitudinal study of therapy with severely disturbed children, and *Visual Perception and Failure to Learn.*

MORRIS VAL JONES, Ph.D. (Stanford University) is a clinical supervisor in the Speech and Hearing Center, Sacramento State College, California. He has been a speech and hearing therapist in the public schools and at the School for Cerebral Palsied Children,

Northern California, in San Francisco. His writings include articles in professional journals and two books. He is active in the American Speech and Hearing Association and the Council for Exceptional Children.

RHODA KELLOGG, M.A. (Columbia University) has been working with the Golden Gate Kindergarten Association since 1945 and now is the Executive Director of the new Phoebe A. Hearst Preschool Learning Center. She has studied children's art for twenty years and has written extensively on their art. She has lectured in many foreign countries and her books are known throughout the world. She is listed in *Who's Who of American Woman.*

LEOPOLD LIPPMAN, B.S.S. (City College of New York) was executive secretary of the Study Commission on Mental Retardation when the Commission was developing California's comprehensive state plan for the mentally retarded. He became coordinator of mental retardation programs, Health and Welfare Agency, when the position was established in 1965. He also has served as executive director of the Washington Association for Retarded Children. He is president-elect of the Sacramento Chapter of the Council for Exceptional Children, and is a member of several other organizations, including the American Association on Mental Deficiency, the National Association of Social Workers and the National Rehabilitation Association.

JOSEPH C. MARX, M.A. (Teachers' College, Columbia University) has been serving the areas of the deaf, cerebral palsied, mentally retarded and dysphasic programs as a teacher, director and superintendent of a residential facility. He is currently principal of two county office operated schools for trainable mentally retarded and director of a program for dysphasic children in San Mateo County, California.

FREEMAN E. McCONNELL, Ph.D. (Northwestern University) is Director of the Bill Wilkerson Hearing and Speech Center and has developed and planned a clinical program and a physical facility which is considered one of the best in the nation. He is also Professor and Chairman of the Division of Audiology and Speech Pathology at Vanderbilt University and Professor of Special Education at George Peabody School for Teachers. He is a frequent contributor to the professional literature in speech and hearing.

RICHARD OUTLAND, M.A. (Ohio State University) is Consultant in the Education of Physically Handicapped Children in the Bureau for Physically Exceptional Children, California State Department of Education. Previously, he was Associate Professor of Education and Coordinator of Special Education at San Jose State College; Director of Special Education, Stanislaus County Schools, Modesto, California; and teacher of physically and mentally handicapped children in the public schools of Ohio. Mr. Outland has served on the summer faculties in special education at the University of the Pacific, University of Oregon, San Francisco State College and Fresno State College.

LAURA LEHTINEN ROGAN, Ph.D. (Northwestern University) is co-founder, with Dr. Alfred A. Strauss and Mrs. Marie C. Strauss, of The Cove Schools and continues to function as its Clinical Director. She is also a consultant to the Winnetka Public Schools' special learning disorders program and the Evanston Hospital Evaluation Center for Learning Problems. In addition to various other publications she is co-author with Dr. Strauss of Volume I of *Psychopathology and Education of the Brain-Injured Child,* and a contributor to Volume II. She collaborated in the authorship of *The Other Child* (a book for parents) by Richard Lewis and Dr. Strauss.

EDWARD RUDIN, M.D. (Temple University) is Director of the Sutter Diagnostic and Treatment Center in Sacramento, California. He has been Chief Psychiatrist and Director of the Riverside State Mental Hygiene Clinic, Chief Administrator of California's Community Mental Health Services Act, and Deputy Director of the California Department of Mental Hygiene. He is also psychiatric consultant to the National Institute of Mental Health, the Sacramento Area Family Service Agency, and the Children's Home Society of Sacramento. Dr. Rudin is a Fellow of the American Psychiatric Association and Fellow of the American Public Health Association.

BERT W. SCHMICKEL (Glassboro State College, N. J.) is Deputy Commissioner of Health, Office of Mental Retardation, Connecticut State Department of Health. He is responsible for many progressive movements in the nation, such as providing both residential and day care services to retarded children and adults, enabling them to remain close to their homes. He has been Superintendent of the Southbury Training School, teacher at the State Colony for Retarded Boys in Lisbon, New Jersey and Supervisor of Special Education in Bridgeton, New Jersey. He was also Assistant Superintendent of the Training School in Vineland, New Jersey. He has served in many organizations and has been given recognition throughout the world.

DELWYN G. SCHUBERT, Ph.D. (Northwestern University) is a professor at California State College at Los Angeles where he teaches professional and therapeutic courses in reading. He is the author of over seventy professional articles and four books. He is also the author of a number of sound filmstrips. He is a veteran of more than three hundred institutes and workshops for elementary and secondary teachers throughout California and has served as a lecturer or consultant in the states of Colorado, Kansas, Michigan, and Washington and in Canada.

MRS. SPENCER TRACY, D.Sc. (Northwestern University) is founder, Director-in-charge, and President of the Board of Directors of the John Tracy Clinic. Because of her dedication to the field of deafness and her leadership in parent-preschool education, she has received many honors, including degrees from Northwestern University, the University of Southern California, Lake Erie College, MacMurray College and Gallaudet College. She has served on various government committees, and is a member of the Honorary Board of the Alexander Graham Bell Association for the Deaf, and an honorary member of the American Orthopsychiatric Association, Incorporated.

ETHEL M. UMPHREY was a staff writer in the Public Relations Department of the Institute of Logopedics. She was primarily engaged in the preparation of Public Education materials and general public information writing on the Institute and the chapter presented was oriented to information concerning the Institute as a whole and not as a professional interpretation of its work. As a public information writer, she was fluent in translating to the public the unique philosophy of the late Dr. Martin F. Palmer, founder and director of the Institute. She died from injuries suffered in an auto accident in the summer of 1966.

EDWARD J. WATERHOUSE, A.B. (Cantab) has been Director of the Perkins School since 1951. He graduated from Queens' College, Cambridge University. He taught at Landon School for Boys, Washington, D. C. and then joined the Faculty of Perkins School for the Blind as a teacher of Mathematics, Physics and English. He was manager of Howe Press, Chairman of the Executive Committee of International Conference of

Educators of Blind Youth, and is now Chairman of the International Committee on Education of Deaf-Blind Children.

ERNEST P. WILLENBERG, Ed.D. (University of Oklahoma) is currently Director of Special Education for the Los Angeles City Schools. He is also a part-time professor of Special Education at California State College at Los Angeles. He was formerly Chief, Bureau of Special Education, California State Department of Education. He was a member of President Kennedy's Panel on Mental Retardation, the Study Commission on Mental Retardation (California), Governor Brown's Committee on Mental Health, Steering Committee, for Los Angeles County Study Project on Mental Retardation and many other such committees. He has just completed his term as President of the National Council for Exceptional Children.

To

my wife Patricia,
who is a Special Education teacher

FOREWORD

IT has been said, "When the tide rolls in, all boats rise." This is true not only for the tides of the great oceans, but also for the tides of progress and education that sweep across the continents of the modern world. Programs for exceptional children have risen during the last ten years as the tide of interest in these exceptional children has swept across our shores.

It has been an indictment of our society that in an age when we have learned to open cans electrically; to broadcast voices and pictures across oceans and continents, even to bounce them from a tiny satellite hurtling through space; to journey below the polar ice; to hurl man, borne by the most powerful engines known to man, literally toward the stars—that while doing all these things—we have failed to give equal priority to the problems of the world's handicapped people.

Over the great temple at Delphi, at the time of the ancient Greeks, was carved the maxim, "Know thyself." For the first time in the more than 2,000 years since that command was given, science is beginning to open the paths to knowledge of ourselves—to knowledge of the mechanisms of the mind and body. We are working, not just to understand the universe around us, but the world within us; not just the matter which surrounds us, but the nature of our own organism; not the forces which affect life, but life itself.

Wherever scientists are laboring to understand the human mind and the human body, wherever they seek to understand fundamental life processes, their work will have consequences for the millions of exceptional youth of today. They will bring new hope and meaning to our work.

Two Wisconsin doctors have discovered another hereditary cause of mental retardation, the lack of a certain enzyme in the blood. This may be comparable to the discovery of the cause of PKU. We now know that PKU can be controlled by regulating the diet of infants. Because of a relatively simple and inexpensive test, over 1,200 of the 126,000 mentally retarded infants born yearly could be saved from needless condemnation to mental retardation. In addition to the saving of heartache to the families involved—the great humanitarian aspects—this would be a savings of $126 million by the end of the lifetimes of those who are born mentally retarded in any one year.

But the twentieth century must have a commitment not just to science—not just to medicine and psychology—but to education. North Carolina's governor, Charles Brantley Aycock, at the start of this century set forth the theme for this commitment when he said that we must seek to give every child the opportunity ". . . to burgeon out the best that is within him." To honor this twentieth century commitment we were obligated to provide education for the blind, and we have begun to provide it. We were obligated to provide education for the deaf, and we have also begun that.

Now we are called upon to provide education for the speech impaired, the visually handicapped, the crippled, the emotionally disturbed and others. Pioneering efforts in education are being made that will work for the benefit of all. On us, and on others with the same commitment, lies the responsibility for assuring that future generations will have cause to bless—and not curse—the light that is now being shed on the nature of man.

Our late President, John Kennedy, supported a new standard of excellence in education matched by the fullest possible access to educational opportunities, enabling each citizen to develop his talents to the maximum possible extent.

My Special Subcommittee on Education heard this testimony:

"Approximately six million American children of school age have extreme or unusual mental, emotional, social or physical conditions. These conditions range from mental retardation to unusual intellectual brilliance; and from blindness and deafness to social maladjustment or emotional disturbance. These exceptional children have a common need. If they are to have a full and equal opportunity to an education commensurate with their ability they must have special educational help."

The Division of Handicapped Children and Youth of the Department of Health, Education, and Welfare recently published figures on the number of children still needing special educational services. Seventy-five per cent of the six million handicapped children, or 4,500,000, need and are not receiving special help. Of this number 48,600 are visually handicapped; 243,000 are hard of hearing; 37,050 are deaf; 1,701,000 are speech impaired; 243,000 are crippled or have similar health disorders; 972,000 are emotionally disturbed; 1,117,800 are mentally retarded, and 486,000 have some other major learning disability.

These figures do not include the thousands of children who have been handicapped by extreme poverty, who have suffered cultural and educational deprivation to the point that special education must be provided at the earliest possible age.

The needs of these children are great. The United States Office of Education has expenditures of $16,500,000 that go into special education for this fiscal year. Of that $16,500,000, $2 million goes into research.

It is estimated that it costs twice as much to educate a handicapped child in a special education class as it does to educate an average child in a public elementary or secondary school.

On January 29, 1963, in his message on a proposed program for education,

President Kennedy said, "For the nation, increasing the quality and availability of education is vital to both our national security and our domestic well-being. A free nation can rise no higher than the standard of excellence set in its schools and colleges. Ignorance and illiteracy, unskilled workers and school dropouts—these and other failures of our educational system breed failures in our social and economic system: delinquency, unemployment, chronic dependence, a waste of human resources, a loss of productive power and purchasing power, and an increase in tax-supported benefits."

He then went on to outline the place the Federal government has filled in regard to education in the last several decades. Then he said, "But all this has not been enough. And the Federal government—despite increasing recognition of education as a nationwide challenge, and despite the increased financial difficulties encountered by states, communities, and private institutions in carrying the burden—has clearly not met its responsibilities in education. It has not offered sufficient help to our present educational system to meet its inadequacies and overcome its obstacles."

It is apparent that within the last few years, especially during the Eighty-eighth Congress, programs have been initiated which open new doors for exceptional children. Although some of the laws were not written specifically for the area of special education they do, in many instances, offer opportunities to be explored.

Those of us in the national legislature who realize the significance and need for greater educational opportunities for all will continue to work for new and expanded programs which will benefit all exceptional children, and I plead with each individual who is concerned about a special handicap to extend that concern to all handicaps. I plead for an end to legislative persuasion for one at the expense of all others. Cooperative effort must be the legislative goal for all organizations.

Conspicuous by its absence in any Federal legislation benefitting exceptional children is the consideration for the gifted child. His needs in education are special needs. Greater efforts in this area, in my judgment, are much needed.

The progress that is being made is encouraging. The climate in the Congress with regard to education, and especially special education, has greatly improved in the last decade. Ten years ago, while appropriating nearly $50 billion for defense without an objection, thirty-one amendments were offered to cut the less than $1 billion budget for health and education.

Legislation is being written and passed now which deals directly with areas such as mental retardation, vocational education, guidance, counseling and testing, teachers of the handicapped, special teaching aids, manpower development and retraining, poverty and economic opportunity, education for the blind, the deaf.

An area of great importance and need is that of socioeconomic exceptionality. A child of three from a slum who has never seen a book, who has never travelled beyond his immediate and narrow geographical area—a child whose parents do not or cannot communicate with him—surely such a child is just as exceptional as a child who is mentally retarded. This child is culturally and educationally retarded and has a desperate need for special education—for compensatory education. This, we now know, must start at age three or four.

The American poet, Vachel Lindsay, wrote a few lines in which he powerfully stated the plight of the poor, the impoverished, and the oppressed.

Let not young souls be smothered out before
They do quaint deeds and fully flaunt their pride.
It is the world's one crime its babes grow dull,
Its poor are ox-like, limp and leaden-eyed.
Not that they starve, but starve so dreamlessly,
Not that they sow, but that they seldom reap,
Not that they serve, but have no gods to serve,
Not that they die, but that they die like sheep.

America must see that her "young souls," whether they are blind, or deaf, or crippled, or emotionally disturbed, or mentally retarded, or speech impaired, or vision impaired, or socially starved, or educationally deprived, or economically impoverished, are *not* smothered out. These children must be free to dream, to reap, to serve, and to live and die in dignity and opportunity—and this they must have through education suited to their needs.

EDITH GREEN
Congresswoman from Oregon
United States House of Representatives

LEGISLATION FOR SPECIAL EDUCATION

NOT too many years ago, virtually all assistance offered those impaired of mind or body came from private sources, the money being furnished on a volunteer basis from people with compassion and the desire to help those less fortunate than themselves.

In today's world, government plays a leading role in assisting those with physical or mental abnormalities. The State of California has moved very rapidly in recent years in its efforts on behalf of those crippled in mind or body.

In the field of special education, we have mandated educational programs in numerous categories of physical or mental abnormality. The state has assumed the excess cost of educating these youngsters.

Existing programs, while providing a good start, are not sufficient. A number of improvements will be considered by the 1967 legislature demonstrating the state's continuing concern in this area.

One proposal would vest greater authority for local special education in the hands of county school superintendents in order that the combined efforts of all school districts within a county may be coordinated so that no child is without equal opportunity for an education suited to his needs. Other legislation would establish laboratory classes in conjunction with state teacher training colleges, in order that our prospective teachers meet, in classroom situations, the youngsters they will eventually face in the field.

We have made a reasonable beginning, but we are not willing to pause in our efforts on behalf of the physically handicapped or mentally retarded in the State of California.

ASSEMBLYMAN LEROY GREENE
California Legislature

PREFACE

THIS is the first of two volumes about special education programs. The second, some years hence, will concern itself with developments abroad.

Numerous men and women, many of them professionally trained, have given their life's blood to build special education facilities throughout the United States. This book presents selected success stories of the fruits of their labor. Porter Sargent has listed more than two thousand facilities for handicapped children in his 1965 edition of *Directory for Exceptional Children*. Here we have only twenty-two but they may be considered among the best.

When I contacted potential authors for this collection, naturally I contacted those whom I knew professionally and asked their advice about additional contributors. Since I have worked for the greater part of my special education career in California, I knew more people and places in the West and the book reflects this orientation. Some directors of special education programs whom I sought as writers were unable to make a commitment for authorship within the time limit set for submission of manuscripts.

The finished product, although somewhat modified from the original concept, meets with my enthusiastic endorsement. We hope the information herein will answer some questions about developing and maintaining special education programs which arise when groups or individuals undertake such activities.

MORRIS VAL JONES

CONTENTS

PART III

CITY, COUNTY, AND STATE PROGRAMS IN SPECIAL EDUCATION

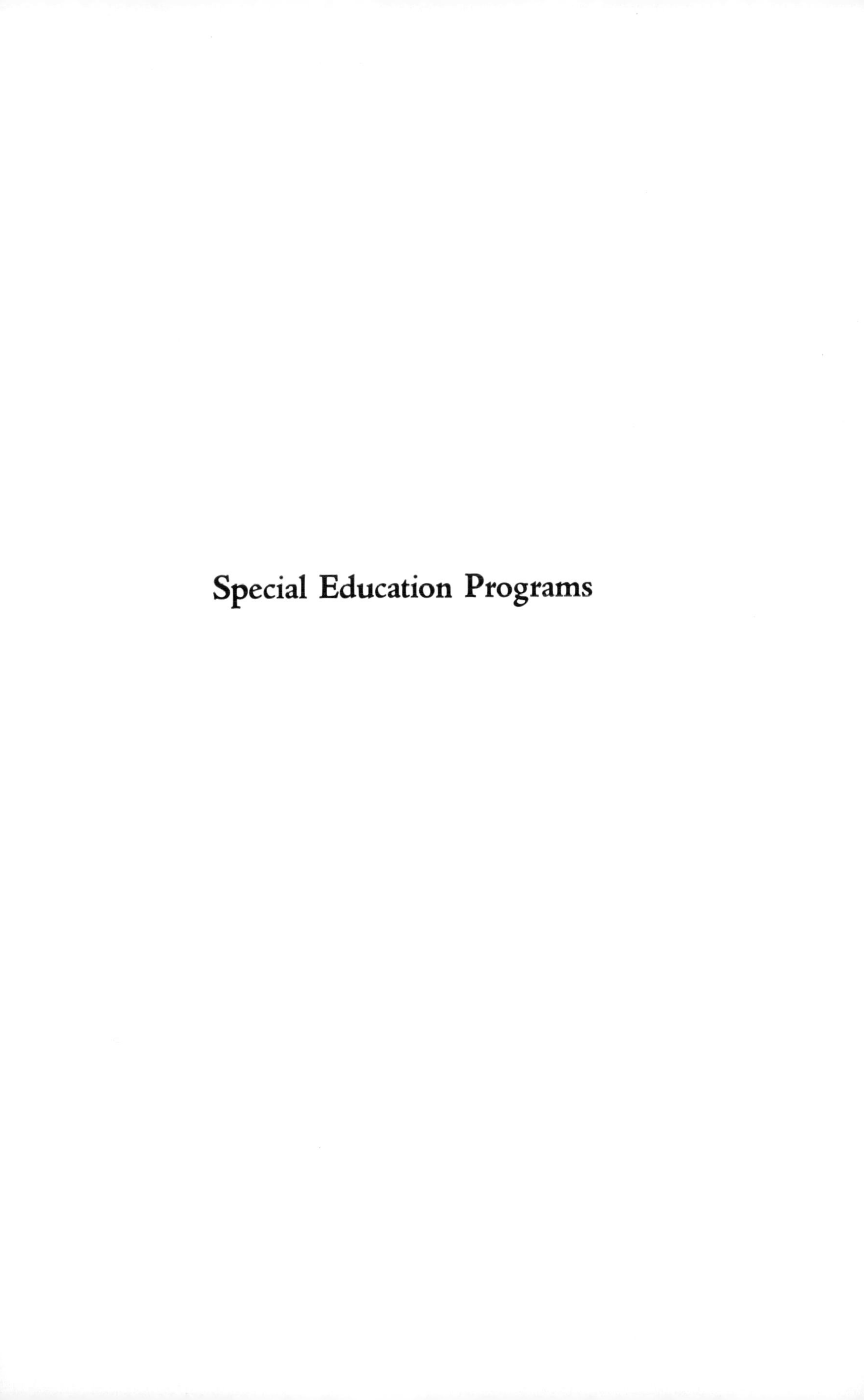

Special Education Programs

Cooperation starts early at the Bill Wilkerson Hearing and Speech Center in Nashville, Tennessee.

Part I

DIAGNOSTIC CENTERS AND SPECIAL SCHOOLS

FIGURE I-1. Perception of sizes and shapes is part of the curriculum at the Frostig School of Educational Therapy in Los Angeles, California.

FIGURE I-2. Dr. Marianne Frostig helps children with body image problems in the Frostig School of Educational Therapy in Los Angeles, California.

FIGURE I-3. Paleontology comes under discussion at the Frostig School of Educational Therapy in Los Angeles, California.

FIGURE I-4. "Tea Time" forms the basis for a language building activity at the School for Cerebral Palsied Children in San Francisco, California.

FIGURE I-5. Dictionary study is stressed at the School for Cerebral Palsied Children in San Francisco, California.

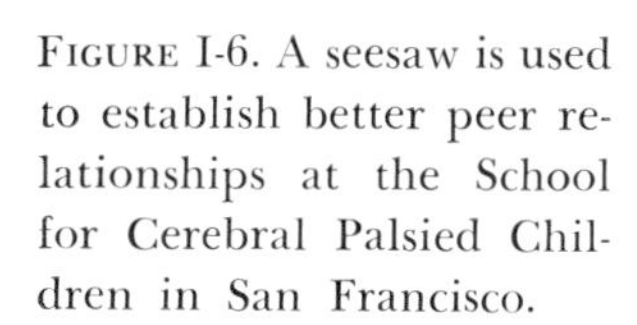

FIGURE I-6. A seesaw is used to establish better peer relationships at the School for Cerebral Palsied Children in San Francisco.

FIGURES I-7 AND 8. Residences for children should be as comfortable and homelike as possible. The larger building pictured above serves as a home for emotionally disturbed teen-age girls. The smaller building is a "halfway house" for ten older boys whose treatment program is vocationally oriented. (Devereux Schools)

FIGURE I-9. The implementation of a residential therapy program revolves around interpersonal relations between staff and child. This is as true on the playing field or in the woodshop *(above)* as it is in a psychotherapy session or an academic classroom. (Devereux Schools)

FIGURE I-10. The development of vocationally useful skills is an important part of the treatment process for many older students. A meaningful work program, such as that provided by Devereux Industries *(above)*, is especially important for rehabilitable mentally retarded adolescents and young adults. (Devereux Schools)

Chapter 1

INSTITUTE FOR CHILDHOOD APHASIA

JON EISENSON

THE Institute for Childhood Aphasia (ICA) was established as a unit of the Division of Speech Pathology and Audiology, School of Medicine, Stanford University, in September 1962. The institute was initially funded by a grant from the Scottish Rite Foundation of California and, for the first two years, was almost entirely supported by Scottish Rite funds. At this time a major portion of financial support continues to come from this source, but additional funds have come from several government agencies including the Office of Education, the Children's Bureau, the National Institute for Neurological Diseases and Blindness, and the Chronic and Sensory Diseases Branch of the United States Public Health Service. In September of 1965 a sizable grant from the United Cerebral Palsy Foundation enabled us to institute and expand a three-year research program to establish differential criteria for nonverbal children.

Objectives

The overall objectives of the ICA may be summarized as follows:

1. To establish criteria for behavioral and linguistic impairments in children with congenital or early acquired (before age two) brain damage. Such criteria, it is hoped, will permit differential diagnoses for nonverbal or severely linguistically retarded children who may be perceptually handicapped (developmentally aphasic) from those who are primarily mentally retarded, severely impaired in hearing, or emotionally (affectively) involved (primary autism or childhood schizophrenia).
2. To provide opportunity for language clinicians, speech therapists and other professional persons concerned with problems of language retardation to develop specific and differential techniques for developing language in brain damaged nonverbal children.
3. To provide a laboratory for experimentation with learning approaches which directly or indirectly may help to establish cognitive functioning in aphasic children.
4. To provide diagnostic evaluations and recommendations as to appropriate therapy and training for children referred to ICA but who cannot be enrolled for long-term treatment. Such diagnostic evaluations may, when indicated, include periods of from one to ten weeks of "diagnostic therapy."
5. To provide interested clinicians, graduate students and other professional persons with opportunities on a trainee, intern, resident, or fellowship basis to obtain experience with aphasic and other nonverbal children in the develop-

ment of diagnostic and therapeutic skills. Training of professional personnel is to be carried on through an apprenticeship relationship with one or more members of the ICA staff.

Staff

The initial staff of the ICA included a director, a pediatric coordinator (physician), a staff psychologist, a senior clinician (supervisor of clinical training) and two language clinicians. As of the present writing, the professional staff consists of the following persons:

Director	Jon Eisenson, Ph.D.
Associate Director	Joel Stark, Ph.D.
Pediatric Neurologist (Medical Coordinator)	Thomas Forrest, M.D.
Staff Psychologist	Sylvia Cohen, B.S.
Social Worker	Bernice Cohen, M.S.W.
Research Psychologist	Susan Singer, Ed.D.
Senior Supervisory Clinician	Robert H. Gottsleben, M.S.
Staff Language Clinicians	Jane Giddan, M.A.
	Teris Wright, M.A.
	Judith Johnson, M.A.

The director, associate director and senior clinician are also members of the faculty of the Speech and Hearing Sciences Section, Division of Otolaryngology, School of Medicine, Stanford University. Their respective ranks are professor, associate professor and instructor.

Roles of Professional Staff Personnel

The nature of the overall operation of the Institute for Childhood Aphasia may be appreciated by a description of the role of each member on what we consider a coordinated team approach to the assessment and treatment of the nonverbal child.

The director and associate director are jointly responsible for carrying out the objectives of the ICA. These responsibilities include financing; selection and supervision of personnel; the development of investigations and research proposals, as well as the supervision of the investigations, related to the work of the institute; liaison with agencies which support research programs, and liaison with the School of Medicine through the Section of Speech and Hearing Sciences. Both also participate in teaching of subject matter (academic courses) related to the work of the institute and to assessment and training of children in the institute.

The Pediatric Neurologist (Medical Coordinator)

As general functions, our pediatric neurologist wants to make his assessment of the child as would any pediatrician or neurologist who routinely and periodically examines a child for health status. He wants to observe the child's reflexes and his sensory and motor abilities. In brief, he wants to determine whether the child has the basic equipment for normal development and for learning what he is expected to learn in and out of school. The pediatric neurologist determines what specialized medical examinations are needed for the individual child and arranges for them through our medical center or through outside physicians.

More specifically, however, the pediatric neurologist wants to have directed questions from other professional persons who have contact with the child so that he can make directed and specialized observations during his own examination. Therefore, he wishes to be informed if a teacher or a clinician observes that a child has lapses of attention, or of memory, or suddenly loses contact with his environment. He wants to know about inconsistencies and liabilities of behavior, of hyperactivity or of hypoactivity, or of catastrophic reactions. He needs to be informed if any behavior has been observed by others that might constitute or resemble a seizure.

Our neurologist makes direct observations about motor difficulties, gross and fine. He observes tongue and hand movements for possible dyspraxic involvements. He listens to the child's vocalizations and, if possible, views the activity of the vocal bands for indication of nerve weakness or paralysis. He also observes inconsistent behavior and sudden extinction of responses as well as the child's ability to attend and to concentrate. All of these observations are correlated with his neurological findings and their implications for the child as to his ability and potential for learning.

Our neurologist, at staff conferences, explains the significance of EEG abnormalities and how these may relate to fluctuations in attention and to deviant behavior. Where indicated, he prescribes medication for control or modification of CNS dysfunctioning. He is also mindful that all concerned —the parents, the teachers and the language clinicians—must be informed of expected changes when medications are administered. Such changes may include temporary depressions in alertness and in the child's affective responses as well as in periods of nausea and dizziness. On the other hand, improvement may also be expected along these lines.

Our neurologist also emphasizes to all who are concerned that most neurological problems are *not fixed*. Many conditions are subject to change and improvement under treatment and with maturity.

The Staff Psychologist

The psychologist, through the use of direct and sophisticated observation, as well as through the use of selected standardized diagnostic instruments and test batteries, seeks to assess the child's abilities and liabilities, his assets and impairments, so that a picture of the child's mental, emotional and social functioning may be obtained The psychologist is concerned not only with present functionings but with potential for future functioning. In a very basic sense, the psychologist is engaged in an "extended neurological." The evaluation of a child's perceptual functioning provides information to the neurologist which may reinforce or set aside suspicion about possible neurological involvement. Sometimes, the psychologist's observation provides clues of a more subtle nature than those readily picked up by the neurologist in a routine examination.

The information and insights obtained by the psychologist provide one basis not only for a differential diagnosis but for training and educational procedures which are consonant with such a diagnosis.

At the ICA reassessments are routinely undertaken for all children who are accepted for training.

The Research Psychologist

The functions of the research psychologist are directly related to specific investigations carried on in the ICA. At the present time such functions include initial diagnostic assessment and reassessment, analysis of data produced by these assessments, and the interpretation of such data. The design and development of relevant investigations are additional appropriate functions. In terms of the overall long-term objective of the institute, the research psychologist is concerned with the identification of the cognitive impairments of nonverbal children. Such identification will be determined not only by describing the children as they are at the time of assessment but by developing training procedures as part of ongoing diagnostic therapy. So, the research psychologist needs to be involved with the training as well as diagnostic aspects of the work of the institute.

Psychiatric Social Worker

The psychiatric social worker is responsible for the nonmedical aspects of the initial interview with the parents. Ordinarily, such an interview seeks to obtain relevant information stated as far as possible in the parents own words about the way the parents view their child and, specifically, as to the nature of the child's problem which brought him to our institute. Information is obtained about the family background with emphasis on siblings and other relatives who may have had or who have similar or related language problems. Information about the child's social development is obtained through informal questioning, through the administration of formal inventories such as the Vineland Scale of Social Maturity, and the Doll Preschool Attainment Record.

The psychiatric social worker also obtains information about parental relationships to the child, to siblings and to one another. In addition, the financial status of the family is determined with a view toward deciding whether any need exists for financial assistance for expenses involved in assessment and therapy. The psychiatric social worker is also available for consultation with the parents should need for more than financial support be required. The usual function of assisting in the placement of a child with an appropriate educational or training agency is also assumed by our psychiatric social worker; so also are the usual duties of consultation with members of the family and the staff relative to problems within the family that influence the child's behavior and may be related to his language difficulties.

Senior Supervisory Clinician

The senior clinician serves in the dual roles of teaching member of the faculty and supervisor of the language clinicians of the institute. In the first capacity, he is directly responsible for the assignment and supervision of student clinicians and student interns, including those he assigns to himself. As a staff member, the senior clinician is responsible for the supervision of the staff clinicians in regard to their work with children who are enrolled for training.

The senior clinician also participates in the initial evaluations and reevaluations of each child by administering diagnostic learning materials for trial periods. Along with all other members of the ICA staff, he also participates in the staffing and the planning of training programs for children who are to be enrolled with us, as well as in outlining recommended programs of training for children who will go to other agencies after our assessments are completed.

The Staff Clinician

Each staff language clinician has dual teaching-training roles—the training of the child and, through an apprenticeship relationship, the training of the student clinician or intern. In accordance with the diagnosis or designation for each child determined during our institute staffing, the language clinician develops an individualized program of therapy. Records are kept of each child's progress in therapy.

Specifically, the language clinician is concerned with the training of the child, individually as well as in small groups, in the establishment of sensory-motor skills basic to language development and in the development of language skills *per se*. The language clinician is also directly responsible for the supervision of student interns. In addition, the language clinician consults with parents regarding techniques and skills that may be practiced and reinforced in the home environment. For those children who attend schools, or other educational agencies, the language clinician consults with teachers and supervisors so that training programs may be maximally coordinated. Each language clinician also serves as a member of the diagnostic team and participates in all staffings.

According to interest, inclination and time, our language clinicians are encouraged to participate in ongoing research. Two of our clinicians are presently involved in the development of programmed teaching for perceptually impaired children.

Facilities

The Institute for Childhood Aphasia presently occupies a building at 1691 El Camino, Palo Alto, California. This building is directly opposite the main part of the Stanford University campus. With funds provided by the California Scottish Rite Foundation, the building was renovated and modified with the installation of four one-way vision areas. Funds were also provided for office equipment and for instruments used in training.

The present quarters are occupied on a short term lease basis. We are looking forward to moving the institute to new quarters which we hope to obtain and occupy on a long term or "permanent" basis. New quarters will be developed so that the construction will reflect the purposes of the institute. It is hoped that we will have specialized areas for observation of diagnoses and training for medical evaluation, for operant conditioning, for individual and small group therapy, and a classroom for instruction of students, as well as conference rooms for staffing. We are also looking forward to inside and outside work-play areas for our children. We also hope to have at least one room set aside for small conferences and coffee breaks. We plan not to overlook the need for a well-designed waiting room in which parents and visitors can learn while they wait, and for appropriately equipped areas for our clerical staff.

Financing

As has been indicated in the opening paragraph, a large portion of the financial support for the ICA continues to come from the California Scottish Rite Foundation. Essentially, these funds cover the rental of facilities, salaries for clerical personnel, and for part of the salaries of the professional staff. Additional funding, for the most part directly related to ongoing research and special investigations, comes from several government agencies, including the Children's Bureau and the Office of Education. The Neurological and Sensory Disease Service Program of the United States Public Health Service is presently funding functions directly related to the patient training services of the institute. The United Cerebral Palsy Foundation is funding a three-year research project (1965-1968) that we hope will enable us to establish differential criteria for nonverbal children. A three year clinical research grant from the National Institute of Neurological Diseases and Blindness became effective September 1, 1967.

An additional but relatively small proportion of our income is obtained through fees for diagnoses and training. It is our intention to keep these fees as low as possible and considerably below actual cost, so that no child will be denied an opportunity for assessment or training because of financial limitation on the part of the parent.

Intake and Training Schedule

Our intake schedule includes one new diagnostic assessment and one re-evaluation a week. During the academic year 1967-1968, ninety-eight such assessments were completed. Our training case load averages fifteen children per ten-week period. (Stanford University academic quarter) with a somewhat greater case load during summer quarters (twenty-two during the summer of 1967). Children in training are seen from three to five times a week, and from one to three hours a day, depending upon the specific needs of the child and the program to which he has been assigned. With few exceptions, most children who receive group training are also given individual instruction. Some of our "graduates" return to us during the summer quarter for "refresher" group instruction.

Future Plans

Our present and future plans are to do all we can to translate our objectives into realities. We hope to be able to establish relatively clear-cut differential diagnostic profiles for nonverbal children. We hope to be able to relate and justify our therapeutic procedures to our diagnostic findings. We look forward to being able to establish differential prognoses as well as differential clinical inventories for children according to age and preliminary findings. Perhaps, above all, we wish to earn and deserve a reputation that all activities undertaken at our institute are proper subjects of investigation and research. These, we hope, will include the medical, psychological, social-behavioral and training procedures.

The staff of the Institute for Childhood Aphasia, as part of the School of Medicine of Stanford University, accepts that its primary function is to engage in research into the nature of perceptually impaired nonverbal children. In keeping with this position, ICA staff members believe that intensive investigation and training with a small group of representative perceptually involved children will ultimately result in a greater contribution to our profession, and to the welfare of such children, than will less intensive work with a greater number of children. At the present time each member of the professional staff, whatever his other duties may be, is also engaged in an investigation—diagnostic, therapeutic, or social-behavioral—in keeping with his interests and the long-term objectives of the institute. Our present and future plans are to continue this practice.

APPENDIX

Following is a list of publications that describe some of our early observations and therapeutic position relative to the work with children seen at the Institute for Childhood Aphasia:

EISENSON, J.: Disorders of language in children. *J Pediat, 62* (1) :20-24, 1963.

EISENSON, J.: Developmental patterns of non-verbal children and some therapeutic implications. *J Neurol Sci, 3*:313-320, 1966.

EISENSON, J.: Perceptual disturbances in children with central nervous system dysfunctions and implications for language-development. *Brit J Disorders of Communication, 1* (No. 1), 1966.

SCHELL, R. E., STARK, J., and GIDDAN, J. J.: The Development of Language Behavior in an Autistic Child. *J Speech Hear Dis, 32*:51-64, 1967.

STARK, J.: Interviewing Parents of Non-Verbal Children. *J California Federation for Exceptional Children, 15*:3-6, 1966.

STARK, J.: Performance of Aphasic Children on the ITPA. *Except Child, 33*:153-161, 1966.

STARK, J.: The Efficacy of Language Training with a Disturbed Child. *Slow Learning Child, 13*:103-106, 1966.

STARK, J.: A Comparison of the Performance of Aphasic Children on Three Sequencing Tests. *J Communication Dis, 1*:31-34, 1967.

Chapter 2

ORTHOPEDICALLY HANDICAPPED CHILDREN IN CALIFORNIA

Francis W. Doyle and Richard Outland

CALIFORNIA'S public schools have had more than thirty-five years of experience in providing educational opportunities tailored to the needs and abilities of orthopedically handicapped children. In serving some of these children, schools have provided little more than the transportation between home and school and minor adjustments in regular classroom programs. For the majority of these children, however, schools have been offering special education programs designed to give each child the help he needs to become as proficient as his potentiality permits. The magnitude of the problem faced by the schools becomes apparent when all the conditions that may cause a child to be orthopedically handicapped are considered.

The Education Code defines a physically handicapped child as the following:

> Any minor who, by reason of a physical impairment, cannot receive the full benefit of ordinary education facilities, shall be considered a physically handicapped individual. . . .

Children with orthopedic handicaps are included under this broad definition of "physically handicapped minors." For the purposes of special educational placement, the orthopedically handicapped are those children whose locomotion, according to the diagnosis of a competent physician, has been severely impaired by crippling due to (1) birth injuries; (2) congenital anomalies; (3) traumas; (4) tumors; (5) infections; (6) developmental diseases; or (7) other conditions such as fragile bones and muscular dystrophy. Other physically impaired children having mobility problems resulting from such conditions as uncontrolled epilepsy, severe cardiac impairment, and in some instances, hemophilia, may be considered as needing to be enrolled in special classes for orthopedically handicapped boys and girls. These individuals, however, should be enrolled in special classes only when it is impossible to make adequate provisions for them in regular classes.

The cerebral palsied, like the orthopedically handicapped, come under the broad definition of "physically handicapped minors" as given in the Education Code. For purposes of educational placement, the cerebral palsied are defined as "those children who have been diagnosed by a competent physician as having an impairment of motor function by injury to certain portions of the brain which govern muscular control." Cerebral palsy characteristically causes such conditions as the following:

Spasticity—hypertension of muscles causing stiff and awkward movements.
Athetosis—constant, irregular, involuntary and aimless motion.
Ataxia—lack of balance and poor spatial relations.
Rigidity—difficulty in extending arms and legs because muscles are partially contracted all of the time.
Tremor—involuntary trembling or quivering of hands, arms, or neck.

The condition of cerebral palsy usually presents a series of problems far more complicated than those typical of most other groups of children with orthopedic handicaps. Children with the impaired neurologic function characteristics of cerebral palsy have, in addition to their problems of mobility, a variety of intellectual, sensory and behavioral signs and symptoms singly or in combinations and in varying degrees. These children, like children with other orthopedic handicaps, are eligible for placement in special schools and special classes because of their problems of mobility.

Services for children with cerebral palsy are an integral part of the total program for the orthopedically handicapped. Children with cerebral palsy may be enrolled in special education classes serving only pupils with cerebral palsy; however, they are frequently enrolled in special classes serving pupils with other crippling conditions affecting mobility.

The primary educational goal for orthopedically handicapped children is identical to that for any other group of children: to enable them to become contributing members of the society. To accomplish this goal, the educational programs for orthopedically handicapped children delineate the obligations to these children in terms of four matters: self-realization, effective responsibility, economic effectiveness and social adequacy.

The process of educating physically handicapped children must be started as early as possible. Everyone working in the field of the orthopedically handicapped sees many children with permanent contractures, atrophied muscles and incorrect motor habits which could have been prevented if the children had received professional treatment early in their lives.

Both educational and medical research indicates that increased physical difficulties, serious academic retardation and social maladjustment can be avoided for many orthopedically handicapped minors by the early treatment and training offered in good preschool programs. In this regard, Arthur J. Lesser, Director, Division of Health Services, Children's Bureau of the United States Department of Health, Education, and Welfare, has written:

> More children would be prepared for regular school if treatment and education were started earlier. From a physiological and social point of view there is

> every advantage for the handicapped child in getting off to an early start. One of the most encouraging developments of recent years has been the increase in the number of nursery school classes for children with cerebral palsy where preschool children can be with other children for several hours a day and have the benefits of speech, physical and occupational therapy. Children who have had the advantages of several years of nursery school are so much better prepared to start school with normal children at the age of six.

Preschool programs are even more necessary for handicapped children than for normal children. Because of their physical disabilities, many preschool children have not had the opportunity to explore their environment or enjoy such incidental experiences as crawling up and down stairs, playing in the grass, or helping their parents water the flowers. A nursery school program can provide a regular opportunity for the team of educators and medical personnel to meet with parents of handicapped children. Through the medium of the preschool program, parents can be helped to carry on a more meaningful and constructive program with their children at home.

The significance of a program in the preschool years has been stressed by Denhoff and Robinault, who wrote that handicapped children have a multitude of problems at every level of growth and development and must receive early help to smooth their road through life.

> The preschool years can never be recaptured. These are vulnerable and pliable years, and they demand keen and precise medical and psychological guidance for the disfunctioning child and his family. . . . This is best accomplished by professional measures that can be facilitated through group therapy in a nursery school setting.

Every effort should be made to coordinate school and home activities by establishing good communication between parents and teachers, therapists, psychologists and school administrators. This is necessary so that parents may become acquainted with the educational goals established for their child; it is equally important for them to learn how to help the child accomplish these goals in purposeful activities outside the classroom. Contacts between the home and school can be accomplished in many ways—scheduled parent-teacher conferences, prearranged home visits, phone calls and written communications sent by mail, pinned to the child's clothing, or handed to the parent by the bus driver.

As school personnel communicate with parents, they need to consider several basic facts: (1) parents are by far the most important persons in the life of a handicapped child; (2) parents are not prepared to accept a child who is not perfect, even though it is estimated that one child in every ten is physically, mentally, or emotionally handicapped; (3) parents want to be good parents, although sometimes they are not; (4) parents often have much greater capabilities than professionals attribute to them; (5)

parents need and urgently want help; (6) parents learn chiefly through participating in the habilitation program of their child; (7) both parents and professionals can learn much about children with handicaps by working together.

Although it is important for teachers to establish positive and strong lines of communication with parents and to help them understand and accept their child, the extent to which an individual teacher can undertake parent counseling has to be determined by the administrator or supervisor of the program. The wise teacher senses when a particular problem posed by a parent is beyond his depth of training and experience, and he makes an appropriate referral. Psychologists, medical consultants and counselors may be used to advantage in the parent counseling program.

Regularly scheduled and well-planned parent-teacher conferences can be a most effective medium of communication with parents. The following guidelines are suggested for conducting such conferences:

1. Indicate the anticipated length of the conference ahead of time.
2. Let the parents know what will be expected of them during the conference. (The teacher should encourage an exchange of information with the parents, avoiding a one-way presentation.)
3. Have available sufficient information about the child, the child's family, the school in general, and referral agencies.
4. Have available some of the child's work to show the parents.
5. Start the conference on a positive note.
6. Limit the number of ideas introduced during any one conference.
7. With the parents' approval, take notes of important points in duplicate. Use these notes to summarize the conference, and give the parents one copy to take home for future reference.

The school cannot be expected to assume the role of meeting all the needs of the orthopedically handicapped. Their needs are so many and varied—physical, emotional, spiritual, educational, social—that they require a program of total community planning. This calls for teamwork at its highest level—a level at which parents, educator, school health personnel, family physician or medical agency, spiritual advisor, health and welfare agencies and recreational leaders pool their respective knowledges and skills so that each child's total needs may be understood and his adjustments improved.

The special education administrator must open lines of communication among the many agencies involved in services to orthopedically handicapped children. By doing so he will not only improve community planning for the children, but he will also make a real contribution in helping to alleviate duplication of services, thereby releasing monies for other kinds of needed services for these children and their families.

It is also incumbent on the special education administrator to plan methods of informing the public about this area of education. He should utilize many techniques of telling the story of special education to the citizens of the community so they will support community programs for the physically handicapped.

The governing boards of school districts having an average daily attendance of 8,000 or more must provide for the education of the orthopedically handicapped as included under the broad definition of "physically handicapped minors." Because of the limited number of these children in certain geographic areas, however, it is not always feasible for every district to establish its own program. Any school district which does not or cannot maintain a program must enter into an agreement with another school or county superintendent of schools maintaining such a facility. The county superintendent of schools must establish and maintain programs for physically handicapped minors who reside in elementary or unified districts which have an average daily attendance of less than 8,000.

The orthopedically handicapped may receive instruction in special schools or classes, hospitals, sanatoriums or preventoriums, or in the home through employment of home instructors. The type of placement for any of these children depends upon his individual diagnosis.

A basic policy in the social as well as the educational development of physically handicapped children is to reduce segregation to a minimum. Children should be assigned to a special class only if they cannot profit from regular class instruction. A special class for physically handicapped pupils is defined as follows:

> . . . a class established for a group of pupils with a similar physical handicapping condition, . . . and taught by a full-time teacher whose responsibility it is to supervise and direct for at least a minimum school day the educational program of all pupils enrolled in the class.

Some of the pupils may be so seriously handicapped that they cannot attend a special class; thus, home instruction may be provided. Such instruction, however, eliminates the social contacts so important for these children, and it should be given only as the last resort.

The cost of educating exceptional children like the orthopedically handicapped is considerably greater than the cost of educating normal children because of the need for special equipment, specially trained personnel and small classes. This cost, over and above the amount required to operate the regular school program is known as "excess expense." Excess expense is reimbursed by the state to school districts and county superintendents of schools in an amount not to exceed $910 per unit of average daily attendance. In addition, an amount not to exceed $475 per unit of average daily attendance may be allowed to school districts or county superintendents for transportation costs for orthopedically handicapped minors attending special day classes.

Financial assistance to school districts qualifying for state school building aid to construct and equip classrooms for orthopedically handicapped was made available in 1952. Some of the special provisions of the law are as follows:

> Three and one-half per cent of any sum appropriated by the Legislature and the proceeds of the same or any state bonds for state school building aid may be used for assistance to school districts in providing housing and equipment for the education of exceptional children.
>
> Space allowance for exceptional children is in addition to the allowance made for nonhandicapped pupils.
>
> School districts receiving an apportionment under Education Code sections 19681-19689 are obliged to repay not more than one-half of the amount of the apportionment.

The area required to provide adequate facilities for educational programs for the orthopedically handicapped in special day classes shall be determined by the department of education upon examining the specific requirements in each applicant district. It is not recommended that two areas of special education be planned to utilize the same school site, inasmuch as integration with normal pupils is limited if multiple special facilities exist.

Transportation of physically handicapped minors is recognized as a function of the public schools. Transportation is not only authorized for pupils assigned to special day schools and classes for orthopedically handicapped minors, but it also must be provided by the district of residence for those pupils whose physical handicap prevents walking to school.

The means of transportation are varied: regular school buses, specially equipped buses, taxicabs under contract and automobiles. In lieu of providing wholly or in part for transportation of pupils attending the special day school or class, the governing board of a school district may pay to the parents or guardians a sum not to exceed the cost incurred in transporting such a pupil.

The main factors to be considered in providing transportation are safety, comfort, traveling time and economy. Sometimes an attendant is employed in addition to the driver, but he should be carefully selected and trained. Routing should be carefully planned to minimize traveling time. Also, the physical condition of each child should be considered in order to make sure his disability is not aggravated by travel. If the necessary safety precautions are taken, the hazards for children being transported to special day schools and classes will be kept to a minimum.

As much as possible, the same curriculum content which has been found to be successful for nonhandicapped children is used for orthopedically handicapped children. Experience has shown, however, that when the regular curriculum is used, not only are adaptations necessary, but changes of sequence in presentation often are required.

One class may have a number of pupils of varied chronological ages and different levels of ability; yet, the following are essential to any class, regardless of ages and levels:

1. Academic training to the maximum of the child's potentiality.
2. Communications by whatever means are possible.
3. Activities involving the training and use of perception.
4. Concepts of learning based upon perception.
5. Highly expressive creative activities in music, art and writing.
6. Self-help skills.
7. Fine motor activities, such as balancing and reaching.
8. Large motor activities, such as climbing and throwing.

For orthopedically handicapped children in particular, long-range educational planning is imperative. This planning must include all of the disciplines involved in service for these children.

The maximum legal enrollment in special day classes for either orthopedically handicapped or cerebral palsied pupils depends upon the chronological age spread and the disability of the pupils. If the age spread is four or fewer years, fifteen cerebral palsied children may be enrolled in a class; if the age spread is more than four years, twelve pupils shall be the maximum enrollment. For orthopedically handicapped pupils, including non-severely handicapped cerebral palsied, the maximum enrollment shall be eighteen if the age span is four or fewer years, or fifteen if the age span is greater than four years.

Children are recommended for admission to the schools or classes for orthopedically handicapped children by an admission and discharge committee, appointed by the superintendent of the school districts with the approval of the district's governing board. The committee is composed of professional people concerned with the child's placement: the superintendent; administrative staff; representatives of the local health department or agency through which crippled children services are administered; the principal of the school; the physician assigned to the orthopedically handicapped unit, and the guidance and counseling service, which usually includes a psychologist. Teachers and therapists contribute information regarding the children, but they may or may not be official members of the committee. The principal of the school or other administrative staff member appointed by the superintendent of the school acts as chairman of the group.

When children are being considered for admission to the program, the committee studies their backgrounds thoroughly in order to determine whether or not their needs can be met effectively in the program. If the committee is determining whether or not a child should be discharged, his total program is reviewed to determine the extent of his progress or lack of progress. The committee's decision is referred to the superintendent for final action.

Children usually are enrolled for a trial period in order to be certain that placement within the orthopedically handicapped program is proper. If a child is discharged from the program he usually is placed in a regular school or another type of special class. Whenever a child is to be discharged, regardless of future placement, the committee works very carefully with the parents in order that the reason for discharge is understood thoroughly and so that the transfer is as smooth as possible for the child. Periodically, the admission and discharge committee should review carefully the progress of all children enrolled in the program and the appropriateness of their placement.

Many complex problems are involved in providing educational programs for children who are orthopedically handicapped. To assist with these problems, the State Department of Education provides consultant services and two residential schools for cerebral palsied children. The consultant services are provided through the department's Bureau for Physically Exceptional Children, Division of Special Schools and Services. The residential schools are supervised by the department's Division of Special Schools and Services. The Bureau of School Planning of the Division of Public School Administration assists school districts in developing adequate physical plants under the state school building aid program.

The Bureau for Physically Exceptional Children, California State Department of Education, provides the services of consultants in the education of the physically handicapped children. The services performed by the consultants follow:

1. Assist in the development, promotion and coordination of statewide policies and practices for the education of orthopedically handicapped.
2. Confer with federal, state and school district officials in the development of curriculums, organization and administration of educational programs for the physically handicapped children.
3. Study and recommend the purchase of appropriate equipment for programs in special day schools.
4. Assist school district officials in planning institutes and workshops for the in-service training of teachers of the orthopedically handicapped.

The Bureau for Physically Exceptional Children also provides the services of consultants in other areas of exceptionality, such as the visually and aurally handicapped and speech defective. These consultants are available on request to assist with the problems of the orthopedically handicapped having additional types of handicaps. The chief of the bureau coordinates the services of the consultants and is also available to serve in special areas.

An educational program for orthopedically handicapped children which fails to include medical services is only half a program. To enable orthopedically handicapped children to attain their full potentialities, their educational programs must provide medical care and treatment and a whole complex of therapies. The State Department of Public Health, through the Bureau of Crippled Children Services, is responsible for administering the medical services.

The Bureau of Crippled Children Services of the State Department of Public Health offers a statewide, tax-supported program, administered locally by county health or welfare departments. In general, the program provides treatment for physically handicapped children whose defects are disabling and can be arrested or corrected.

Local agencies responsible for crippled children services have the following responsibilities in the program for cerebral palsied children:

1. Administration of the program, including arrangements for clinics, clinic physicians and therapists.
2. Location of handicapped children and assistance for their families in finding facilities for care.
3. Determination of a family's financial eligibility for assistance for specific medical and surgical care and receipt of family reimbursement.
4. Coordination of services for each child so that maximum benefit can be achieved through available facilities.
5. Assistance to families in making travel arrangements and providing home care following treatment.

No specified length of residence in California or in a particular county is required in order to secure the services of this program. It is necessary, however, for the family to establish the fact that it intends to make the county its normal place of residence, barring any unforeseen circumstances.

Through the Bureau of Crippled Children Services, the State Depart ment of Public Health establishes administrative policy insofar as the medical care program in the therapy units of the schools for orthopedically handicapped children is concerned.

The Bureau of Crippled Children Services and the locally administered county crippled children services provide medical case management, medical supervision of cerebral palsy clinics, and also physical and occupational therapy in the schools for orthopedically handicapped children. These clinical services, including physical and occupational therapy, are provided without charge. Physical and occupational therapy are prescribed either by the cerebral palsy clinic's physician or the private physician treating the child.

Parent counseling is a vital aspect of the total services of the special school program. It is a policy of the Bureau of Crippled Children Services to take the provision of these counseling services into account in the planning of programs and facilities.

Physical and occupational therapists are hired by the local crippled children services agency on a contractual agreement with the Bureau of Crippled Children Services, State Department of Public Health. The Bureau of Crippled Children Services provides service to local therapy units in the schools through physical and occupational therapist consultants. Supervision and management of the therapy unit are responsibilities of the local crippled children services agency.

The Bureau of Crippled Children Services must approve therapy positions before they can be filled on a reimbursable basis. Such approval is contingent upon the need for therapy service, the adequacy of space, and the provision of appropriate supplies and equipment in the therapy unit.

In the construction of new therapy units or the expansion of an existing unit, local crippled children services administrators and the Bureau of Crippled Children Services personnel should be included in the planning stages of space and equipment are met. Plans for therapy units must be approved by the Bureau of Crippled Children Services before therapy positions are assigned.

Cerebral palsy clinics, administered by the local crippled children services agency, are held periodically within the districts maintaining special schools or classes for orthopedically handicapped children. Diagnosis and prescribed medical treatment, including therapy services, are included in clinic services. The clinics usually are conducted in the therapy unit. Their frequency depends upon the number of children being served by the unit.

Physicians who serve in these clinics are specialists in one or more of the following: pediatrics, orthopedics, neurology and psychiatry. Others who participate may include the public health nurse, school psychologist, teacher, therapists, school administrators and the parents. To protect the privacy of parents and children, however, the intent is to keep the clinic members to a minimum, including only those whose information is pertinent to the education and medical treatment of the child.

Diagnostic centers for neurologically handicapped children are financed by the Bureau of Crippled Children Services and provide coordinated diagnostic services for children who are suspected of having an organic brain lesion and who require evaluations by several specialists before a diagnosis can be established. No treatment is given in these centers; they provide the following diagnostic and consultative services:

1. Medical consultation in all necessary specialities, including neurology, orthopedic surgery, neurosurgery, psychiatry, speech and hearing, psychology and others as needed.
2. Social casework evaluation.
3. Laboratory and x-ray diagnostic services.

CALIFORNIA STATE SCHOOLS FOR CHILDREN WITH CEREBRAL PALSY AND SIMILAR HANDICAPS

In response to the requests of parents and a few medical and educational leaders that the state provide a specialized program for cerebral palsied children, the California State Legislature, on April 23, 1943, passed a resolution requiring the State Department of Education and the State Department of Public Health to investigate "the number of such children in the state who are in need of and can be benefited by special treatment and education . . . and to report to the Fifty-sixth Session of the Legislature the result of its investigation and make recommendations as to the treatment and education of such children, together with the facilities required for such purposes and the costs thereof." This report was provided, and it resulted in the Fifty-sixth Session of the California State Legislature authorizing the establishment of two state residential schools for cerebral palsied children in conjunction with the state cerebral palsy clinics. The California State Department of Education was designated as the agency responsible for the administration of the schools.

In 1946 the school for northern California was established in temporary quarters near Redwood City, and the one for southern California was established at the Convalescent Home of Children's Hospital in Los Angeles. In 1948 the southern California school was moved to temporary quarters in Altadena on property leased from the Pasadena Health Foundation. The school in Redwood City was named School for Cerebral Palsied Children, Northern California; the one at Altadena, School for Cerebral Palsied Children, Southern California.

In 1955, the next major step was taken to meet the needs of children with central nervous system disorders when the legislature, at the request of the State Department of Education, broadened the scope of the program to include "other similarly handicapped children." The two schools for cerebral palsied children were authorized by this legislation to extend their services to children with central nervous system disorders even though the children did not have motor handicaps.

In 1953, the legislature authorized funds for the construction of facilities for the northern California school in San Francisco, at Lake Merced Boulevard and Winston Drive and adjacent to the San Francisco State College. In 1955, the northern California school was moved from Redwood City to these facilities. In March, 1964, the southern California school was moved into new facilities near the California State College at Los Angeles.

Objectives

Because brain-injured children frequently have multiple handicapping conditions—sensory, emotional, intellectual and motor in varying degrees and combinations—it is necessary to make a thorough differential diagnosis of all aspects of each child's ability to function in each of these areas before the programs of treatment and education he needs can be determined. The children must be worked with in small groups, and highly specialized and individualized teaching techniques must be employed. Therefore, the objectives of the schools are as follows:

1. To diagnose the degree and extent of each child's disorder.
2. To determine the kind of educational programs best suited to meet the needs of children with cerebral palsy and other similar handicaps.
3. To determine the type of medical program that will enable each child with cerebral palsy or a similar handicap to progress to the extent his capability permits.
4. To provide services for children with cerebral palsy and for others similarly handicapped whose need for education and treatment programs cannot be met in the children's communities.
5. To serve as a resource in the training of teachers, therapists and other professional personnel.
6. To serve as a demonstration laboratory for the inservice training of professional persons interested in special education.
7. To provide counseling and education services for parents of children enrolled in the state schools for children with cerebral palsy and other similar handicaps that will help to secure for each child the type of treatment and educational opportunities he needs.

Eligibility for Enrollment

To be eligible for enrollment in one of the schools for children with cerebral palsy and similar handicaps, a child must be a resident of the state and must be "of suitable age and capacity . . ." (Education Code Section 26501). Suitable age is considered as being age three or over. Generally, children who are less than three years of age have not reached the stage of developmental maturity at which they can fully benefit from the programs offered by the schools. Children who are known to be severely mentally retarded, especially those who have been accepted for placement in a state hospital or other program for the severely retarded, are not deemed to have suitable capacity to benefit from the program offered by the schools.

To avoid needless duplication of services, the schools endeavor to secure all the information regarding a child that is available from the individuals or agencies in his home community that have provided any special services for him. This information includes the child's medical and educational records.

The residential schools provide temporary residence for children. Enrollment in the schools is therefore limited to one year or less, except in special cases that require additional time to secure the necessary diagnosis and to determine the educational-medical treatment required. In their diagnosis and determination, the schools make maximum use of the child's previous medical and educational history. Additional educational-medical data are gathered while the child is enrolled in the school if needed to determine the types of educational, medical and physical and occupational therapy programs that he requires. For example, one child may require a new approach to bracing, another may require therapy twice a day for five days a week to achieve ambulation, and another may require special help to improve his communication skills. Intensive presurgery and postsurgery therapy is provided as required.

Referral for Enrollment

Any individual between the ages of three and twenty-one who is a resident of California and who is suspected of having a central nervous system disorder (brain damage) may be referred to the schools for evaluation and enrollment by the following individuals, groups and agencies:

1. The physician directing the medical program of the school or school district in which a child is enrolled.
2. The consultant physicians of the State Crippled Children Services Cerebral Palsy Clinics that are conducted in various communities throughout the state.
3. The county superintendent of schools of the county in which a child resides, the superintendent of schools or the director of special education of the district in which the child is enrolled, or the principal of the school in which the child is enrolled.
4. The child's family physician who, as a result of his study, has found or suspects central nervous system damage and desires to have an intensive study made of the child.
5. The State Neurological Diagnostic Clinics operated under the auspices of the State Department of Public Health and conducted in hospitals in different communities throughout the state.
6. The staff of a state school.

Steps in the Referral Process

Copies of the referral forms are available, upon request, to appropriate personnel of the school in which the child is registered, to private physicians, to hospitals and to a State Crippled Children Services Cerebral Palsy Clinic. In addition to the completed referral forms, the state schools require copies of all available physical, psychological, educational, social and occupational, physical and speech therapy reports which have been written on the child.

Before the child arrives at one of the state schools, his referral has been processed as follows:

1. Information forms are sent to the referring source. The forms are filled out by the parents, the child's physician and other persons who have worked with the child.
2. Upon return of the information forms, the state schools' Admission and Discharge Committee, which consists of educational and medical staff members assisted by local school officials, reviews each form to determine whether the child shows any evidence of having a central nervous system disorder; the state schools' program would appear to benefit the child; services comparable to those offered by the state school cannot be secured locally; there is a specific objective to be met by the child's enrollment; the services the child will receive at the state school will assist in the development or maintenance of a local program designed to meet the child's needs.
3. If the state schools' Admission and Discharge Committee believes that the program to be offered will benefit the child, the referring agent or agency is notified, and a tentative enrollment date is given. If the state school cannot accept the child for enrollment, the referring agency or person is notified in writing as to the reasons.
4. When a tentative admission date is agreed upon, final forms are sent to the child's parents for completion and for their approval of the admission date.

Upon completion of the referral process and acceptance by the parent or guardian of an admission date, the child is enrolled in a program which is appropriate for him. Upon completion of the initial study of the child, a transfer to another type of program offered by the state school may be made. The child's parents or guardian must approve his transfer to the type of program deemed appropriate by the school authorities.

Diagnostic Evaluation

Each state school maintains a facility for a short-term diagnostic study of the child. Each child who is accepted for enrollment is initially diagnosed to determine the scope of his problem and to determine the period of enrollment.

The study, which usually lasts from one to two weeks, includes an evaluation of the child's immediate physical, intellectual, education and emotional status. It is an integrated and coordinated study by a staff of educators, medical personnel, psychologists and therapists. The medical evaluation is supervised by the school's medical director, and medical specialists are employed to examine the child whenever such services are to be found to be appropriate.

The cost of the medical examinations is borne by the state through the Crippled Children Services, the State Department of Public Health, or by appropriations to each school for medical services. Parents and guardians are expected to pay the costs of transportation for the child to and from the school, the cost of meals eaten at the school by siblings and adults other than the child's parents and the child's personal expenses. If surgery, braces, glasses, prosthetic devices and the like are found to be necessary, the parents or guardian may, under certain circumstances, apply to the State Department of Public Health, Bureau of Crippled Children Services, for financial assistance to help defray the cost of surgery or of the required devices.

Under the school's program, a child may be enrolled on an inpatient or outpatient basis, depending upon the place of residence of the child or upon his family's financial circumstances. At least one parent or the guardian is expected to remain with the child during the initial evaluation period, a period ranging from two to five days.

Upon completion of the short-term diagnostic study, the child may be treated in one of the following ways:

1. Referred to a special education class in his home community.
2. Referred to an appropriate agency for further service.
3. Enrolled in the school's program as a residential or day student, depending upon his requirements. (Such an enrollment is based upon the necessity to work intensively with the child in order to determine the kind of program which will be of the greatest benefit to him.)

Long-term Residential Program

The long-term enrollment program is designed to meet the educational-medical needs of each child. Special education programs are conducted by the state school's teaching staff at the nursery, elementary, and secondary school level. The medical program, under the supervision of a licensed physician, includes prescription of routine nursing care, medications and regular consultations by medical and dental specialists. Special drugs are used when approved jointly by the medical director and by the child's family physician. Group and individual physical, occupational and speech therapy is scheduled according to the need of the child. Social casework and psychological counseling are available for parents and children when need for them is indicated. Board, room, laundry and minor repairs to the child's clothing are provided by the school without cost to the parents. Children are generally enrolled for a period of from three to nine months for intensive study and determination of a meaningful program. There are several purposes for which a child is enrolled. Among the most important are the following:

1. Diagnosis and the determination of the treatment and the educational programs for children crippled by cerebral palsy and other similar handicaps, as outlined in the Education Code.

2. Treatment in occupational, physical and speech therapy, dependent upon the needs of the child, and instruction designed to minimize the child's particular educational handicaps.
3. Service as demonstration schools for teacher training purposes for California State College at Los Angeles and San Francisco State College. Students studying to be physical, occupational and speech therapists, as well as medical, nursing and psychology students, are provided training in the specialized techniques needed by individuals working with cerebral-palsied and other brain-damaged children.
4. The development of teaching techniques that will assist the child to acquire the knowledge and skills that will help him to develop to the extent of his capacity and ability.
5. A program of parent education designed to develop understanding of the child's potential and the role of the parent and child in the family and community. All parents of children enrolled in one of the state schools are required to attend scheduled individual and group counseling sessions.

Residential Program

Children in residence at a state school are assigned to homogeneous teaching groups under the direction of special education teachers who are trained and experienced in analyzing the educational problems of brain-damaged children. Children whose primary problems are language defects are grouped, and, when possible, so are those who are hyperactive and distractible and those who have severe physical disabilities. Each group is given an educational program especially designed to meet its needs.

Each child's educational program is individually designed to help him in the areas where he has the most difficulty, as demonstrated by psychological and educational testing. The teacher's goal is to discover techniques and approaches to help the child make gains in the fundamental academic subjects.

The program for the children enrolled is coordinated by educational and medical personnel who understand each other's viewpoints and who employ all known techniques in their effort to secure for each child a diagnosis and prognosis that may be used as a basis to determine the treatment program he must have if he is to have a life that is as productive as his abilities permit.

Physical and occupational therapy is continued as prescribed by the medical consultant. Occupational and physical therapists assist in evaluating the child's physical problems and, under medical supervision, assist the child in the development of coordination of body skills which are necessary to establish a sound basis for the acquisition of self-care, feeding, reading, writing and vocational skills.

Language comprehension and expression (oral, written, or by gesture) are essential for living and learning. Speech therapists contribute to the overall program by evaluating the children's language skills and by giving the children intensive training in the skills which enhance self-expression. The audiometric center provides the special equipment the speech therapist uses to obtain a hearing evaluation of each child.

The staff psychologists serve an integrative function in the diagnostic and treatment program by providing a comprehensive appraisal of the child's intellectual and emotional capacities. The findings of the staff are interpreted to all school personnel who work with the child.

Social workers assist in making the appraisal of the child by providing social casework to his family on an inpatient or outpatient basis.

Attractive four-bed dormitory rooms provide bed space for the children in residence. Each dormitory has a bath and dressing area designed to encourage the physically handicapped to help themselves. "Roommates" chosen for compatibility of social maturity and interests become close friends in this environment.

A staff of registered nurses and resident attendants provides personal care for the children day and night. Infirmary rooms are available where children who become ill are given nursing care.

Recreation rooms and playgrounds are provided for evening and weekend recreation. The children are divided into compatible recreation groups and are encouraged to participate in suitable recreation activities under the supervision of an attendant staff. The aim of the recreation program is to provide each child with opportunity to learn appropriate leisure-time activities. Every effort is made by the staff to carry out activities that are appropriate to classroom work.

When deemed necessary by the staff, separate dining rooms are used for training the children in skills of self-help. Those who are learning the basic skills of self-feeding receive individual training at each meal, while those who have mastered these skills are encouraged in social graces and table manners during the meal periods. The school's menu patterns are planned by the food service supervisor in cooperation with the medical director. A nutrition consultant from the State Department of Public Health helps with the development and preparation of menus that meet the nutritional needs of the children. Meals are prepared by a staff of skilled cooks and trained food service assistants.

Minor repairs to each child's wardrobe are provided by the school seamstress. Sturdy clothing is sent to a local laundry, while more delicate articles are laundered at the school. Clean, neat clothing and attractive hairstyles for both boys and girls are necessary to enhance self-esteem. The children are encouraged to learn the skills of self-grooming, with supervision and assistance as needed, and instruction in personal hygiene is provided.

Parent Visitation

When children are enrolled for periods of time in excess of the short-term evaluation enrollment period, their parents are encouraged to visit the school. During their visits, the parents of a child may observe him in the classrooms, therapy rooms, dormitory, dining room and play areas. At the southern State School for Cerebral Palsied Children, observation booths are available in the educational and testing facilities. During special visiting days, arrangements are made for parents to have conferences with staff members.

Weekend Program

Each state school endeavors to have a weekend program that will enrich the regular program. Visits to parks, zoos, museums and other points of interest are arranged for recreational and educational purposes. Every effort is made to coordinate the weekend program with the regular classroom program. Parents are encouraged to have their children remain at the schools on weekends so that they may have the advantage of participating in these experiences.

Weekend home visitation by the child may be arranged by the parents with the superintendent of the school. If possible, parents should make such arrangements well in advance, since the school must take absences into consideration in planning the program for each child.

Community Personnel-Staff Conference

Educational and medical personnel from the child's home community, as well as representatives of authorized social agencies, are invited to join with the school staff in the conference that it holds for each child on the results of his evaluation study. In this conference the group has opportunity to share information and data about the child, to discuss findings by the staff of the school, and to study the resources of the child's home community as a means of developing a long-term plan for the child. If it is decided that the child's development can be significantly accelerated by a longer enrollment for the purposes of instruction, treatment and training, then such an enrollment is suggested to the child's parents and to the officials of the school in the child's home community. Occasionally, this enrollment is deferred until after the child receives surgery or after he has participated in an appropriate local program for a given length of time.

Staff-Parent Conference

A conference of staff members of the State School for Cerebral Palsied Children and the parents or guardian of a child is held during the enrollment period if the members of the staff think that the conference will produce results that may be helpful in making the diagnosis of the child's needs and in determining the kind of program that is likely to be most beneficial. During the enrollment period and at the end of it, the parents or guardian of the child meet with members of the professional staff of the school to discuss recommendations which the members have made. Every effort is made to assist those responsible for the child to understand and accept the staff evaluation and the recommendations of the staff regarding the program that the child should have.

Reports

At the close of each type of enrollment, a report is prepared by the educational-medical staff team that participated in the study of the child. This report is classified as *confidential.* The report is for the sole purpose of summarizing the findings and recommendations of the persons representing the several disciplines involved in the study. Professional staff members of the state school may interpret the findings and report the recommendations to the parents or guardian. The information in the report regarding the child's educational needs may be made available to the child's parents or guardian by the professional staff of the school from which the child was referred to the state school, and the medical findings in the report may be explained to the child's parents by the family physician or by other physicians in the child's home community.

Each state school endeavors to forward a report to the child's home community at the earliest possible date so that the findings may be used to plan the program he needs. Comments and suggestions from the recipients of the report are solicited by the state school.

Special Education Programs

The State Schools for Cerebral Palsied Children have as one of their objectives the providing of service to school districts and must, therefore, offer the kinds of services that have value to the districts and that the districts need. To consider the needs of local schools, the superintendent of public instruction appointed an advisory committee consisting of medical, educational and lay leaders interested in programs for brain-injured children.

After reviewing many possible programs, the advisory committee recommended to the superintendent of public instruction that each school be organized to provide the following:

1. A classroom for children with cerebral palsy or orthopedic handicaps.
2. A classroom for children with aphasia or similar language disorders.
3. A classroom for children with essentially visual perceptual disorders or dys-

lexia. (The admissions and discharge committee of each school will determine if hyperkinetic children are to be admitted.)

4. A classroom for selected children whose learning problems are associated with a neurological deficit.

The following brief descriptions of each type of program offered by the state schools will be helpful to all who are interested in being fully informed regarding the services offered for children with cerebral palsy and similar impairments.

NEUROMUSCULAR IMPAIRMENTS (CEREBRAL PALSY). The State Schools for Cerebral Palsied Children are organized for the purpose of providing diagnosis and intensive treatment for children with neuromuscular impairments. Enrollment in the schools is a phase of a long-term program planned by interdisciplinary personnel of the child's community. After referral to one of the state schools, the length of enrollment is established in cooperation with the several disciplines involved and with the parents. All are responsible for the child's long-term educational-medical supervision. Enrollees are usually between the ages of three and nine. The classroom teacher in the program offered emphasizes preschool or school activities and academic work; the children are scheduled for the therapies—physical, occupational and speech—as determined necessary during the evaluation enrollment.

The medical consultants hold clinics at the schools to assess the physical potential of each child referred and to recommend treatment. All children who are receiving physical or occupational therapy are examined periodically at these clinics.

Special speech teachers work intensively with the children to assess the extent of any physical problems which will prevent acceptable speech development. Speech therapy is given to each child who needs it and as often as necessary.

The teacher must know the general characteristics and needs of each such child and plan the instructional program for him accordingly. She must also know the ways the child's physical disability has prevented his reaching higher levels in certain areas and ways in which the child may be helped to avoid letting his disabilities handicap him unduly.

LANGUAGE DISABILITIES (APHASIA). Children who have been diagnosed as language handicapped are enrolled in the class for language development. The language handicap is of a symbolic nature, i.e., aphasia (which may be receptive or expressive), alexia, agraphia, or acalculia, or some combination of these. The language retardation is not due to a hearing loss but to a brain injury, to mental retardation, or to emotional problems. Varying degrees of these conditions may be manifest in the disorder.

Children are enrolled for periods up to one year for language therapy and study. The primary emphasis is upon determining methods by which each child can learn language, and this emphasis results in special attention being given to the educational techniques required to help the child progress academically. The program is individualized, and attention is given to avoiding the undesirable effects which frequently accompany neurological impairment, such as distractibility, perseveration and perceptual problems.

In general, the teacher uses methods which follow the pattern of normal language development. Those situations, persons and objects most immediate to the child's daily experiences supply the materials utilized. Materials are selected or prepared on the basis of their relationship to the child's present level of language development. Attempts are made to work with the parents of each child and with the school personnel in the child's home community who will continue working with the child when he leaves the State School for Cerebral Palsied Children so that improvement in the child's language development while he is in the state school may be furthered by the school he attends.

PERCEPTUAL DISORDERS (DYSLEXIA). The class is for children of normal and above intelligence whose major problems are in the area of reading and who exhibit a degree of neurological involvement. Some neurologically impaired children are unable to achieve mastery of basic academic skills even though their measured intellectual capacities are within the educable range. The primary handicap of these children is inability to integrate visual stimuli into meaningful information. They may have normal visual acuity but be unable to interpret relationships of size or relative position, to coordinate eye movements with body movements, or to attend to a major visual stimulus while screening out extraneous stimuli. Sometimes they are also unable to retain visual symbols in their memory. Any of these inadequacies can interfere with their profiting from participation in preschool activities to the extent that they have the prerequisites needed to acquire skills such as reading. These inadequacies are also responsible for many social and behavioral disorders as the child attempts to respond to a world which he perceives in a confusing and disorganized manner.

These children do not necessarily have additional handicaps of orthopedic involvement, speech problems, visual impairment, lack of hearing acuity, or mental retardation, but they may exhibit the characteristics associated with such handicaps. The major emphasis in a training program for perceptually handicapped children is to help them develop visual perceptual skills. Specially prepared materials that require the use of all forms of sensual impressions—touch, muscle sense, hearing—are used for this purpose.

READINESS AND REMEDIAL CLASS. The readiness and remedial class is for children who have a variety of problems, such as are caused by immaturity or visual or auditory difficulties that have prevented the children from being successful in school. Children in the younger age group with such problems usually need an intensive reading readiness program and a considerable amount of individual instruction before they can participate successfully in regular school programs.

The older children who have major problems in the basic school subjects, such as reading, writing, arithmetic and spelling, are given the individualized help each one requires. Their problems may be due to a variety of causes: visual or perceptual problems, or both; visual-motor coordination problems; visual or auditory discrimination difficulties, or both, and the like.

After the learning disability is differentially and definitely diagnosed in the Medical-Educational Diagnostic Clinic, a child may enter the remedial program, where he will be given the specific type of help that he needs. The teacher's primary aim in this program, as in the other programs, is to reduce the discrepancy between a child's ability and his achievement.

Availability of Information. The state schools, as part of California's public school system, desire to assist whenever possible with local programs that are being offered for brain-injured children. In addition, both schools offer college students training for work in the field of special education or opportunity to observe and participate in clinical and educational situations. The State Department of Education encourages persons interested in the diagnosis and intensive training of brain-injured children and those persons interested in training of medical and allied personnel to write either the southern or northern School for Cerebral Palsied Children for information regarding the program of the schools.

SUMMARY

The California program for orthopedically handicapped children is an integral part of the educational program offered by the public schools. This program was made possible by legislation passed in 1927. Legislation passed since that time has made provisions for these programs to be improved and expanded as necessary. Special classes for orthopedically handicapped children including the cerebral palsied are maintained by the public schools, and the schools also provide individual instruction for these types of children who are confined to hospitals, sanatoriums, or their homes.

The problems encountered in educating orthopedically handicapped children require the well-coordinated attention of both educational and medical personnel. Services of the State Department of Education and the State Department of Public Health are available to school districts operating programs for these children.

To assist further with the complex problems involved in providing educational programs for children who are orthopedically handicapped, the State Department of Education provides two residential schools. These schools are known and designated as the School for Cerebral Palsied Children, Northern California, and the School for Cerebral Palsied Children, Southern California. These schools provide diagnostic services and temporary residence for children who, by reason of their handicaps, cannot be taught in regular public school classes.

Chapter 3

PROGRAM AND FACILITIES OF THE EXPERIMENTAL EDUCATION UNIT OF THE UNIVERSITY OF WASHINGTON MENTAL RETARDATION AND CHILD DEVELOPMENT CENTER

NORRIS G. HARING AND ALICE H. HAYDEN

INTRODUCTION

THE Experimental Education Unit is one of four basic elements which together comprise the Mental Retardation and Child Development Center, a state facility utilizing a multi-disciplinary approach to the problems of children. The other units are Medical Research, Behavioral Research and Diagnosis. Each unit has specific concerns for the individual child. The principal responsibilities for the Experimental Education Unit are professional training, research and service centering around the development and testing of procedures, methods, materials and devices which will permit the attainment of each child's fullest potential for learning. The learning environment is adapted to allow the child to learn at his own rate and to modify ineffective or inappropriate behavior.

Before a description of the present and proposed programs and facilities is elaborated, some background about the unit and the center may help the reader understand the interest in and the need for a multi-disciplinary and unified approach to the problems of children.

Excerpts from the introduction to "A Proposal for a Research and Training Center in Mental Retardation and Child Development" provide a clear statement of the problem and its scope:

> There are probably over six million persons in the United States who are handicapped by mental retardation. In our increasingly complex and technologically oriented society, the cost to the community, both in personal tragedy and in non-productivity poses a growing problem that must be solved. The challenge is great; the responsibility must be faced and accepted. The task of solution will require intensive effort of all of those sciences and professions related to the study of man. In the immediate future, we must develop facilities to provide proper care and education of the mentally retarded so that they may develop their faculties to the maximum potential. For this purpose, new diagnostic and educational techniques must be elaborated and personnel must be trained to bring to the community without delay the fruits of current and future research. Concomitantly, we must seek means to prevent this handicap. Epidemiologic and

> diagnostic studies, to characterize and define the number, nature and location of the retarded population are required. Finally, we need to develop understanding of those basic biologic mechanisms which may lead to retardation, for only through such understanding can the means of prevention be provided.
>
> We believe that the strength of our program lies in the extraordinary support that has developed within the State and University over the past years. The concept of a Center has evolved from our experience in the advantage of cooperative effort. . . .

It would be no small task to acknowledge the contributions of the many people throughout the state and at the University of Washington who have cooperated in the planning and developmental stages of the center. Many individuals and groups can take justifiable pride in the roles they have played over a period of years in laying the foundations for the achievement of their dream—the construction of a state facility that brings together various professional disciplines to work with and concentrate upon the many problems presented by exceptional children.

The need for a multi-disciplinary approach to the problems of mentally retarded children was recognized early in the State of Washington. In 1936, a local group of interested parents and professional people was organized to work in behalf of mentally retarded children. This organization, known as the Children's Benevolent League, was the forerunner of the Washington Association for Retarded Children. The latter organization, along with several other state groups formed the National Association for Retarded Children in 1950. In fact, a Seattle man, Alan Sampson, was elected to serve as the first president of the National Association for Retarded Children.

University of Washington faculty members working in different departments and clinics at various locations on the campus felt and expressed the need to work together on the problems presented by handicapped children as they participated in informal and formal discussions and deliberations. Organizations of parents' groups and resolutions passed at state meetings of the Washington Association for Retarded Children emphasized the necessity for a concentrated attack on these problems which seemed to become ever more apparent and numerous.

The University of Washington took great strides forward when it began, in 1955, the operation of Clinic VIII—The Clinic for Child Study—and in 1960, when it accepted the offer of financial assistance from a private donor for the establishment of the Pilot School for Brain Damaged and Mentally Retarded Children. These two units and other ongoing programs established a solid foundation for the development of plans for the Mental Retardation and Child Development Center.

Between 1957 and 1960, three state committees were reactivated, reconstituted or appointed by the governor of the State of Washington to correlate, integrate and study programs and services for the mentally retarded. In 1960, the governor augmented the Inter-Agency Subcommittee on Mental Retardation by appointing seventeen citizen advisory members and eighteen professional advisory members "to assist the subcommittee in studying the needs of the mental retardation program in the State of Washington and in formulating a report of its findings and recommendations." The report of the total committee, *Everybody's Child,* was published and presented to the governor in 1961. The report was circulated widely not only in the State of Washington but throughout the United States. The principal recommendations of the report were the following:

1. A State Mental Retardation Center be established to carry on research and professional education and to provide diagnostic services for regional and local centers;
2. The staff of the proposed Center serve as the nucleus of a State-wide committee to foster research on all aspects of mental retardation;
3. Multi-disciplinary education be made available to all professional groups that work with the mentally retarded.

Everybody's Child was not a report which was filed and forgotten. The University Center Planning Committee was appointed by the president of the university. In 1962, this group was combined with a committee representing the various interested agencies of the state government to form what was known as the Joint Working Committee. This latter group was instrumental in organizing the State Citizens' Committee consisting of nearly 200 members to inform citizens throughout the state and members of the legislature of the need for authorization and financial support for the proposed center. Legislation was drafted and presented as Senate Bill 170. The Senate Bill was passed by both Houses by an almost unanimous vote and is recorded in the Washington State Session Laws of 1963.

The cooperative efforts exerted in the development of the center plans were abundantly rewarded on May 1, 1962, when representatives of the President's Panel on Mental Retardation held a hearing in Seattle. Spokesmen for the interested disciplines within the university appeared as a group to state the need for a center to be located on the university campus. Other representatives of state agencies and organizations gave evidence of their full support of the plan.

In August, 1963, an application for Federal construction funds under Public Law 88-164 was submitted to the National Institute of Child Health and Human Development. The year 1964 saw the granting of Federal funds to the University of Washington for one of the first two such centers to be established in the United States. The announcement of this grant was not the end of hard work for those involved, but was the beginning of renewed efforts.

Since the Pilot School for Brain Damaged and Mentally Retarded Children was the forerunner of the present Experimental Education Unit, a brief historical review of its establishment and development seems pertinent to this discussion.

THE PILOT SCHOOL

The initial proposal for the establishment of the Pilot School for Brain Damaged and Mentally Retarded Children was prepared and presented to the private donor, John H. Hauberg, Jr., for his consideration on September 1, 1960, by a university committee appointed by the president of the university, Dr. Charles E. Odegaard. A memorandum of agreement based on this proposal was approved by Mr. Hauberg and a representative for the University of Washington Board of Regents, John L. King, on September 29, 1960. In accordance with the agreement, the president of the university on September 1, 1960, appointed a University Committee on the Teaching and Research Program for the Mentally Retarded Child, composed of the university representatives who had made the initial proposal, and delegated to this committee responsibility for the operation of the Pilot School. The school was established as an administrative unit of the Graduate School, and the dean of the Graduate School, Dr. Joseph L. McCarthy, was named chairman of the administrative committee.

The original proposal provided for an advisory board, but in January, 1964, in preparation for the reorganization of the Pilot School as a unit of the new Mental Retardation and Child Development Center, the Pilot School Advisory Board was dissolved by agreement and replaced by the new Advisory Committee. Both the Advisory Board and the Advisory Committee have included well-informed lay citizens interested in mental retardation as well as professional representatives.

The Advisory Board and the Pilot School administrators had many initial tasks, among them the matter of obtaining facilities appropriate for the operation of a school. Several possibilities with respect to housing the school in temporary or permanent quarters were investigated during the late summer and fall of 1960. These possibilities included moving and remodeling buildings owned by the university, the building of new facilities or the rental of space. An architect was engaged to look into the possibility of moving and remodeling a large portable building, the Harborview Hospital Annex. The estimated cost for this operation did not seem to warrant the investment. Plans for the construction of a new building on university property at some distance from the campus were then discussed. The architect was asked to prepare plans for a building with costs not to exceed

$42,000. A review of preliminary plans and estimates indicated that this budget would provide approximately 2,800 square feet of space, which would not be adequate for the needs of the Pilot School program. It was also felt that a site closer to other university facilities and clinics would be desirable if one could be obtained.

Initially, quarters were provided in Miller Hall (education building) for an intermediate class and in the nursery school of the Institute of Child Development for a preschool class. Subsequently arrangements were made for the temporary occupation of two university owned houses with an adjacent vacant lot within two blocks of the main campus. On February 20, 1961, the intermediate class moved into the first house which had been remodeled and painted. The second house became available on March 20, 1961, and was remodeled to accommodate the preschool and primary classes.

The objectives of the Pilot School as stated in the proposal for the establishment of the Pilot School in 1960 were as follows:

1. *Teaching.* To provide for teaching, training and experience for appropriate university students who will serve during their professional lives to assist handicapped children. Students from such fields as education, psychology, speech and hearing, medicine, nursing, social work and others may participate.
2. *Research.* To provide for research on brain damage and mental retardation to be carried out by university faculty and graduate students, and other interested and qualified persons.
3. *Public Service.* To provide high quality therapeutic and educational assistance to a small number of brain damaged and mentally retarded children and, in addition, to provide a model applicable elsewhere for establishment and maintenance of special schools for mentally handicapped children.

Dr. Alice H. Hayden, professor and director of graduate studies in education, was appointed as director of the Pilot School in September, 1960. This part-time assignment was in addition to her other responsibilities and was assumed with the understanding that the appointment would be temporary. On April 5, 1961, Dr. C. R. Strother, professor of psychology and psychiatry, was appointed director on a half-time basis. In 1962, a doctoral candidate in education was made part-time principal of the school. In 1963, Dr. Hayden became associate director on a half-time assignment. In September, 1964, a position was established for a full-time principal, and Mr. R. Vance Hall was appointed to this position.

The school staff consisted of a head teacher and two teaching assistants for each class, a speech therapist, a secretary, and for 1964-65, a social worker and part-time psychologist.

In addition to the regular staff, a consulting staff participated regularly in the evaluation of pupils, curriculum, methods and materials, and provided liaison with their respective departments and clinics. The consulting staff included representatives from the following disciplines: education, pediatrics, psychiatry, psychology, social work, and speech pathology and audiology.

In the original agreement, the school was established to provide a pilot, or experimental, program for brain-injured children. General policies were established by a university committee consisting of representatives from the disciplines mentioned above. The committee formulated three basic criteria for admission of pupils to the school: (1) a presumption of brain injury; (2) evidence of inability to secure placement in the schools; (3) an acceptable degree of compatibility with those children currently enrolled in the class in which the applicant would be placed.

In general, children have not been admitted if public or private schools could offer appropriate placement, or if it appeared that the child could not be prepared for transfer to other school facilities within a two-year period. All of the children enrolled have been markedly retarded in one or more aspects of development—in perceptual and motor skills, in language, in emotional maturity, or in social behavior. The largest number of applicants has been in the six to eleven year old age range. They typically exhibited problems of behavior such as distractibility, hyperactivity, or withdrawal or special learning disabilities which were sufficiently obvious to exclude them from the public schools. Applications have been initiated by clinics, physicians, school personnel and parents or other relatives.

Close cooperation with parents has been an essential part of the school program. Regular parent conferences were held between a child's parents and his teacher or whenever any specific need arose. If any serious problems of child-parent relationship existed, a social worker provided parent counseling services. Regular parent education meetings were held. Pilot School staff members or outside speakers discussed selected topics. Such meetings were alternated with parent discussion sessions. Parents were asked to express their ideas of programs which would be of special interest to them. The group sessions for parents were well attended and resulted in an exchange most valuable to the school as well as to the parents.

The achievements of the Pilot School project are probably best expressed in the final report submitted by the director of the school on July 17, 1965.

> The Hauberg grant was offered to the University to stimulate a multi-disciplinary program of research and training in the area of brain injuries in children. In the five years during which the grant has been in effect:
>
> 1. Fifty-nine children for whom no other suitable educational facilities were available have been given the advantages of an intensive and specialized program.

2. One hundred and three graduate and undergraduate students, from seven professional fields, have been given training in work with brain-injured children.
3. Six hundred lay and professional observers from more than fifteen states and five foreign countries have visited the school to see a model program in operation.
4. Over 3,000 lay and professional leaders, in national and regional conferences, have heard papers presented by the school staff and observed demonstrations of procedures used in the school.
5. New programs in special education have been established by the College of Education to train teachers of the mentally retarded and other handicapped children.
6. Programs of research in education, speech pathology and psychology have been initiated.
7. Developmental and training grants totaling approximately $140,000 have been received from Federal agencies to date.

More important than any of these consequences is the fact that this grant has stimulated, and provided a solid foundation for, a multi-disciplinary program in mental retardation and child development which has: (a) drawn together a large number of departments and colleges in one of the most significant inter-disciplinary projects ever undertaken by the University; (b) aroused widespread interest among citizens of the state, lay and professional organizations and state legislators; (c) created a fruitful partnership between the University and other agencies of state government which are concerned with mental retardation; (d) been recognized by the National Institutes of Health, through the award of more than $6,000,000 in construction funds alone, as a major national center for research and training in mental retardation and child development.

In the summer of 1965, the university concluded its contract for its five years of operation of the Pilot School insofar as any commitment of this type can ever be completely fulfilled. The Pilot School was exactly what the title implies, a pilot or a beginning of a larger program and operation of a facility, and to this extent, the obligations of such a commitment are never really fulfilled except as progress is made in the ongoing and expanded programs.

PRESENT EXPERIMENTAL EDUCATION UNIT

Principal among the changes in 1965-66 were the following: (1) the change in the name of the school to the Experimental Education Unit of the Mental Retardation and Child Development Center; (2) the change in the location of the facility to temporary quarters in two buildings presently leased by the University of Washington in the Coach House at 4701 24th N.E. where the unit is located in the same physical facility as the Division for Child Health; (3) the transfer of the Experimental Education Unit budget from the Graduate School to the College of Education; and (4) the change in administrative personnel with the appointment of Dr. Norris

G. Haring as director of the unit, thus leaving Dr. C. R. Strother free to devote more time to his responsibilities as director of the Mental Retardation and Child Development Center. Another administrative change was the appointment of Harold Kunzelmann as principal of the Experimental School and lecturer in education.

The above changes have had an influence on the philosophy of the unit, criteria for admissions and administrative organization and practices. Effort in the Experimental Education Unit is directed toward the improvement of classroom instruction as well as toward improvement of instruction for professional personnel at the pre-service, graduate and in-service levels through application and demonstration of newer techniques in behavioral measurement and the utilization of modern educational technology. The application of procedures inherent in the functional analysis of behavior of children in group-classroom situations provides a basis for determining appropriate group and individual instruction. The efficiency and objectivity gained from these procedures have been especially valuable in studying the effects of programmed instruction and materials and the influence of environmental consequences upon behavior. Through the use of these procedures and the adaptation or development of new equipment for recording data, the academic responses of all the children enrolled in the unit may be recorded. Teachers and other professional personnel or university students also record nonacademic behavior as a basis for research and modification of environmental consequences.

Administrative Organization

The administrative organization of the unit is designed to permit maximum exchange and communication within the unit itself, to facilitate communication among the units, and to maintain the exchange from the four units to the center administration. In addition to its operation under the policies and procedures established by the Executive Committee of the Mental Retardation and Child Development Center, the Experimental Education Unit has its own Advisory Committee. This committee includes informed citizens as well as professional members. The Advisory Committee meets with the Administrative Committee of the Experimental Education Unit on a quarterly basis.

Another advisory committee, called the consultant advisory committee, works with the Experimental Education Unit Administrative Committee and includes all of the professional consultants from the cooperating disciplines. This committee meets every two weeks although additional meetings may be called if specific situations or problems need to be discussed.

The internal organization of the unit has four divisions and presently three branches which relate to and serve all the divisions. Each of the four divisions of the unit: training, research, service and behavior analyses, is headed by a member of the Administrative Committee who in turn works with a committee in his particular division. The branches in operation at this time are Program Development and Evaluation; Instrument Development and Evaluation, which includes data-recording and processing for computer input and data-photography; and Administrative Systems Development.

All divisions and branches are set up to provide periodic information "readouts" to assist in locating and correcting specific problem areas within the unit. The administrative organization must be able to accommodate modifications and expansion of staff, facilities and programs as the unit prepares to make the transition to its new and much larger facilities in the center complex. Every effort is being made through the individual units, the center organization, and the university administration to permit the four units of the center to work together and to coordinate their programs in advance of occupying the new facilities which should be ready for use in 1968. For example, a third building in the Coach House complex was leased by the university in the summer of 1966 to permit the further drawing together of personnel from the several disciplines which will be working together in the center programs.

The School Program

The school year at the Experimental Education Unit follows the quarter system as does the university. Classes for children are provided in the summer quarter as well as during the academic year. This system allows not only for the utilization of the physical facility to its fullest extent, but also permits coordination with other university programs.

The Experimental Education Unit which includes the school area, consists presently of seven converted apartment units located on the ground floor of two of the buildings which comprise part of the Coach House complex. Initially five apartment units were converted to accommodate the classes and the personnel housed in the Pilot School. Thus three apartments were converted into three classroom units each of which had observation and storage space. Chart 1 shows a typical classroom arrangement. The other two apartments were converted into offices, therapy rooms, an instrumentation laboratory, a conference room and reception areas.

Two additional apartments in a second Coach House building were made available for establishing two more classrooms after January, 1966. One of these apartments was remodeled and equipped for use by children admitted to an intermediate level class in January, 1966. The second apartment was designed to serve as the behavior analysis area where the efforts of profes-

TYPICAL CLASSROOM ARRANGEMENT AT THE EXPERIMENTAL EDUCATION UNIT

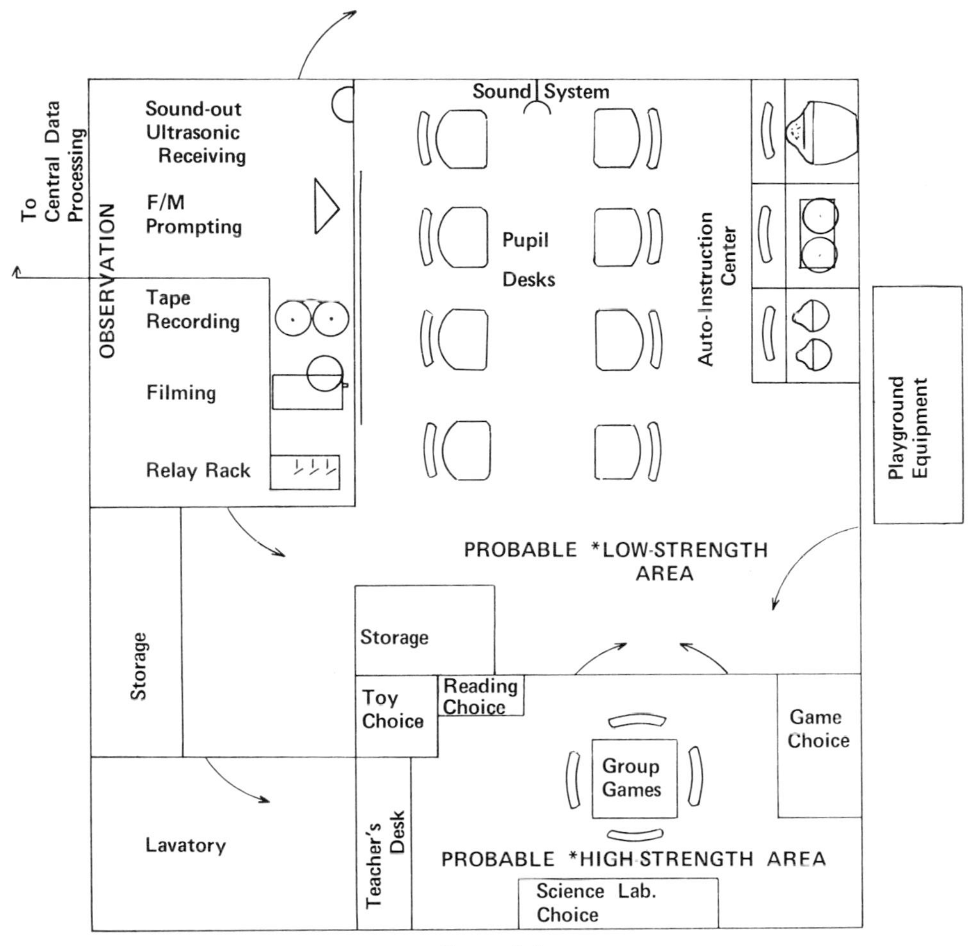

CHART 3-1

sional personnel from a number of disciplines could work together on diagnostic and remediation procedures.

Presently, five classrooms serve six groups of children between the ages of three and sixteen years. One classroom is shared by two groups of preschool age children with one group meeting from 9:00 to 11:00 A.M. and the other meeting from 1:00 to 3:00 P.M. The behavior analysis program occupies a second classroom. Three remaining classrooms provide demonstration and research programs at the primary, intermediate and junior

* Probable low strength area is basically programmable for teacher control of stimulus and consequence variables. For each pupil, probable high strength activities are contingent upon ratios of academic work.

high age levels. Each of these programs will be described in some detail subsequently.

The children enrolled in the unit have been referred largely by school officials in local school districts and pediatricians in the metropolitan area. All children who are admitted to the unit are evaluated, staffed and diagnosed by the staff of the diagnostic unit. Following the diagnostic process, the children are placed into diagnostic categories such as mentally retarded, brain injured or emotionally disturbed.

Following the diagnoses, or often as a part of the diagnostic process, the children are seen in the behavior analysis program. This analysis involves the direct measurement and direct observation of the child's responses within a controlled environment. In the program particular attention is given to stimulus environment, i.e., the stimulus that occurs both before and after the response and the effect these stimuli have upon the child's responses.

Two preschool programs extending over a two-hour period per day meet five days per week. Presently, an Experimental Communication Program is being carried on with the preschool group which meets in the mornings. In addition to the usual admissions procedures and criteria for enrollment in the unit, children considered for instruction in this program must have had a complete evaluation of their speech, language, and hearing. The basic criteria for admission to the Experimental Communication Program are as follows:

1. The child's primary disability should be in the area of communication.
2. Any behavioral problems which the child may exhibit should be minimal and adjudged as those resulting from the communication problem.
3. The parents must be willing to accept an experimental approach to their child's communication problem and demonstrate a willingness to participate in learning activities which must be extended to the home environment.

Although other preschool skills receive attention, the primary focus in this program is upon the development of communications skills. The program is both diagnostic and instructional. A speech therapist and a preschool teacher work together with this specially selected group of not more than six children and have the assistance of a consultant from the area of speech pathology and audiology as well as services from the instructional materials specialist when such services are appropriate for advancing the readiness and academic skills of the children.

Another preschool age group of children, not to exceed eight in number, occupies the preschool classroom in the afternoons, and their activities and program are directed by a teacher and an assistant. The preschool children are given tasks which have academic skill value. These tasks are carried on in a separate area of the classroom and provide each child with some exposure to a semi-classroom environment. Thus, besides usual preschool activities, these children have specific responsibilities to perform that help develop their academic learning skills.

The most important development in the preschool program is a sequence of work that leads to writing, language and number skills. The program material now consists of 300 pages of work which, in time, should approach two thousand pages. Within this program the child moves at his own rate of progress, and consequently, he directs the construction of his program by his rate and level of achievement.

Since two preschool groups occupy the same classroom and follow programs designed to accomplish different objectives, careful planning has been necessary to attain a high degree of flexibility in arrangement of equipment and materials. Attractive materials are placed in storage units and may be secured by the teacher and the contents released for the children's use at her discretion and direction. Different types of objects and teaching materials may be used by the persons responsible for the two groups of children and these learning stimuli must be under the teacher's control. Children's activities with these objects and materials may be recorded subsequently for analysis of individual and/or group pupil activity.

The primary classroom has been the focus of much attention from the speech therapists on the Experimental Education Unit's staff. The significant language problems exemplified by all the children in the primary class have called for the integration of many techniques of the speech therapist into this classroom procedure. The program created for the children consists of a readiness sequence which leads directly into a programmed reading series. This is coupled with graphic manipulations that allow for visual-motor development in terms of manuscript writing. The entire program eventually leads to the attainment of writing skills. The mathematics program, comprised of many manipulative type skills, also uses speech techniques in overcoming the language difficulties encountered in the presentation of number concepts and skills in naming numbers.

Probably the most interesting development in the primary classroom is that of an individualized or a near tutorial presentation of instruction within a group setting. The teacher allows the child to function and progress at his own level and rate of development on each program presented without interfering with the progress of the total group's social behavior. Although there exists a wide range in skill development among the children in any one group, by using these tutorial techniques the social activities remain common to all, thus providing a naturalness in the setting and permitting common group and social behaviors.

Research in the primary class has led to the use of individually programmed instruction for the children. The reading series for the children centers about a fundamental, linguistic approach which concentrates upon the learning of sounds. When the background in terms of their language difficulties is known, a sound-oriented program can be presented to them which will allow each child to progress at a relatively high rate of reading skill attainment.

The intermediate class includes children who range in age from eight to twelve years. The class, begun in January of 1966, started initially with five severely disturbed boys. Four of the five children in the group were referrals from Clinic II, child psychiatry. The severity of their adjustment problems necessitated the gradual introduction of these children to a group situation. Carefully recorded information about children's responses to the learning stimuli has been the basis for selection of subsequent presentations to them and has led to an increased rate of response. Such information has also increased the accuracy of prediction of each child's performance. The teacher has come to realize that by increasing the stimulus value of selected presentations to elicit certain types of experiences necessary for academic learning, she can help the disturbed child concentrate on productive activities.

Twelve children are scheduled for the intermediate classroom for the 1966-67 school year. The teacher and her assistant may call upon consultant help in special areas as well as upon the services of the instructional materials specialist and instrumentation specialist for selecting and utilizing appropriate academic programs for each child and for recording information on academic and social behavior.

The junior high program is for pupils between the ages of twelve and sixteen who are markedly retarded in academic achievement. There are usually eight to ten children in the junior high classroom. Emphasis is upon remediation of learning disabilities. The careful study of each pupil's academic or classroom behavior enables the teacher to investigate objectively some of the learning environment variables which affect academic progress. Results from such research support the use of programmed instruction for teaching basic academic skills which had not been acquired by these children at an earlier period. Beginning with programs with which these pupils can cope effectively, they usually respond at high rates to these academic materials and are motivated by their successful performance. The programs which progress by small steps and are corrected or graded by the teacher promptly provide a source of data for the teacher as well as motivation for the pupils.

In the junior high classroom the record of the pupils' responses on academic tasks is the basic source of information used by the teacher to investigate the variables in the environment which affect the pupils' academic processes. The academic responses of each pupil are recorded by the hour and graphed each day. This information is used by the teacher to individualize the pupil's academic program. A record is also maintained on the environmental consequences which occur subsequent to the responses. Both the academic program and the consequences of responses are systematically prepared and studied. The analysis of both the program and the responses of the environment (correction from the teacher) forms the basis of investigation of the learning of children in the junior high class.

Thus, from the classroom data, it appears that older children who lack needed academic skills will work independently on programmed materials. These children are able to maintain a high rate of accurate responses over a long period of time. The measurement of these responses gives important information concerning the effect of immediate correction upon the rate of responding.

The pupil's progress in the junior high classroom, as well as in the other classes, is never left to chance. With an accurate recording of what the teacher has asked the child to do as an assignment, of what the child actually does when working on the assignment, and of how the child spends his time immediately after completing the assignment, the teacher insures the progress of the child through the constant analysis of such records.

Research and Professional Training

With the use of timers and counters which help to quantify the responses of the children in the learning environment, the teacher secures an accurate measurement of the children's responses to programming and, thus, is able to give the child a successful experience through some consequation satisfying to the child after he has worked on the assignment. This objectively recorded information provides the teacher with data which can be used to investigate methods of behavior management in the classroom. By having a record of two specific parts of the learning environment, namely the program and the consequences, teachers can determine their value to the child's ongoing progress in the classroom. Hopefully, at a time when the child is making considerable progress on his program, an entire assignment may be given to him similar to that which a child may receive in a regular classroom.

The research and training possibilities stem from two sources: first, the utilization of technological devices for recording information from the learning environment; and second, the systematic analysis of this information. Such situations allow for a systematic investigation of the many facets of the classroom that in the past have been without definition or have not been within the realm of researchable ideas. These learning environment records form the basis for research designs which can be carried out with student trainees as an integral part of their collegiate program.

The utilization of modern technology characterizes the activities in all of the classrooms at the Experimental Education Unit. Exemplifying this is the development of a wireless listening center which records the child's verbal behaviors. This listening center can be utilized both in the classroom and in the speech therapy area for children with language disabilities. With this wireless listening center a complete analysis of a child's auditory input and verbal emission can be made from the recorded data. From this type of record, verbal behavior of a child may be studied scientifically. This research will in turn provide important data for the logical sequencing of information to the child.

Multi-disciplinary research that will expand the service given to the children at the Experimental Education Unit as well as services given throughout the area to children with any exceptional problems has been initiated at the unit through a coordinated effort with the Division of Child Health. At the present time, many of the children in the Experimental Education Unit are on medication prescribed by the medical personnel in the Clinic for Child Study of the Division of Child Health. This united attention of the educational and medical staffs to the children allows a quantitative assessment of behavioral change vital to medical and educational research.

Expectations are that a terminal station connected with the University Computer Center will be installed for the joint use of the Division of Child Health and the Experimental Education Unit in the fall of 1966. The staff of the Experimental Education Unit anticipates its use not only for the storage and analysis of classroom data and streamlining administrative operations, but for carrying out research related to computer assisted instruction as well.

Through the cooperative efforts of the multi-disciplinary professional investigators with the teaching staff at the Experimental Education Unit much can be accomplished for the benefit of children, teachers and other professional personnel involved in training and research which never could have been realized through any single discipline.

There has been a substantial use of the Pilot School and the Experimental Education Unit as a teaching resource through directed observation by students from educational psychology, educational sociology, nursing, pediatrics, psychiatry, psychology, social work, special education and speech pathology and audiology. Faculty and students from other nearby institutions, colleges, and universities also make use of the facility. Some interns from other universities spend periods ranging from several days to several weeks at the unit when special arrangements for such work can be accommodated.

Visitors and observers who registered during 1965-66 numbered 374. The visitors included students, teachers, parents, staff members from the University of Washington and other institutions of higher learning, administrators of special education programs, social workers, school psychologists, pediatricians, speech and hearing therapists, interested lay persons and staff members from different institutions in the State Department of Institutions, as well as staff from the State Department of Public Instruction. Present facilities provide observation space for each therapy room and classroom, thus making possible the easy assimilation of visitors and observers in the unit. Each observation room adjoining the classrooms has a sound system and one-way glass. Visitors are, however, asked to schedule their visits in order that the facilities are not overcrowded at any particular time. An orientation for visitors and observers is also provided.

Staff members of the Experimental Education Unit participate in in-service programs upon request if their schedules will permit. In 1965-66, members of the Experimental Education Unit administrative staff participated in forty-three in-service sessions for professional personnel working with exceptional children. This was in addition to the in-service and orientation sessions for Fellows on traineeships and staff members of the Experimental Education Unit and related units.

Communication

Members of the Experimental Education Unit administrative staff are not unmindful of the need for good public relations and communication with all those who work for and with the unit. Communication has been facilitated in a number of ways, such as the following:

1. Bulletins and announcements to various groups.
2. Exchange of information and discussion opportunities afforded through committee participation.
3. Teacher orientation and staff meetings.
4. Observer orientation sessions.
5. University student training orientation sessions.
6. Staffings.
7. Parent meetings.
8. Parent-teacher and parent-principal conferences.
9. Follow-up of pupils transferred from the Experimental Education Unit.
10. Follow-up of personnel formerly associated with the Pilot School or the Experimental Education Unit.
11. Orientation sessions for visitors to the unit.
12. Participation of EEU staff members in radio and television programs.
13. Participation of EEU staff members in special programs.
14. Participation of EEU staff members and Fellows in national, regional, state and local meetings of professional organizations.
15. Participation of EEU staff members in in-service programs.
16. Publications by EEU staff members in periodical and book sources.

Members of the Experimental Education Unit recognize the need for feedback for the evaluation of programs and for determining their practicability for use in public and private schools serving similar types of children. The Experimental Education Unit Service Committee therefore includes directors of special education programs who serve staggered terms as committee members.

The foregoing discussion has included a history of the events leading toward the development of the new Mental Retardation and Child Development Center. Each step has represented a gradual expansion in preparation for occupying the larger center facilities. Many innovations in programming and educational technology are being utilized in the present facilities. Particular emphasis has been placed upon developing cooperative working relationships with other disciplines which can be continued as the program moves forward. The program which has been described has served the several initial objectives; these and other goals should be more easily realized in the new facilities. The discussion of the Mental Retardation and Child Development Center is included as the final portion of the chapter which follows.

THE EXPERIMENTAL EDUCATION UNIT FACILITY IN THE NEW CENTER COMPLEX

Following the appointment of the University Center Planning Committee by the president of the university in 1961, an assessment of the tasks required for making the center a reality was undertaken and priorities were established. Some of the immediate needs were to obtain legislative authorization for the establishment of a center on the university campus; to secure funds for costs of planning, constructing, furnishing, equipping and operating the several facilities within the center; to select an adequate building site; to develop programs appropriate to the aims and objectives of the different units and of the center; to plan and consult with experts in various areas and with informed personnel in preparation for developing building plans appropriate to serve the programs in training, research and service in the several units and in the center organization; and to determine the most effective administrative structure for integrating, coordinating, and operating such a multi-disciplinary facility encompassing widely diverse but related programs.

The committee was ever mindful of the recommendations and objectives stated or implied in *Everybody's Child* that the project should do the following:

1. Provide housing for the much needed expansion of ongoing programs in the field of mental retardation at the University of Washington.
2. Establish the Center in Mental Retardation and Child Development at the

university with service available to university students and retarded children from all over the state.

3. Provide in this center the opportunity for extensive interdisciplinary exchange of information and cooperation through the proximity of the different programs and personnel.
4. Provide a model center for training and education of future workers in the field of mental retardation.

The Center Planning Committee did not, of course, attempt to accomplish all the tasks itself. For example, the Mental Retardation and Child Development Center Building Committee with a number of subcommittees undertook responsibilities for developing plans for the several units. Reference has already been made to the excellent cooperation received from many quarters in achieving authorization for the establishment of the center and for funding center complex construction.

Careful study was undertaken to determine the most adequate site location to permit the uniting of the several facilities which comprise the center. In addition, proximity to related facilities and programs was recognized as necessary to effect liaison with the parent disciplines represented in the center. The needs of the different units in terms of space and other requirements received long and careful consideration by the university administration, the university architect's office, and other committees and groups concerned with near and long-range planning for the university. After all the pertinent information had been collected and carefully analyzed, it was finally decided that the Diagnostic, Behavioral Research, and Experimental Education Unit Center facilities should be constructed on a portion of land which was formerly part of the university golf course located directly south of the University Hospital. One unit, Medical Research, will be part of one wing of the hospital. The site is bounded on the north by Columbia Road, on the west by Fisheries buildings and a proposed university parking garage, on the east by Montlake Bridge, and on the south by the Lake Washington Ship Canal. The south boundary respects an arbitrary right-of-way line approximately one hundred feet from the bank of the ship canal.

Considerable thought has been given to the use of the land, and schematic plans have been examined and debated. On one hand is the prime factor of land availability, particularly the pressing need for expansion space in the area of the health-science-hospital complex. On the other hand is the mandatory need of the Experimental Education Unit to relate directly to the outdoors, its need for extensive play and recreation areas, and its need for space at one level considering the multiple problems of supervision and elimination of barriers for mobility of handicapped children. The relationship of multistoried elements of structure at the canal line to structures on the opposite canal side, and the logical sequence of existing building masses as they approach the canal line were also given careful consideration. Other factors taken into account were (1) future hospital expansion; (2) service roads and utilities; (3) concepts of flow of the south campus plan; (4) future structures to be built to the east and west of the center facility; (5) existing traffic and potential parking problems; (6) preservation of the green belt along the canal; (7) grade changes from an elevation of forty-two feet to the lower hospital level which has an elevation of sixteen feet, and (8) the triangular size of the site.

In addition to land-use considerations, careful attention has been directed to the following: (1) indoor-outdoor relationships; (2) adult-child relationships, and (3) within unit relationships, unit-unit relationships, and unit-center relationships.

Before any specific planning was done relative to the Experimental Education Unit, criteria were developed and agreed upon as bases for the development of the school unit plan. These criteria were that maximum effort should be made to insure the following: (1) flexibility; (2) safety; (3) elimination of architectural barriers; (4) informality in the school environment; (5) work efficiency; (6) control of traffic flow, and (7) ease of maintenance.

Main traffic arteries favor the children. See Chart 3-2. Traffic links within the Diagnostic Unit are part of the scheme, but are planned to limit the extent to which adult traffic can and should intrude upon the school.

For the most part the Experimental Education Unit, which accommodates pupils between the ages of three and sixteen, is patterned after elementary school concepts inasmuch as the numbers of children served will favor the younger age groups. It is a one-story structure which has a part basement and affords approximately 39,809 gross square feet and is not designed for additional floors. The service aspect of the facility is limited to the professional training and research needs of the center.

This unit houses the Experimental School, teacher training facilities, data recording and closed circuit television elements in the instructional center facilities for the three-building complex. Also included in the Experimental Education Unit are various therapy rooms, testing facilities and spaces for consultants and teaching and research assistants. Prime consideration in the design development has been the location of the adult instructional center. This is in reality a special ninety-nine-seat-seminar television and film production studio-demonstration room. Facilities are also provided for multi-media projection, telephone conferencing, programmed instruction requiring active student response for instructor feedback and data processing. The instructional center is located for ease of use by adults without interference with programs involving the children, and can be readily used separately in off hours.

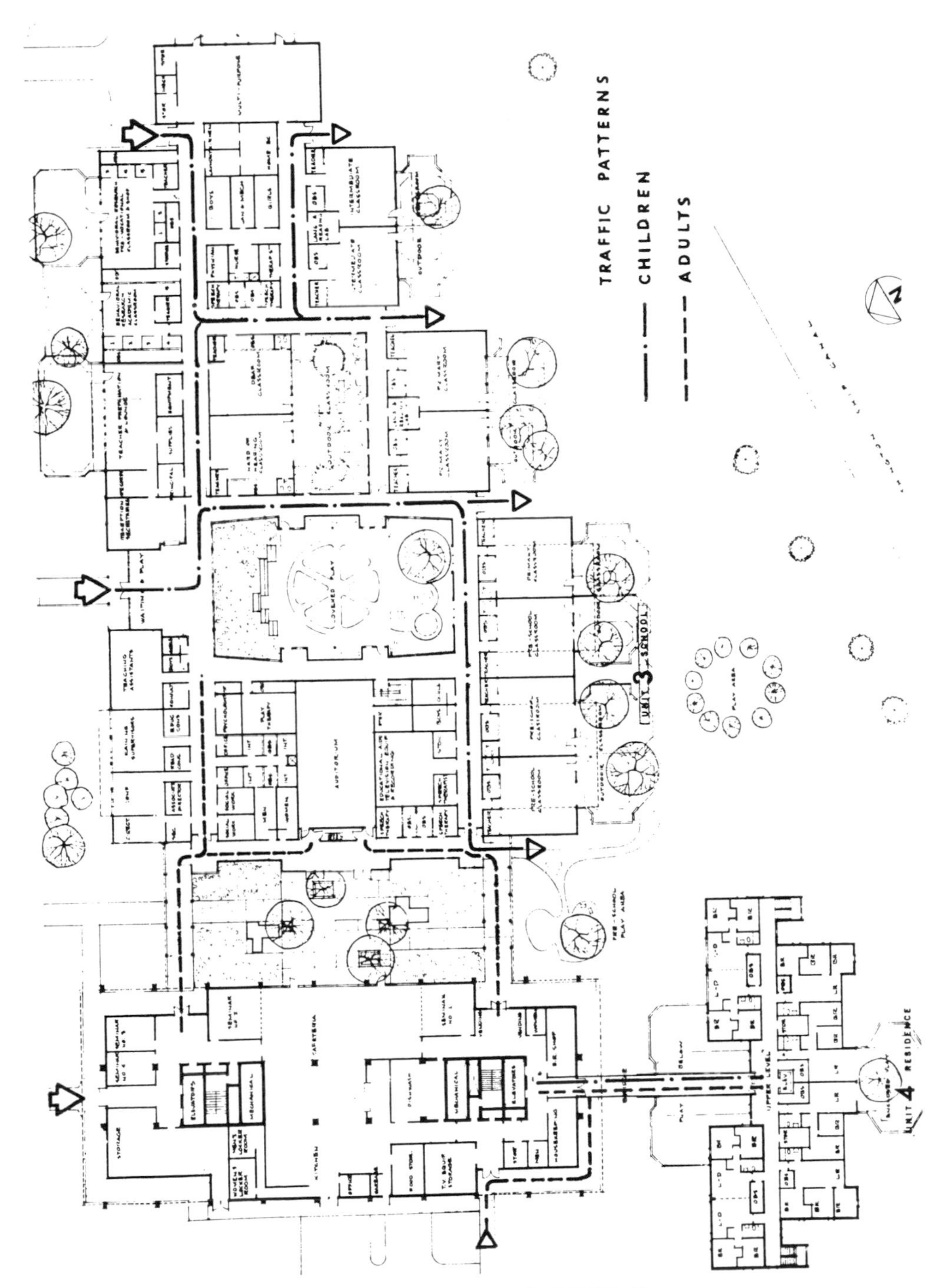

CHART 3-2. Traffic patterns in MRCD Center.

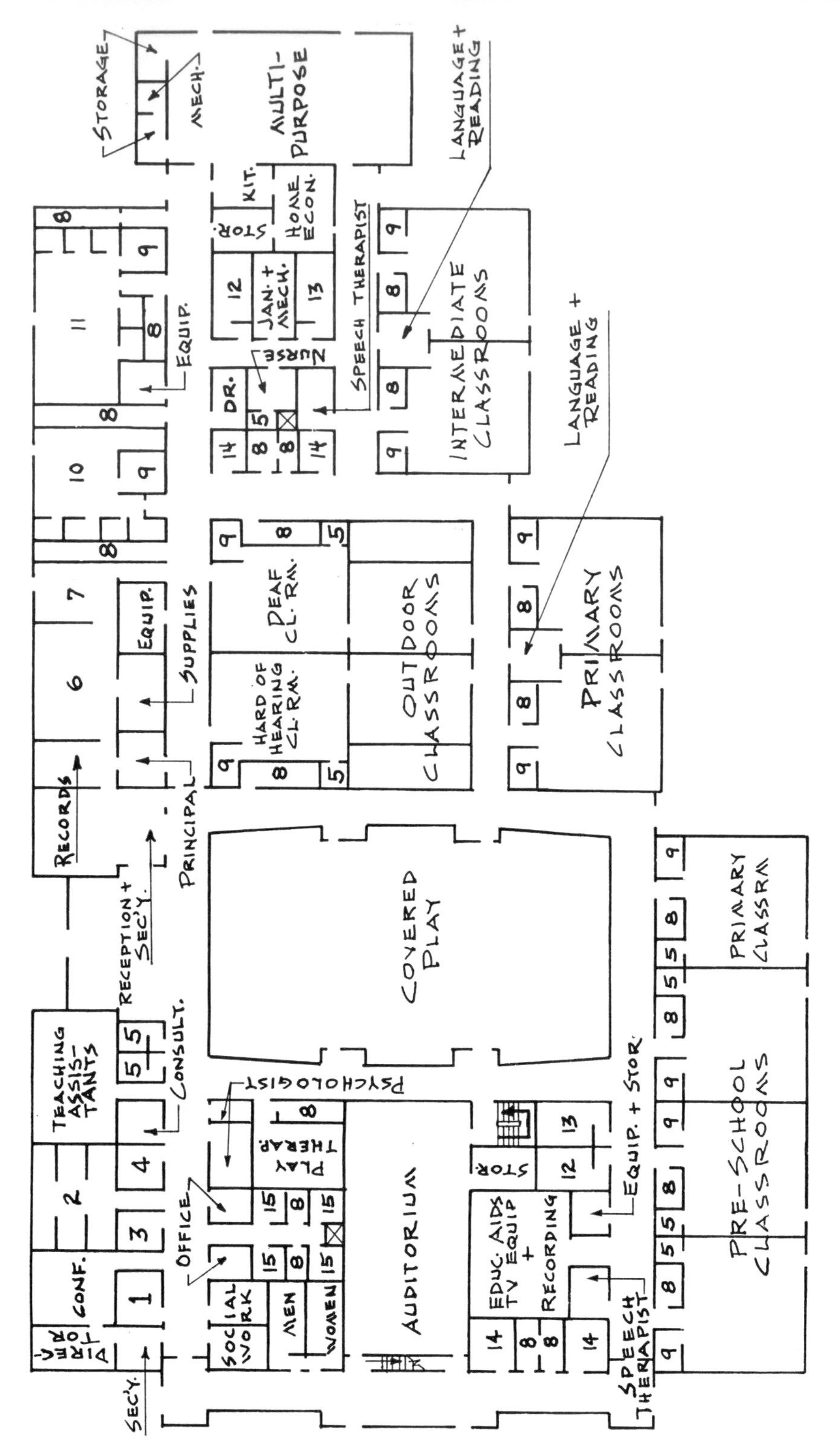

CHART 3-3. Floor plan of the Experimental Education Unit in the New Center Facility. Every classroom has an outdoor extension which includes an eight-foot overhang for protection. *Key:* 1. associate director; 2. training supervisors; 3. reading consultant; 4. educational consultant; 5. lavatory; 6. teacher preparation; 7. teachers' lounge; 8. observation; 9. teacher; 10. behavioral research academic classroom; 11. behavioral research pre-vocational classroom and shop; 12. boys' room; 13. girls' room; 14. speech therapy; 15. interview.

The Experimental Education Unit is designed on a basic classroom net size of approximately thirty feet by thirty feet. The design module is essentially ten feet and all rooms and corridor systems are multiples thereof. The nine and one-half feet clear corridors were considered highly advisable for handicapped children. Chart 3-3 shows the floor plan. It will be noted that fixed equipment has been kept to a minimum to insure flexibility. Moveable walls have also been used where possible to serve this same purpose. Some classrooms will be used by more than one group of children during the day. Classrooms may also serve different groups at various times. For example, a greater number of older children may be provided intensive training programs in the summer than during the regular school year.

It is anticipated that the Experimental Education Unit will continue to work primarily with children who, for one reason or another, cannot be accommodated in a community school program. When a child can be provided an adequate program in his own community and can make a satisfactory adjustment to that program, he will be transferred from the Experimental Education Unit. Members of the EEU staff will work with teachers and other school personnel to make the transition as easy as possible for the child. In some cases, however, an intensive summer program at the unit may enable the pupil to remain in his own school community and to progress at a more rapid rate in his academic program. School districts wishing to work with the unit in the selection of pupils for such intensive summer training programs will be invited to start the selection process early, in order that all necessary information about each child may be obtained well in advance of the summer session. Selected teachers will also be given opportunities to participate in special summer training programs for different groups of pupils normally accommodated in school community programs. In addition to regular year and summer programs for teachers and other professional personnel, there will be increased opportunities for conferences, workshops and in-service programs in special areas.

Attention is presently being focused on programs and classes on human growth and development which will include information about deviant as well as normal development. In addition to programs for university students and professional personnel, effort is being directed to the development of programs for parents whether they have children enrolled in the Experimental Education Unit or not. A great need seems to exist in this area and will no doubt continue to exist until all adults are better informed about human growth and development and the role of parents in this vital process.

Chapter 4

PHOEBE A. HEARST PRESCHOOL LEARNING CENTER

RHODA KELLOGG

HISTORICAL BACKGROUND

THE Preschool Learning Center is operated by the Golden Gate Kindergarten Association, a nonprofit, nonsectarian, incorporated organization which was founded by Sarah B. Cooper in San Francisco. In 1879 she gathered twelve young children of poverty-stricken families off the streets of the Barbary Coast district into a rented room and began to educate them according to methods developed by the Froebelian kindergartners. She opened a second school the next year. By 1895 she had secured enough funds from local citizens to maintain forty schools attended by more than 3,500 children. During this period three wealthy women—Phoebe Apperson Hearst, Jane Lathrop Stanford and Miranda Lux gave substantial sums to support this work. They also left money in trust to the association, annual income from which is still received. Hundreds of other San Franciscans contributed annually to the association.

When Mrs. Cooper died in 1896, the Golden Gate Kindergarten Association was known throughout the world. She carried on an enormous correspondence, wrote thousands of letters every year and published lengthy annual reports, of which more than 85,000 copies had been circulated in the United States and abroad. Visitors came from nearly every state in the Union, and Mrs. Cooper received admiring letters from such women as Julia Ward Howe, Frances Willard, Clara Barton, Elizabeth Peabody, Susan Blow and Susan B. Anthony. She was president of the International Kindergarten Union in 1892. The association received a Gold Medal Award for an exhibit at the World's Fair in Chicago in 1893, and at the Columbia Exposition in Antwerp.

Some of Mrs. Cooper's writings are in basic essence timely for today, as the following quotes show: "The foundation of character and national welfare are laid deep down in our infant schools." "The most elementary teaching is the most potent in shaping human destiny, and the infant school is more vital than college." She thought a child's education should begin at age two.[1]

The kindergarten classes were attended mainly by children whom she called "waifs" and "street urchins," but Mrs. Cooper believed that all children should receive free education in the preschool years, as children in the association's schools did. Only by concentrating on children of the slums, however, could she obtain money for these schools. Though the majority of children enrolled were ages three and four in her day, children over age two and under age seven were also accepted. Never did the association operate a day nursery program. Eventually in 1917 the San Francisco Board of Education took over some of the association's classes and opened more kindergartens as part of the public school system.

The association developed a teacher-training program in 1915, under the direction of Anna Stovall, and became affiliated with the San Francisco State Normal School when Dr. Frederic Burk was its president. This affiliation lasted for many years. The association's three-story brick training school, built by Phoebe A. Hearst, was destroyed by fire and earthquake in 1906. In 1911 Mrs. Hearst's son, William R. Hearst, rebuilt on the site at 570 Union St. a school with two classrooms. This building had outlived its usefulness by 1965. The Hearst Foundation of New York and the W. R. Hearst Foundation of California then gave funds needed to build the Preschool Learning Center, which is owned by the W. R. Hearst Trust for the lifetime use of the Golden Gate Kindergarten Association.

After 1926 and the death of Miss Stovall, the association concentrated on nursery education for children under age four years and nine months—the eligibility age for a child's entrance into a public kindergarten in San Francisco. Since that date there have been four directors of the association's educational program. Dr. Helen Christianson 1925-1931, Lynette Mass Messer 1931-1932, Dorothy Henry 1933-1945, and Rhoda Kellogg 1945 to the present time. Programs were conducted in various locations in North Beach, in Chinatown, on Potrero Hill and in the Sunnydale district. In the Fillmore district, a school having a 50 per cent Negro enrollment was operated from 1944 to 1947 under a Rosenberg Foundation grant, though an interracial admissions policy has always existed in the association's schools. The first parent cooperative nursery school in San Francisco was set up by the association in 1941, and taken over by the board of education in 1946 under the adult education program. During the war, the association opened its first "child-care" nursery school at Sunnydale, which also was taken over by the board of education in 1946 when state funds were made available for public child care centers. That same year a new school at 350 Union Street was opened, only to be closed after two years by a lease cancellation, leaving the association with only Hearst and Stanford schools in operation from 1948 to 1965.

Obtaining housing and financial support was always a struggle over the years. With the new Preschool Learning Center, the housing problem is solved for years to come. The financial ones will still exist, unless the school enrolls high numbers of children who pay full fees. Fees are set on a basis of family ability to pay, but children from all economic groups are admitted. This brief historical statement suggests that the association's longevity and vitality are based on its educational integrity and ability to change with the times. Mrs. Cooper got the association off to a good start by her dedication to the child-centered approach, and never has it wavered toward other emphases. Needs of the poor, the working mother, the teacher in training, the war effort, social casework, and research were always secondary to the primary aim of providing the best possible daily educational experience to the children enrolled, no matter what benefits adults might also receive from their enrollment.

Through eighty-seven years of operating many schools in buildings which ranged from store fronts, family dwellings, tents (after the fire) and two specially designed buildings, the association has accumulated ample evidence to prove that properly designed housing is of paramount importance to preschool education. Its new building has been designed to provide as many desirable features of a nursery school as could be obtained in an urban setting. In addition, this building provides space for classes in visual arts for older children, space for the continued research in child art, which it has pursued for twenty years, and space for education of adults about the needs of human beings in early childhood. The architect, William B. Fox, working closely with this writer as technical consultant, has incorporated many features in this building which are unique and highly desirable for the smooth functioning of a nursery school.

THE NEW BUILDING

The Nursery School Area

The new building is located in Western Addition, an area of apartment houses, mainly built on land obtained from the San Francisco Redevelopment Agency. The building is flanked on the rear by a huge San Francisco Housing Authority Project, occupied mainly by Negroes, with a high proportion of families on Aid to Families with Dependent Children. Across the street from the front entrance is another housing group called St. Francis Square, which covers four square blocks. This integrated, low-cost housing development was built as an investment by the International Longshoremen's and Warehousemen's Union. Nearby are high-rise apartments for families of middle and upper class income. More than 500 young children live within a five-block radius of the new center.

The building site of 22,000 square feet of land is on sloping ground. There is an upper building of 7300 square feet and 6500 square feet of playground located on the roof of a lower building of 6500 square feet. Set backs and off street parking take up the balance of the lot. This entire site of expensive urban land has been utilized to a maximum consistent with its purpose. The upper building, of redwood frame construction, is a nursery school for eighty to ninety children. The lower-level building, of poured concrete, has no playground, and has multipurpose usage. The two separated buildings blend together as one pleasing whole, with long lines and low roofs which scale it suitably for occupancy by young children. Inside the nursery school, a large lobby and wide, long hall are pleasantly spacious, as are the three large classrooms most pleasingly proportioned. The nursery school building and playground are on one floor level, with no steps, ramps, or door sills, on which children can stumble or fall. The playground is smooth cement with drains to the sewer so that frequent hosing down keeps the play area surface free of city dirt. Rubber mats under equipment prevent falls onto cement.

Toilets are located off each playroom near the exits to the playground, which is divided so that each room has its own separated play area. Teachers' toilets, with individual lockers, are located off the children's toilets. A teacher standing at one end of the toilet has good view of playground and playroom, keeping her in touch with the entire flow of traffic, and giving her opportunity to guide it to and from the three areas. A toilet off the entrance hall is available to parents, cook and housekeeper.

Radiant heat makes warm floors for the children, and the high windows keep drafts off the floor and opened windows out of children's reach. Clear plastic upper window panes and opaque plastic lower panes give a view of sky, but not of streets or playground: so that the children inside are not distracted by children outside or by pedestrians looking in. Plastic window panes cannot get broken by young vandals in search of thrills. Doorknobs are 48 inches high, except for the fire exit doors to the street and on the lower half of a small Dutch door between playground and playroom. The program allows children to go inside and outside as they care to with independence, and these doors permit varying degrees of ventilation control in the classrooms. Classrooms can be locked from the outside but not the inside. Walls in classrooms are sheetrock covered with a pale yellow vinyl plastic which looks like woven grass cloth. This durable surface defies scratches and is easily washed. Floors are gray sheet vinyl, lockers and cupboards are natural finished birch. The sink for teacher use is made to hold two paint trays from the easel, so that keeping easels clean and mixing paint can be done with no trace of washing-up in evidence on the stainless steel sink and drainboard. A wet mop can be left standing over the sump in the corner of the toilet and is readily available for wiping up urine on the playroom floor.

Visitors can observe at any time from one-way-vision booths in the playrooms, where the screening makes impossible their identifying faces. Thus teachers and children need never wonder if "someone is looking," but neither need they make social contact with visitors, as they have to do when visitors come into the room.

The rectangular playgrounds have seven-foot-high fences with no hidden corners. There is no vegetation within the fence (outside tree tops appear above it), no dirt-digging corners to attract local cats in the evening. Both the usual and some unusual playground equipment is placed for safe, vigorous outdoor play. An overhanging roof gives a small place to ride tricycles on rainy days and gives shade on hot days, the latter being little needed in San Francisco's windy climate. The A-frame separating fences, with a few openings, give places for children to crawl into and space for storage of wheel toys at night.

Teachers can go from classroom to classroom without having to go through the entrance hall. The three classrooms have children aged twenty-four to fifty-four months separated by age level into three groups. Cupboards in the rooms are mostly low and available to children, a few are for teacher-controlled materials. Tables and chairs are scaled to size of age level, chairs range from five inches to eight inches, tables from fifteen inches to eighteen inches in height.

A large central room, called the multi-purpose room, is used by children in the morning for music and finger painting and, on occasion, by adults for meetings of the board, the auxiliary, or visiting groups.

The kitchen, with its own entrance, is at one end of the building and is lined on three sides by stainless steel counters and equipment, built for efficiency and sanitation, and long life with little upkeep. The electric ovens are standard, but the gas burners are set in a row accessible to a woman cook, and easy to clean. A hood over the stove and an electric fan remove kitchen odors. There is a small sink, and a large one with garbage disposal for washing big pans and preparing dishes for the electric dishwasher. Dishes and silver are sterilized and air dried. Washed dishes are set on the food carts ready for the next meal. Food carts with three shelves are used to serve food to three tables in each playroom. Food removed from stove goes into heated stainless steel bowls for serving at the tables, with family style service.

A pantry off the kitchen houses food supplies bought in quantity at wholesale prices. A freezer holds the frozen vegetables. Fresh meat, salad vegetables and milk are bought daily and kept in a refrigerator until used. One cook can prepare the food in this kitchen for seventy persons. Garbage is placed in the gardener's room near the kitchen and the garbage collector has a key to this room. Service entrance has space for a laundromat for washing the bibs used by the two-year-olds and the pillowcases used by children who sleep at school.

There is a staff lounge for teachers' use on their ten-minute morning coffee break, or their thirty-minute afternoon rest period. The space is adequate for several teachers to sit or to lie down during these periods. Coffee is available all day to staff.

There are two office rooms, one for private interviews and one for the secretary, whose desk is placed near a window opening into the lobby. She can see all who enter or leave the building, but her desk is protected from children's reach.

Between the two offices is a small room and toilet, required by law, for the isolated care of a child who becomes ill, until such time as the parent can call for him. This arrangement means that the child can be supervised by the office staff and thus avoid the teacher having to leave the classroom. Before being admitted children must be given medical examinations by their own physician or at a public health clinic, and regularly checked thereafter by a physician.

An intercom system on the secretary's desk provides communication between classrooms, offices and kitchen, saving many steps for everyone, and providing a teacher with any immediate assistance she may require without having to leave the classroom. Arrival of parent can be announced to the teacher and the child will be sent from the room, or the mother may go in to get the child. To complete this description of the nursery school area, the janitor's closet and the storage room for school supplies must be mentioned.

The entire building is esthetically pleasing and functionally efficient. The furnishings in the rooms are arranged to please the eye and to give a sense of order wherever one looks. A relatively small staff is needed, because so many "conflict traps" between teachers and children have been eliminated by the skillful planning of every feature. A director, secretary-bookkeeper, ten teachers, housekeeper and janitor comprise the staff.

Child Art Area

This building, which has the playground of the nursery school as its roof, has windows on two sides only, and therefore has forced air ventilation and heat. It can accommodate three programs: child art classes for children aged four to twelve years, adult education, and child art research and exhibition. There is an auditorium which seats 150 and is suitable for classes in child art during the day, for evening meetings of adults and for art display. A kitchenette is located between this room and a good sized parent's lounge. A smaller room is allotted for classes for younger children and has its own toilet. These rooms open off a hallway which goes the length of the building, with an exit at each end. Four outside rooms contain the archives of the Rhoda Kellogg Child Art Collection, space for research work in child art, a large lobby and one office. This building also contains the mechanical room for the two buildings.

The above description of the architectural aspects of the new building has given some information about program, next to be described in more detail.

NURSERY SCHOOL PROGRAM

The association is committed to pioneer work in the theory and practice of preschool education. As an independent organization, it is free to experiment and is able to proceed on a basis of its own long previous experiences. Experimentation in depth rather than in breadth is its role, though the contributions it makes are applicable on a wide scale. The Preschool Learning Center will continue to demonstrate the value of certain educational theories and practices which it has tested out with success over the years, and also some new ones.

The modern urban home is not equipped to educate the young child properly without the assistance of schools which provide some experiences in group life among peers. The family group provides only older or younger persons, and in the family children cannot learn to feel "equal" and adequate, as they can in peer groups. A democratic society should therefore provide organized education for the very young.

Nursery education, unlike later education, is not a pouring out of content of adult minds into children's minds. Rather it is a living experience with peers in an environment which stimulates the individual's physical, mental and social growth, under guidance from adults who devote their entire attention to the children. To be effective, education must be agreeable to children in the sense that the satisfactions of group life make it worthwhile to sacrifice individual behavior which is considered detrimental to the group. We think that in the nursery school there must be no teacher-imposed rewards or punishments, that undesirable behavior must be benignly corrected so that the child learns to obey because the resulting reward is the self-approval reflected from teachers and peers. Only positive, rather than negative, discipline builds such self-esteem and brings cooperation which enables children to utilize the environment for learning. To learn from the curricular materials, every child must feel safe from attack, physical and psychological, by adults. Then he learns to coordinate body movement, in response to sensory and mental stimuli, with a resulting feeling of emotional satisfaction in learning.

Nursery education is the most important phase of child education because it lays the foundation for all later learning. Brain growth between two and four years makes this time a critical one for mental development. The most important year for preschool training is between age two and three. After more than twenty years of successfully conducting classes for young two-year-olds from all walks of life, we have found that this age level is most responsive to group life, if the physical environment is scaled to their body size and if teachers are skillful with this age level. Women who have learned, through apprentice teaching, to be knowledgeable about and comfortable with children this age, and who are able to view toilet training as educational, are able to teach two-year-olds in a group situation.

Age two is a more difficult one for mothers at home than it is for teachers in a nursery school. Therefore, mother and child need some daily relief from each other, and the child needs to learn at this early age that there is a benign world outside the home. If his own home is not benign, this learning can be a life-saving experience. If his home is all that is generally considered desirable, he profits from learning very early in life that the world is not the small oyster which he first inhabits. At age two children can best learn to have confidence in the authority of adults other than their own parents. Baby-sitters who inspire this confidence are not easy to find. We have found that children who, at two, seem to be emotionally disturbed or somewhat retarded, often do not appear to be so after attending one of our nursery schools for a year.

Unhappy children, entering at age three, show less change of behavior after a year in school. Nursery school attendance, after age four, cannot easily correct undesirable behavior patterns which have been firmly established by the exclusive environment of the home. The nursery school should not try to be like the home, because it cannot be. We realize and admit freely that most children and mothers are eager to be separated from each other for a few hours a day, and we recognize this desire as wholesome.

The idea that every nursery school should have formal or compulsory parent education is one to which we do not subscribe. The school's job is to provide education for children, and this by itself is a very large order to fill. Parents automatically do get some new ideas simply by talking with teachers and director incidentally as they care to, and by observing how teachers handle children. Formal classes and scheduled interviews with parents are not desired by most of them, in our experience. Furthermore, teachers who are skillful with young children are usually not the best teachers of parents, partly because teachers often lack the experience of parenthood. The association's open-door admissions policy brings to school children of differing races, creeds, color, social and economic status and educational backgrounds. Therefore, though teachers can deal with children from all walks of life, they cannot be helpful to all their parents. When forced to try to be so, beyond the normal exchange of casual conferences on specifics of child behavior, women who are potentially good teachers can be alienated from nursery school work. Also parents who do not want to divulge family affairs can be alienated and keep their children home rather than risk the loss of privacy.

Having a special social worker or parent educator on the premises only complicates matters. The director is capable of deciding which children will not fit into the school—all others are welcome and best off in nursery school if the school is of good quality. We know that more separation of parent education and nursery education is possible and very desirable. We also believe that the best parents are those who themselves had good childhood experiences, and the nursery school's best parent education program is preparing boys and girls for good future parenthood. Education for parenthood, in the nursery school, is too often too little and too late, and can be dangerous or superficial. Parents who do not feel the need of it are made uncomfortable by group education with others who are not their peers, and those who feel the most in need of enlightenment may be persons who require far more complex instruction and help than the nursery school can or should try to give. Other agencies exist for this function, and we recommend parents to them when necessary.

What most parents need is less criticism, implied or overt, from the school, and more moral support for doing the best they can, which all parents are really doing. If their best is not good enough, all society is to blame for the many complex conditions which affect parents' misguided behavior, and the nursery school should not assume that parent-teacher contacts can do much about them. For this reason we minimize reports to parents on child misbehavior, so as not to add to family anxieties, knowing from experience that home and school do not evaluate behavior similarly, and that much of it will improve with time and further nursery school experiences of good quality. We live and let live, and try to make children as happy as they can be in school, and parents more satisfied with their children.

We rarely employ a mother as a teacher, and then only when her child can be in another room. We do not have substitutes or volunteers in the classroom. We are convinced that the three regular teachers in the room are enough adults for the children to learn to like and to obey. Since the adults must be compatible and behave consistently in one classroom, the fewer the better.

Our experiment with a parent-cooperative nursery was short-lived and deemed an unsatisfactory method of trying to reduce costs both of nursery education and parent education. There is no safe way to reduce the cost of good preschool education. It is costly, compared to elementary school, not to college education. Endorsing the desirability of such reductions leads society to give excuses rather than good reasons for placing children under the instruction of adults who are present, not because they are qualified teachers, but because this arrangement seems to provide a condition whereby the taxpayers have their cake and eat it, too. The child is entitled to have his mother be special to him, as his mother, and she cannot be this special person to him when she is acting as teacher to him and others. We employ graduates of teacher-training institutions as teachers when we are able to. We also employ women who seem to be "naturals" but lack a college degree. Permanent employment is given only after a trial period, as this policy insures the best morale in staff performance. We train our new teachers on the job by having them work directly with the children under supervision of the experienced teachers. Student teachers get similar training, and their practice work is backed up by selected reading and conferences which support our methods and our curriculum. We do not burden them with purely academic approaches.

The curriculum at the Preschool Learning Center encourages children to learn by doing, and by being themselves, under supervision of teachers who enjoy their society. The program is planned to promote well-being in body, mind and spirit of both children and adults. The school day is balanced with periods of enjoyable play activities, rest periods and times for eating nourishing foods. The center opens at 8:00 A.M. and closes at 4:00 P.M. so that part-time working mothers can enroll their children. Children of nonworking mothers can be enrolled from 9:15 to 11:45, or 9:15 to 12:45. Breakfast is served at 8:30, after the early-comers have had a rest period on cots. From 9 to 12 children play indoors or outdoors, as they care to, weather permitting. There is no group instruction, other than for short music and story periods. The yard is equipped with safe apparatus and wheel toys which encourage vigorous movement that builds good muscle coordination, under eye and brain control, developing powers of observation, ability to evaluate risk situations and awareness of the activities of others. Misuse of equipment is discouraged by corrective remarks from teachers—not by disallowing further use of it, except on occasion by temporary removal of the child to another activity.

Physical force of teacher is used, however, in any situation destructive to children or to property, but such force is not used punitively. The distinction between punitive and nonpunitive use of force is a subtle one. When the teacher is able to admit her own anger or annoyance, and is also able to have conscious control of her speech and actions, she can act nonpunitively. Thus she is not being hypocritical, but wise, for she knows that children respond best when she controls her own behavior, but acts decisively; thus she condemns the deed but not the doer. Above all, teachers try to be polite to children. Rudeness we have found to be very destructive. For this reason, we select teachers who, by habit, are polite to their inferiors as well as their superiors. Only long experience develops the capacity of teachers to use nonpunitive discipline habitually. While adults tend to justify their hostile attitudes toward children as educationally sound, the wise teacher does not, because she knows that mistakes of the learner must be corrected, and precluded by force only if need be, but never by punishment or fear of it. Teachers have an easier time than parents regarding discipline, because they are not with children twenty-four hours a day.

A hot lunch is served at 12:15, after which the children sleep on cots until 3 P.M., then play inside or outside until they go home. Orange juice and 100 milligrams of vitamin C are given at 9:30; cheese and milk at 3 P.M. Lunch consists of twelve different menus served in rotation. Meat, potato, rice, cooked vegetable, bread, margarine, milk, lettuce salad and fruit are the lunch foods. Food combinations and recipes used are those we have found over the years to be the favorites of most children. We want children to eat enough body-building food to sustain good energy levels. By rotating, every two weeks, menus consisting only of their favorite, nutritious foods, they eat well in school. We leave it to the home to provide other favorite foods and new varieties. No child is ever pressured to taste a food or to "clean his plate," and each may have several servings of one food item while uneaten ones remain on the plate. One tablespoon of each food is always served. We discourage those who would eat only bread by limiting the amount available on the table beyond one piece for each child.

There is little food waste in the school because first servings are small, and few children decline to eat almost everything served. We have found that "eating problems" are best treated by lack of pressuring children to eat, by the company of peers who enjoy eating. We think that the small amounts of food "wasted" are worth it for building better habits and attitudes toward eating. One cook prepares the food, the housekeeper brings it to the room where it is served in family style to the groups of six to eight children at a three- by six-foot table. The housekeeper removes the dishes and cleans the table while the teachers are settling the children for nap.

We think that young children should have an afternoon nap and that conducting afternoon classes for young children is not desirable nursery education. Lack of building space explains, but does not justify, the scheduling of afternoon nursery school classes, as it long has with kindergarten classes. A child is not likely to develop good learning habits if exposed to school learning situations only when fatigued. To set up classroom space for morning use only is wasteful, but there are many children needing food and sleep away from home who could be making afternoon use of this space. We keep children in the afternoon whose homes are not, for good reason, a better place for the child to be. Overcrowded slum housing, mothers in ill health or with excessive home duties are prevalent good reasons for keeping a child in school until 4 o'clock. Another one is a very poor mother-child relationship. Hopefully the day will come when certain children can come to school on a Saturday or Sunday, or overnight, if need be, because of stress situations in the home. Once the public views the nursery school as a wholesome, necessary service which strengthens family life, voters may decide to build enough schools for all children, believing them to be good protection against family breakdown in urban communities.

In the present climate of opinion, nursery schools seem to be valued more as coaching schools for kindergarten and the ensuing road to college. The Preschool Learning Center has no such concept. Its aim is to let children develop their learning capacities, in noncompetitive cooperation with others on the here-and-now level, leaving the future to unfold as it will, but presumably with consequences brighter than they would be without a good educational start at age two. It is not a head start—head start over whom? Nursery school can help most children to get along better in school; it can also sour them on life in classrooms too regimented. It certainly cannot guarantee to do a good coaching job for success in substandard public school classrooms.

Premature offering of the letters and numbers, for it can only be that at the nursery school age, will no doubt prove to be founded currently on mistaken optimism in the minds of some researchers, parents and taxpayers. We feel that since adults do not yet know enough about the workings of the child mind, they cannot be sure that the three-year-old reader will not later become more a reader of word symbols than a fluent reader of word meanings, unless those words are supported by pictorial visual stimulus, or audio stimulus such as "the voice" as heard on television and radio, or the sound from a $30,000 typewriter.

Adults fail to realize that any specific new learning can not be disassociated from the total physical, mental and emotional stimulus to the brain which occurs while that learning is taking place. Undesirable aspects of any learning situations become fixed in the brain while the desirable ones are being fixed. Educators like to oversimplify the situation for themselves by ignoring the negative aspects of any given bit of learning, so long as the adult's specific objective is achieved. Because the adult's mind is so different from the child's and can never again become like a child's, a "mind-gap" between teacher and pupil must always exist. Love, or empathy, does not bridge this mind-gap, but only mitigates misunderstandings. For this reason, it is better for adults to note carefully the total responses of the child to new learning situations than it is to ignore some of them. Traditional attitudes about child learning hold that much af it has to be unpleasant to children, and they must learn to bear it. (The doctrine of original sin is far from dead.) No one can guess what far-reaching benefits to the human race would result if adults could guide child learning without poor side effects. The great value of nursery education is that teachers can take time to be aware of the child's total behavior, and they are trained to weigh relative values in learning situations. In nursery schools which do not have well-trained teachers the children's total learning will not constitute desirable development of the mind.

The association has never endorsed any kind of prereading exercises in its nursery schools, but it maintains an indoor curriculum designed to develop the very young child's mind to recognize and to memorize form, shape, color and other aspects of sensory materials. This kind of development is pleasurable and is valuable as a foundation for learning the three R's at a later date. When each child in his play moves ahead at a rate of speed decided by his own mind, this development is wholesome and sound.

As for language development, we do not encourage children to learn mainly from adults by having them repeat, singly or in unison, phrases of rhymes which adults have composed. Instead, we seek to make the environment one where children speak spontaneously to adults and to other children, without fear of being humiliated when they "say the wrong thing." We respect their desire to say little, knowing that coaxing children to verbalize is not wise. However, there is always the sound of children verbalizing in our classrooms. It is not true that children in our schools who come from the so-called "culturally deprived" families speak less well than children from middle class homes, unless their families do not speak English. Children can be disinclined to speak when there is too much verbalizing at home or at school, or because it is unsafe to verbalize freely. Most children hear English spoken on radio and television, but they may not listen to much of the speech from these media. In the nursery school we try to minimize adult verbalizing to those words which have immediate significance to the child being spoken to.

Over the years we have learned that an indoor curriculum based mainly on the visual arts is the best one for developing cognition, memory, powers of concentration, satisfaction with work done, willingness to do more of the same until "learning" is achieved, and eagerness to use materials creatively. Art materials include the obvious ones of clay, easel paint, finger paint, crayons; less obviously, they include large blocks and a large variety of small table toys which can be used as units for making abstract constructions. Whatever the child may label these productions, the eye and brain register them as abstract esthetic formations, or gestalts, and for this reason they can be called art materials.

Non-art materials are books, dolls, doll furniture and toys, picture puzzles, pounding devices, toy trains, and the various other types of playthings which are used with regard to their informational meanings—meanings which derive largely from the adult mind and hopefully have similar meaning to the child's mind. These toys always give the same visual gestalt with their fixed forms and meanings, whereas art materials are abstract, fluid, ever changing, and require no projected meanings or labeling, though they can also be added.

As we know, children may project their own meanings on whatever they play with. A doll may be a doll, or a mama, or a superman, but the visual stimulus of a doll, or of a picture, is always the same, no matter what the labeling. A child's painting or a scribbling is fluid, not static or duplicable, and the art of drawing keeps stimulating the senses and the mind to work with dynamic abstract, structural processes, no matter what verbal label is put on the final results. Thus art materials are richer in visual and mental stimulus than non-art materials, because the former can forever be combined into organized structural wholes having new entities for eye and brain to detect and "learn" or "memorize."

From our twenty-year study of one-half million art products of preschool children, we have learned a great deal about the natural unfolding of the child mind in its ability to recognize and to retain abstract line constructions, or gestalts—the ability needed for learning to read at a later date. We have also learned that there is a biologic schedule for this development which roughly corresponds to age level maturation. Though children vary individually in this development, as they do in growth, the appearance in art works of certain gestalts, in sequential order, is similar for children the world over. Thus we believe that a curriculum founded on the arts is biologically sound, and lets the child mind naturally unfold, as Froebel and Montessori thought it would and should, and avoids the dangers of stuffing it like a goose with valuable content of the adult mind. Of course, the didactic materials in use today are far more plentiful and superior to those devised by these two great educators.

The history of education shows that it has been dominated by the stuffing process. To extend formal education downward to preschool children nursery education mainly for promoting benefits to adults, economically, politically, or socially is to proceed at great risk. Experience and research have given evidence that the association's art-centered curriculum seems to be a wise one.

CHILD ART RESEARCH PROGRAM

This program is a continuation of research done by the association over the past twenty years. During that period, the drawings and paintings made by children have been saved and studied as objective records of child development. In 1955 a report was made, based on examination of 100,000 works of preschool children. Since that date 200,000 more works of preschoolers have been collected, plus half a million made by elementary school children living in the Bay Area of California, plus some 5000 drawings and paintings done by children in thirty foreign lands. This collection, known as the Rhoda Kellogg Child Art Collection, constitutes the largest collection of child art work in one location and will be available for research purposes at the Preschool Learning Center early in 1968.

Research to date shows that young children, the world over, draw line gestalts of such similarity that they can be viewed as expressions of a biologic rather than sociologic nature, and that they constitute a reliable record of how cognitive ability in the young child naturally develops.[2] Since 1955, many new findings about this development have been discovered and reported in two books.[3, 4] What makes this collection especially valuable is that it contains a large quantity of work of young two-year-olds, difficult to obtain, and of basic importance to the understanding of cognitive ability of that age level. For example, we have discovered that scribblings made at this age, and later, are placed on the paper in what are called placement patterns, and that work done at a later age, up through the early pictorial stage of drawing, shows how these self-taught, "learned" patterns dominate child art. Therefore, interpretations of what are called distortions in child art can be misleading, unless one recognizes the role which placement patterns play in the child's spontaneous production of art gestalts.

The aim of this research program is (1) to develop objective descriptions of the gestalts made by normal young children; (2) to record the age levels in which these gestalts are generally made by children; (3) collate the drawing performance of children with their other behavior which indicates developing cognitive ability; (4) determine which gestalts can be reliably used as measurements of cognitive development in art.

The above paragraphs merely indicate the nature of this research; space does not permit further comment on this important work. Funds are being sought to do the necessary statistical work to establish the incidence of identifiable gestalts in child work as they appear on the age level scale. With this data as a base line, a teacher could be trained to "read" children's scribblings objectively, as a measure of child ability to see, to remember and to construct line gestalts. From these readings, adults would be able to set the timing of a child's readiness to learn word gestalts. The writer thinks that the important role which scribbling plays in developing the child's mind for comprehending abstract line gestalts is too little understood by educators. This research can give needed understanding.

CHILD ART CLASSES

As a result of our research to date, the association decided that many young children could benefit greatly by having access to art materials in classes which could be conducted in space not qualifying for a regular nursery school program. In 1964, in a small space in the North Beach Housing Project, experimental classes were set up and operated until April, 1966. Classes ran from 9 A.M. to 12 noon and from 1 P.M. to 4:30 P.M. in space made available by the San Francisco Housing Authority. Children living in the project could attend for as short or as long a time as they cared to, so long as they concentrated on working with the art materials. Mothers had to bring the two-year-olds and return for them after an hour. Most of the children, aged three and older, came by themselves and left when they wanted to. The room opened off the project's playground where the children were accustomed to playing without parents being present.

The class schedules called for separation of age levels by hours of the day, but this did not work out. Some children stayed all morning, several returned in the afternoon. School age children made so much trouble if we did not let them come in the afternoon, that we had to admit them. In only 600 square feet of space, this mixing of various age children has serious disadvantages, but the space could not be enlarged. Even with the poor facilities, the program was a great experimental success. It proved that children are starved for art materials and thrive when exposed to them. More than half the children in the project regularly used the facilities, though only twenty-two could be crowded into this small space at one time. Some children stayed only for short periods, others regularly spent two or three hours a day here. Two teachers were always in attendance. The children were from families of various national origin; some spoke no English. Since only residents in the project were eligible, the racial and social mixture was that of the tenants. There was no charge for these classes.

In the new center, there is sufficient space for daily attendance of a hundred children separated by age level into three groups. Because of the density of population in this area, there are great numbers of children needing to be given the opportunity to develop their minds through use of art materials which they do not have at home or in public school. Though the public school offers some opportunities for art, each child is allotted little time for this work, and has almost no access to the table toys which develop esthetic cognition. The center can offer many of these valuable materials to play with, as well as crayons, paint, finger paint, clay and collage—the usual art materials.[5]

The art classes in North Beach project closed down for lack of funds and the desire to keep the association's program under one roof. These classes are popular because they can be attended voluntarily for periods of time which the child sets according to his interest and ability to concentrate. There is no pressure to have a child stay or go, except to leave when his interest in art lags and he becomes troublesome to others. Then he is asked to leave. but can return when he is ready to concentrate on the materials. There is good sociability among the children, and freedom to go from one table to another at will. Dramatic play of disturbing nature is not allowed. Discipline problems are minor for the children who want to do art, but there are a few neighborhood toughs and delinquents who want to come in only to rumble. The program is not set up to be helpful to them, but hopefully, the oncoming crop of such unfortunate youth can be reduced in number as a result of attending art classes, after school hours during the school year, and in summer from 9:30 to 12:00 and 1:30 to 4:00.

ADULT EDUCATION PROGRAM

Parents of very young children who attend art classes are required to remain in the building, but not in the classrooms, except to observe. A lounge and kitchenette provide a natural setting for Negroes, Orientals and Caucasians of varying economic backgrounds to mingle comfortably and be sociable with each other because they are all there for a similar purpose—helping their children to learn. We think the advantages of the art class services will be an inducement to most women in the area to accept each other as parents with common purpose. Whatever kind of "adult education" these parents request, we will try to provide, but no classes or interviews will be urged upon them.[6] We expect them to pick up from the school's atmosphere many valuable insights. We will accept them as adequate parents and not try to reform their ways.

The teacher-training program will be in-service training for teaching in the nursery school or in the child art classes. For the latter, neighborhood women whose home duties permit can be trained and employed.

The adult education which the center expects to do in greater volume is education of the visiting public about the value of nursery school and child art classes for all children. Visitors are always welcome, and seeing is believing. Conferences and meetings for adults can be scheduled, with speakers and films of interest to special groups. Publications, films and art exhibits enable the Association to spread its influence.[7, 8, 9, 10] Correspondence with inquiring persons from far and wide continues, though not on the scale which Mrs. Cooper maintained. In short, the Phoebe A. Hearst Preschool Learning Center expects to be a valuable example of special education programs within the United States, which will bring the Golden Gate Kindergarten Association a future record worthy of its eighty-seven-year old past record of achievements.

BIBLIOGRAPHY

1. Third Annual Report of the Golden Gate Kindergarten Association, 1882.
2. KELLOGG, RHODA; KNOLL, M., and KUGLER, J.: "Form Similarity Between Phosphenes of Adults and Preschool Children's Scribblings." *Nature, 208*:1129-1130, December 11, 1965.

3. KELLOGG, RHODA: *Analyzing Children's Art.* Palo Alto, N-P Pubns, 1967.
4. KELLOGG, RHODA with SCOTT ADELL: *The Psychology of Children's Art.* CRM Publishers, Random House, New York, 1967.
5. KELLOGG, RHODA: *The How of Successful Finger Painting.* Palo Alto, Fearon, 1958.
6. KELLOGG, RHODA: *Nursery School Guide.* Boston, Houghton, 1949.
7. KELLOGG, RHODA: *Child Art Collection of 7500 Drawings of Children Ages 2-5 Years on Microfilm.* Washington, D. C., Microfilm Editions, 1967.
8. KELLOGG, RHODA: *Discipline in the Nursery School.* San Francisco, Golden Gate Kindergarten Association, 1967.
9. KELLOGG, RHODA: *The Biology of Art.* Brooklyn, N. Y., Anthology of Impulse Publications, Dance Horizons, 1967.
10. *Early Expressionists,* 16 mm film, New York, Contemporary Films, Inc., 1965.

Chapter 5

THE DEVEREUX SCHOOLS

Edward L. French

THE Devereux Foundation is a multi-faceted organization. It conducts residential treatment and special education centers for the emotionally disturbed and mentally retarded in Devon, Pennsylvania; Santa Barbara, California; Victoria, Texas, and Rutland, Massachusetts. Plans are under way for a day center in Phoenix, Arizona, and a residential tutoring school in Washington, Connecticut.

In addition, the foundation operates a day school and summer tutorial camp in Pennsylvania; a therapeutic residential camp in Maine; the Devereux Foundation Institute for Research and Training, with an ongoing research program into the causes and treatment of childhood problems, and a professional training program in clinical psychology, school psychology, vocational counseling, child psychiatry, special education, child care services and others; and the Devereux Foundation Press, a publishing house specializing in educational, psychological and psychiatric books, journals, monographs and materials.

This paper, however, will be concerned with Devereux's residential treatment program.

DEVEREUX: A RESIDENTIAL TREATMENT CENTER

As of this writing (late 1966), Devereux's resident student population numbers approximately 1,350—with 910 in the Pennsylvania Schools; 180 in California; 200 in Texas; and sixty-eight in the Massachusetts branch.

Although the children in residence present a wide variety of problems, all fall into one of two general groups: The emotionally disturbed and the mentally retarded, with about 50 per cent of the facilities designed for each.

Subsumed under each general group is a broad spectrum of diagnostic categories, including psychoneurotic disorders, chronic brain syndromes, academic disabilities, behavioral reactions, psychoses, aphasias and autism. The age span is wide, from preschool into adulthood, although some 90 per cent of the student population is in the school age range.

The children are grouped homogeneously, according to age, type of problem, social maturity and similar factors. They reside in geographically separate units, each with complete facilities for from twelve to one hundred students. Each unit has a unique program, with its own home, school, recreation areas and specially trained staff. On many campuses there are several small residential cottages, each with its own homogeneous subgroup.

This paper will concentrate on the treatment philosophy and methodology evolved during the past fifty-four years. However, it may be helpful first to outline Devereux's history and organizational structure.

Devereux was founded in 1912 by a young Philadelphia school teacher, Helena T. Devereux. It was a logical step for a woman who had been instrumental in establishing one of the first special education classes in the country. Six years later Miss Devereux moved her small school to Devon, Pennsylvania, which is still the organization's headquarters.

Here, in the midst of the Main Line section of suburban Philadelphia, the school flourished. In 1944, Devereux became a nonprofit corporation, and since then has operated under a self-perpetuating board of trustees comprised of patrons and employees of the foundation. Helena Devereux remained as the elected director until 1957, when she voluntarily retired from that position. The organization retains strongly her orientation and principles.

Research, both formal and informal, has always played a major role in Devereux's work, as has the training of qualified personnel in the field of childhood mental health. In 1955, the Devereux Foundation Institute for Research and Training was established. Since that time, the institute has conducted extensive organized research projects and training programs in the areas of clinical psychology, school psychology, counseling psychology, rehabilitative counseling, child psychiatry and child care training. The research and training programs are financed by Federal grants and individual contributions. The recent establishment of the Devereux Foundation Press has made possible the publishing, marketing and distribution of a considerable volume of relevant material developed by both Devereux personnel and others.

Community service obligations are met through the operation of day schools, summer day camps, consulting relationships with nearby public school systems, outpatient diagnostic studies and the active participation of Devereux staff members in various local organizations.

Devereux's staff can, for practical purposes, be separated into two primary groups: the unit staff, comprised of personnel who work directly with the children on a day-to-day basis, and the central staff, which consists of department heads and other administrators, secretarial and clerical workers, clinical practitioners, therapists and other professionals.

Each unit staff includes a clinical administrator (usually a special educator), a home supervisor, a group of house parents, a nurse, a school principal, teachers, recreation personnel, cooks, gardeners, etc. Attached to every unit is a team of clinical consultants from the central staff, including a psychiatrist, a psychologist, a social worker and a physician. In addition, consultants in areas such as vocational rehabilitation and speech therapy are available when indicated.

The children's programs are highly individualized, with a staff-to-student ratio of approximately one-to-one. Considerable emphasis is given to individual tutoring, and efforts are made to have every student engaged in individual, small group and large group activities.

The approach, therefore, is multi-disciplinary. Education is the central, integrative discipline, but every child's program is fashioned after the guidelines provided by the multi-disciplinary team of consultants described above.

At this point, the matter of costs usually arises. A recent survey made by the author reveals that the cost of residential therapy programs available in the United States ranges from $6,000 to $12,000 or even more per year per child. This cost factor presents, of course, a serious problem for many families, and unfortunately prohibits such services for many children who could benefit from them.

Invariably, attempts to reduce the cost of residential therapy programs result in the simultaneous lessening of services. This is never desirable, for without a wide-ranging program, intense individualization and the availability of professional staff members, the program itself becomes therapeutically meaningless and reverts to custodial care.

Even in state-supported schools for the emotionally disturbed, the costs of maintenance go as high as $12,000 per year per student. Because these costs are financed from tax funds, individual families do not, in such instances, bear the full burden.

The problem, however, is not so much how to reduce costs as how to help families to meet them. There are several potential avenues to this goal, which we will discuss later.

WHAT RESIDENTIAL THERAPY IS

Residential therapy is a treatment technique in its own right. It borrows from and uses other treatment tools, but also offers unique contributions of its own. It has its own indications for use, along with its own advantages, limitations and problems. In certain situations, it may be an actual treatment of choice.

Residential therapy is *not* psychotherapy given in a residential setting, plus schooling, plus a recreation program. Rather, in its true sense, it is an *integrated* program, with many interweaving facets which are consistently and integratively designed. Many children within a residential therapy program may receive psychotherapy. On the other hand, many may not and yet be in treatment.

The tendency to equate treatment with psychotherapy may be traced to the usual outpatient setting, in which psychotherapy is often the only treatment tool available. In a residential setting, however, many additional means of treatment are possible. It is frequently true that psychotherapy is an important—and occasionally imperative—part of the overall treatment program. It remains, however, but one phase of a total plan.

Just as *psychotherapy* and *treatment* are not synonymous terms, so *residential therapy* and *environmental therapy* are not equivalent.

Residential therapy is an inclusive form of therapy, incorporating psychotherapy, environmental therapy, relationship therapy, recreation therapy and, when indicated, numerous other approaches.

It is true, of course, that environmental therapy constitutes an important phase of a total residential therapy program. Briefly stated, the concept of environmental therapy is that, ideally, *every* aspect of the child's living situation is therapeutically planned. That is to say that *every* daily experience, *every* relationship with both peers and adults, *every* activity in which he takes part is consciously designed for therapeutic purposes.

Such an ideal, of course, can never be achieved. However, certainly more progress can be made toward such a goal within a residential treatment setting than in the usual outpatient setting.

Also implied in this concept is a thorough knowledge of the child's history—particularly of previous experiences and relationships which have been traumatic; of his personality dynamics; of his intellectual pattern and any specific learning disabilities; of his physical abilities and disabilities (including the degree and type of central nervous system impairment, if any); and, above all, of the practical implications these factors hold for programming and controlling behavior.

Perhaps it will be helpful, at this point, to clarify further the term *residential treatment center.* A treatment center for children should, and ordinarily does, differ markedly from either a school or a hospital.

While it usually does have a school program, the educational regime is flexibly designed for therapeutic purposes, and not merely for the acquisition of skills as ends in themselves. This is not to suggest that skill acquisition in itself does not have ego-building implications, but in a treatment center, skill acquisition is the means and ego-building the end.

The distinction between a residential treatment center for children and a hospital designed primarily for adults is discussed by the author at length in an earlier paper,[2] the basic premise of which is the following:

> In general, the excellence of an adult program (in a mental hospital) is judged largely in terms of the amount of psychotherapy and other individual psychiatric attention. It is customary to emphasize comfortable surroundings, full nursing coverage and certain ancillary services, for example, occupational therapy. For young

people, not only do we need more, but more important, we need something different—a change in *attitude* and *criteria*.

Implicit in this broad definition of residential therapy is the necessity for a carefully defined treatment plan which emphasizes implementation in practical aspects of the child's daily life. For example, the child is encouraged to build relationships with the types of adults who can best fulfill his needs, and the competition which he meets is, in actual fact, controlled.

It is also obvious that a multi-disciplinary approach must not only be used, but must be expanded beyond the usual multi-disciplinary team role. The most vital function of the team in a residential treatment center is to provide a structure through which the contributions of all disciplines represented may be brought to focus on (1) an understanding of the child's problems and needs, and (2) practical and specific program plans for the child.

The representative of each discipline (at Devereux: education, psychology, psychiatry, pediatrics and social work) brings to the team his own unique background and experience. It is axiomatic that no single discipline "has all the answers," but that the contributions of all are necessary.

INDICATIONS FOR RESIDENTIAL THERAPY

Indications and contraindications for residential treatment are inherent within its unique treatment opportunities and limitations. It is not, certainly, a panacea, but neither is it merely a last resort, to be considered only when all else fails.

Within a very general context, residential therapy is indicated in the case of emotional disturbance: when environment is a factor in the child's illness; when harmful aspects of present environment cannot be eliminated; when an environmental change is necessary for, or would be helpful to, treatment; when the child exhibits strong resistance to the forms of treatment, such as psychotherapy, available in an outpatient situation; when continuation in the present environment is dangerous either to the child himself or to others in the environment; or when community outpatient facilities are unavailable or inadequate.

With the mentally retarded, factors to be considered when weighing the advantages and disadvantages of residential placement include the following:

The availability at home of adequate companionship at his age level; the degree of competition from neighborhood children; the attitude of the community regarding acceptance of a mentally retarded child; the opportunity for social interaction; the availability of special education facilities which are oriented to individual needs; the relationship to siblings (the retarded child's effect on them and vice versa).

Admittedly, separation from home and parents may constitute a major trauma for children. However, the crucial consideration is the fact that the child is deteriorating in the home environment. Every therapist who has attempted to help a child within the framework of one or a few therapy sessions per week knows the frustrating situation that exists when the child must continue to live in the very environment which is causing or contributing to the problem.

Among the types of problems for which residential therapy is indicated are the following:

Mental Retardation, With or Without Emotional Overlay

A mentally retarded child is inevitably faced, both in the home and in the community, with insurmountable competition from his chronological peers and from younger siblings. This frequently results in frustration reactions of various types.

To prevent or ameliorate such reactions, use of a residential setting, in which the child is placed with a functional as well as a chronological peer group, can be very beneficial. The programs in such cases are not merely educational, but therapeutic, and frequently the ability to learn improves as the emotional overlay is ameliorated.

Use of residential placement for the higher-grade mentally retarded is particularly indicated with the relatively newer emphasis being put on rehabilitation of such children through intensive vocational rehabilitation programs.[3] Training in self-care and social maturity skills for the trainable and educable retarded is often facilitated in a residential setting, where home-care staff can be educationally oriented.

Situation Reactions

It is generally accepted that some childhood problems and emotional disturbances can be caused, or at least exacerbated, by the situation in which the child lives. Of particular significance, naturally, is the family situation. Frequently a circular reaction is found, with the situation irritating the child's problem, and child's problem, in turn, causing a reaction by the family, which reacts on the child, etc. Removal of the child from the family can be, in itself, a mutually healing move, as will be discussed later.

Acting-out Problems

The "acting-out" child is often very difficult to treat directly in an outpatient setting. There are many reasons for this, including the following: potential danger to the community; community and police reaction to his behavior; his usual distrust, suspicion and resistance to psychotherapy, and his tendency to dissipate treatable anxiety through impulsive behavior. A residential setting incorporating a degree, at least, of containment and the utilization of a total therapy program including skill acquisition for ego-building purposes has, in many instances, proven successful.

School and Learning Problems

Children who fail in school may do so for one or more of a variety of reasons, including intellectual retardation, specific language disabilities, physical handicaps, or emotional problems. Residential placement may be indicated in some instances.

The flexible, individualized school program usually found in a residential treatment center permits freer scheduling in terms of each child's strengths and weaknesses. In addition the therapeutic program, as well as the school program itself, may prevent or ameliorate emotional problems associated with learning difficulties, as cause or effect, or both.

An excellent summary of indications for residential treatment is given by Scott[5] who writes the following:

> Highly expert treatment for a child and adolescent can be and often is largely or wholly nullified if other needs of the child are not recognized and supplied. This is far more true in the treatment of children and adolescents than in the treatment of adults. The therapist usually correctly avoids the use of environmental manipulation as much as possible in the treatment of adults. This rule for adults easily may be incorrectly applied to the treatment of children.
>
> As insights and the freedom from disabling conflicts are achieved, most adults are capable . . . to accomplish changes in their environment. Children are unable to change their environment to any extent, both because of dependency and the subjection to authority which is inherent to childhood. If allowed and encouraged to do so, the child's own immature ego and lack of independent resources not only disqualify him to arrange things for himself, but being thrown on his own resources often only increases his confusion and anxiety.*

Scott goes on to emphasize that, if the therapist feels that treatment would be facilitated by environmental manipulation, "then he should seriously consider as a first choice and not as a last resort, a residential treatment program."

BASIC PROGRAM PHILOSOPHY

We have already emphasized that residential therapy is an integrated program which includes *to a planned degree* such treatment tools as environmental therapy, educational therapy, relationship therapy, psychotherapy, play therapy, drama therapy, art therapy, music therapy, etc. The unique quality of residential therapy lies in the opportunities it presents

---

* Quoted by permission of the author.

for the utilization of a variety of treatment procedures within a therapeutically designed milieu.

There are three basic considerations in the implementation of residential therapy: complete diagnostic study as a foundation for program planning; a multi-disciplinary orientation to both study and treatment, and a thorough understanding of the principles of environmental design. We will attempt to discuss each at some length.

Diagnostic Study

The admissions process is vitally important to the entire treatment program, and careful structuring of this step increases the chances of success at all points. Referral to a residential treatment center is usually made by a professional person or agency, and often detailed clinical studies have been made prior to referral which are of great help in screening and initial evaluation procedures.

Special techniques, committee structures, etc., for admissions vary widely among residential treatment centers, but most have three major objectives as follows: the screening of the applicant in terms of the applicability of program (unless the center must accept all referrals, as in the case of some state and community centers); the securing of clinical and historical material so that placement into an appropriate peer group can be decided and a tentative program begun immediately; and the enlistment of active family participation in planning.

To these ends, preadmission clinical reports are obtained and studied. Clinical evaluations are made by the staff of the center prior to or at admission; detailed case history is obtained through parental interview, and admission case conferences are held by the evaluating team. Parents are interviewed to discuss preliminary findings, the decision regarding acceptance and placement, the tentative program plan and goals and the philosophy and methods of the treatment center.

Preadmission studies, history and admission evaluations are used essentially for screening and initial planning. More intensive studies in all areas are made during the first few months of residence. In addition to the usual clinical evaluations by psychiatry, psychology, medicine and education, it is of great importance to obtain *direct observation* reports of the child's residence and school adjustment, relationship to peers, relationship to authority, reaction to success and failure, etc.

These studies are then synthesized through group discussions. Short-term and long-term goals are refined, and program implementation techniques decided upon.

At relatively frequent intervals, the child's changing situation is evaluated on the basis of direct personal observation in the home, in the school and, when applicable, in psychotherapy. Formal studies in any indicated area may, of course, be done at any time. Changes in program may thus be initiated as the child's needs change. In the evaluation studies, emphasis is at all times placed on the implementation of findings into actual program content and method.

Multidisciplinary Orientation

The multidisciplinary group at Devereux, as mentioned earlier, consists of the unit clinical administrator, school principal, home supervisor, psychiatrist, psychologist, physician and social worker. Both the school principal and the home supervisor are members of the department of education, due to our conviction that it is unwise to separate administratively the home and the school. The clinical administrator, who is usually also an educator, is responsible for the implementation of professional recommendations.

Each consultant functions both as an individual representative of his discipline and as a member of a group. In general, the role of each discipline is as follows:

EDUCATION. The education department is administratively responsible for the home, school and recreation programs, and, therefore, for the implementation of the environmental therapy program, with the guidance of the other clinical departments.

In addition, this department is looked to for consideration of group dynamics and group balance—both extremely important in a residential setting—and for clinical educational studies of learning levels and patterns. In other words, the education department—which is, of course, really a special education department in every sense—functions as the environmental administrative department.

PSYCHIATRY. This department is the one primarily responsible for elucidation and interpretation of the child's personality dynamics, for guidance of program planning based thereon, and for the conduct or supervision of individual and group psychotherapy, music therapy, play therapy and art therapy.

MEDICINE. The medical department is responsible for the physical welfare of the children, and also for medical studies relating to neurological impairments, endocrine deficiencies, visual and auditory problems and similar matters.

PSYCHOLOGY. The department of clinical psychology is concerned with psychological assessment in all areas, including personality, emotional development, intellectual and learning patterns and etiology. Vision and hearing screening tests are conducted by this department, and speech therapy is in its jurisdiction. Psychologists may, if qualified, conduct psychotherapy under psychiatric supervision. The research and training departments are under psychological administration.

Social Work. The securing and synthesizing of preadmission studies is the responsibility of the social work department, as is the obtaining of case history material through parental interviews and the making of a social diagnosis. Social work also carries considerable (but not exclusive) responsibility for follow-up parental contacts and for implementation of post-discharge planning. Communication with community agencies is, for the most part, handled by social workers. As in the case of psychologists, qualified social workers may do supervised therapy.

In group discussions, the educators contribute particularly from the standpoint of the child's educational performance and patterns, relationships to other students and staff and group interactions, as well as reporting direct observations of class, residence and recreation situations. The psychiatrist contributes from his knowledge of personality dynamics and emotional problems and of psychotherapeutic development. The psychologist brings information concerning the child's intellectual strengths and weaknesses, learning patterns and personality structure. The physician adds information concerning physical, neurological, endocrinological and similar defects. The social worker contributes information concerning the social background, from which the child came and to which he will presumably return, and relates the program planning to parental goals and community facilities.

It is the responsibility of the professional group, after studying all available information concerning the child, to design an overall treatment plan and to outline, as specifically as possible, staff attitudes and procedures. In other words, a therapeutic "program prescription" is designed, involving the types of therapy to be used, the amount of each, the types of staff and peer relationships to be encouraged, the amount and type of competition to which the child should be exposed, the degree of support to be afforded, etc.

While this multidisciplinary approach has proven advantageous, there are a few cautionary factors which should be borne in mind. Unless appropriate precautions are observed, team functioning can result in individual responsibility being sacrificed to group action. It is mandatory, therefore, to emphasize the administrative authority which the representative of each discipline has in his own area.

Clinical decisions cannot be made on the basis of a democratic majority vote. Rather, each member of the group must have an area in which he makes the final decision after having considered the contributions and advice of his fellow team members. For example, in matters of unit administration and environmental therapy, the educator is fully responsible; the psychiatrist is the decision-maker in psychotherapeutic questions; the physician decides on the advisability for neurological referrals and medical treatment.

Principles of Environmental Design

Probably the least understood—and the least codified—aspect of residential therapy is the environmental program. Perhaps the best organized presentation of the principles involved is that of Alt.[1] While the following discussion acknowledges Alt as a source, it also incorporates other material derived from experience and theoretical formulation at Devereux.

Among the basic assumptions of environmental therapy is the belief that an individual's "living space" can be healthful or traumatic, and that environmental experiences can either contribute to emotional growth or be stultifying. Such factors as interpersonal relationships with peers and adults, along with the degree of competition and success inherent in the environment, are also considered important to the development of a mature personality.

The implementation of an environmental therapy program must, to a large extent, revolve around interpersonal relationships between staff and child. These relationships, to be therapeutically effective, must in turn be solidly based on staff attitudes of acceptance and realistic understanding. It is mandatory that the child comes to feel that staff members are sincerely interested in his welfare and accept him as an individual—even though they may not condone his behavior.

From this standpoint, as from many others, communication is crucial if staff attitudes are to be consistent and nonmanipulatable. Even when the roles of individual staff members are clearly differentiated, all must act within the framework of a thoroughly understood overall plan. Thus, general attitudes on the part of the staff should be such that even unanticipated spot decisions will be made on the basis of the child's needs, rather than for ease of management.

This all-important communication should certainly include formal reports, frequent staff meetings, interpretations of day-to-day behavioral exchanges and agreement on program modifications. Unmatched for the exchange of significant information, of course, is the kind of informal communication which takes place over coffee or lunch.

Group dynamics constitute another major factor in environmental control. Group balance, the relationship of children with each other and peer pressures can be either negative or positive. For instance, in placing a newly admitted child in a group, one must consider the degree of concentration of problems already existing within that group and whether this particular child's problems can be absorbed or will tend to overbalance the group.

A history of consistent failure is shared by most children in a residential treatment center. One of the central goals of a therapeutic environment, therefore, is to reverse this trend. This must not, however, be attempted via artificial means. In order for the experience of consistent success to be meaningful, it must also be realistic.

Such an approach, of course, implies the gearing of competition to the child's abilities, the encouragement by staff of participation on the part of the child in activities in which they feel confident he can succeed, and the furnishing of just enough support to ensure success. It also implies a scale of values on the part of staff so that success for one child in a certain activity can be as meaningful as success in another activity for another child.

> The school program . . . functions as part of the total milieu therapy by developing skills which build ego. With normal young people, every new skill acquired, whether in reading, algebra, basketball foul-shooting, art or automobile mechanics, is a step toward maturity, toward ego growth. But this matter assumes an even greater importance with emotionally disturbed (and mentally retarded) young people. The one common denominator for all our students is previous *failure;* success, because they are not accustomed to it, is of special significance. Thus, an educational program carefully individualized within a group setting is in itself a therapy; it increases contact with reality and builds self-control and confidence.[3]
>
> All of this, of course, involves much conscious attention to goal-setting. We have found that it is very difficult for many disturbed children to work for a long-term goal, and therefore, it has been necessary to devise techniques to substitute a series of short-term realistic, attainable goals with immediate rewards.[4]

The setting of limits for children's behavior is an inherent part of environmental therapy, and is probably a factor in increasing the children's sense of security. These limits vary from one group to another, depending on the levels of emotional growth, but the procedure is facilitated by our system of separate campuses for different groups. However, a minimum standard is articulated, understood and insisted upon, even in the most disturbed groups. Each child is led to understand that the staff will do everything possible to help him stay within the limits.

Environmental therapy also involves the principle of gradual substitution of internal behavior controls for external. When the child is unable to control his own impulses, he needs, and usually unconsciously welcomes, controls being imposed on him, because of his fear of his own destructive impulses. However, in the growth process, he must have the opportunity for an increasing degree of freedom to the level at which he can handle it. This process must be carefully designed and controlled, for it can be as harmful to give too much freedom too soon so that the child fails, as to restrict below the child's level of internal control.

In speaking of the necessity for external controls, we do not mean to imply that closed facilities play any role in a residential treatment center. It is advisable, on both theoretical and practical grounds, that the center be operated in an open setting where the child is held by positive motivation and relationship with the staff. Runaways do occur, but, considering the types of problems being treated, on a surprisingly infrequent basis. Usually, the runaway is accepted back with the knowledge that his action is disapproved. In most instances where a child cannot maintain himself in an open-group therapeutic setting, hospitalization is indicated.

In carrying out external controls, in setting realistic limits, and in helping the child to develop self-control, staff members must tolerate—and, indeed, expect—difficult behavior. It is therefore evident that the adults in an open setting must be personally secure individuals who are not prone to panic, and who do not regard incidents of misbehavior as being directed at them.

SPECIFIC TECHNIQUES AND METHODS

The uniqueness of residential therapy lies in the vast array of avenues through which the general principles described above may be implemented. The following will incorporate only a few examples of specific techniques and methods but will, hopefully, suggest many more. For purposes of organization, we will restrict the discussion to five major areas: physical facilities, individualized programming, school program, work program and eventual transition to community living.

Physical Facilities

The program needs of a residential treatment center should dictate the kind of physical facilities available. Small, cottage-type residential groupings are usually desirable. About twelve to fifteen children is generally the best number for homogeneous grouping, although the number may vary with age and type of problem.

Large school buildings present numerous problems. We have found it preferable to have no more than thirty to sixty children in a given school, with classes ranging from individual tutoring situations to groups not exceeding seven or eight students. Because all young people need "elbow room," it is necessary to have an adequate number of athletic fields, gymnasiums, swimming pools, bicycle yards, theaters, etc.

Residences should be designed with both age groups and types of problem in mind. For example, young children need a play-bedroom arrangement for the period before bedtime, whereas preadolescents and adolescents should have individual desks for study and hobby activities. Each child, of course, needs a private bureau and closet.

Both single and double bedrooms should be provided. Most children want and need a roommate, but single rooms should be available for certain situations. It is usually inadvisable to room more than two youngsters together.

Although residences should be as comfortable and homelike as possible, an exception may be made in the case of acting-out adolescent boys. At the beginning of the treatment program, these students often benefit from being placed in relatively primitive surroundings—sometimes even with furniture they have made themselves. Later, as the boys grow in self-control and there is a reduction of overt acting-out behavior, they can be gradually promoted to more comfortable quarters.

Individualized Programming

No matter how homogeneous the group, no two children will present exactly the same needs. Within each general program, therefore, there must exist provisions for a wide range of individualized programming.

To take as an example only one facet of a total plan, the sports program, the offerings must go from individual sports such as track, gymnastics, weight lifting, tennis and golf to integrated team athletics such as football, soccer and hockey. Also, skill demands should range from relatively non-competitive skill training work, through activities such as croquet and quoits to interscholastic baseball, basketball, hockey, track and football events.

We mentioned earlier the relative difficulty which disturbed children encounter in striving toward a long-term goal. With this in mind, we have found it helpful in certain of our units to maintain a weekly report and reward system in which students are graded on general citizenship, home adjustment, school effort, etc. Allowances and special privileges, such as trips with varying degrees of freedom, are awarded on the basis of these grades.

The use of such a technique, of course, depends upon the degree of illness and objective symptomatology presented. Children must never be punished for exhibiting the very behavior which led to their enrollment in the treatment center. Therefore, such a technique is employed only at certain levels of emotional development, and is administered with staff attitudes of accomplishment and reward rather than failure and punishment.

Another practical method of implementing the gradual substitution of internal controls for external ones is through the use of promotional transfers. We have found it very advantageous to establish for each child a rather finely graduated series of steps through which he can progress, with each step offering a slightly greater degree of freedom and privilege. This series should be made known to the child at the onset of the treatment program, along with an understanding of the concept that increased freedom is accompanied by increased responsibility.

School Program

There are many reasons why it is advisable for a residential treatment center to offer its own school program at all levels. Attempts to utilize local public schools have, through no fault of the public schools, generally proven unsatisfactory.

The goal of the public school is education. In a treatment center, however, the primary goal of the school program is therapy, with education being secondary. Consequently, the necessary degree of rigidity which typifies the public school limits the classroom as a therapeutic tool.

Public school classes are bound by certain rules and regulations with which disturbed and/or retarded children often cannot cope. If a child is scheduled for an English class, for example, he must at least attend the class and remain for the full period. In the treatment center, however, if the child's emotional condition is not equal to the study of English on any particular day, he may instead go to an art class or the woodshop. If his emotional problem limits his attention span to ten or twenty minutes rather than the usual forty-five, he should be able to leave the class for another activity without being disgraced.

Balanced scheduling is frequently an important aspect of the school program in a treatment center. In practice, it means simply that an abstract activity such as an algebra or reading class is followed by a concrete activity such as arts and crafts or physical education.

We have also found the utilization of "normal" adolescent school activities of proven value. Several Devereux units publish student newspapers and year books; the high school units for the emotionally disturbed are divided into freshman, sophomore, junior and senior classes, depending upon academic credits; a student council and other committees, such as home councils and recreation councils, function well; graduation is with caps and gowns and traditional commencement ceremonies.

In a similar manner, we feel it advisable to use school rather than hospital terminology. Thus, children are *students* rather than *patients*. The residences are *homes* and not *wards*. At the same time, it is a thoroughly understood, accepted fact that the students have problems and are in the residential center for treatment.

In the educational program for the mentally retarded, full use should be made of such individualized approaches as teaching tapes and single learning booths, as well as especially adapted techniques including mechanized teaching aids and the Initial Teaching Alphabet System. A language development program is of utmost importance.[6] It goes without saying that flexibility of programming is necessary.

Work Program

A work program in which positive staff-student relationships may be built is vital to the success of a treatment program for adolescents and older children. In addition to teaching students the importance of individual contributions to group welfare, it also offers them the acquisition of specific work skills, the satisfactions of a job well done and a sense of personal worth. Even the youngest child can be held accountable for some work role, if only the emptying of a wastebasket.

It is necessary, of course, for a residential treatment center to offer strong services in vocational evaluation, training and counseling. Rehabilitation at the adolescent level should be, if not to a normal school setting or college, then to a meaningful work situation.

Few children come to a treatment center possessing vocationally useful skills. Consequently, the development of such skills is an important part of the treatment process. Such an undertaking must, in turn, be based on a study of aptitudes and interests, the setting of realistic goals and the development of motivation through counseling.

While many graduates of residential treatment centers go on to further academic training, many others possess performance skills which far outweigh their verbal abilities, or cannot be motivated academically. For the latter group, appropriate goals may be found in such fields as electronics, automobile mechanics, carpentry, hairdressing, dietetics, or clerical work. This area, of course, is of great significance for the rehabilitable mentally retarded adolescents and adults.

Transition to Community Living

After the period of initial adjustment to life in a residential treatment center is over, most children develop a sense of security from the familiar surroundings and carefully nurtured relationships. Therefore, unless steps are taken to ease the situation, separation anxiety may be intense as the time for discharge draws near.

Such steps may include the gradual extension of home vacations for as long as a full "trial" summer, and the utilization of halfway houses. The latter technique was instituted at Devereux several years ago,[3] and has proven encouragingly successful. Students who are judged to be within a few months to a year of readiness for discharge may be transferred to one of the small (ten children) cottages which are located in the local community. Their community contacts are greatly increased, even to the point where students may work or attend school in the community. Considerable freedom is given; the students may go about the community largely as they please; bedtime is flexible; community friendships are encouraged; public transportation is used. At the same time, there is a measure of supportive supervision. Counseling or psychotherapy may be continued, and staff relationships are maintained but gradually diminished to decrease dependency.

PROBLEMS ENCOUNTERED IN RESIDENTIAL THERAPY

While we are convinced that residential therapy is frequently the most complete and practical treatment method available for the rehabilitation of emotionally disturbed and mentally retarded children, it would be unfair to neglect the fact that its unique advantages are accompanied by certain unique problems. Among the basic areas of concern are the necessity for practical implementation of findings; the demands made of staff; the implications of the family situation; the extremely wide range of direct and indirect services required, with concomitant administrative and cost factors; and the uniqueness of community relations.

To an extent, a modification of conventional orientation on the part of professional workers is required in a residential setting, as opposed to the usual outpatient situation. Evaluations, reports and recommendations are significant, in residential therapy, to the degree to which they are directed to practical implementation in programming. Thus, the psychologist, psychiatrist or other professional must emphasize the practical, not only with regard to his own relationship with the child, as in psychotherapy, but to all aspects of a total living situation. This implies thorough familiarity with program possibilities and limitations. Some difficulty in this may be encountered by those professionals who are trained to think in terms of an individual client, without a balancing knowledge of group dynamics and group management.

The ultimate key to the success of a residential therapy program rests in the hands of those adults who work on a direct, day-by-day basis with the children. This is particularly true of members of the education, home and recreation staffs. Theirs is the task of the actual, detailed implementation of program plans formulated in relatively general terms by the clinical consultants. When crises occur—when a child explodes in rage, or becomes without warning unduly depressed, or spontaneously starts a small riot in the cottage—the teacher, housemother or recreation instructor cannot defer action until he consults with the appropriate clinician. Immediate staff response is necessary, not only for control of the individual and the group, but for therapeutic purposes. This fact—that staff members are not only teachers and caretakers, but also models, identification figures, parent surrogates and administrative therapists—may pose major problems.

The overriding problem, of course, is in securing individuals who possess the innate qualifications necessary to assume such responsibilities. It is relatively simple to list the desired characteristics in terms of intuitive understanding, empathy, warmth, dedication, firmness combined with flexibility and inner security. In other words, what we are looking for is a group of nearly ideal human beings. Unfortunately, there are very few such creatures to be found.

The problem is compounded by the fact that not only must we set high standards for personnel whose jobs require constant association with the children, but also for such apparently fringe staff members as cooks, gardeners and drivers. These workers also come into contact with the students, and such contacts can be therapeutically important. Many hours of careful ego-building can be undone by an unwise word or reaction, whether it comes from a teacher in the classroom or a driver transporting the child to a psychotherapy appointment. Therefore, the *first* quality we look for in all staff members is an inherent liking for and ability to work with children. Only when this qualification is met do we consider specific job skills.

There is an undeniable shortage of personnel at all levels and in all job categories within residential treatment centers. Devereux has attempted to meet this challenge through professional courses in child care services, wide-ranging recruitment efforts and intensive inservice training programs.

It is also important that special consideration be given to staff functioning in terms of role differentiation. It was pointed out above that significant treatment can sometimes be administered by staff members not ordinarily identified with therapeutic roles. Administrative action within a residential treatment center invariably carries treatment implications.

On the other hand, it is usually inadvisable for psychotherapists to become involved in obvious environmental manipulation on behalf of students whom they are seeing in therapy. This is not to imply that the psychotherapist should remain entirely apart and conduct his psychotherapy in an ivory tower, or that the deep insights gained through psychotherapy should not be utilized in planning the total program for the child. Quite the contrary, the psychotherapist's findings and recommendations are conveyed to the consulting team and form an integral part of the gradually increasing knowledge of the child, which is the basis for the program prescription.

However, for many of the children in a treatment center, manipulation has become a characterological manifestation. It has been our experience that the psychotherapeutic program—as well as other facets—is hindered if the child has cause to believe that his psychotherapist exerts any degree of control over his living situation. The therapeutic hour is then transformed by the child into a campaign to receive privileges. This inevitably leads either toward intensification of the demands or rejection of the therapist by the child if the therapist does not accede to the demands. In a similar fashion, members of the educational staff deal with the students at the conscious level only, and do not become involved in the interpretation of unconscious material. Thus, each staff member must be ready to recognize the limitations, as well as prerogatives, of his role.

If the adults in the environment are clear and consistent regarding their roles, their areas of competency and their limitations, the children very rapidly absorb and respond to the distinctions, no matter how fine they may be. Such staff understanding requires training, as well as a high level of personal security.

Another major area of concern is the vast complex of situations involving the family. In a residential treatment center it is necessary to include the family in planning for all phases of the program, from enrollment to discharge. This is true in three interrelated aspects: the relief of separation anxiety and guilt reactions; the development of a role for the family in the treatment process itself, and the preparation of the family for the child's ultimate rehabilitation.

Almost inevitably, parents faced with the prospect of placing their child in a residential treatment center experience feelings of failure and guilt. Consequently, most parents, either consciously or unconsciously, exhibit such obvious defense mechanisms as denial, projection, self-recrimination, and overprotection or rejection of the child.

To facilitate the implementation of the child's treatment, the center's staff must aid the family in making the necessary emotional adjustments. This process starts at the time of enrollment and basically includes two aspects: the establishment of confidence on the part of the family in the professional integrity and judgment of the staff, and the development of a feeling of participation and sharing between family and staff.

The fact that the family usually lives some distance from the treatment center makes frequent personal contact impractical and precludes direct therapeutic intervention in the family situation. Therefore, other measures must be taken to ensure family participation and cooperation. These measures may include the following: written professional and observational reports; conferences between staff and family held as frequently as circumstances permit, preferably twice a year and once annually at a minimum; close communication of the treatment center with an agency or professional person in the family's community, accompanied by strong encouragement for the family to utilize such a resource to the fullest; family days at the center, with emphasis on education of the family through staff-led seminars and individual conferences; dissemination to families of various types of brochures, pamphlets, form letters, etc., discussing childhood problems in general and the center's treatment philosophy; frequent personal letters outlining the child's program, changes therein, and progress; and regular vacations for the child at home, unless specifically contraindicated. Visits by the child to his home should, of course, be preceded by letters or personal conferences embodying staff advice on management and family attitude, and should be followed by a direct invitation for the family to report observations, experiences and difficulties.

In addition to maintaining avenues of close communication between center and family, it is sometimes helpful to refer certain members of the family to a facility in their local community where they can receive psychotherapy or counseling. In such instances, close liaison should be maintained between such facilities and the treatment center.

Since the ultimate goal of residential therapy is to rehabilitate the child and return him to his home community, the treatment center obviously cannot keep itself or its students in a state of isolation. It is important that opportunities for community contact be developed and utilized to whatever degree the individual student is capable of handling.

One obvious means of accomplishing this is through trips to town for shopping or entertainment. Such trips can be made in supervised groups or, when indicated, individually and without supervision. Other means include the following: Participation in athletic leagues, with home and away games in the usual sports; utilization of community cultural and educational resources such as museums, historical sites and concerts for scheduled class educational trips; encouragement of local church activities by the students (on a selective basis); and membership by some students, when they are ready, in local youth groups. A halfway house program such as that described earlier can also be a valuable tool in making the transition from treatment center to community.

Of course, if community facilities are to be used advantageously, it is important that potential prejudices and anxieties on the part of the local community be alleviated. It is reasonable to expect an uninformed community to react with apprehension, fear and distrust to a residential treatment center in its midst. Therefore, it is part of the responsibility of the center to overcome such feelings even before they arise.

This can best be achieved by acquainting the community with the actual nature of the treatment center via such means as open house programs, explanatory talks by staff members to local organizations, positive relationships with local newspapers and tours of the center by leading citizens and influential groups. We have also found it valuable to issue general public invitations to student-produced dramatic productions, high school graduation ceremonies, athletic contests and similar functions.

It is also wise to make the center a functioning part of the community by extending its services in such directions as professional assistance to the local public schools, sponsorship of local lay and professional educational programs, training workshops for community teachers and the establishment of a speakers' bureau. All activities designed for the benefit of the community will result in a better general understanding of the center and the children it serves, and are bound to be advantageous to all concerned.

While the bulk of this report has been concerned with the direct service functions of a residential treatment center, it is important to point out that indirect functions also play a vital role in overall administration. This includes such areas as dietetics, construction, building maintenance, purchasing, transportation, office management, finances, budget control and housekeeping. The task of the administrator is to make certain that such departments operate for the purpose of enhancing the therapeutic program, rather than independently toward different goals.

We mentioned earlier the necessarily high costs of residential therapy and the need to find ways of helping families to meet these costs. Considering the shortage of trained personnel in the field and the high initial cost of purchasing or building physical facilities, it would appear logical to concentrate on the full utilization of existing facilities rather than the inauguration of new ones. Some states and other governmental agencies (e.g., Massachusetts, Connecticut, Cuyahoga County of Ohio, etc.) have recognized the advantage of this approach. In such cases, tax funds can be diverted to the treatment of emotionally disturbed and mentally retarded children in existing centers, to the relief of individual taxpayers.

Many residential treatment centers are nonprofit organizations. Those which are may build scholarship and endowment funds for the financial support of those children whose families cannot afford the full costs of an optimal treatment program.

All efforts to reduce nonprofit fees without reducing the range of services are, of course, dependent upon the concrete support and contributions of interested organizations and individuals. The solicitation of such support is not an easy undertaking. The task becomes greatly simplified, however, in instances where there is widespread and sympathetic recognition of the fact that untreated emotionally disturbed and mentally retarded children are and will remain a major public liability.

The estimated number of such children in the United States today varies according to definitions, but it is safe to assume a *minimum* figure of 5,000,000. With specialized help, most of these children can at least cease to be liabilities, and many of them can become contributing members of society.

BIBLIOGRAPHY

1. Alt, Herschel: Residential Treatment for the Disturbed Child. New York, Int. Univ, 1960.
2. French, Edward L.: A treatment program for emotionally disturbed children and adolescents. *Ment Hosp, 14* (7) :386-389, 1963.
3. Kukoda, Louis; Jacobs, Abraham, and French, Edward L.: *Vocational Rehabilitation in Residential Treatment Center.* Devereux Foundation Monograph Series, Devon, Pa., The Devereux Foundation, 1963.
4. Levine, Murray, and Spivack, George: Incentive, time conception and self-control in a group of emotionally disturbed boys. *J Clin Psychol, 15* (1):110-113, 1959.
5. Scott, J. Clifford: On the Indications for Residential Treatment of Children and Adolescents. Devereux Schools Forum, December, 1962, pp. 8-13.
6. Kleiser, John R., *et al.: A Language Arts Program for a Residential Special School.* Devereux Foundation Monograph Series, Devon, Pa., The Devereux Foundation, 1964.

Chapter 6

THE COVE SCHOOLS

LAURA LEHTINEN ROGAN

THE history of an organization—its coming to being, its growth and existence reflects the currents of its time. Some twenty years ago, the commitment of its founders* to a radical new concept in special education and the dedicated support of a few imaginative and enthusiastic laymen† led to a small, experimental adventure in education which was to have far-reaching effects. The Cove Schools (at Racine, Wisconsin and Evanston, Illinois) was organized in 1947 as a very small private, nonprofit school for "brain-injured" children—the only term of designation in use at the time. Its objectives were several. One was to provide education through new understanding and specialized methods for children with diagnosed mild brain damage unable to learn effectively or function behaviorally according to the expectation held out by their tested intelligence level. A second was to provide a working model of an educational laboratory which might serve as an example or inspiration for public school systems desirous of extending their special services to the same classification of children. A third was to provide opportunities for the training of teachers so that they might translate the learnings and experiences gathered at The Cove Schools into local programs adapted to the conditions and needs of their own communities. A fourth was to continue research and studies in the psychology and education of these children. The school was the embodiment of twenty years of treatment and research into the psychological sequelae of neonatal and early brain damage by the late Alfred A. Strauss in the United States and in Germany. As an educational unit it was the culmination of an idea which began with the reeducation of brain-injured war veterans in Germany, led to a pedagogical clinic in Spain and thence to an experimental class at the Wayne County Training School in Northville, Michigan. Because it sought to relate educational procedures in a close alliance with medical and psychological knowledge, its approach was unique.

At the time of the schools' founding the special education philosophy in the United States identified several major classifications of handicap with resulting special need: sensory defects of vision and audition, orthopedic

---

* Alfred A. Strauss, Laura E. Lehtinen, Godfrey Stevens, Marie C. Strauss.

† Robert P. Gardiner, H. M. Benstead, Harold Sporer, Racine, Wisconsin.

handicaps and mental retardation of varying degree.[4] For children afflicted in any of these ways classrooms staffed by teachers with special training were provided in most large school systems. State legislation recognized the particular needs of these children and in many cases provided financial reimbursement to school districts with special classes. Additional educational problem areas were identified in the children with speech defects and reading problems and these were usually met by providing specialists to work with such children individually or in small groups for limited periods of time during the school year until the problem was resolved.

Children with severe emotional or social maladjustment difficulties constituted still another group, but one about which there was no unanimity of opinion in respect to appropriate educational or management approaches. Another sizeable group of children did exist, however, who presented a variety of learning and behavior difficulties, but who did not qualify because of sensory losses, physical crippling, mental retardation, or severe social maladjustment for the special programs provided by the schools. In the studies of remedial reading, suggestions of a central integrative difficulty were advanced as possible causes of the reading problem and case studies of children with known brain damage were included.[3, 6] However, this factor was not independently investigated. Lack of integrity of the child's central nervous system had not yet been definitely implicated as a significant contributor to his success or failure as a school pupil.

The early researches of Dr. Strauss and his collaborators on the psychological and behavioral consequences of early brain damage were done with mentally retarded children. It was demonstrated in a succession of studies[8, 9, 12–14] that children with exogenous mental retardation performed differently from endogenous mentally retarded children on tests of visual perceptual organization and concept formation. Children in the exogenous group were observed to be generally poor in the performance of skilled motor activities, and many of them exhibited speech and language deficiencies reminiscent of adult aphasia yet not quite the same. Difficulties in sustaining attention, erratic thinking and restless or hyperactive behavior were commonly observed. The researches sought to revise the prevailing treatment concept based on the presumed homogeneity of mental deficiency by establishing a relationship between etiology and mental organization. In the groups studied it was shown that while the Stanford-Binet IQs used as measures of intelligence were the same, the children who were retarded mentally because of early brain damage and who came from normal families with presumably normal genetic patterns differed in important ways from those children who were retarded intellectually because of familial, presumably inherited, mental feebleness. The distinction between exogenous and endogenous types of mental deficiency seemed to have greatest significance for the educable group with IQs ranging from about 50 to 80.

Despite the limitations in experimental procedures and perhaps even conceptualization of the problem, which critics of these studies have pointed out,[7] one of the profound effects of this "new look" in mental retardation was the ferment of discussion and investigation which was stimulated in a long-quiescent field. Another was the courage it gave to normal parents to admit publicly to having a mentally retarded child without fear of being judged genetically inadequate themselves. This attitude was to provide much of the thrust behind the parent movements in behalf of "brain-injured" children which burgeoned in the succeeding years.

Gradually Dr. Strauss' investigations were extended to include children other than the mentally retarded: the cerebral palsied, deaf and those with known brain damage who retained a normal intelligence test score on standardized testing.[10, 11] In these children, as in the retarded group, problems of attention, hyperkinesis and mild motor awkwardness without actual palsies were found along with specific deficits in visuo-motor development, language, memory and abstract thinking. Characteristically these children had very irregular test and learning patterns, performing as well as normal children in a few areas and very poorly in others.

Such was the climate when The Cove Schools was organized: normal intelligent children failing to learn despite apparently adequate educational environments, mildly retarded children functioning normally in some areas and very poorly in others, concerned parents seeking answers which the local schools were not yet able to provide.

It was this group of needful children which The Cove Schools was designed to serve—those with learning and adjustment problems resulting from perceptual, attentional, memory, conceptual, language, organizational and coordination deficits due to early minor brain damage, but with normal or close to normal tested intelligence levels. Since the schools were intended to serve as a demonstration or exemplary facility, the number of children enrolled was limited so that those enrolled might be studied in depth and worked with in small groups. At the present time the schools enroll twenty-four children in the residence unit and thirty-three in the day program (initiated in 1950). The central focus was on a rather homogeneous group to a large extent free of the complicating variables of disadvantaged socio-economic circumstances and primary emotional problems. These were children of parents who wanted to provide opportunities but were frustrated by their lack of knowledge and the child's deficiencies. The complicating emotional factors which were present were judged to be secondary, having been brought about by the child's inability to respond effectively to the riches around him or by his anger or retreat in the face of the expectations imposed by parents, peers and school. In a controlled environment with appropriate demands, many of the unacceptable reactive behavior patterns could be expected to change for the better as the primary problem improved. Although the major emphasis was on the group described above, room was always left for a few children who differed in a more extreme way, that is, who presented severe deficits in language, perceptuo-motor development, behavior controls and emotional development, or who had additional complicating conditions of sensory losses or motor involvement. The latter were children who would normally not be considered the responsibility of the usual public school special education program in contrast to the main group who, it was felt, belonged within the sphere of public instructional provisions. With a few exceptions, therefore, the group served was and is today composed of children between the ages of six and twelve years, with an established medical diagnosis of central nervous system damage or dysfunction, no primary emotional disturbances, tested ability levels in the normal range or on the borderline of the educable mentally retarded classification, and failure to progress in the available school situation.

Most of the referrals are initiated by the public school because of the child's unsatisfactory progress. As the relationship between central nervous system damage and learning and behavior difficulties has become better known among the lay public many inquiries and self-referrals come from parents when their children are still in their preschool years.

While the specific enrollment figures relative to sex distribution, ability levels and types of deficits shift somewhat from year to year, those in any given year may be taken as broadly representative. The sex ratio is always heavily weighted toward boys; three to one is common. In the present group, three-fourths of the children in attendance had developmental problems of sufficient severity to have been noticed by the parent and diagnosed by the pediatrician or other child specialist in the preschool years. These were in motor development (delay, immaturity, neurological deficits, cerebral palsy), speech and language development (delay, dysarthria, aphasoid language problems), health problems such as seizures, or psychomotor problems such as hyperkinesis.

In almost all instances, children who were subsequently found to be functioning within the educable retarded or borderline retarded range gave evidence of early and significant developmental deviations, mainly in language or visuo-motor development. A smaller number of the group enrolled manifested delays in motor or speech development or generally poor coordination but were not seen by a specialist during their preschool years and were not diagnosed as having central nervous system dysfunction until school age. In these instances the parents were aware of developmental slowness or motor awkwardness, but either through inexperience or their own wish to believe that everything was well they saw the child as only a little slow and hoped he would catch up. Another smaller number of children presented nonspecific behavior and management difficulties together with mild motor clumsiness or minor speech delays. The behavior difficulties reported were usually hyperactivity, stubbornness, aggressiveness, inability to get along with peers, irritability, impulsiveness, and difficult to discipline in that they did not learn to modify their behavior after correction or punishment. Because of family circumstances the emotional factors received the focus of diagnostic and therapeutic efforts with generally favorable effects on behavior but little influence on learning.

All of the children presently enrolled have had nursery school and kindergarten experience with normal children. If the problem had already been diagnosed, some special care and thought were given to the selection of the kindergarten so that one with few children, an especially interested teacher or a particular philosophy was chosen. In most instances except those where behavior problems were prominent, the parents felt that the child had benefited from the social experience at least and had enjoyed this introduction to school. It appears that the emphasis on socialization and the respect for maturational influences which is part of the philosophy of early childhood education permits acceptance of a wide range of individual differences in capacities and personality. It is also probable that the social awareness of the handicapped child and his preschool contemporaries is as yet so undeveloped that he does not feel too keenly out of step or very different from the other children. A very few children had received specific help at a preschool age directed toward speech and language or visual perceptual development.

Many of the children progressed on into regular first grade with nonhandicapped children. There were various reasons for this decision: The problem had been diagnosed as something other than a neurologically based learning problem; no problem had yet been diagnosed; the problem had been diagnosed as a central nervous system dysfunction, but no facilities were available in the community, or parents and professionals adopted a wait-and-see attitude because of the minimal nature of the child's problems.

In working with children who have learning disabilities it is easy to focus so narrowly on the details of their disabilities that one loses sight of the character of the forest while studying the trees. For this reason we find the broad test patterns as revealed by the Children's Wechsler and supplemented by other tests when indicated useful in maintaining our bearings. In a very general way these test patterns seem to be associated with observable learning characteristics and academic prognosis.

Both Verbal and Performance Quotients on Children's Wechsler Clearly Within Normal Range (IQs over 90)

Despite the discrepancy in favor of the verbal score often seen in these children and the irregularities in development reflected on the subtests these children usually respond well to special teaching. They utilize the information given by the teacher and respond with insight when relationships are pointed out. They are frequently quite resourceful in developing compensatory behaviors to accommodate to or minimize the deficits they become aware of. Despite their erratic and confused approach to learning they give the impression of being alert, normal and capable of some introspection and analysis of their own difficulties. Although they may have conceptual confusions they do not have significant difficulty with the process of conceptualization. Once having mastered the basic academic skills they can apply them in a meaningful way but usually continue to need help in higher level integrative processes such as summarizing and organizing. They often continue to experience inefficiency in various aspects of mentation for an indefinite period of time, making what appear to be careless errors of omission, transposition, substitution, etc.

Children with a discrepancy in favor of the performance score usually present a picture of relatively well organized behavior, competence in table and group games, and enjoyment of visuo-motor activities for recreation. Generally they demonstrate auditory discrimination and retention difficulties and almost always have severe reading and spelling problems. Insight into arithmetical relationships is usually good but recall for automatic combinations is poor. They progress slowly in academic learning, especially in reading and spelling but often do very well in art, crafts and mechanical areas.

Verbal Quotient Clearly Within Normal Range (IQ 90 and above), Performance Quotient Borderline Retarded or Low Dull Normal Range (IQ 70-80 and occasionally lower)

These children present the familiar pattern of good vocabulary, relatively good acquisition of specific knowledge and relatively good understanding of social information. Unless specifically limiting factors are present they learn well the mechanics of reading but perform less well in comprehension of the conceptual aspects of the material read and still less well in arithmetic. They avoid activities requiring the use of visuo-motor skills, preferring to talk to adults, engage in fantasy play, or watch television. They frustrate and surprise adults by the contrasting aspects of their development. They are able to learn and remember many things well, yet are often ignorant or unaware of the most basic and obvious perceptual and conceptual relationships affecting their daily lives. Parents complain, "I don't understand him—is he stupid or is he smart?" With special help in visuo-motor organization, academic skill development and conceptual thinking these children can fit into regular classes after the basic mechanics of academic learning have been mastered. However, they continue to need tutorial help at various points along the way. They almost always fail to grasp the abstractions of algebra, geometry and science and "pass" these courses in a mechanical way. Map and graph reading skills are learned with difficulty and the spatial organization of written work is usually poor.

Verbal Abilities Dull Normal (IQ in low 80's), Performance Abilities Normal Range (IQ 90 and above)

Children with this pattern usually demonstrate various auditory discrimination and retention difficulties, their thinking is often descriptive rather than generalizing, their vocabularies small. They are successful in games and activities depending upon good visuo-motor organization and usually have good grapho-motor skill. As academic work becomes progressively more verbal-abstract in the upper grades they find it increasingly difficult but continue to perform well in practical courses.

Verbal and Performance Quotients Ranging Borderline Range to Dull Normal Range (IQ's in 70's and 80's)

These children show the effects on their intellectual functioning of frank brain damage. Although they may score well on one or two subtests such as vocabulary, comprehension, or object assembly, these areas of relative competence are not sufficiently broad to compensate for the marked deficits which exist in the other fields. They learn slowly, require many clues and special adjustments for long periods of time, tend to be concrete in their thinking and forget without a great deal of review. They learn details and find it difficult to integrate them into whole patterns of thought and action. Despite their areas of rather good skill, these children usually require a special class for their further education.

The ultimate objective for these children is the same as for all children—to realize as fully as possible their individual potentialities for development and eventually to become self-sufficient adults able to function in society. To this end the immediate objective of The Cove Schools is to prepare its pupils for return to the general stream of education whenever the child's individual capabilities and existing community resources permit. Two to four years depending upon the child's general ability level and the extent of his disabilities is the usual length of stay.

In its most general sense, "learning" whether it occurs in school or out refers to the process by which experience leads to change. In this sense it is a continuous process of interaction between organism and environment, the effects of which become manifest in behavior change. Experience may be organized and offered in ways which directly influence the responses of the individual as in prepared lessons, thus shaping his behavior in more or less well defined directions. A vast amount of learning occurs incidentally and informally through the spontaneous activities and explorations of the individual.

At The Cove Schools four major areas of learning receive attention. These are the acquisition of the commonly called academic skills—perhaps better referred to as literacy skills (the mechanics of reading, spelling, writing, written English and fundamental arithmetic processes), the improvement of basic mental functions (motor, perceptual, language and conceptual abilities) fundamental to all learning, the development of specific knowledge and skills important in daily life activities, and growth in social and group living skills. The cultivation of individual interests and aptitudes is not neglected and is often a natural byproduct of the other efforts. Only the first two will be discussed here.

Several aspects of the child's total development, whether handicapped or normal, have important bearing on his capacity to learn. As we view them these are developmental readiness, general intelligence, disabilities in mental functioning, motivation and emotional freedom to learn.

Developmental Readiness

Students of child development have long emphasized the importance of biologic readiness as a prerequisite for certain learnings.[1, 5] The concept is particularly relevant to early childhood education since biologic maturational and integrative patterns of the central nervous system do, in fact, largely determine the child's early development. Neurological integration appears to have a major role in the development of basic sensorimotor and perceptual accomplishments such as sitting, standing, walking, speech, being able to give attention and responding to the teaching of primary reading and arithmetic skills. Test measures devised for determining school readiness include a sampling of those abilities most closely related to success in the first grade and have been employed with considerable success in identifying children with slow maturation patterns for retention in kindergarten or for special grouping in first grade.

In addition to the mental abilities which mature at various time points during the preschool years there are others which do not mature until later but which are also important for learning academic skills. Studies of children with reading problems indicate that auditory discrimination for speech sounds and the directional orientation of letters which are opposites of each others do not reach full maturity in many children until well into the eighth year of chronological age.

The child with organically based learning impairments presents unique problems inasmuch as he has had superimposed upon his natural biological timetable the effects of the central nervous system damage. In children with diffuse damage, the maturation of all of the various mental abilities is differentially retarded. In others with more selective damage, unimpaired mental abilities mature at a normal rate while others develop more slowly. The result is a child with a very irregular profile of abilities. It is a subject for future research to determine whether it is more correct to conceptualize such retardations as developmental lags or neurological deficits and whether they are ever actually made up either through growth or learning.

It is therefore possible for the child with minimal brain damage to have matured to a level of readiness for beginning academic work in many important areas of mental ability and to be significantly lacking in others. The effect of his exposure to a regular learning experience is that he will acquire those skills for which he has developed the requisite neurological readiness and will grasp feebly or only partially those dependent mainly on the abilities he has not yet developed. A common example is a child who has learned to read words skillfully but who cannot visually keep his place on the page, print or write legibly, or comprehend number concepts beyond the level of unit counting. A child with this achievement pattern will usually be found to have developed the visual-perceptual ability to discriminate detail differences in forms and simple patterns, the memory for names given to the forms, simple verbal concepts, and the basic motor skills required to perform these activities. He may be severely retarded in his ability to do spatial thinking, in fine motor skill, in motor-pattern organization, auditory discrimination for speech sounds, and the capacity to translate percepts organized through one modality to percepts in another modality. Consequently he has learned what his abilities allowed despite the existence of many areas of deficit. The latter will not only continue to prevent his learning of those skills which they undergird, they will gradually interfere with further progress in the area in which he started out with such apparent success.

In The Cove Schools' special environment, a child who shows evidence of interest in and neurological maturation for any of the academic skills is started on a program for their development. On a continuing basis he is given every assistance to prevent his disabilities from interfering with his progress; at the same time, however, he is given a program to improve them. Thus if he has the verbal, memory and basic visual perceptual abilities for beginning reading but has visuo-motor or attention difficulties affecting his ability to keep his place on the page, the interfering disabilities will be offset by encouraging him to point with his finger, use a marker or use a mask for the page. If he confuses similar letters or words, his poor discrimination will be offset by marking differentiating details in color, by framing, underlining, etc. If he has auditory discrimination difficulties, adjustments such as articulating distinctly, speaking somewhat more slowly, prolonging a sound or amplifying sounds will be made for them.

In the meantime, the child will also have a program directed toward improving the lagging or deficit functions. It is characteristic for children with perceptuo-motor difficulties to have avoided games and activities relying heavily on some degree of efficiency in this area. Parents discover this when their handicapped child takes no interest in the puzzles or educational toys they bring him, preferring to listen to records instead. Consequently, through his own avoidance and selection behavior the child often stringently curtails his opportunities for spontaneous learning through daily play experiences. An important part of the child's day in a special program consists in bringing these experiences to him in order to provide him with the opportunities for learning which he has missed either because of his slow rate of maturation or because of his own selectiveness.

It cannot yet be said that neurological maturation can be accelerated by specific practice. However, the functional application of neurologically based skills in complex integrated activities can be improved decidedly through practice. It also appears to be true that the more adequate the maturation of an ability or the better the existing potential, the greater will be the improvement through practice.

General Intelligence

There has been a tendency in discussing the mental and behavioral characteristics of brain-damaged children to ignore the contribution of general intelligence or cognitive adequacy to the symptom picture. The child who tests in the normal range intellectually will function in many ways like a nonhandicapped child despite his various areas of learning difficulty. Because of his more adequate capabilities he will benefit from verbal explanations, process more information from a greater variety of experiences, deal with material on a level of generality and categories, and produce organized responses.

However, while intelligence in the normal range will usually insure that the child will grasp concepts and meanings and fare well when general comprehension is involved, it does not insure adequate function in such nonconceptual areas as retention and recall, motor dexterity, right-left orientation, topographical orientation and reliability and efficiency of intake and output. Neither does it assure adequacy in the higher level integrative and organizational operations required for the insightful use of models and diagrams, the ability to extract pertinent material from reading and the ability to summarize and organize.

The teacher needs to be able to meet the child on the level appropriate to his general intelligence and maturity, yet not be surprised by the many gaps in understanding, conceptual confusions, or missed steps in learning which soon become apparent. These relate to the areas of disability or inefficiency of the system. It is not unusual to find that a child can comprehend the concept of the equator as an abstraction, yet be unable to locate it correctly on maps with different angles of projection. It is possible for a child to be working at a fourth grade level of reading and arithmetic and not know his own telephone number or the months of the year, or just be learning for certain the spelling of his last name.

When well motivated and unencumbered by interfering emotional problems the minimally brain-damaged child is often a highly cooperative learner, interested in his own learning processes and able to share actively in his own rehabilitative experience. He can understand and appreciate his need for various procedures suggested by the teacher and learn to apply them independently. On the other hand, by virtue of his good capacity, the normally intelligent minimally brain-damaged child is highly vulnerable to the school and parental pressures that follow upon his poor achievement, often confused and resentful about his limitations, and sensitive to peer group evaluations. The attendant negative feelings may lead him to cling defensively to inefficient methods of learning or problem solution and be unwilling to accept procedures which would ultimately be more beneficial to him. Obviously skill and sensitivity on the teacher's part are absolutely essential in helping the child with these additional problems to make his understanding work for him so that he can accept the remedial measures he needs. If motivational and emotional factors are positive, the more intelligent the child the more rapid will be his learning of new material, the more effective his effort to compensate for his deficiencies and the better his scholastic prognosis.

Disabilities

No attempt will be made to detail all of the areas of disability noted in minimally brain-damaged children or the various teaching approaches devised for their improvement. Prominent among the mental abilities impaired by brain damage are the visual perceptual functions. We view the process of perception as the capacity to experience form and pattern in an organized, meaningful way, and the development of perception as ranging from the earliest levels of simple awareness to the differentiation of progressively more complex stimulus configurations. Simultaneously, a process of integration of perceptual and motor development, language and concepts is in progress. The entirety of the visual perceptual function in children is far from being completely understood either in respect to its characteristics or the ontogeny of its development, and present training efforts represent only the first steps in our ultimate understanding of the problem.

Children with impairment in their capacity for visual perceptual organization will reveal inadequacies in their perception of unitary form, pattern, size, figure against disturbing ground, the relationship of parts to a whole, the analysis of wholes, discrimination of small differences, simultaneous awareness of several features of a stimulus configuration, and the ability to deal with space coherently by filling it and sectioning it in an organized way.

A vast number of the child's daily nonscholastic activities such as games, play, crafts, construction projects and self-care routines will be adversely affected by a visual-perceptual impairment. On the other hand, his adequacy in handling these activities can be significantly improved through appropriate learning experiences. To this end experience with a variety of materials requiring visual-motor organization and response is planned into the child's day just as reading and arithmetic are planned.

The first level for children enrolled in our setting is that of awareness of some of the characteristics of the material and an interest in exploring its possibilities in any coherent, organized manner, no matter how simple. This may consist in making a response based on awareness of color, placing shapes or blocks into matching depressions, fitting pegs or sticks into holes, etc. From this level of exploration and limited awareness the child is led to become more discriminating in his perception of various other characteristics of the material or other possibilities for its use. Materials used may include such items as peg boards, cube block designs, parquetry block designs, magnetic form boards, mosaic tiles, colored sticks, Tinker Toys®, puzzles, picture materials, plastic building blocks, etc. Keeping one's place or reaching a goal despite interfering background is required for success in many board and table games like checkers and dominoes.

As he improves, the child progresses to the recognition of whole-part relationships of increasing complexity, as in duplicating geometrical designs or drawings or building three dimensional constructions. Activities tapping visual-perceptual capacities are unlimited, as they comprise many of the multitude of games and spontaneous activities of the child. They exist as commercially produced play materials, and they can be devised by imaginative teachers and parents. Indeed, cutting, coloring, painting, pasting, folding, lacing, modeling with clay, constructing with blocks, arranging a bulletin board and so on through a host of other common activities all involve visual-perceptual organization and provide learning opportunities. For the non-handicapped child every game and leisure activity involves learning as he spontaneously experiments with new combinations, appraises the results, corrects unsatisfactory efforts, remembers previous successful operations, and applies them—in this way constantly trying, checking, and revising. The handicapped child working without the advantages of a normal, perceptual, data-processing and feedback system does not recognize his errors as readily and does not possess the flexibility and resourcefulness to correct them. The teacher's role in these perceptual learning situations is the same as in any other learning experiences. If the child encounters difficulty with some aspect of the task because he does not identify the problem area or possible solutions, she offers him leading questions or suggestions or verbally delineates the part to select for attention, directing visual attention by blocking out confusing detail or outlining a part with pencil or finger, suggesting kinesthetic or tactual discrimination as an aid, helping to organize procedures so as to maximize opportunities for success, etc. If she notes that a particular aspect of the activity continues to offer difficulty, she directs the subsequent choice of an activity so as to give the child additional practice with that feature in another context.

To the extent that acquisition of the academic skills requires well-developed visual perceptual abilities, their mastery will also be impeded. Learning the academic skills is one specific and highly important area of application of visual as well as auditory perceptual abilities, and specific task-related assignments are given to promote the development of the specific skills required. Typical of assignments directly relevant to the perceptual aspects of academic skill development are matching letters, words, number patterns, separating words into syllables or structural parts, dividing geometrical figures into fractional parts, etc.

Difficulties in auditory discrimination and organization are important problems which often require specific attention. It is usual for children enrolled in our setting to have developed mastery of such fundamental auditory perceptual processes as identifying a sound with the object which produces it and being able to sense its localization and intensity. Many, however, have not developed very keen discrimination for some of the speech sounds or the awareness of stress as heard in syllable accenting. Other problems involving the verbal-automatic levels of speech and the auditory memory functions are seen in problems in patterning (sequencing) sounds in words and words in sentences. The former leads to mispronunciations like "bisgetti," "aluninum," "memeber" and the latter to problems in establishing automatic patterns of word order in sentences. Group work in discrimination and auditory analysis is given to all children in preparation for the learning of phonics. Individual attention is provided for the child with more severe problems for whom the group work is insufficient. Here again specific task-related exercises such as rhyming and sound blending are planned in reading and spelling.

Awareness of how one's body moves and how to relate oneself to the space in which one lives is usually also disturbed in the child with nonmotor brain damage and contributes to the impression of clumsiness he often presents (his impulsiveness, his hypertonic grasp and jerky or poorly modulated movements do also). Three types of activities relating to knowledge of the body and its movement are a part of our program. Body image activities are used to help the child become aware of the various parts of his body and their relationship to each other; this knowledge will eventuate in an internalized scheme of body-awareness or body image. Group activities in the form of games, such as "Do as I Do," "Did You Ever See a Lassie?" "Simon Says," are enjoyed by the children and permit a wide range of bodily movements.

A somewhat more complex level of body awareness, involving sequential patterning and recall is required in moving according to a defined pattern. The latter requires the corollary innervation and inhibition of movements and their integration into a smooth whole. Jumping, hopping on one foot, gliding, galloping, walking on all fours, skipping, walking backwards, jumping jacks, circling, are all movement patterns which require that the limbs be innervated in a particular sequence. Mastery of these activities, just as the mastery of any new learning, requires attention, perception, memory, feedback awareness and integration and so is a valid learning experience. These activities, furthermore, form the basis for a large repertoire of later game, dance and gymnastic patterns and so have a highly functional goal.

A third level of coordinative activity consists in bringing the self into relation with an external object as in running to a goal, climbing a jungle gym, jumping from a box, etc. The problem is further complicated if the object also moves as when it is another player or a wagon, a bicycle, jump rope, swing, or balls. All of this motor learning leads up to the mastery of organized games on various levels of complexity, with their attendant requirements of spatial awareness, organization, strategy, etc.

An important part of the educational experience of the child with minimal brain damage includes activities which stress the integration of perceptions from different sensory modalities. The child with a disability tends to do most of his thinking in the areas in which he is most adequate, so that if the has high verbal abilities and poor visual perceptual skills, he thinks in words but tends not to translate them into their visuo-motor counterparts. In a comparable fashion the child with good performance skills and poor verbal development performs well in a visuo-motor sense but finds it difficult to give words to his actions. Specific practice in the form of games is useful in helping to make the child aware of the need to think in a fuller, more complete sense, but more important is the teacher's awareness so that she can emphasize such thinking wherever possible in the child's work. Scarcely an area of academic learning is untouched by the need for this type of thought process. In learning to write, the child needs to relate visual, auditory and motor inputs into a whole. In reading he must relate visual and auditory-verbal stimuli in order to know what the words are, and in order to comprehend their meaning fully he needs to relate the auditory-verbal word stimulus to his visual or experiential recall of real objects or events like those referred to by the words. In arithmetic learning he must translate his visuo-motor percept of objects and their relations in space into verbal statements. Later the verbal statements found in his "story problem" need to be translated once more into images representing real visuo-motor-spatial experiences. Listening requires the translating of the auditory-verbal input into visual-spatial-experiential terms. The effort to help a child think in as integrated a way as possible must be a part of all of his learning experiences.

Concept development is also given special attention through such activities as describing objects, discussion of functions, classifying according to likenesses and categorizing. Other aspects of thinking involving word meanings, thinking in sequential terms, anticipating consequences or logical outcomes, following directions and answering riddles. Summarizing and organizing are done on different levels from beginner to more advanced pupil.

Further handicapping problems which seriously reduce the efficiency of learning or output of the minimally brain-damaged child relate not so much to actual disabilities as to the manner in which the central nervous system performs its work. When a task involves difficult material or much information to be processed (solving arithmetic problems or reading), successful performance requires elimination (or inhibition) of all irrelevant input. The minimally brain-damaged child experiences difficulty with this process and is called distractible or inattentive. Irrelevant information interferes with the processing of the focal information, so that the task requires longer to complete or is inefficiently or automatically done. On the other hand the minimally brain-damaged child often seems to overdo the need to admit only part of the information entering by the sense organs. It is as though much of the nervous system needs to be reserved for the task in order to insure its successful performance, and all other information is held back by the central filtering process. Written composition work seems to suffer characteristically from this kind of narrow focusing of attention or inhibition of input. The child is not able simultaneously to keep in mind successfully the many aspects of the task—conceptualizing, organizing, selecting vocabulary and syntax to formulate the ideas, writing, spelling, punctuating and spacing, at the same time maintaining feedback of what has been put down. The process of proofreading suffers from similar problems of inhibition. Intent on his meaning the child neglects to notice spelling, punctuation, capitalization, or indenting.

Always the teacher needs to be aware that working to improve an area of disability may become frustrating and difficult. In any learning area, but most especially when working in an area of weakness, the learning should begin at the child's level of competence—his level of success and strength—and progress from there. The teacher needs to determine where the child's performance breaks down and then proceed to develop his skill in carefully graded steps from that point.

Motivation

Psychologists and educators have defined motivation in many different ways but for our purposes the word refers to the impetus to learning or achievement, the push or drive to accomplish which the child brings to his tasks. Ekstein[2] traces the growth of motivation from the initial state of learning for love to love of learning. Early, extrinsic motivations are provided by adults in the words of praise and commendation given for a task accomplished satisfactorily in any area of learning. A somewhat less personal source of motivation exists in the social reward and satisfaction that comes from carrying out a responsibility. Being permitted to select an interesting, pleasurable activity to do after having finished his task offers anticipation of a pleasure awaiting the child after he has fulfilled his responsibility to the class, his teacher, and of course ultimately to himself. The hoped for goal is that the child develops the intrinsic motivation to work because he enjoys the satisfaction of learning new things or has so internalized the need for achievement that he recognizes it as a largely self-imposed or at least accepted goal rather than as externally imposed.

A selective factor is operative in the enrollments at the schools, and so any generalization about motivation must naturally take into account the fact that the children come from middle class environments. It is of course entirely possible and largely probable that standards of achievement are set by parental expectations and that the parents of all of the children enrolled value learning highly. On the other hand one is also inclined to attribute some of the drive seen in the children to the sheer wish to master aspects of the environment wherein they themselves feel uncertain or lacking. Once shown that learning is within their grasp they often make heroic efforts at mastery. The cumulative effect of many experiences which have demonstrated to the child that his peers seem to know all the answers, or that they develop rapidly and easily many skills which he must struggle to master is to leave him feeling uncertain, discouraged, or left out. In a low-risk situation offering little threat to his self-esteem with a teacher who can show him how to master the learnings he has missed he often develops a strong thirst for achievement and is willing to invest much of his energy in it. The prime importance of a high level of motivation for the child's future school success is self-evident.

Emotional Freedom to Learn

In the search for organic factors as an explanation for the child's learning difficulty, the very important question of his emotional development and the freedom from emotional problems which may impair his capacity to participate actively in the learning process is often overlooked. Various workers concerned primarily with the influence of emotional problems not directly related to learning have emphasized the major role which such problems may have in leading to learning difficulties, in this case, secondary in nature. Certainly the emotional factors should be considered just as carefully in planning for the child with known symptoms of central nervous system involvement as the organic ones in planning for the child with known emotional difficulties. Often the diagnosis is best made on a longitudinal basis, and only after exposure to one form of treatment or the other can a conclusive statement be made about the differential weight to be assigned to each. It is entirely possible for the child with minimal brain damage to be additionally disturbed by anxiety, negativism, a need to fight back through aggressive or passive reactions, to become self-depreciating or to be unable to accept or enjoy personal gratification. A child with learning disabilities based on central nervous system dysfunction may be suspected of having more basic emotional problems if he continues to demonstrate behavior difficulty or inability to invest his energies in learning despite the fact that he is in a situation in which school permits achievement, the classroom offers protections, competitive pressures and evaluative procedures are minimized, and the teacher can develop a positive relationship with him. The minimally brain-damaged child does not grow up in an emotional vacuum or necessarily in an emotional environment always enhancing to his development.

Power conflicts between parent and child or child and siblings will be transferred to the arena of the classroom, a passive-dependent method of gaining help and attention will manifest itself in school, anxious preoccupations will interfere with concentration and so on. These manifestations of emotional problems will persist until help is given to the child and parents to correct the conditions from which they stem. It is entirely possible, in fact usual, for the child with such problems to make progress in a small classroom in which the total environment reaches out in as positive a way as possible. However, he will not make as much progress as he might if he were free to be more actively engaged in learning. Most parents of the minimally brain-damaged child are confused and uncertain of their ability to perform their child-rearing functions satisfactorily. Reassurance, management suggestions and the opportunity to learn new and more suitable techniques for modifying the child's behavior can help them to become more effective to the resulting benefit of the child. Where the problems are deeper, the help of a therapist for parents or the child or possibly both is suggested.

Within the framework of understanding outlined above, the teaching of the child is individualized according to his maturational level, specific limitations, cognitive or intellectual development and motivational strength. Many of the materials and techniques used are adaptations of those known in general education with specific adjustments or approaches necessitated by the child's disabilities. The teaching is programmed in detail to insure understanding or mastery of the many steps which the child with intact learning processes leaps over with ease.

Review and overlearning are indispensable. Because he has understood a process on one day is no guarantee that tomorrow the child will still be able to recall the steps involved, and the teacher must be ready to repeat the lesson (although in a slightly different format with different examples) for several days or weeks. On each successive presentation her goal is to withdraw little by little her promptings, leading questions, reminders and admonitions to "think" until the child is actually able to direct his own way through the task from beginning to end. When mastery is achieved, the material is then combined with other similar material so that it becomes part of a larger repertoire of skills. Always the new process is presented in different contexts with different types of materials so that it becomes generalized rather than remaining an isolated and specific accomplishment. To check on the permanence of the learning and to provide continuing review, a process is presented after progressively longer intervals of nonpractice. Progress under these conditions is slow, and patience is required from the teacher as well as the learner. Additionally, interest must be maintained through frequently changing some aspect of the material no matter how superficial. Boredom leads to loss of attention, and freshness and interest need to be maintained along with the necessary repetition.

Throughout the child's learning experience the emphasis is placed first on the process, then on the end result. It is therefore most important that the teacher attempt to present the lesson in such a way that she can be aware of the thought process the child is using to reach his goal. An effort is made to elicit from the child some form of report about how he solved the problem or thought through an answer. He may do this by giving a verbal account of his thinking, by diagramming it in drawing or by indicating it through gesture. In this way the teacher becomes aware of whether the child's successes are accidental or real and whether he is developing the type of integrated thought process required for further progress.

Left to his own devices in a large group, the child with faulty equipment for learning does the best he can and emerges from the experience with incomplete understanding or actual disabilities. In the small situation no new skill or step in learning is practiced without close supervision to make certain that the child does not practice errors. The child does not work independently until the teacher is certain that he can do so essentially without error; until that point his practice is all done with supervision.

Another important consideration is the work environment. A quiet, orderly, disciplined classroom is essential. For children who find the sounds and movements of the classroom disturbing, an individual study carrel is made by using a screen to block out the distractions. An attitude of self-discipline and individual responsibility is established as early as possible. Since the lessons are planned so that the child will be successful, he can be held responsible for their completion.

For most children with minimal brain damage, rehabilitative education is a long-term process. Intensive short-term measures applied during the years critical for the development of literacy skills, work habits and expectations for one's self may provide the foundation for later educational efforts. The effectiveness of the latter will depend upon the strength of the child's drive to achieve despite what are sometimes long odds, and the willingness of the regular school to program intelligently and sensitively for one more category of handicapped child.

BIBLIOGRAPHY

1. Breckenridge, Marian E., and Vincent, E. Lee: *Child Development.* Philadelphia, Saunders, 1965.
2. Ekstein, R.: The learning process: from learning for love to love of learning. *Reiss-Davis Clin Bull, 1* (No. 1), Spring, 1964.
3. Fernald, Grace M.: *Remedial Techniques in Basic School Subjects.* New York, McGraw, 1943.
4. Garrison, Karl C.: *The Psychology of Exceptional Children.* New York, Ronald, 1940.
5. Gesell, Arnold, *et al.: The First Five Years of Life.* New York, Harper, 1940.

6. MONROE, M.: *Children Who Cannot Read.* U of Chicago, 1932.
7. SARASON, SEYMOUR B.: *Psychological Problems in Mental Deficiency,* 3rd ed. New York, Harper, 1959.
8. STRAUSS, A. A.: The incidence of central nervous system involvement in higher grade moron children. *Amer J Ment Defic, 45*:548-554, 1940-41.
9. STRAUSS, A. A.: Typology in mental deficiency: its clinical, psychological and educational implications. *Amer J Ment Defic, 44*:85-90, 1939.
10. STRAUSS, A. A., and KEPHART, N. C.: *Psychopathology and Education of the Brain-Injured Child.* New York, Grune, 1955, vol. 2.
11. STRAUSS, A. A., and LEHTINEN, L. E.: *Psychopathology and Education of the Brain-Injured Child.* New York, Grune, 1947.
12. STRAUSS, A. A., and WERNER, H.: Disorders of conceptual thinking in the brain-injured child. *J Nerv Ment Dis, 96*:153-172, 1942.
13. WERNER, H., and STRAUSS, A. A.: Pathology of figure-background relation in the child. *J Abnorm Soc Psychol, 36*:236-248, 1941.
14. WERNER, H., and STRAUSS, A. A.: Types of visuo-motor activity in their relation to low and high performance ages. *Amer J Ment Defic, 44*:163-168, 1939.

Chapter 7

MARIANNE FROSTIG CENTER OF EDUCATION THERAPY

MARIANNE FROSTIG AND DAVID HORNE

The perceived world is the always presupposed foundation of all rationality, all value and all existence.*

INTRODUCTION

THE Marianne Frostig Center of Educational Therapy is a nonprofit institution operated by the Foundation of Educational Therapy for Children. It is situated in central Los Angeles and currently occupies a number of small buildings. The center has outgrown its present quarters and the Board of the Foundation of Educational Therapy for Children is currently negotiating for a much more convenient and attractive site and building complex, not too far from the present location. The staff numbers sixty to seventy persons who serve the needs of about 220 children and their families.

The Frostig Center has three main functions—service, professional training and research. Services involve educational, psychiatric and psychological evaluation, and training and treatment of children with learning difficulties.

Learning difficulties may be due to brain dysfunction, environmentally caused emotional disturbance, or to an apparent lag in development without known cause. Usually both causation and symptomatology are multiple with emotional disturbances a frequent factor in the total clinical picture. Moreover, a child's problems do not affect him alone, but involve the entire family. Therefore parents often need psychotherapy; nearly always they need advice on how to help their handicapped youngster, and support in carrying it out.

To meet these difficulties the Frostig Center has developed a multi-disciplinary approach, which brings together in one place the services of psychiatrists, psychologists, social workers and educational therapists. Each child is provided with a comprehensive evaluation and treatment program, which covers all developmental areas and takes into account the needs of the whole family. The remedial training programs are precisely geared to the individual child's test results.

---

* MAURICE MERLEAU-PONTY: *The Primacy of Perception,* M. Edie (Ed.). Evanston, Northwestern University, 1964, p. 13.

The professional training programs of the center are designed to acquaint educational therapists, psychologists and social workers with the special needs of children with learning difficulties, and with the appropriate evaluative and remedial measures. The research is concerned with the construction of evaluative instruments and the development and assessment of educational and psychological treatment methods.

The overall concern of the center is with the preconditions of learning: the developmental abilities which enable a child to achieve success in school. Remedial techniques are used to develop abilities which are lagging. Subject matter and academic skills are taught in such a way as to develop them.

The aim of the remedial programs is to enable each child to function at his optimum level and enter, or return to public school competent to succeed to the best of his ability with whatever method he may be taught. To achieve this remedial goal, the center concerns itself not with a single remedial technique, but with a great variety of teaching and therapeutic techniques, and not with one facet of a child's development, but with every facet.

EVOLUTION OF THE CENTER'S PHILOSOPHY AND PRACTICE

The philosophy and practice of the Frostig Center are rooted in the work of former educators, some of whom lived and worked prior even to the early part of this century, and who were themselves but links in a chain stretching even further into the past. But it is in the last two or three decades that the greatest advances in special education have been made. The Frostig Center is proud to have been one of the contributors to this new progress in the art and the science of educational practice.

Long before this century, Itard,[48] Froebel,[19] Pestalozzi[73] and later Seguin (see Talbot[92]), and Montessori[66, 67, 80] developed effective methods of teaching very young children, both retarded and normal.

A common characteristic of their efforts was the inclusion of sensory-motor training in their educational programs. They used manipulative toys and made the children aware of the form, color, size, sound and of all other physical characteristics of their environment. Montessori brought sensory education to a high point of development, but although her methods were based on excellent clinical judgment, they were not yet sufficiently underpinned by theoretical formulations or systematic research. Consequently, there were no means of showing when they would work, why they were helpful, and how they should be modified to help optimally in specific cases. Nevertheless, their success stimulated hope and underscored the necessity for establishing a scientific rationale.

Dr. Frostig had sporadic contacts with Dr. Montessori and with several of her students. Montessori was a warm, kind person, who always approached children with a spirit of love and great understanding. At the Montesorri School in Vienna the child's needs for art, poetry, music and social relationships were always taken into account. To use Montesorri's sensory-motor teaching techniques without concern for these other aspects of child development is to confuse her aims altogether. Montesorri's goal of educating the whole child while emphasizing sensory motor and perceptual training in the preschool child has been a lasting influence on the philosophy of the center.[67]

The years of the First World War saw the occurrence in Europe of encephalitis epidemics, which left many children as well as adults with typical symptoms of brain damage. The professional workers of this time recognized that disorders in children with a post-encephalitic syndrome were inaccessible to the usual counseling and psychotherapeutic methods, but they did not believe that the condition was amenable to any medical, psychological, or educational help.

Interestingly enough, no one at that time realized the remedial significance for such children of the wealth of ideas contributed by Montesorri, especially her methods of sensory-motor training.

Other contributions to the theory and practice of the center came from studies in child development. Marianne Frostig first became acquainted with the available knowledge on child development through Charlotte Buhler,[10-12] who lectured at the University of Vienna. Later Werner,[101] and Wapner and Werner,[96] Erikson[16] and most particularly, Piaget[74-79] were most influential in developing her educational practices. Their writings taught her developmental principles and the importance of observing various aspects of a child's behavior, and then comparing the findings with the progress of other children *in terms of the developmental sequences* through which each child must pass.

The voluminous literature available demonstrates that the exact time at which many developmental abilities emerge is in part determined by individual differences, and in part by a particular culture, but the sequence in which the abilities unfold is set and independent of culture.

Several distinct phases are postulated. During the *sensory-motor phase* the child becomes aware of the world around him through applying all his sense modalities and movements simultaneously to the exploration of the environment. He also masters locomotion. Maximum developmental progress occurs during the first eighteen months of life. During the phase of maximum *language* development, from approximately eighteen months to three and one-half years of age, the child learns to understand and to express ideas through speech.

Maximum growth for the *perceptual abilities* (or in Piaget's terms, intuitive intelligence) is during the period from approximately four to seven and one-half years of age. The child develops the ability to discriminate and to recognize stimuli present in the environment. Manipulation of concrete objects is no longer necessary.

After about the age of seven and one-half, the development of *higher cognitive processes* becomes predominant. The child develops the abilities which enable him to understand temporal and causal relationships in his environment, but without being bound to perception of the here and now —to immediate and present stimuli. The development of these more abstract abilities such as memory, classification, concept formation, drawing conclusions and checking hypotheses helps the child to connect the experiences of the past and the expectancies of the future with the observation of the present, and so weld his thoughts and perceptions into a firm representation of the world in which he lives.

The final two developmental areas, *social adjustment* and *emotional development,* are modified throughout the individual's life span in a more gradual way. The child's continuously changing needs as he progresses through school, his slow growth toward independence, his growing ability to integrate with wider social groups, and his changing attitude to authority, are among the characteristics of which all teachers are aware, but which may take different forms in the child with learning difficulties. The educational therapist has to learn to understand these deviations.

The procedures for evaluation and general program planning at the Frostig Center are based upon developmental psychology. The staff of the center learns from the writings of those scientists who study development as well as from those who have themselves developed educational methods on the basis of the research findings of others. For instance, Piaget's research has many applications in the classroom which have been developed by Aebli,[1] Legrand,[55] Peel,[71] Lovell[58] and Levi[56, 57] among others. The center's staff attempts to add to these methods. For example, Piaget's[74, 79] theories of how a child acquires number concepts provided ideas for developing methods of teaching arithmetic. Piaget's observations in regard to perception have promoted new methods in perceptual training. At the center specific methods are used to help the child to achieve what Piaget terms *decentration*—the ability to relate the different parts of the visual perceptual field to each other. These methods apply to training in figure-ground perception and spatial relationships, but transcend perceptual abilities by helping the child to gain increased freedom from dependency on immediate stimuli. (See publications of Piaget, J. and Lambercier, *Arch Psychol,* Geneve, from 1942-1956.) Piaget's theory of the development of thought processes has been adapted to helping children develop their abilities to judge, classify, draw inferences and so on. These are only a few samples from Piaget's rich storehouse of ideas that are applicable to education.[74-79]

Similarly, the theories of Russian scientists, especially Luria,[59] Luria and

Yudovich[60] and Vygotsky,[94, 95] concerning the development of language have yielded suggestions for remedial techniques in the area of language and thought.

Other contributions to the center's philosophy and practice have come from neurophysiology. Neurological and neurophysiological research and theory have only lately become applicable to psychological understanding and educational practice. They impress on the educational therapist the importance of giving equal consideration to the promotion of sensory input, motor behavior and body awareness.[38, 74-76, 87, 96, 101] They elucidate the influence of both motivation and alertness on the function of the nervous system,[61] on the significance of laterality,[72, 102] and generally give much significant information in regard to the functioning of the nervous system and its relation to behavior[6, 64, 65] and the influence of learning on brain anatomy and physiology.[84]

Hebb's[43, 45] theory of cell assemblies and phase sequences is particularly useful for understanding the learning process from the point of view of neurophysiology. It suggests the importance in teaching of providing multiple associations, much repetition in varied forms, multi-sensory reinforcement, the accretion of new skills and knowledge through step-by-step progression, and careful integration of new subject matter with what has already been learned.

During the last years, research in many fields has helped to open up new avenues for education. Jerome Bruner,[7-9] in studying the learning processes in children, has demonstrated how children can be taught to explore and arrive inductively at a solution to a problem at a much earlier age than is normally thought possible. Aurelia Levi[56, 57] has shown how children's higher thought processes can be enhanced by educational methods. Her work in turn is based on Piaget's studies of cognitive development and on those of Harlow who explored the formation of learning sets.[39, 40] Learning set is defined as a basic strategy applicable to the solution of various problems. Study skills, such as outlining or the ability to use phonic clues for spelling, are examples.

Other learning theories have lately become applicable to the classroom. Especially influential is the Skinnerian[89] method of operant conditioning, which shapes behavior by careful reinforcement in step-by-step procedures.*

This latter theory is an example of the contribution of learning theory to everyday educational procedures. A broad scope of research findings in the area of learning has to be considered in educational practice.[4, 44, 46]

---

* This method is not regularly used at the center. It is regarded as possibly being useful for a limited period in a circumscribed segment of a child's program, when other methods have failed to stimulate progress in that particular area.

Of equal importance are the examples of educational methods introduced by educators themselves, such as the already mentioned Montesorri, and Ann Sullivan, whose work with Helen Keller[49] is especially instructive; or the pioneer work with brain injured children of Strauss and Lehtinen[90] and Strauss and Kephart.[91] In present day America, Kirk[50-51] Bateman,[3] Cruickshank,[13] Kephart,[49A] and Myklebust[68-69] are among the leaders.

In giving recognition to the various trends which are influential in the educational policy of the center, a somewhat broad discourse seems to be warranted in regard to psychoanalysis. Today the medical and psychiatric direction of the center is conducted by two psychoanalysts, and the developmental theories basic to every educational measure taken at the center are strongly integrated with psychoanalytic theory, which of course is a developmental theory also.

Psychoanalysis and education have this in common: both are concerned with the profound and lasting influences of childhood experiences on the formation of the adult, and consequently of society. Both take into account the set sequence of behavioral changes and unfolding abilities which occur during childhood and adolescence.[83]

As psychoanalytic findings became influential, there was an increasing tendency in education to try to "liberate" the child—to permit him free expression of his feelings and drives. This tendency is described in such books as *Summerhill*.[70] This is not the practice at the center, where the teacher's role is conceived as that of a mature adult who guides the child with firmness as well as gentle understanding toward adulthood and a meaningful role in society.

A pioneer psychoanalyst/educator whose influence on the theory and practice of the center has been profound is August Aichhorn,[2] with whom Dr. Frostig worked for several years during her training in Vienna. Aichhorn was the first psychoanalyst to take social and cultural factors into consideration in his evaluation of the significance of psychoanalysis for the treatment of behavior disorders. He believed in an attitude which confronts the child with the demands and rewards of reality. Aichhorn had a great gift for adapting his handling of a child to the child's individual requirements. He could be gentle or strict, patiently working through a problem step-by-step with a frightened child, or becoming appropriately forceful and demanding.

He was well grounded in many disciplines, and of great cultural breadth. He was the exemplar of an educator: a man who studied and integrated findings from a variety of fields, and who firmly believed that optimum educational therapy can only be provided by an integration of psychoanalytic and educational principles.

Anna Freud's[17, 18] studies are also most important for education. She pointed out that what was called delinquency, as well as what is termed neurosis, is an expression of early unresolved conflicts rooted in the family structure. Many nonlearners become able to learn when they are helped to resolve these paralyzing conflicts. The resolution of these conflicts results in a modification of their outlook and behavior, and their relative freedom from guilt and anxiety, permitting them to marshal the capacities for learning which had previously been denied or immobilized.

Heinz Hartman,[41, 42] by redefining the concept of the ego and emphasizing its importance as the mediator between the individual and external reality, served further to bridge the gap between psychoanalysis and education. By helping the child to achieve initial satisfaction in mastery,* education promotes the wish to master even more, to attempt new tasks and to enjoy the growth of skills and new achievements.

Applying the concepts of ego psychology to education and its practitioners, Sheldon Rappaport[83] has postulated that the teacher should have positive personality factors which enable the educational process to take place in what he calls the "relationship structure." The teacher is instructed to provide the pupils with a sense of mastery, a desire for genuine achievement, and an ability to accept limitations and to master impulses which would bring them in conflict with their environment. The teacher should use warmth and love to help children face their difficulties.

Erikson's work, as well as Hartman's, is most important for the education of children with learning difficulties. Erikson[16] shows how endangered the child feels who cannot master his developmental tasks. Everyday observation in the classroom confirms his view; progress is indeed often at a standstill because the child is paralyzed by all-pervasive anxiety which may rise to panic when he is confronted with a task which seems too difficult for mastery, or with a relationship which seems threatening. He is afraid to perceive and understand the everyday world and to face himself. In the center's classrooms, therefore, a great effort is made not only to help the children master their learning tasks but also to help them understand the significance of their act of learning—to perceive and to enjoy their own progress. When they begin to feel more positive about themselves and the world around them, ego development takes place.

It has been necessary to give these examples of the influences of other research workers and their significance for the policy of the center, because to our knowledge until recently no comprehensive formulation derived from the many valuable theoretical contributions to remedial methods has existed or at least has not been accessible to the majority of educators.

Nor, to our knowledge, has there been a school or center in which psychia-

---

* See also DAVID RAPAPORT: *The Autonomy of the Ego.*[82]

trists, psychologists and general educators interested in special education have worked together as members of a team, with equal responsibility for leadership and for carrying the burden of everyday tasks. The equal emphasis at the center on each of the necessary tasks of evaluation, treatment, education and research and professional training makes possible a deep understanding of the child with learning difficulties and a broad range of services to help him.

Even today the teaching of special education often seems to be rather narrow, mechanical, or without scientific foundation. Too often, too little of what is taught in theories is translatable into educational procedures, and too little of what is taught in regard to practice is based on sound theory. At the Frostig Center an attempt is made to coordinate information and suggestions from various areas of scientific research and apply them to educational, treatment and evaluative procedures. At the same time new procedures are developed, and are validated by research, often undertaken in conjunction with public schools, as well as by clinical observation conducted at the center.

SERVICES OF THE CENTER

> The capacity to make considered decisions and to act on these with confidence is only acquired by the adult with a well trained brain and whose motivations are influenced by properly balanced feeling responses.*

At the head of the Frostig Center, and responsible for coordinating all its efforts, are the executive director and the medical director. The organization of the center can be regarded as divisible into five departments, although in fact all are interdependent. They are psychiatric diagnosis and treatment, education, psychological evaluation, research, and professional training. The administrative staff of the center helps to coordinate and facilitate the functions of these branches.

Psychiatric Services

> Feelings can give us knowledge: They can give us knowledge of [other's] feelings—and only feelings can do so.†

In charge of the psychiatric department are the medical director and the chief psychiatrist, both psychoanalysts. The medical director is responsible for the overall medical supervision of the center. He oversees the intake conference, formulates a diagnosis on the basis of the comprehensive evaluation, and approves and is responsible for the final treatment plan. He works together with the executive director in charting the future course of the center,

---

* W. Ritchie Russel: *Brain Memory Learning*. Oxford, Clarendon, 1959, p. 130.

† H. S. Burr: *The Neural Basis of Human Behavior*. Springfield, Ill., Thomas, 1960, p. 68.

and interprets professional concerns to the lay board and to the community at large.

The chief psychiatrist is responsible for the day-to-day psychiatric treatment. He supervises all therapists, including educational therapists insofar as they are concerned with behavior disturbances in the classroom. The supervisory meetings of both the chief psychiatrist and the medical director constitute seminars for the fellows in educational therapy or psychology. The chief psychiatrist works closely with the executive director and the medical director in formulating clinical policy.

Psychotherapy and Counseling

Psychotherapy may be necessary for children with learning difficulties when emotional disturbances or social maladjustment are at the root of their failure to learn. More often it is necessitated by the acute feelings of incompetency and worthlessness which commonly ensue from a child's perception of his failure to learn and the anxious or derisive reactions of significant adults and peers.

Children with perceptual disturbances are often confused by faulty interpretation of the environment, and this, too, can lead to emotional disturbances, usually characterized by extreme anxiety. Withdrawal, aggression or sudden swings to either extreme are often the behavioral result of the unstable, unpredictable and anxiety-arousing nature of his environment as he experiences it.

Newly enrolled children too disturbed to take part in classroom instruction are often seen individually until they can be integrated into a group. They then usually enter a preschool or school group of not more than six children.

The educational therapists at the center are trained to understand and handle upset behavior in the classroom. Should the classroom routine become affected, however, a disruptive child may be excluded temporarily from the classroom. He will usually spend the time with an adult and not in isolation. Educational therapists consult frequently with the therapist of any child who is receiving psychotherapy, and psychiatric supervision is always available to them.

About a quarter of the children require formal psychotherapy as part of their program. Psychotherapy may be conducted by a psychiatrist, a psychologist, a psychiatric social worker or the research therapist. Currently all psychotherapy for children is individual therapy, but group therapy for boys of ten to thirteen years of age will be instituted soon.

All parents are required to take part in at least three group sessions at the center, called *Parent-orientation Groups*. According to the recommendation of the chief psychiatrist, they may then enter a child-centered therapy group termed *Parent Education,* or a group concerned primarily with the problems of the parents, which is termed *Parent Group Therapy*. Other parents may receive individual counseling or psychotherapy. Parents may be seen together, or individually, or with the child, or the entire family may attend together, according to the diagnostic assessment.

Parents are involved in treatment in about 25 per cent of the cases.

Psychological Evaluation

. . . The aim of testing is to select the best treatment for every person.*

The psychological evaluation is under the guidance of the director of psychological services, while the psychologists engaged in psychotherapy are under the direction of the chief psychiatrist.

Extensive psychological evaluation is available for children from three years of age to adolescence, who present a wide variety of problems. The major reason for referral to the Frostig Center may be a learning difficulty, but sometimes the emotional or social problems are even more serious. As a rule multiple disabilities are found, and it is necessary to pinpoint the child's strengths and weaknesses in all developmental areas. A wide battery of assessment measures are used, which are reinforced by observation. The child is evaluated by a team of several clinicians (two to three usually), working independently. While the parents are seen by the social worker, the same child is usually seen more than once by each clinician, and altogether four to six times.

The psychological test battery explores motor skills, language development, perceptual functions, intellectual aspects of the personality (verbal and nonverbal), emotional and social aspects of personality functioning and academic achievement. Four tests are regularly employed with children of the appropriate age level: the Frostig Developmental Test of Visual Perception (1964),[31] the Wepman Test of Auditory Discrimination (1958),[100] the Illinois Test of Psycholinguistic Abilities (1961),[52] and the Wechsler Intelligence Scale for Children (1949),[97] but others are added at the discretion of the director of psychological services or of the examining clinician. Usually a great variety of tests are employed.† The findings obtained are integrated with the case history, and with psychological, educational and medical findings obtained from other sources.

One of the senior psychologists summarizes the findings gathered by his

---

* LEE J. CRONBACH: Psychological issues pertinent to recent American curriculum reform. *Child and Education,* G. S. Nillson (Ed.). Copenhagen, Munksgaard, 1962, p. 147.

† See Appendix for the full list of tests used at the center, and for charts based on the test results which help the teacher plan educational strategy for both individuals and classes.

team, makes recommendations based on these findings and submits his report to the director of psychological services for extensive review. At the weekly psychology staff conference some of these reports are discussed; *all* are reviewed by the director of the department. Final recommendations and dispositions are made by the psychiatric intake team headed by the medical director. The findings are interpreted to the parents, and recommendations made by the social worker who did the intake interview, together with one of the psychologists who participated in the test evaluation. The parents thus have direct contact with one of the clinicians who studied their child. Approximately 250 children are evaluated during the year.

Educational Services

> Man is defined as the speaking animal, but of equal importance is the fact that he is also the only animal capable of forming the detailed and differentiated perceptual learning sets that underlie a vast range of intellectual processes, including those of mastering or being mastered by the printed page.*

The educational services offered by the center are as follows:

1. Full-time school program: first to sixth grade, 9:00 to 1:30 P.M. daily.
2. Junior high school program: seventh to ninth grade, 2:00 to 5:00 P.M. daily.†
3. Preschool groups: 9:00 to 11:30 A.M., three days a week.
4. Training in basic abilities or tutoring in specific subjects for individuals or very small groups.

The importance of the educational services in regard to the total services of the center is implicit in the fact that nearly all children use the educational services and that most of the staff members are engaged in them. More than twenty educational therapists and ten fellows engage in classroom and individual teaching.

Of the 200 or 220 children enrolled in the school, about 120-140 are taught individually or in very small groups for about two hours weekly. They receive special training or tutoring in addition to attending public school. About eighty children are enrolled in the day school, and are taught in groups of five to seven children. All classes with more than five children are conducted by two teachers, so that attention can be paid to individual children when necessary. An afternoon play group is available.

The teacher's task is to help each child acquire as much as possible of the academic skill and knowledge expected of a child of his age level. At

---

* HARRY F. HARLOW: Learning theories. *Current Trends in Psychological Theory,* Dennis, Leeper *et al.* (Eds.). Pittsburgh, U of Pittsburgh, 1951, p. 82.

† An arrangement is made with the public schools permitting the children in this program to continue to attend public school for those activities in which they are relatively proficient, while attending the center for subjects in which they need special help.

the same time, the teacher must develop each child's lagging abilities and help him toward greater emotional and social maturity (see above). In order to achieve this, individual curricula are developed by the head teachers according to the basic test results, which indicate the areas in which each child requires remedial emphasis (see chart p. 147).

Organized remedial programs have been developed at the center for the various developmental areas. These can be used as total programs, or a selection can be made of the specific measures required for the particular child. For example, a program of physical education has been developed for sensory-motor training based on factor analytic studies of movement. The program aims at the development of various attributes of movement: speed, agility, flexibility, balance and so on. About half an hour per day is devoted to it with all of the children enrolled in the day school, but children who attend for tutoring may only do exercises in certain areas, such as rhythm or coordination or laterality, according to their individual needs. Training in fine motor coordination is done within the framework of an arts and crafts program as well as through the eye movement (tracking) exercises described in the Teacher's Guide to the Marianne Frostig Developmental Program of Visual Perception.

This program for training visual perception[30] is precisely geared to the Frostig Developmental Test of Visual Perception, and includes exercises in figure-ground perception, perceptual constancy, perception of position in space and perception of spatial relationships, as well as eye-motor coordination. A language program has also been developed, based on the Illinois Test of Psycholinguistic Abilities; this program is still in the experimental stage. In the area of higher cognitive processes, however, the program being developed can not be geared exactly to the basic test used for this area (The Wechsler Intelligence Scale for Children[97]) because most of the items in this and other intelligence tests tap a variety of abilities rather than one specific ability. The program for higher cognitive processes therefore, consists of methods similar to those suggested by Aurelia Levi,[56, 57] for helping children to classify, to work with sequential material, to perceive and manipulate relationships, to work with symbols and to form learning sets. This procedure leaves the WISC and other intelligence tests uncontaminated by direct training. They can thus be used as instruments for evaluating the performance of experimental and control groups after specific training has taken place.

As mentioned before, a chart is prepared by the head teacher, which illustrates the specific needs of each child in the class according to the test results, and guides the teachers in grouping the children and selecting areas of remedial emphasis (see Class Chart in Appendix).

The class illustrated by this chart consists of children nine to eleven years of age. The ITPA test results indicate that all of the children have difficulties in visual-motor association and most of them in vocal encoding (verbal expression) and visual motor sequencing (memory for visual sequences). These disabilities make writing, spelling, composition and oral expression very difficult. Considerable training in these skills therefore has to be done. Written expression, incidentally, also helps the children with auditory-vocal automatic skills (grammatically correct expression) in which most children in this group are lacking. Although writing skills differ from the abilities tested by the visual-motor association test of the ITPA, the latter abilities may also be developed by training in writing skills.

Most children in this group also show difficulties in planning and in the analysis and synthesis of patterns, abilities which are required in all school learning and in art and construction work. The curriculum itself may therefore provide training if academic skills and subject matter are taught by careful step-by-step procedures; in addition, appropriate exercises may be given from the perceptual and language programs. All of the day school children in the center participate in the physical education program as a matter of course.

A few children in the group discussed have specific difficulties not shared by the rest of the group. They are given specific exercises in these areas by the assistant teacher during periods in which the others are engaged in work less essential for them. For example, Robab, Simsy and Rotro have more difficulties with visual perception than the others, and require more exercises from the Frostig Program. Simsy and Robab also need auditory perceptual training (see Wepman test). Instruction in phonics is especially necessary for them. The same two children also have great difficulties in making abstractions, keeping a thought in mind, and remembering sequences of events and visual patterns. For both of them methods similar to those suggested by Aurelia Levi may be helpful.

The lagging abilities of the children are thus strengthened through teaching the regular curriculum in a manner which takes their difficulties into account, by administering specific exercises from the language and perception programs and by training in higher cognitive functions.

PROFESSIONAL TRAINING

> The value of man should be seen in what he gives, and not in what he is able to receive.
>
> ALBERT EINSTEIN

A one-year Fellowship training program in educational therapy is conducted at the center. Educators and school psychologists from various parts of the United States participate. The program is designed primarily for experienced school personnel or graduates in special education or psychology, and includes seminars, staff meetings and intensively supervised teaching with individual children and groups. Graduate credit for this work is given by the University of Southern California.

Less comprehensive training programs currently offered at the center include summer or single semester programs; two-week orientation programs designed primarily for administrators; periodic workshops; and formal training in testing. Fees are required for these programs, though a few scholarships are available. The responsibility for the training programs lies with the director of training, who also supervises the work of the permanent educational staff.

The trained educational therapist should have at his disposal a very well stocked arsenal of remedial techniques. It is quite common for a teacher to be skilled in teaching reading by a particular method; but he must know many methods, and which one to use with a given child. Educational therapists also need to know theories and principles as well as the body of knowledge pertaining to their craft, if they are not to be limited in their ability to modify, innovate and select the appropriate teaching procedures. For example, it is quite simple to learn to use sandpaper letters as a special technique, but it is another matter to be aware that tactile learning is not necessarily easier than visual learning nor applicable to all children. A child who has finger agnosia (diminished tactile awareness in the fingers) is poorly equipped to learn by touch; and a child who is oversensitive to tactile stimuli might be inhibited from learning by the repellent roughness of the paper. In addition, children do not necessarily transfer information readily from one sense modality to another.[5]

The educational therapist is also taught to understand test reports; but as test results tend to give an incomplete picture, he is taught to augment them with his own observations. For example, it is possible to test a child's ability to remember auditory sequences of numbers presented in a certain way, but the result will not indicate the circumstances in which he will learn to remember and recall number sequences as part of his permanent repertoire. After recognizing and understanding the deficit, the teacher must find out by experimentation and careful observation of the child's reactions the best remedial technique.

He must also learn how to treat the emotionally disturbed child in the classroom. In many instances, a child can improve his emotional health in the context of the class or the one-to-one tutoring or training relationship without formal psychotherapy if the educational therapist understands his plight, and is neither too angry to be loving nor too anxious to be firm.

In seminars, the various methodological problems are discussed together with the theories and principles which guide the educational therapist in the accomplishment of his main task: the amelioration of the child's problems whatever the origin and nature of the presenting symptoms.

RESEARCH

> We have hypothesized that there are few, if any, visual properties that are not greatly modified by learning, and that learning is the key both to understanding perception, and to integrating this psychological faculty with other time-and-tradition-honored facilities in psychology.*

The center's ongoing research in perception received its first impulse with Dr. Frostig's study of the work of Pestalozzi, Froebel, Montessori and Itard, who all employed sensory-motor training. Schilder's[86, 87] work on body image suggested also that training in sensory-motor functions, especially that which emphasized the development of the body image might be effective with emotionally disturbed and brain damaged children. Dr. Frostig's experiments with such a program at a Viennese school for children with emotional disturbances and behavior disorders seemed to bring about improvement, and she later used the same approach at a psychiatric hospital in Poland with equal success.

While in Vienna, Dr. Frostig's observations of post-encephalic children (see page 124) also indicated that such children might have perceptual disturbances, and she concluded that they, too, might be beneficially affected by training in sensory-motor functions and development of body image. Unfortunately, no standardized instruments were available to measure either a child's perceptual efficiency, or the nature and degree of his improvement after training. The observations remained only "hunches" which could not be proved. Much later, in England and in America, psychologists interested in perception, such as Thurstone,[93] Wedell[98, 99] and Cruickshank[14] found that the process of visual perception included several relatively independent abilities.

The inception of the center in 1947 made possible a close study of children with learning difficulties, which seemed to confirm the conclusions of these psychologists that a number of perceptual functions could indeed be differentiated. Five visual motor and visual perceptual abilities seemed of particular relevance to school performance: eye-hand coordination, figure-ground perception, perception of form constancy, perception of position in space and perception of spatial relationships.

To explore these abilities, and to provide age norms, construction of a developmental test of visual perception was begun in 1958. Pilot studies

---

* HARRY F. HARLOW: Learning theories. *Current Trends in Psychological Theory,* Dennis, Leeper *et al.* (Eds.). Pittsburgh, U of Pittsburgh, 1951, p. 74.

were conducted throughout 1959 and 1960. Criteria used for the final selection of items in each subtest area were good age progression and low degree of contamination with other abilities.* An attempt was made to differentiate tests of reproduction from those of recognition of visual stimuli.

The third, and current, edition of the test was first published in March, 1961. The child is required to attempt carefully graded tasks in the five areas of visual perception mentioned above. Current norms for the test are based on over 2100 nursery school and public school children between the ages of three and nine years, living in Southern California. Normative curves drawn from the standardization sample indicate that the maximum perceptual development in the areas measured occurs between the ages of four and seven, with little progress after the ages of eight and nine years. After the age of about seven and one-half, the development of higher cognitive processes begins to predominate.

Perception is thus the chief developmental task of the child at the age of beginning school entrance. Correlations found between teacher ratings of classroom adjustment and scores on the Frostig Test for 374 kindergarten children indicate that a child at this grade level who scores low on the test is highly likely to have difficulties with initial school adjustment.[62] These findings are congruent with Knobloch and Pasamanick's contention[54] that a lack of integrity of the nervous system is most clearly expressed in the main developmental task during any phase of development.

Not only are visual perceptual disabilities frequently reflected in disturbed behavior during the four- to seven-year age period, but a child's ability to learn to read is also affected by his visual perceptual development. A study reported by Maslow, Frostig, Lefever and Whittlesey[62] suggests that a child with difficulties in this area will not voluntarily attempt to learn to read. Research was reported in the same monograph on other reading situations in which the children were required to read. It showed a correlation coefficient of between .4 and .5 between the Frostig Test and reading achievement in first grade. These studies indicate that, while other skills are also involved, visual perceptual abilities play an important role in the acquisition of reading, and visual perceptual dysfunctions make beginning reading difficult and unrewarding.

The test enables the educational therapist to gauge the range of perceptual dysfunctions directly and to infer the existence of other dysfunctions if no perceptual disabilities are evident. Perceptual disturbances, especially visual ones, are so frequently the cause of learning difficulties, and probably of

* Research done at the center (Maslow, Frostig, Lefever and Whittlesey,[62] p. 487) and by Silverstein[88] has substantiated the hypotheses that the test does measure five relatively distinct abilities, and that training in the different abilities is warranted.

behavioral difficulties, that there is a temptation to believe that they are *always* the main or the only precondition for successful school progress.* In the same way intellectual or emotional disturbances have been considered the essential cause. Usually, none of these factors occurs alone; the causation is nearly always multiple. *All developmental abilities of a child have to be explored to find possible reasons for a learning deficit.*

The current research of the center therefore focuses on exploration of specific lags in each of six developmental areas (sensory-motor functions, perception, language, higher cognitive functions, emotional and social development) evidenced by children referred to the center. It is concerned with what relationships, if any, exist among these deficits; how the deficits manifest themselves in school behavior and achievement; whether such deficits may be ameliorated, and if so, by what means.

The various departments of the center contribute basic data: results of assessment at initial intake, including a developmental history; observations and progress reports by educational therapists; psychotherapy notes; the social worker's report on family attitudes and practices; public school reports; results of retesting, and so on. Many public school districts, not only in the Los Angeles area but throughout the country, cooperate with the center by field testing various experimental programs, by contributing suggestions and criticisms and by sharing research findings.

A cluster analysis is now being conducted on the test scores† obtained by children between the ages of six and one-half and nine referred to the center because of severe behavior or academic difficulties. This sample of children all have either performance or verbal WISC IQ scores of 77 or over, and no known sensory defects or severe psychopathology. The study is primarily designed to indicate possible interrelationships between disabilities in this group.

A study is also being conducted on a sample of children who have had a year of training at the center and who have been retested with the original battery. This is conceived as a pilot study in the evaluation of the total remedial programs.

NOW AND THE FUTURE

> Reality involves relationship, and as soon as you have relationship you have, for human beings, emotions.‡

---

* For instance, in a sample of 78 children aged 9 years or younger referred to the Frostig Center because of learning difficulties, 66.7 per cent had a total perceptual quotient of 90 or below (lowest quartile). These were children with a full scale WISC IQ of 77 or above. In a similar study of 89 children of 9 years or older, 78 per cent did not reach the maximum possible age equivalent on one or more of the subtests.

† On the Frostig, the Wepman, the WISC and the ITPA.

‡ Sir Russel Brain: *The Nature of Experience.* London, Oxford U P, Amen House, 1959, p. 58.

In the past the center consisted of a small school, inadequately housed, but with a most enthusiastic staff. There were no fully trained people to fill the positions because no training facility was available. The staff members learned while working and were always eager to experiment until they found what would best help a child.

To build a center adequate for the tasks at hand, much had to be created —theories and methods, tests and teaching materials, buildings to work in and a team of trained personnel. These tasks are now well in hand, though much remains to be done.

At the present time, a vast network of contacts and common interests connects the center with other facilities in nearly every state, and in many countries abroad. The instructions for the Frostig Developmental Test of Visual Perception have been translated into French, German, Polish, Czech, Spanish, Portugese, Japanese and the Scandinavian languages. The Perceptual Program is also used in many institutions in the United States and abroad.

The results of much of the testing and training are fed back to the center, to facilitate the further refinement of methods of evaluating and training. Joint research is undertaken with a number of public school systems in this country and abroad. Physical education programs currently under development at the center are being used in some public schools on an experimental basis.* Some of these school districts have constructed "Frostig playgrounds" on the basis of recommendations in the Teacher's Guide to the Frostig Program for training in visual perception, and others are developing specific three-dimensional training materials.† Yet others are carrying on research with the language program developed at the center.‡ An adaptation of the Frostig Program to preschool training has been made, with the needs of Head Start programs specifically in mind. It is currently being applied and further developed.§

Close liaison with school systems if of importance for validating and refining teaching and training methods. Liaison with institutions of higher learning is equally important for filling the enormous need for personnel trained in educational therapy. Among the institutions at which courses have been given are the extension divisions of the University of California at Los Angeles, Davis and Riverside, and the departments of special education of

* Particularly in the Cupertino School District under the direction of Dr. Charles S. Knight, Superintendent and Secretary to the Board of Education, with the cooperation of Mary Webster and Erika Bauer, Adjustment-Remedial Teachers and Elementary Counsellors.

† As in Tucson, Arizona, under the direction of Mrs. L. D. Ganoung, Supervisor of Special Education and Mrs. Genevieve Klein, Special Education Teacher.

‡ The most active in these respects is Coffeyville, Kansas under the direction of Betty Shewell, Psychologist.

§ In a Head Start Program in Hartford, Connecticut, under the direction of Mrs. Geraldine Withycombe, director of the program, and Ann-Marie Miller, Head Teacher.

San Fernando State College, and Los Angeles State College. Countless workshops have been held in all parts of this country and in Canada and England.* Two training films have been made at the center, one demonstrating therapy with multiple handicapped children with severe ego disturbances; the other showing the relationship between disturbance in visual perception and failure to learn. For publications by the center staff see Bibliography.

The Fellowship training program is now well established, and currently includes students from the University of Southern California, University of Arizona, and graduates from Syracuse University and Wayne University.

Much remains to be done. The current procedure of trying out methods developed at the center in public school systems will be continued and the feedback from public schools will help us to refine the methods and modify them so that they are optimally applicable to public school purposes. Longitudinal studies will, we hope, provide us with the data which will permit prediction of improvement in individual children and the selection of the most effective teaching methods. More films are planned to demonstrate teaching techniques to public school personnel. When enlarged facilities are available professional training will be expanded to help meet the staffing needs of our center and of other institutions.

It is hoped that as these tasks are undertaken and the slower and more orderly growth of the center's maturer years takes place, the enthusiasm and desire to experiment of the pioneer days will be maintained. The center has recently become the training school for the University of Southern California. A fruitful partnership with the university is anticipated.

CONCLUSION

The emphasis on developing scientific testing and teaching methods, which is the natural result of attempting to remedy the disabilities of children with learning difficulties, must be balanced by the recognition that education, in both its means and its ends, is a matter of human relationships. The aims of the educator for all children are, in Einstein's view,[15] "the training of acting and thinking individuals who, however, see the service of the community as their highest life problem."

It is of especial importance for children with learning handicaps to acquire self-fulfillment as contributing members of society. Their frequent failure to achieve individual competitive success and their difficulty in integrating

---

* For example during the period of September 1964-June 1966 major lectures and workshops given were: California—56, British Columbia—3, Toronto, Canada—1, London, England—1, Hawaii—1, Oregon—2, Washington—2, Texas—2, Oklahoma—2, New York—8, Illinois—2, Michigan—2, Washington, D. C.—1, Arizona—1, Kansas—1, Indiana—1, Wisconsin—1.

with the society of the average public school classroom often produce irritable, depressed feelings of helplessness and impotence. The special methods which the teacher uses can help to improve the child's basic abilities and provide him with the antidote to the ills which all children with learning difficulties have in common—the lack of self-respect and the sense of failure. However, improved ability and greater success and self-respect are only part of the educational goal.

Each child needs to be helped to learn that he can find satisfaction in respecting others' needs and joy in helping others, at whatever social, professional or intellectual level he may function. When he knows that his contributions are appreciated, an inner glow of purpose and self-respect will give him direction throughout his life.

Although he must learn many "methods" the teacher must in the last analysis select for himself and effect them through the medium of his own personality. He must understand that no method will be maximally helpful, without the vehicle of his relationship with the child, and the child's awareness of the teacher's sensitivity to his needs. The convictions and the personality of the teacher, as well as his training are thus of utmost importance for the child's welfare. Education, as any endeavor involving human relationships, must always remain an art as well as a science, with a philosophy as well as a rationale.

ACKNOWLEDGMENTS

The authors are grateful to the staff members of the Frostig Center who provided time and material in the construction of this paper. They are Janet Switzer, Ph.D., Zev Wanderer, Ph.D., and Helmut Wursten, Ph.D. Special thanks are due to Phyllis Maslow, M.A., who was most active and thorough in her assistance and advice, and gave generously of her time.

The three secretaries working with us on this paper, Phyllis Gedge, Irene Tamosaitis and Beulah Wilson, have contributed the careful typing and the charts. They have helped with advice and worked with skill and devotion. To them, too, go our heartfelt thanks.

BIBLIOGRAPHY

1. Aebli, H.: *Didactique Psychologique. Application à la didactique de la psychologie de Jean Piaget.* Neuchatel, Delachaux and Niestle, 1963.
2. Aichhorn, August: *Wayward Youth.* New York, Compass, Viking, 1965.
3. Bateman, Barbara: An educator's view of a diagnostic approach to learning disorders, in *Learning Disorders,* J. Hellmuth (Ed.). Seattle, Special Child, 1965, vol. 1, pp. 219-239.
4. Bigge, Morris L.: *Learning Theories for Teachers.* New York, Harper, 1964.
5. Birch, H. G., and Lefford, Arthur: Intersensory development in children. *Monogr Soc Res Child Develop, 28,* No. 5, 1963.

6. Brazier, Mary A. B. (Ed.): *The Central Nervous System and Behavior,* Transactions of the Second Conference, Princeton, 1959, sponsored by Josiah Macy, Jr. Foundation and the National Science Foundation. Madison, New Jersey, Madison Printing Company, 1959.
7. Bruner, Jerome: *The Process of Education.* Cambridge, Harvard U P, 1960.
8. Bruner, Jerome: Learning and Thinking, in *Readings in the Psychology of Cognition,* R. C. Anderson and D. P. Ausubel (Eds.). New York, Holt, 1965, pp. 76-86.
9. Bruner, Jerome, and Olver, Rose R.: Development of equivalence transformation in children, in *Readings in the Psychology of Cognition,* R. C. Anderson and D. P. Ausubel (Eds.). New York, Holt, 1965, pp. 415-434.
10. Buhler, Charlotte: *The First Year of Life.* New York, Day, 1930.
11. Buhler, Charlotte: *Testing Children's Development From Birth to Schoolage.* New York, Ferrar and Reinhart, 1935.
12. Buhler, Charlotte: From Birth to Maturity. London, Kagan, Paul, Trench, Trebner, 1935.
13. Cruickshank, W. M.; Bentzen, F. A.; Ratzenburg, F. H., and Tannhauser, M. T.: *A Teaching Method for Brain-Injured and Hyperactive Children.* New York, Syracuse University Press, 1961.
14. Cruickshank, W. M.; Bice, H. V., and Wallen, N. E.: *Perception and Cerebral Palsy.* Syracuse, Syracuse, 1957.
15. Einstein, Albert: On education, reprinted from *Out of My Later Years* (Philosophical Library, 1950), in *Human Development,* M. L. Haimowitz and N. R. Haimowitz (Eds.). New York, Crowell, 1960, pp. 534-538.
16. Erikson, Erik H.: *Childhood and Society.* New York, Norton, 1950.
17. Freud, Anna: *The Psycho-Analytical Treatment of Children.* London, Imago, 1946.
18. Freud, Anna: *The Ego and the Mechanisms of Defence.* New York, Int Univs, 1946.
19. Froebel, Friedrich: *The Education of Man.* New York, Appleton, 1900.
20. Frostig, Marianne: Motion and emotion. *Claremont College Reading Yearbook,* 1948.
21. Frostig, Marianne: The treatment of blind and seeing autistic children in a clinical school. Digest of paper presented at the 36th Annual Meeting of the American Orthopsychiatric Association, April 1959. Abstract only.
22. Frostig, Marianne, and Horne, David: Language development in a psychotic child during successful therapy—a method of evaluation. Presented at the 38th Annual Meeting of the American Orthopsychiatric Association, March 1961. Published in abstract form.
23. Frostig, Marianne; Lefever, D. W., and Whittlesey, J. R. B.: Developmental test of visual perception for evaluating normal and neurological handicapped children. *Percept Motor Skills, 12*:383-394, June 1961.
24. Frostig, Marianne, and Horne, David: Assessment of visual perception and its importance in education. *AAMD Education Reporter, 2*:1-12, April 1962.
25. Frostig, Marianne: Education of children with learning difficulties. *Distinguished Lectures in Special Education.* University of Southern California, Summer 1962.
26. Frostig, Marianne; Maslow, Phyllis; Lefever, D. W., and Whittlesey, J. R. B.: Visual perceptual development and school adjustment and progress. *Amer J Orthopsychiat,* March 1963. Abstract only.
27. Frostig, Marianne, and Horne, D.: Changes in language and behavior in psychotic

children during successful therapy—method of evaluation and findings. *Amer J Orthopsychiat, 33*:734-737, July 1963.

28. Frostig, Marianne: Visual perception in the brain-injured child. *Amer J Orthopsychiat, 33*:665-671, July 1963.
29. Frostig, Marianne; Lefever, D. W., and Whittlesey, J. R. B.: Disturbance in visual perception. *J Educ Res, 57,* November 1963.
30. Frostig, Marianne, and Horne, D.: *The Frostig Program for the Development of Visual Perception* (Pictures by Bee Mandell). Chicago, Follett, 1964.
31. Frostig, Marianne; Lefever, D. W., and Whittlesey, J. R. B.: The Marianne Frostig Developmental Test of Visual Perception, 1963 Standardization. *Percept Motor Skills, 19*:463-499, 1964. Monograph Supplement 2-V19.
32. Frostig, Marianne: The implication of developmental diagnosis of children with learning difficulties, and applications in the normal classroom. *J Humanistic Psychol,* 1964.
33. Frostig, Marianne: Corrective reading in the classroom. *Reading Teacher, 18*:573-580, April 1965.
34. Frostig, Marianne, and Horne, David: An approach to the treatment of children with learning difficulties. *Learning Disorders, 1*:293-305, Seattle, Washington, Special Child Publications, 1965.
35. Frostig, Marianne: The needs of teachers for specialized information on reading. *The Teacher of Brain-Injured Children: A Discussion of the Bases of Competency.* Syracuse, Syracuse, 1966, pp. 87-109.
36. Frostig, Marianne: The education of children with learning disabilities. *Progress in Learning Disorders,* Helmer Myklebust (Ed.). New York, Grune, 1966.
37. Frostig, Marianne, in cooperation with Hart, Wilma: Developmental evaluation and the institution of remedial programs for children with learning difficulties. *Principals' Journal,* Nov. 1966 (in British Columbia); also *Academic Therapy Quarterly,* Summer 1966.
38. Goldstein, Kurt: Sensoritonic theory and the concept of self-realization, in *Perspectives in Psychological Theory,* B. Kaplan and S. Wapner (Eds.). New York, Int Univs 1960, pp. 115-123.
39. Harlow, Harry F.: The formation of learning sets. *Psychol Rev, 56*:51-65, 1949.
40. Harlow, Harry F.: Learning set and error factor theory. *Psychology: A Study of a Science,* S. Koch (Ed.). New York, McGraw, 1959, vol. 2, pp. 492-537.
41. Hartman, H.: Comments on the psychoanalytic theory of the ego. *The Psychoanalytic Study of the Child.* New York, Int Univs, 1950, vol. 5, pp. 79-96.
42. Hartman, H.: Ego psychology and the problem of adaptation (abbreviated, annotated version), in *Organization and Pathology of Thought,* D. Rapaport (Ed.). New York, Columbia, 1951, pp. 362-396.
43. Hebb, D. O.: *The Organization of Behavior.* New York, Wiley, 1949.
44. Hebb, D. O.: *A Textbook of Psychology.* Philadelphia, Saunders, 1958.
45. Hebb, D. O.: A neuropsychological theory. *Psychology: A Study of a Science,* Sigmund Koch (Ed.). New York, McGraw, 1959, vol. 1, pp. 622-643.
46. Hilgard, E. R.: *Theories of Learning.* 2nd ed. New York, Appleton, 1956.
47. Horne, David: The loneliest children of all. *Light,* Autumn, 1959.
48. Itard, Jean M. G.: *The Wild Boy of Aveyron.* New York, Appleton, 1962.
49. Keller, Helen: Teacher—Anne Sullivan Macy in *Human Development,* M. Haimowitz and N. Haimowitz (Eds.). New York, Crowell, 1960.

49a. KEPHART, N. C.: *The Slow Learner in the Classroom.* Columbus, Charles E. Merrill, 1960.

50. KIRK, SAMUEL A.: *Educating Exceptional Children.* Boston, Houghton, 1962.

51. KIRK, SAMUEL A., and BATEMAN, BARBARA: Diagnosis and remediation of learning disabilities, in *Exceptional Children.* 1962, vol. 29, pp. 73-78.

52. KIRK, SAMUEL A., and MCCARTHY, JAMES P.: *The Illinois Test of Psycholinguistic Abilities.* Urbana, U of Illinois, 1961.

53. KIRK, SAMUEL A., and MCCARTHY, JAMES P.: The Illinois Test of Psycholinguistic Abilities. *Amer J Ment Defic, 66*:399-412, 1961.

54. KNOBLOCH, H., and PASAMANICK, B.: An evaluation of the consistency and predictive value of the 40-week Gesell developmental schedule. *Child Development and Child Psychiatry,* C. Shagrass and B. Pasamanick (Eds.). Washington, Amer Psychiat Assn, 1960. Psychiat Res Rep No. 13, pp. 10-31.

55. LEGRAND, LOUIS: *Psychologie Appliquée a l'Education Intellectuelle.* Paris, Delachauex and Niestle, 1961.

56. LEVI, AURELIA: Treatment of a disorder of perception and concept formation in a case of school failure. *J Consult Psychol, 29* (No. 4) :289-295, 1965.

57. LEVI, AURELIA: Remedial techniques in disorders of concept formation, *J. Special Ed., 1*:3-8, 1966.

58. LOVELL, K.: *The Growth of Basic Mathematical and Scientific Concepts in Children.* New York, Philosophical Lib, 1961.

59. LURIA, A. R.: *The Role of Speech in the Regulation of Normal and Abnormal Behavior.* New York, Liveright, 1961.

60. LURIA, A. R., and YUDOVICH, R. I.: *Speech and the Development of Mental Processes in the Child.* London, Staples, 1959.

61. MAGOUN, H. W.: *The Waking Brain.* Springfield, Ill., Thomas, 1958.

62. MASLOW, PHYLLIS; FROSTIG, MARIANNE; LEFEVER, D. W., and WHITTLESEY, J. R. B.: The Marianne Frostig Developmental Test of Visual Perception, 1963 Standardization. *Percept Motor Skills, 19*:463-499, 1964. Monograph Supplement 2-V19.

63. MCCARTHY, J. J., and KIRK, S. A.: *The Construction, Standardization and Statistical Characteristics of the Illinois Test of Psycholinguistic Abilities.* Urbana, Univ of Illinois, 1963.

64. MCCULLOCH, W. S.: *Brain and Behavior in Current Trends in Psychological Theory.* Pittsburgh, Univ of Pittsburgh, 1951, pp. 165-178.

65. MILLER, G. A.; GALANTER, E., and PRIBRAM, K. H.: *Plans and the Structure of Behavior.* New York, Holt, 1960.

66. MONTESSORI, MARIA: The Montessori Method: scientific pedagogy as applied to child education, in *The Children's Houses.* New York, Stokes, 1912.

67. MONTESSORI, MARIA: *Dr. Montessori's Own Handbook.* New York, Schocken, 1965.

68. MYKLEBUST, H. R.: *Auditory Disorders in Children.* New York, Grune, 1954.

69. MYKLEBUST, H. R.: *Development and Disorders of Written Language.* New York, Grune, 1965, vol. 1.

70. NEILL, A. S.: *Summerhill.* New York, Hart, 1961.

71. PEEL, E. A.: *The Pupil's Thinking.* London, Oldbourne, 1960.

72. PENFIELD, W., and ROBERTS, L.: *Speech and Brain Mechanisms.* Princeton, Princeton, 1959.

73. PESTALOZZI, JOHANN HEINRICH: *Letters on Early Education.* London, Sherwood, Gilber, and Piper, 1827.

74. PIAGET, JEAN: *The Child's Conception of Numbers.* New York, Humanities, 1952.

75. Piaget, Jean: *The Origins of Intelligence in Children.* New York, Int Univs Press, 1952.
76. Piaget, Jean: *The Construction of Reality in the Child.* New York, Basic, 1954.
77. Piaget, Jean: *Judgment and Reasoning of the Child.* Paterson, Littlefield, 1959.
78. Piaget, Jean: *The Child's Conception of Physical Causality.* Paterson, Littlefield, 1960.
79. Piaget, Jean: How children form mathmetical concepts, in *Readings in the Psychology of Cognition,* R. C. Anderson and D. P. Ausubel (Eds.). New York, Holt, 1965.
80. Rambusch, Nancy McCormick: *Learning How to Learn,* 2nd ed. New York, Helicon (Taplinger), 1963.
81. Rapaport, David: Psychoanalysis as a developmental psychology. *Perspectives in Psychological Theory,* B. Kaplan and S. Wapner (Eds.). New York, Int Univs, 1960, pp. 209-255.
82. Rapaport, David: The autonomy of the ego. *Psychoanalytic Psychiatry and Psychology,* R. P. Knight and C. R. Friedman (Eds.). New York, Int Univs, 1954, pp. 248-258.
83. Rappaport, Sheldon R.: Personality factors teachers need for relationship structure. *The Teacher of Brain-Injured Children: A Discussion of the Bases for Competency,* Wm. M. Cruickshank (Ed.). Syracuse, Syracuse, 1966, pp. 47-55.
84. Rosenzweig, Mark R.: Environmental complexity, cerebral change, and behavior. *Amer Psychol, 21*:321-332, 1966.
85. Sands, R.; Frostig, Marianne, and Horne, D.: Educational therapy in learning difficulties: the role of the pediatrician in prevention, diagnosis, and therapy. *Amer J Dis Child, 107*:155-159, February, 1964.
86. Schilder, Paul: The psychological implication of motor development in children. *Bull Wood School, 4*:38-59, 1937.
87. Schilder, Paul: *The Image and Appearance of the Human Body.* New York, Int Univs, 1951.
88. Silverstein, A. B.: Variance Comments in the Developmental Test of Visual Perception. *Percept Motor Skills, 20*:973-976, 1965.
89. Skinner, B. F.: *Cumulative Record,* Part III. New York, Appleton, 1959.
90. Strauss, A. A., and Lehtinen, L.: *Psychopathology and Education of the Brain-Injured Child.* New York, Grune, 1947.
91. Strauss, A. A., and Kephart, N. C.: *Psychopathology and Education of the Brain-Injured Child.* New York, Grune, 1955, vol. 2.
92. Talbot, E. M.: *Edouard Seguin.* New York, Teachers College, Columbia, 1964.
93. Thurstone, L. L.: A factorial study of perception. *Psychometric Monographs,* No. 4. Chicago, Univ of Chicago, 1944.
94. Vygotsky, L. S.: *Thought and Language.* New York, Wiley, 1962.
95. Vygotsky, L. S.: Learning and mental development at school age. *Educational Psychology in the U.S.S.R.,* Brian and Joan Simon (Eds.). London, Routledge and Kegan Paul, 1963, pp. 31-33.
96. Wapner, S., and Werner, H.: Experiments on sensory-motor field theory of perception. *J Exp Psychol, 44*:126-131, 1952.
97. *Wechsler Intelligence Scale for Children.* New York, The Psychological Corporation, 1949.
98. Wedell, K.: Variations in perceptual ability among types of cerebral palsy. *Cereb Palsy Bull, 2*:149-157, 1960.

99. Wedell, K.: The visual perception of cerebral palsied children. *J Child Psychol Psychiat, 1*:215-228, 1960.
100. Wepman, J. M.: *Wepman Test of Auditory Discrimination.* Chicago, Language Research Associates, 1958.
101. Werner, Heinz: *Comparative Psychology of Mental Development,* 2nd ed. New York, Int Univs, 1957.
102. Zangwill, O. L.: *Cerebral Dominance and Its Relation to Psychological Functions.* Springfield, Ill., Thomas, 1960.

APPENDIX A
ASSESSMENT OF SIX MAIN AREAS OF DEVELOPMENT
Examples of Tests Used at the Frostig Center

Sensory-Motor
- Oseretsky Scale
- Kraus-Weber Test
- Harris Test for Laterality
- Observation for the Prechtl syndrome
- Test for finger agnosia
- Test for ability for kinesthetic memory
- Observation of eye movements

Perceptual
- Wepman Test of Auditory Discrimination
- Frostig Developmental Test of Visual Perception
- Bender-Gestalt
- Goodenough
- Memory for Design (Benton, Kendell, Graham)

Language
- Illinois Test of Psycholinguistic Abilities
- Eisenson Test for Aphasia (where indicated)
- Recording and assessing the child's spontaneous language

Higher Thought Processes
- WISC, WAIS
- Binet
- Developmental Scales for Pre-School Children
  - Merrill-Palmer, Bühler
  - Cattell
  - Leiter

Emotional Development
- Rorschach
- Children's apperception Test (TAT)
- Thomas Completion
- World Test

Social Development
- Vineland
- Observation and description of behavior, play observation
- Reports from parents and others

(Achievement)
- Wide Range (include an oral test)
- CAT
- Metropolitan
- Stanford
- Durrell Oral Reading
- For kindergarten and first graders, an estimate of reading ability and arithmetic ability

Other test may be given at the individual psychologist's discretion.

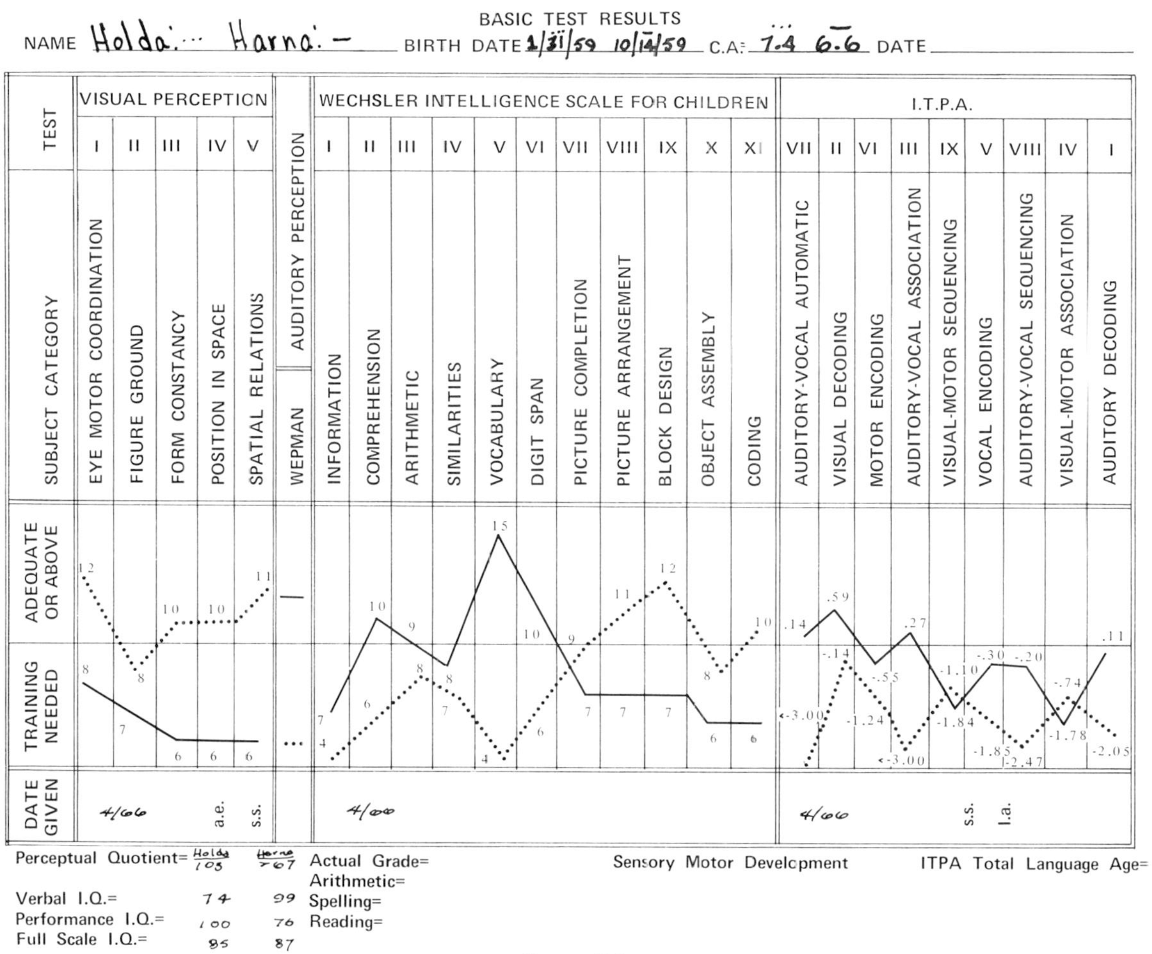

BASIC TEST RESULTS

NAME Holda... Harna... — BIRTH DATE 1/31/59 10/14/59 C.A.= 7.4 6.6 DATE

TEST		SUBJECT CATEGORY	ADEQUATE OR ABOVE	TRAINING NEEDED	DATE GIVEN
VISUAL PERCEPTION	I	EYE MOTOR COORDINATION	12	8	4/66
	II	FIGURE GROUND		7, 8	
	III	FORM CONSTANCY	10	6	
	IV	POSITION IN SPACE	10	6	a.e.
	V	SPATIAL RELATIONS	11	6	s.s.
AUDITORY PERCEPTION		WEPMAN	—	...	
WECHSLER INTELLIGENCE SCALE FOR CHILDREN	I	INFORMATION		7, 4	4/66
	II	COMPREHENSION	10	6	
	III	ARITHMETIC	9	8	
	IV	SIMILARITIES		8, 7	
	V	VOCABULARY	15	4	
	VI	DIGIT SPAN	10	6	
	VII	PICTURE COMPLETION	9	7	
	VIII	PICTURE ARRANGEMENT	11	7	
	IX	BLOCK DESIGN	12	7	
	X	OBJECT ASSEMBLY		8, 6	
	XI	CODING	10	6	
I.T.P.A.	VII	AUDITORY-VOCAL AUTOMATIC	.14	<-3.00	4/66
	II	VISUAL DECODING	.59	-.14	
	VI	MOTOR ENCODING		-.55, -1.24	
	III	AUDITORY-VOCAL ASSOCIATION	.27	<-3.00	
	IX	VISUAL-MOTOR SEQUENCING		-1.10, -1.84	
	V	VOCAL ENCODING		-.30, -1.85	s.s.
	VIII	AUDITORY-VOCAL SEQUENCING		-.20, -2.47	l.a.
	IV	VISUAL-MOTOR ASSOCIATION		-.74, -1.78	
	I	AUDITORY DECODING	.11	-2.05	

	Holda	Harna
Perceptual Quotient=	105	767
Verbal I.Q.=	74	99
Performance I.Q.=	100	76
Full Scale I.Q.=	85	87

Actual Grade=
Arithmetic=
Spelling=
Reading=

Sensory Motor Development

ITPA Total Language Age=

CHART 7-1

BASIC TEST RESULTS

GROUP CHART

NAME ______________ BIRTH DATE ______________ C.A. = ________ DATE 12/65

Test group	Test	Subject Category	Adequate or Above	Training Needed	Date Given
VISUAL PERCEPTION	I	EYE MOTOR COORDINATION	◇□△○●◆■	▲	
VISUAL PERCEPTION	II	FIGURE GROUND	◇□△○●■	▲◆	
VISUAL PERCEPTION	III	FORM CONSTANCY	◇△○	□●■▲◆	
VISUAL PERCEPTION	IV	POSITION IN SPACE	◇△○●	□■▲◆	a.e.
VISUAL PERCEPTION	V	SPATIAL RELATIONS	◇□△○●▲	■◆	s.s.
AUDITORY PERCEPTION		WEPMAN	△○▲	◇□●■◆	
WECHSLER INTELLIGENCE SCALE FOR CHILDREN	I	INFORMATION	◇△▲◆	○●■□	
WECHSLER INTELLIGENCE SCALE FOR CHILDREN	II	COMPREHENSION	◇□△○▲	●■◆	
WECHSLER INTELLIGENCE SCALE FOR CHILDREN	III	ARITHMETIC	◇△●	□○■▲◆	
WECHSLER INTELLIGENCE SCALE FOR CHILDREN	IV	SIMILARITIES	◇□△●▲	○■◆	
WECHSLER INTELLIGENCE SCALE FOR CHILDREN	V	VOCABULARY	◇□△●▲	○■◆	
WECHSLER INTELLIGENCE SCALE FOR CHILDREN	VI	DIGIT SPAN	◇□▲	△○●■◆	
WECHSLER INTELLIGENCE SCALE FOR CHILDREN	VII	PICTURE COMPLETION	◇□△○●	■▲◆	
WECHSLER INTELLIGENCE SCALE FOR CHILDREN	VIII	PICTURE ARRANGEMENT	◇□○▲	△●■◆	
WECHSLER INTELLIGENCE SCALE FOR CHILDREN	IX	BLOCK DESIGN	◇△●	□○■▲◆	
WECHSLER INTELLIGENCE SCALE FOR CHILDREN	X	OBJECT ASSEMBLY	◇□○●	△■▲◆	
WECHSLER INTELLIGENCE SCALE FOR CHILDREN	XI	CODING	△○□◆	◇□●▲	
I.T.P.A.	VII	AUDITORY-VOCAL AUTOMATIC	◇○□	△●■▲◆	
I.T.P.A.	II	VISUAL DECODING	◇△○●▲□◆	■	
I.T.P.A.	VI	MOTOR ENCODING	◇○●■▲□	△◆	
I.T.P.A.	III	AUDITORY-VOCAL ASSOCIATION	◇△○●▲□	■◆	
I.T.P.A.	IX	VISUAL-MOTOR SEQUENCING	△●	◇○■▲□◆	s.s.
I.T.P.A.	V	VOCAL ENCODING	◇●□	△○■▲◇	l.a.
I.T.P.A.	VIII	AUDITORY-VOCAL SEQUENCING	△○●▲□	◇◆■	
I.T.P.A.	IV	VISUAL-MOTOR ASSOCIATION		◇△○●▲■□◆	
I.T.P.A.	I	AUDITORY DECODING	◇△○■▲□	●◆	

Perceptual Quotient =

Verbal I.Q. =
Performance I.Q. =
Full Scale I.Q. =

Actual Grade =
Arithmetic =
Spelling =
Reading =

Sensory Motor Development

ITPA Total Language Age =

MARRU ◇ MORJO □ MOSSO △ RECHA ○ RHOJE ● ROBAD ■ ROTRO ▲ SIMSY ◆

CHART 7-2

Part II

PROGRAMS FOR COMMUNICATION DISORDERS

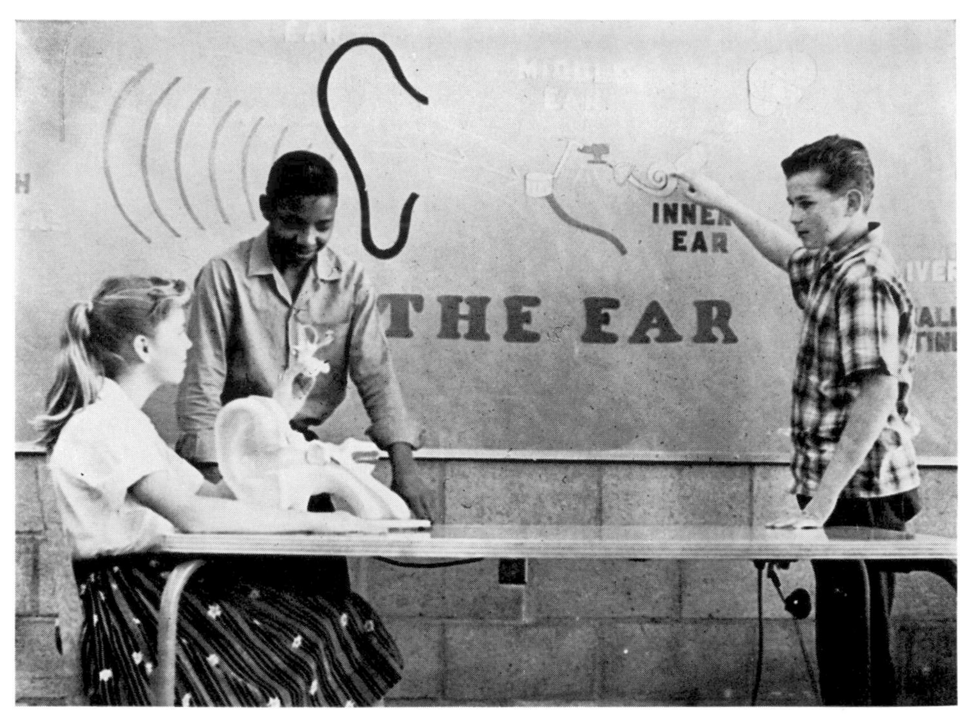

FIGURE II-1. An explanation of the mechanics of hearing is useful at the School for the Deaf, Riverside, California.

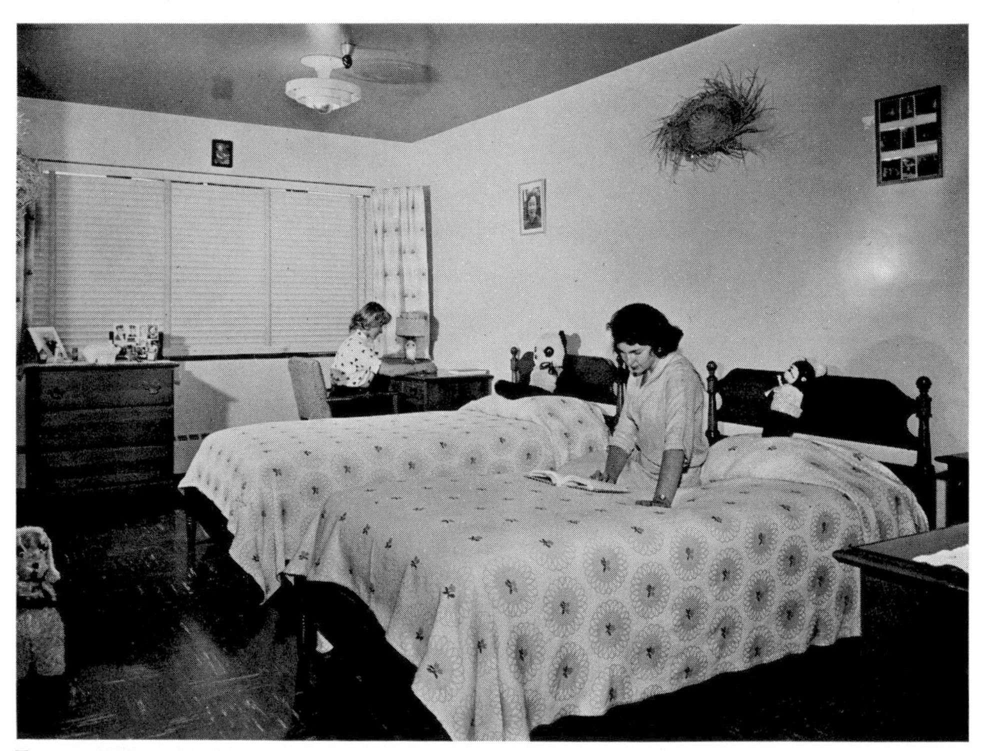

FIGURE II-2. This high school girls' dormitory room is homelike—State School for the Deaf, Riverside, California.

FIGURE II-3. The audiologist is an important member of the team at the Sutter Diagnostic and Treatment Center, Sacramento, California.

FIGURE II-4. The tape recorder is utilized in the Speech Clinic at the School for Cerebral Palsied Children in San Francisco, California.

FIGURE II-5. Children wearing binaural hearing aids —Cleveland Hearing and Speech Center. (By permission, Western Reserve University Press)

FIGURE II-6. Dr. Ruth Bender and Dr. Nancy Wood work with deaf children at the Cleveland Hearing and Speech Center.

FIGURE II-7. Present main building of the John Tracy Clinic.

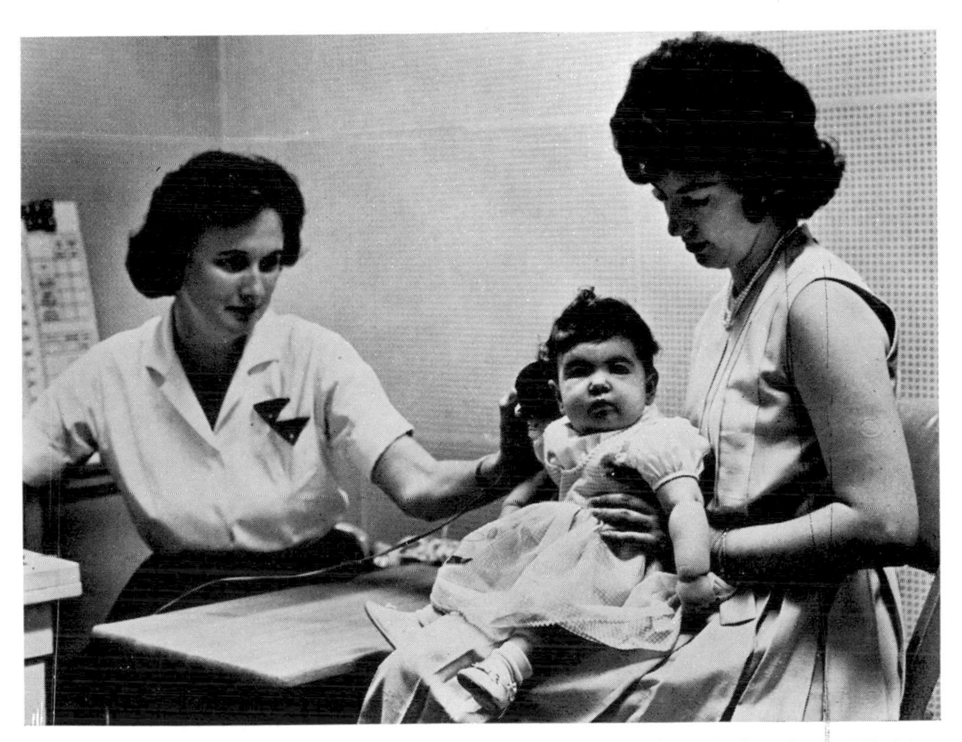

FIGURE II-8. It is seldom—if ever—too soon for initial testing. (John Tracy Clinic)

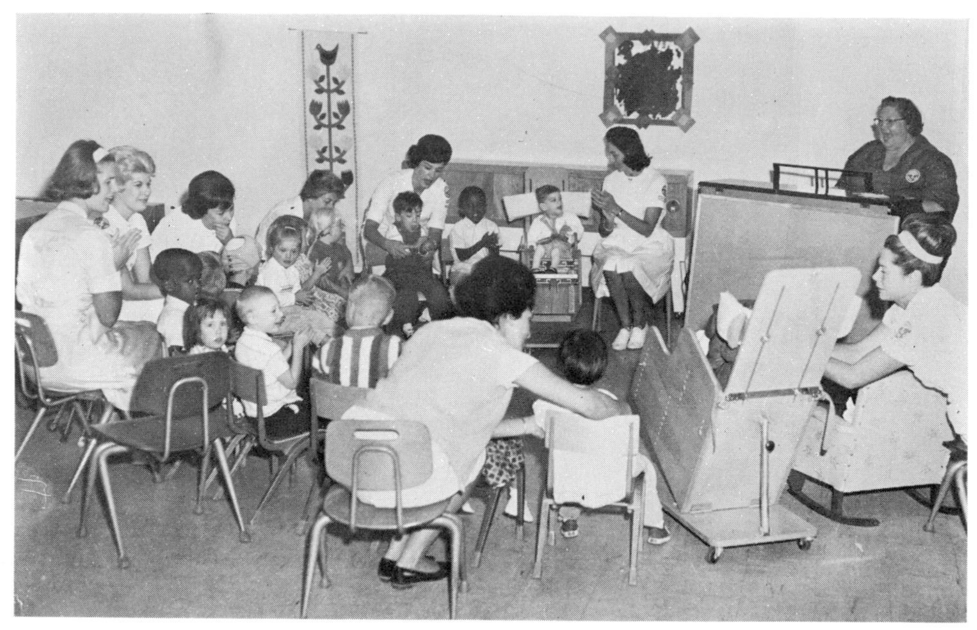

FIGURE II-9. "Sing Your Way to Better Speech" is one method of language building, employed at the Easter Seal Rehabilitation Center, Sacramento, California.

FIGURE II-10. "I'm Forever Blowing Bubbles" is utilized as a method of gaining breath control as a basis for speech production at the Easter Seal Rehabilitation Center, Sacramento, California.

Chapter 8

JOHN TRACY CLINIC

MRS. SPENCER TRACY

JOHN TRACY Clinic is a parent center, a place where parents of preschool deaf and hard of hearing children may come or may write for information, encouragement, guidance and training. It is unique in its philosophy, its methods and its program.

Back in 1943, some evening toward dusk, if an aware and discerning person had paused in front of the small house at 924 West 37th Street, Los Angeles, he might have caught a glimpse of covered wagons and the scent of campfires, for, from its beginning, the clinic has been a pioneer engaged in pushing back frontiers. It has offered a new concept of parent-preschool education in the field of deafness. It was not the first effort to help parents nor the first to offer a preschool or nursery school program, but it is, as far as we know, the first to offer all parents intensive training along with some type of service to their children—whatever can best be taken advantage of by individual parents. The purpose is, first of all, to reach babies and young children during what has often been referred to as man's fastest and most important learning years and to reach them in what seems the most natural and obvious way—through their parents—and secondly, to help parents for their own sakes, because as people they badly need help, perhaps need it at this point more than do their babies.

The philosophy supporting this purpose is simple. All learning for each and every child begins at birth. He learns. It is only a question of what he learns. What he learns during his early years, the extent and the quality, depends almost entirely upon his environment and the people in it, that is, upon his parents. It depends, as we have said many times, not only, nor perhaps primarily, upon their knowledge, their educational background, but it depends upon their love, their support, their understanding and upon their attitudes toward him, toward themselves, and toward the world in general. Not only are the years under five widely claimed to be man's fastest learning years, a period that even determines to a great extent what he is able to learn later on, but these years are the communication years, the language years, the speech years. And it should be added, the imitative and the habit-forming years. *They are the great years.* By the age of six, on entering school, the average hearing child is well on his way.

Because he cannot hear the speech of others nor the sound of his own voice, a young deaf child is deprived of the opportunity to acquire language and speech in the natural, normal way. He must be taught. Like hearing children, the large majority of deaf children do not enter school until the age of five-and-a-half or six. Unless they have managed in some way to get special training before this time, when they enter they cannot understand others, nor can they express themselves except by gestures and facial expression. In order to narrow at least this gap between the school-age hearing child and the school-age deaf child, in order to salvage to some extent these deprived, these empty years, the education of a deaf child, the clinic believes, must begin with his parents in his home and as early as possible. This is the "running start" it has talked about for so many years.

With this belief as an incentive and a guide, the clinic, though at this point only a movement, got under way. In the early fall of 1942 thirteen mothers, twelve of whom had deaf children ranging from eighteen months to seven years of age, hungry for information and guidance, formed a kind of study group to learn more about the problems and needs of young deaf children and particularly, of course, what each might do to help her own child.

By a happy chance, almost immediately they were provided with a place to hold their informal meetings. Through the interest of Dr. Rufus B. von *KleinSmid,* then President of the University of Southern California, the university gave the group the use of a small house just off the main campus, one which only days before had been acquired as part of its future expansion program. It stood, a most dejected, unprepossessing prospect. Apparently long empty, with wallpaper hanging in strips, plaster falling in heaps, old newspapers and nameless debris strewn about, and dirt, dirt, dirt everywhere, it looked a most unlikely place in which to launch such a movement.

But the "small house," when put in shape by some of the boys at the university, the mothers themselves and several of their husbands, provided much more than a place to meet. It provided an address. It could be given a name. It carried with it the tacit approval of the university and so lent stability, dignity and importance to this movement and to the efforts of the little group which gathered there.

In casting about for a starting point and the guidance that was needed, it was suggested, and with some hesitation on the part of several mothers finally agreed to, that a good way to begin learning more about little deaf children might be to learn more about children. So by late fall of that year, weekly classes were being held in what was called Child Development and Parent Attitudes. The material presented by the parent-teacher leader under a program sponsored by the Adult Education Division of the Los Angeles Department of Education might seem at first glance to have nothing to do with deaf children and the needs of their parents. As a matter of fact, the instructor had had no experience with deaf children and knew nothing of their special training and education; but she did know something of children, of their growth and development, and did understand how the attitudes of their parents affected this development.

In a few months most of the mothers were beginning to see that a deaf child is first and above all a child, and that what was discussed in those classes in most instances applied equally to hearing and to deaf children. At first there was often to be heard a plaintive protest, "But our children can't hear what we say," or "But we can't explain *why* to our children." However, these objections occurred less and less frequently as the parents began to see the child rather than his deafness, and recognize, for instance, that no two- or three-year-old hearing child obeys because he understands what is said to him, the *why* he should do so and so, and that a pleasant—if possible—but firm *expectancy* is usually what gains cooperation.

The group began to understand what is meant by "the whole child" and the whole child in his total environment, which was to become such a basic part of the clinic's philosophy. There was a growing awareness and understanding of attitudes and the effect of their own attitudes upon their children. As I remember, when these classes started there was not even more than the haziest idea of what was meant by an "attitude," what it was, or where it came from! The fact that attitudes are part of a kind of chain reaction beginning with experiences, whether remembered or not, which trigger feelings which in turn beget attitudes, resulting in a certain kind of action or behavior, was a concept that was presented to parents later. However, it can be seen that a faint outline of the clinic's philosophy and its approach to parents already could be detected. Indeed, this first tentative and modest effort to find help for parents is given more space and more emphasis than ordinarily such a one might warrant because it did so much toward setting the direction and much of the emphasis of its program. We often say that the clinic's program might be divided roughly into facts and feelings. There is a large amount of information which in a number of ways is made available to parents, almost spoon-fed in some instances, but which often they have trouble in using because of their feelings; indeed, sometimes they cannot even hear the information.

The weekly class with which the clinic began its program continued for three years. The one which followed it under the same title was given by a psychologist who had been engaged as a parent counselor. Even at this early period of the clinic's development, and when money to support this new and little understood movement was very hard to come by, when the occasion arose, Alathena Smith, who had in her background preparation nursery school, exceptional children and parent counseling, was engaged as a full-time member of the small staff. The "chain reaction" concept to which I alluded a moment ago, with its emphasis on feelings, was introduced by Dr. Smith, and her classes and philosophy ever since have continued to color and to strengthen the total parent program.

Let it not be thought for a moment, however, that deafness and the specific problems—and problems there are—relating to young deaf children which had brought these mothers together were being neglected. Shortly after the attitude classes had begun, a teacher of the deaf from the nearby city of Long Beach, Katherine FitzGerald, who felt it was quite reasonable to believe that mothers could play a part in the education of their children, offered her help. She came to the clinic, without any charge, every second or third Saturday morning and talked to the mothers, talked about the many little things they could do at home to encourage and develop language, lipreading and speech, and illustrated with the children who happened to be there. This was in no way a class except, perhaps, in that one person was teaching and others were learning. There was not a teacher-to-class atmosphere. Instead they talked *with* one another and there was the easy warmth and informality of good friends talking together. This same atmosphere insofar as possible has been preserved and continuously fostered.

By the end of the year the little house and the program which was already solidly and comfortably ensconsed in it had been named John Tracy Clinic, and a small framed sign to this effect had been hung beside the front door. A listing now being possible, a telephone had been installed. By early in January the number of inquiries both by phone and by mail argued for engaging a secretary and setting up an office. This we did, although the "setting up" consisted primarily of a table, a bookcase which had been an early contribution, a rented typewriter, a small filing cabinet and stationery with our letterhead. However, the secretary we were fortunate enough to engage was extremely competent and had an "air." It was constantly demonstrated during those early years that it is the quality of people that is important, not the equipment.

In February of 1943, John Tracy Clinic was formally opened, with a program in the university's Harris Hall. Dr. von KleinSmid sat on the platform and welcomed the guests. Although to those present he represented the university—such representation ordinarily could not have been hoped for—really, he represented his own belief and deep interest in what the clinic was trying to do, a belief and an interest which lasted and grew throughout his lifetime.

For this occasion, the clinic had been scrubbed and tubbed to the limit its paint could endure. The mothers themselves had beautifully recovered some old furniture given us, and new carpeting covered part of the downstairs and one room upstairs. All in all, we felt it was quite presentable when the three hundred or so parents, relatives, friends and well-wishers trooped through it, following the program which had explained the reason for the clinic and what, in one way or another, it hoped to accomplish.

In March, the first mother and child were enrolled in our correspondence course. This was a somewhat simplified version of the Wright Oral School's course. Inasmuch as it was not being used at the time and its use was not contemplated, the school generously permitted the clinic to use it, provided it was given, as was promised, without charge and that it could be recalled if the school ever did want to use it again. Much of the old Montessori material had accompanied the installments of the course, and Miss Matie Winston, then principal of the school, boxed up all that remained and sent it along with a copy of the course. We adapted some of the material to fit our purse and the talents and time of the parents—yes, parents helped to make the sense-training material which we sent to the first correspondence course families. We asked that this material be returned within the month in order to send it to other parents; however, so few returned anything, and so many new parents began to contact us, that, rather sadly, we had to abandon sending out anything. At the same time we felt the parents themselves, with a little imagination and effort, could make material that would be quite as effective. Parents do not need elaborate or expensive material. Years later, we had one mother, who, living in the country and apparently with nothing much but the necessities for keeping alive, used for some of the matching games leaves from the great variety of trees which grew nearby. It is not things, it is imagination; it is not time, it is thought. It is taking advantage of the material and the moment-to-moment opportunities that exist in and around almost every home.

Sometime during the spring, there began to be considerable discussion among the mothers regarding the possibility of having a nursery school where they and their children might learn together, a nursery school where they would feel free at any time to visit and quietly to observe, and where the philosophy which they were absorbing—and helping to develop—could be put into practice. No one knew where the money would come from to support such a project, but on the basis of a somewhat miraculous six months, they were beginning to believe that anything was possible. After some investigation, two teachers were suggested who, it was thought, might fill our specific and unusual needs. We wrote to both in glowing terms of the wonderful opportunity waiting at John Tracy Clinic for one who would accept its challenge. Somewhat to our surprise, both teachers expressed interest in our maverick program and were willing at least to explore this "wonderful opportunity" further. I promptly left for New York to meet these forward-looking and, I felt, rather courageous women.

The trip had several far-reaching results. First, I met Mary C. New of the Lexington School who was to contribute so much both to me personally and to the clinic and leave an indelible mark on the clinic's program. Second, I had an opportunity to observe the nursery school setup at Lexington School, which in general was to serve as a model for the one the clinic opened that fall. The program presented not only a fresh approach to nursery school education in a school for the deaf, but one which was in complete harmony with the clinic's philosophy of the whole child. Both trained teachers of the deaf and trained nursery school teachers were responsible for things taught and things learned. The teachers of the deaf were called tutors and each child was taught—or tutored—individually so that each child, getting undivided attention, might start where he *is* and go at his own rate of speed. Throughout the rest of the day under the watchful eye and sometimes guidance of the nursery school teacher, he was busy learning with blocks, with cars—from miniature toy ones to cars in which he could sit and pedal—with poster paints, clay and all the other equipment and material present in any good nursery school through which children learn and develop dexterity, curiosity and assurance, and—through their association with other children—develop socially and emotionally. It was instantly and clearly obvious that if the clinic were to start a nursery school, it would need two teachers, not one. Third, I met Hattie Harrell, then with the Rochester School, now principal of the Tucker-Maxon Oral School in Portland, Oregon, whom we finally engaged to come to Los Angeles.

We might add a fourth to the list. It was here that the clinic received one of its earliest financial contributions, and I was suddenly and forcibly struck by the realization that we had not only something new, unique and of tremendous importance to a fair-sized group of people all over the world, but also something which had a potential for arresting the quick interest and enthusiasm of a public untouched by the problem and, for the most part, quite unaware of its existence. At the suggestion of Dr. Clarence O'Connor, superintendent of the Lexington School, I talked for about ten minutes to a group of students, and presumably some teachers, at Hunter College, where children attending Lexington were rehearsing a dance program which was to be given shortly as part of the graduation exercises and festivities. Before I left I was given a check for twenty-five dollars from one of the student organizations. It was quite evident that many of these young women had been quite moved by the story about parents and their needs. I knew at this point the clinic was going to need money—lots of it—and it behooved us to get out the word, with reference not only to the clinic and its purpose and its needs, but to what deafness means, wherein lies its handicap and what can be done about it—not just at John Tracy Clinic but in all schools and by people everywhere.

The immediate result of my long, endlessly interesting and exciting discussions with Miss New and several talks with both Dr. O'Connor and Miss Groht, the principal of Lexington, was the suggestion from Dr. O'Connor that, if agreeable to Miss New and to the clinic, Miss New would be relieved of her teaching that summer at Hunter College and be free to give six weeks or so to the clinic to try out some methods and develop a pattern for a parent-child program in a nursery school setting. It would mean that the clinic would provide such a setting with enough parents and children to facilitate the experiment. Miss New said, "I don't know how to teach parents, but if you're willing, we'll work this summer and find out." I was more than willing. She also said, "I don't want any salary. Just pay my expenses, and they won't be much!" So almost on the spur of the moment, with only a few weeks to complete plans, a summer session was announced.

There was no problem in getting enough parents and children. There were thirteen although, as I remember, about four of them were overage and already in school. Our first, most urgent, need was for a nursery school teacher. Our second was to improve both the usability and the appearance of the clinic's back yard, which we would scarcely be able to do without. It was overrun by a variety of very substantial weeds, and the long-neglected, ramshackle fence not only had to be repaired but cried out for paint. The nursery school teacher we would have to look for; but the yard we could move in on. Keeping our eyes on the best feature, the large fig tree which stood in the center of it, spreading welcome shade and considerable charm, we went to work. The university came to our assistance, as it so often did, and the maintenance department sent over a crew to do a clean-up job. My guest, Mary Kennedy, who arrived on the scene at this moment, said, "Why, we can paint that fence!" I had no idea how much time and hard work those yards upon yards of picket fence would take to paint. We learned, and on three of the hottest days Los Angeles could offer! We also planted some grass seed which, as we might have known, was a lost cause because of both the short growing period it would have and the treatment to which it would be subjected with the arrival of the children; but it did look nice for a few minutes on Opening Day.

We eventually found a nursery school teacher. She was loath to come, principally, as I remember, because she did not know anything about deaf children, but she finally did agree to do so. She found that deaf children in a nursery situation were not very different from hearing children, and she continued with us in the fall when we opened the nursery school program.

The summer session was a continuously stimulating and rewarding experience. We all learned—parents, children and our staff of two. I don't know into just what category I fitted—promoter, most likely—but I learned more, it seemed to me, in those six weeks than I had learned in years. We looked forward to the fall nursery school program with an enthusiasm which swept away any misgivings we might have had, as we sometimes were reminded that we would not have Miss New, and also that we had quite a lot—for us—of money to raise.

In addition to working out a method of teaching parents along with their children, before she left Miss New helped us in further revising the correspondence course, adding some material that came as a result of the summer's experiences. She continued through her lifetime to be a source of information and solid, practical advice.

I have mentioned several times people the clinic has been fortunate to interest, people who have contributed generously and helped substantially in a variety of ways to make the clinic what it is. It has been greatly blessed.

The nursery school clearly was a big step for the clinic's very new, very small, group of parents to undertake. There was now a full-time staff of three: a trained teacher of deaf children, with whom the mothers were delighted, a fully trained nursery school teacher and a secretary. In addition, there was the parent-teacher leader, still provided by the Los Angeles Board of Education, but whose salary was soon to be taken over by the clinic; and a cook—an excellent cook—who, of all things, chanced to live next door. We were not only "blessed," but sometimes we were inordinately *lucky!* Eight mothers and their children were enrolled. Although now, as in the summer, we were to work directly with the children, this was still parent education. While in the minds of some of the parents perhaps the emphasis appeared to be transferred to the children and doubtless the feeling was that here at last was some real help for their children, in the clinic's book *it was still parent education.*

The nursery school provided the "picture that is worth a thousand words," not only for the mothers who were enrolled with their children, but for all mothers who wished to observe. It also would furnish a visitor a look at what we were doing—a vital ingredient in "educating" the public. It was a kind of laboratory. No child could be enrolled without his mother, who was obligated to spend one full day each week at the clinic observing and possibly teaching under guidance, as well as to attend regularly the two weekly classes, the one in attitudes and a new one, given by Miss Harrell, in communication skills, which focused principally on lipreading and speech. It was later that language development, really the most important, the *basic* factor in all communication, was added and emphasized, along with auditory training. To these classes, as in the case of the one the previous year, *all* mothers, not only of preschool children but of deaf children of any age, were welcome, and as we managed to make contact with them, urged to attend. It was this "making contact" that bothered some of us. I, personally, had been naive enough to think that immediately after the existence of this new resource for parents was known, they would flock to it. They did not. Why?

There were a number of reasons which gradually became apparent. Most parents of young deaf children simply were not aware of the clinic. At this point it had had very little publicity. Few otologists were aware of what was going on in that little house on 37th Street, and fewer pediatricians. Schools for the deaf resented what they felt was interference in what was strictly their bailiwick, so no referral of parents from the Los Angeles public day school could be hoped for. There was no understanding of what the clinic was trying to do—no appreciation of the role parents played, willy-nilly, good or bad, in the learning of their children.

However, the clinic had managed to gain the ear of one otologist and to enlist his interest, advice and support, which through the years have proved invaluable. It was, I believe, initially at least, because of Dr. Victor Goodhill that other otologists and otolaryngologists, notably Dr. Mackenzie Brown, sometimes called the father of otology in Los Angeles, and later Dr. Leland Hunnicutt, Dr. Howard P. House and others became interested, and I eventually was asked to talk briefly before their various organizations, where some awareness was spread and some misconception corrected. In October 1947, through Dr. Goodhill and Dr. Dean Lierle of the State University of Iowa, I spoke to the members of the American Academy of Ophthalmology and Otolaryngology at their annual meeting in Chicago, and the following winter to the members of the Research Study Club of Los Angeles at a meeting of ear, nose and throat specialists from all over the country. Following this latter occasion, the clinic received a check for $5,000 toward research and, in the accompanying letter from Dr. Hunnicutt, the hope was expressed that "this means the beginning of a closer cooperation on the part of doctors and the clinic."

The pediatricians have been much harder to reach. Perhaps our own pediatrician at the time described a part of the problem when he said, "Why, Mrs. Tracy, in my years of practice I remember only once seeing a deaf baby." But, of course, one doesn't "see" a deaf baby! We have often suggested that if pediatricians, family doctors and general practitioners, when asking questions about a baby, sick or well, in the home, doctor's office, medical clinic, or hospital, would ask this simple question, "Does he seem to hear well?" it might be that this alone would bring to light quite a number of deaf children. Thus, getting acceptance and referrals from the medical profession as well as the schools was then, and was to remain for some years, one of the clinic's chief problems.

In addition during its early period, particularly during the first four or five years of the program, it was hard to "sell" this intensive parent participation to the parents themselves. One would tend to think—we did—that practically all parents would want to help their deaf youngsters who, without understanding and positive help, face a narrow and often lonely existence. But many parents, we found, in their misery, frustration, defensiveness, in their fears and feelings of inadequacy, shied off, continuing their not really hopeful search for a cure, or grimly waiting for the time when the child could be sent to school where "someone who understands these things" would take over. So from one cause or another, it was still several years before we got more than a trickle of parents.

In October 1943, an important and necessary step was taken. The clinic was incorporated under the laws of the State of California as a nonprofit organization, with a board of directors composed of five members. This was necessary if people were to contribute financially, and important also in that it gave the clinic stability and stature. That original board was composed of Walt Disney, Neil McCarthy, Mrs. Orville R. Caldwell (long-time friends of the Tracy family), my husband Spencer Tracy and myself.

In March of 1945 Harriet Montague came to the clinic from the Volta Bureau in Washington to take charge of the burgeoning correspondence course. She was ideal for the position, peculiarly fitted by temperament, talents and background. Deaf herself from the age of eighteen, she had great empathy with the parents and understanding of many of the problems they faced, even though the problems of one born deaf are quite different from those of a person who becomes deaf after he has acquired speech and language. She had a magnificent command of language, had done newspaper work and among her writing credits was her collaboration with John Dutton Wright in writing and compiling the Wright Oral School Correspondence Course. With her warm, outgoing personality, keen sense of humor, direct, practical and uninhibited approach to all matters, together with her knowledge and facile pen, she fitted the needs of the correspondence course like a fine French glove.

Previous to her advent, this service had been a joint effort of the staff—Miss Harrell, Mrs. Berg, our parent-teacher leader, and the Clinic's secretary, Doris Jackson—now Doris Chambers—and, occasionally, myself. It was one example of the "doubling in brass" which everyone did. Though far from a satisfactory arrangement, we still felt that only good could come of it. It was infinitely better than nothing, and like everything else we were doing it was a start.

In 1946, as previously mentioned, Dr. Smith joined our small but now in one sense complete staff. We could boast of a trained teacher of the deaf, a fully trained nursery school teacher, a psychologist, some one well qualified to handle our correspondence course and an excellent secretary.

At that time the services open to parents were consultations, classes for parents, a nursery school in which the *family* was enrolled, psychological counseling, a correspondence course, and a six weeks' summer session. The consultation service, with respect to hearing tests, was of necessity somewhat sketchy, judged by present standards—ours, as well as those of people and organizations responsible for setting standards. However, I think they were comparable to those given at that time in most schools for deaf children, where one of their teachers was assigned to test hearing. The words *audiology* and *audiologist* were not even coined until 1945. It was in the speech and hearing clinics which began to spring up after the close of the war, many of them in connection with universities, that the field of audiology was developed. Our current teacher did the testing, and that primarily through noisemakers—gross sounds of many kinds. Of course, we had no sound-treated—no "quiet"—room.

We did well, I believe, in the psychological tests although Dr. Smith seldom referred to them in such terms. There was a series of simple performance tests and "observations" to try to determine how a child used or manipulated certain material in relation to his chronological age and to indicate how he might feel about his world and the people in it.

In conclusion, we all sat in on the counseling and guidance which followed. Remembering specifically a few of these informal, warmly enthusiastic sessions, I think we sometimes were able to do as much toward getting parents started on the right road as we are today.

In the summer of 1946, in association with the University of Southern California, a course in preschool-parent education was made available for already trained teachers of the deaf. This was carried on simultaneously, of course, with the summer session.

In the July 1949 issue of our *Bulletin* there is a short report on our new "Open Friday Clinic." It reads:

> To expand the nursery school program to include mothers and children who, because of lack of space, could not be enrolled in the regular nursery school, a Friday Clinic was inaugurated. Regular nursery school mothers and children now attend only four days a week in order to make this activity possible. Six mothers and children started in February. Replacements were made from time to time and a total of seventeen mothers and children have been enrolled. Parents observe nursery school routines and individual instruction of children by teachers of the deaf. At noon the children have a hot lunch while the mothers meet with Mrs. Smith and Mrs. Hollzer to discuss the morning's observation. In this way there is, in many instances, an immediate follow-up after the initial consultation.

This explains briefly the main purposes of this important addition to the program and the way in which it was handled.

In the case of so many of the developments and changes which occurred, I remember how they started. In this instance, I instantly see Dr. Smith,

Rose Hollzer, our then-current nursery school teacher, and myself late one afternoon sitting on the narrow stairway, midway between the first and second floors, discussing this need to give more mothers and children something approximating, even over a short period of time, the experience shared by the few mothers and children in the nursery school. We also were disturbed by the obvious fact that the lack of any direct service to their children was undoubtedly the reason why the interest of mothers not in the nursery school ranged from casual to nonexistent. It was quite evident that those families who were not enrolled in the nursery school felt they did not really "belong." It was an attitude which, try as we might, we had been unable to change. We were still "selling parent education." Perhaps we always will be, to some parents. We also remembered the visitor who upon leaving said, "All I can think of is that there are a few children getting a big turkey dinner and in the rest of the world they're starving to death!"

I can almost hear Dr. Smith say, "We could cut the nursery school from five days to four and on Fridays invite another group of mothers and children." Although I have no recollection of this now, Dr. Smith says I objected at first, saying, "But we promised these nursery school parents a five-day week." Dr. Smith felt that these parents would be more than willing to relinquish one day. It would be a day to "get their house cleaned up, to have the weekend free, and would provide a healthier family life." In any event, we decided that afternoon to try it out and the next day we cleared the decks for action. The regular nursery school was shortened—the parents did not object—and a group of mothers and children who had been seen in consultation was invited to participate in the new service on the following Friday. We never have hesitated to change horses in the middle of the stream when the other horse looked better.

Prior to 1949 there were three important developments I have not mentioned. In the spring of 1946 the parents formed John Tracy Clinic Auxiliary, an organization aimed primarily at raising funds for the clinic's operation. Gradually another purpose developed, that of helping the new parents in one way or another. Later this group changed its name to John Tracy Clinic Parents' Auxiliary. During a twenty-year period it has raised a magnificent sum of money. This has been done primarily through an annual bazaar.

In the fall of 1948 during the opening session of Dr. Smith's class in Child Development and Parent Attitudes—the one where the parents' feelings are brought so strongly into focus—one of the mothers said, "I can tell my husband what I do here, but I can't tell him how I feel here." The result of this observation was to change the class from daytime to evening, when the fathers were invited to attend. They came and continued to come. Why we had assumed that they would not be interested in taking an active part in the clinic's program and in their child's education, I do not know. Somewhat belatedly, they were recognized as part of the family and half of the parents we were always talking about. They both strengthened and enlivened the program.

The third development staggered us at first mention. Sometime in 1945 an inspector from the Los Angeles Fire Department, one who called regularly to inspect the clinic cottages, which eventually numbered three, said in effect that six months after the close of the state of emergency which had been declared because of the war, we could no longer occupy our present buildings. The department had always complained that they were highly unsuitable for children, and it was only because there was always a ratio of at least one adult to one child that we were permitted to occupy them. He said that there were many so-called nursery schools and child care centers that had grown up almost overnight because of the war and working mothers. "Most of them will have to go," he said. Pause—"Why don't you build?" "Build!" we gasped, "Where would we get the money? It's all we can do to raise enough to take care of costs." "Other organizations find the money. Why not you?"

Well, eventually, we did. The years before we managed to get together enough for the ground breaking, which occurred on July 28, 1951, were spent in enlarging our small board of directors, developing—and redeveloping many times—our building plans, finding a site and working with various fund raisers. It was a rugged but enlightening experience, leading to a really fine building and a far better program to put into it. Indeed, on looking back, we were grateful we were not able to raise the money immediately. Our needs, and consequently our plans, changed constantly not only in the overall size and the special facilities needed, but in many small details. Although the end of the emergency has never been declared, we bear no grudge. Had it not been for the possibility of it hanging over our heads, goodness knows when we would have built!

By 1949, the pattern and philosophy and services had assumed distinctive form and structure, and are clearly recognizable as those of the clinic today. There has been, and I am certain will always be, development, refinement and expansion of services in a continuing effort to provide more effective ways of helping the now steadily increasing flow of parents, and through them their young deaf children. The only really new kind of service which has been added since 1949 is the Demonstration Home, which was opened in September 1964.

The Demonstration Home carries the philosophy of parent help in the home away from the schoolroom, the "rigged" situation, right back into the home, reaffirming this philosophy on which the clinic was built. This new part of the program will be described later.

To be sure, a full Teacher Training Course in association with the University of Southern California also has been added, but this is not a service to parents, and might be designated, as might our research program, which got under way in 1954, as an auxiliary activity, although much help has been derived by the clinic from both. Research projects have contributed substantially to developing new material and developing and refining services, while Teacher Training has helped to staff the clinic and its branches and to spread, both in this country and in other countries, an understanding of its philosophy and methods in both the guidance and training of parents and the education of very young children.

In view of the importance of the roles—the various roles—she has played at the clinic, I should not leave 1949 without mentioning the fact that in the fall of that year Marguerite Stoner came to us from Lexintgon School. Although her first role was that of a teacher, she soon became the supervising teacher and later, in addition, had charge of the clinic's teacher training programs. Her contributions have been many.

In June of 1952 the clinic was able to move into its new home at 806 West Adams Boulevard. The long, low building, looking out from behind a magnificent old Moreton Bay fig tree, with its ample play yards and parking space, was well planned, extremely functional and attractive. In design, color and texture, those responsible for both buildings and furnishings managed to keep the warm, informal and comfortable atmosphere of the little cottages. It was thought that it would provide for the needs of the program for some time to come. Yet the period of rapid development seemed to have no more than begun, and the opportunity to stretch itself, to flex its muscles, seemed not only to provide for but to stimulate its growth.

In four years it was found necessary to build a substantial addition, almost doubling its facilities. With this addition we at long last had sound-treated testing rooms, and, instead of one room, almost the whole second floor for the Correspondence Course Department. More parking space was a great need in this sprawling city where cars are almost a necessity. Also, the board believed it must have protection for future expansion, to the possibilities of which no one could shut his eyes, so adjoining lots on both sides of the clinic property were purchased. On one lot stands a large old dwelling which, when it was built, must have ranked as one of Los Angeles' finest. The "old mansion," as it is called by many has been a conversation piece, but since its acquisition four years ago, it has provided space for our research program, and more recently, for the Demonstration Home, which itself started as a research project. It is expected that this one-time handsome relic will soon make way for a research center of more suitable, convenient design.

In 1954 a step was taken which contributed tremendously to the growth and eventually to the widespread recognition of the clinic's work. Dr. Edgar L. Lowell was engaged as administrator and to head the Research Program. He came to us from Harvard where he was assistant professor in the Graduate School of Education and research associate in the Laboratory of Human Development. We might say the clinic had come of age.

Although I have devoted by far the greater part of this article on John Tracy Clinic to its history—to the story of its development—for that has seemed to me in some ways to be its most imporant aspect, it has, possibly, the most to say to other groups which are just starting out, bursting with ideas and enthusiasm, and looking for road maps and encouragement. I feel the clinic's story provides both. Certainly it is far from complete but in it I have tried to include all of those events, those circumstances, which not only engineered our course, but which color and flavor the philosophy and program which are John Tracy Clinic today. It also should provide—as all history provides—a greater understanding of what we are and what we are doing now in October of 1966.

If you were to look through the clinic's most recent brochure and to compare it with one of fifteen or sixteen years ago, you probably could note very little difference. The purpose and philosophy are identical but the services, with the exception of the Demonstration Home, the Teacher Training Course and Research Program, referred to earlier, *only appear* not to have changed. Here they are: Consulting Service, Classes for Parents, Nursery School, Weekly Clinic Day, Psychological Counseling, The Demonstration Home, Correspondence Course, Summer Session, Teacher Training Course and Research Program. However, each service has experienced seventeen years of development, refinement and expansion. It is not only that the number of parents served in some instances has more than trebled—and numbers alone bring change—but in many ways the content, the quality, the *reach* have resulted in virtually a new program.

Consulting Service

In outlining our present services it seems logical to begin with the consulting service, which usually provides our introduction to the family. However, in case there are parents' classes previous to their appointment, it is sometimes suggested by the consultation secretary that they attend, and the staff is alerted so that they may be identified and welcomed. Although these classes in some respects may be confusing to brand-new parents, it is felt that the opportunity to be a part of a large gathering of parents with the same general problems, to feel its friendliness and support, to savor its warmth and often its humor, more than outweighs any possible confusion or dismay due to the amount and the level of the information being given. An appointment can be made by either telephone or letter. Except immediately following staff vacations, consultations ordinarily can be scheduled within a week or ten days. If for one reason or another a particular urgency is evident, we arrange to see the family immediately even though a second and full consultation, if indicated, will have to follow a little later.

Both mother and father are asked to be present at the consultation. It is essential, we believe, that both parents hear the same thing at the same time, or at least be exposed to it. They are also asked to bring with them a third person who can stay with the child while the parents talk with the audiologist, the psychologist and any other appropriate member of the staff.

The consultation begins with a hearing test. And yet, it actually begins a few minutes earlier when the audiologist and, when possible, the psychologist come to the waiting room to welcome the family. As they walk the little group up the hall to the testing room, they are warm, relaxed, unhurried, accepting and reassuring. The attitude is catching. Confidence takes the place of anxiety.

The sound-treated testing room is quite large as such rooms go and accommodates comfortably the child, his parents, the accompanying relative or friend and, of course, the audiologist and equipment. It is carried out in pastel shades, and the shelf at one end as well as the floor underneath it display inviting toys and material used in the tests. As the test progresses, the audiologist in simple language and by demonstration tries to help the parents to understand what she is looking for. They may or may not fully comprehend at the moment either the meaning or the implications of what is said, but what is important is that they do not feel ignored or left out.

After the test has been completed, the third person takes the child back to the waiting room, and the audiologist talks to the parents about the results of the test and their meaning in terms of their child's special educational needs, particularly as they relate to language and speech. We are fortunate in having an audiologist who is also a trained teacher of deaf children. It is not enough to plot an audiogram. An audiologist should know what such an audiogram means educationally, and without using the technical jargon which is almost completely unintelligible to most parents, be able to tell them what it means and to translate it into action, offering immediate support and guidance.

However, this talk between the audiologist and the parents cannot follow a set pattern. It depends upon the test findings and it depends upon the parents. I might say, with no pun intended, that much of the consultation is played by ear. It may be that no hearing loss is indicated. In this case, the family makes a relieved and happy exit. Or, it may be that problems other than hearing are suspected; if so, parents and child go to our psychologist—the child for further observation and tests, and the parents for counseling and possible recommendations.

Although in these instances it may be that the clinic will have nothing to offer the child, we sometimes can be of further help to the parents through the parents' classes. The Child Development and Parent Attitudes series has much to offer the parents of *any* child. At all times when there is a possibility of helping the *parents,* the clinic tries to establish and maintain contact.

Then sometimes it happens that one or both of the parents are in such an emotional state that they are unable to follow or even listen to what the audiologist is saying. So further discussion of educational needs and opportunities must wait until some of their feelings can be resolved. Here again, our psychologist takes over. But when this happens I remind you that the attitudes of those people involved, their acceptance and support, are crucial.

When there are no special problems encountered either with the child or the parents, when it is believed that the child has a hearing loss, even though he may be too young to say how great—babies as young as three months have been tested—and the Clinic's program is thought appropriate, a developmental test is given. Again we shy away from the term "psychological" and tend to place more importance on observing the general behavior of the child, how he seems to feel about his world and the people in it and the interrelations of the family. Following this the parents have an opportunity to talk with the psychologist, to understand and relieve some of their pent-up feelings—all parents have them. They are advised of the services which immediately can be offered to them: the Correspondence Course, Parents' Classes, and depending upon the age of their child, the Demonstration Home and the Friday Clinic. If their child is not yet two, they are taken to the Demonstration Home for a talk with the head teacher, and an appointment is made for their first visit. If their child is two or older he and his parents are eligible not only for the Demonstration Home program but for the next series of Friday Clinics, and an opening date is given them. If time permits and circumstances are favorable the parents are given a glimpse of the nursery school.

Once it is determined that the child and his parents can use our services, you can see that the effort of the consultation staff is to encourage, to support, and to involve them as soon and as fully as possible.

Classes for Parents

Parent classes is one of the services in which the growth of the clinic is most evident—one in which the number of parents has more than trebled.

To the two classes which for so long served our purpose—"Child Development and Parent Attitudes" and "Development of Communication Skills"—has been added "Nursery School Philosophy and the Education of the Preschool Child." But more revealing is the fact that "Communication Skills" now provides for first, second, third and fourth year levels; "Parent Attitudes" is on a first, second and third year level—the second year is almost pure group therapy, and the third, at a still deeper level, is available only with the permission of the leader; and "Nursery School Philosophy" is on two levels, making a total of nine weekly classes. It seems clear that in the process of providing for growth in number these classes have inevitably increased the scope of the material presented, both in breadth and in depth, as well as strengthened and refined it. From close and continuous observation, we believe we also continue to improve the method of presentation.

These classes I consider to be the backbone of our program. They further fortify all other services and continue to be available to all parents of deaf and hard of hearing children—indeed to their uncles and aunts and grandparents—regardless of the age of the child and whether or not he is receiving any of our services. However, all parents enrolled in the nursery school are obligated to attend the classes. Except for the "Nursery School Philosophy" and the advanced "Parent Attitudes" classes which are held certain mornings, all classes continue to be held on Tuesday evenings from eight to ten thirty. They are so scheduled that all parents are able to take the particular two courses to which they have been assigned.

Weekly Clinic Day

Each series of weekly Friday Clinics now runs for ten Fridays instead of the original five. These overlap, the new series starting the Friday following the completion of the first five. This enables us usually to have seven such programs during the year. The first five weeks are generally similar in plan to those inaugurated in 1949, but the present program does much more and does it better. As has been mentioned, at the time of the family's first consultation, if the child is a good solid two years of age, they are invited to attend the next clinic series. The parents receive an intensive, streamlined we might say, orientation to deafness and its problems as reflected in young children, to communication, to the learning process in all young children both hearing and deaf, to what they as parents can contribute to this learning process and to communication with their own child. Meanwhile, the children are having a nursery school experience and giving various staff members an opportunity to study them further, aiding the planning of their program as well as that of their parents. I cannot emphasize enough the individual quality of the help we give.

The succeeding five Fridays parents and children come by appointment. The children are given a lesson with the parents observing and often with their participation. "Lessons" sounds rather formidable when talking about a two-year-old, but in this case they are really play with a purpose.

The parents of younger children, children who are not yet eligible for the Friday Clinics, may still and really should attend these first five orientation periods. Although parents may choose to join the parents' classes immediately, if they have not happened to have had their consultation, or to have learned of the clinic's services until midwinter, they may find that they feel very confused and lost in the amount and the level of the information being given. It would be the same situation one would find in any course one might take. The Friday Clinics serve as a very substantial stepping stone. At the same time, as I suggested when talking earlier about parents attending classes even before their consultation, sometimes what parents gain on immediately joining a class outweighs the hazards.

Correspondence Course

The correspondence course is available to parents of children between the ages of two and five, anywhere in the world—within the reach of a postage stamp, we say. The twelve lessons include the first lessons in sense training, lipreading, language, auditory training and speech preparation. Theoretically this is a year's course, but actually the period over which these lessons are sent is flexible. A two-year-old may require two years, while the parents of a three-year-old may need but a year. The only requirements for enrolling in the course are that the child has a hearing loss, that the parents are able to read and write English or Spanish, in which we also give it, or have the lessons and their reports translated for them, and that they do report regularly to us after each lesson. If their child is quite young, and if illness, moving, or other disruptions occur, there may seem to parents little or nothing to report, or they may feel they cannot find the time, but we explain that we want a note, a postcard—something. Although we will continue to send one or two lessons, together with a "jogging" letter, after that we send no more lessons until we hear from them. Unfortunately, we suspect that sometimes parents envision the course as being some kind of little pamphlet on "How to teach speech in twelve easy lessons."

We also now have a pre-correspondence course, one which is called "Letters to the Parents of Deaf Babies." The youngest child to "participate" in this service was but six weeks old! Since its inception seven years ago, over eighteen hundred parents and their babies have been enrolled. From the baby course they enroll in the regular course. At present, a total of 3,581 parents are enrolled in both courses. In all, since 1943, we have enrolled more than twenty-four thousand families in ninety-eight countries. With our blessing the course has been translated, giving the clinic credit, into fifteen languages. These translations have been used in diverse ways. The clinic was not able to do more than suggest the various ways in which it might be conveyed to parents, but it was felt that as we were in no position to enroll the thousands of parents having neither English nor Spanish at their command, the important thing was to make the material available in one way or another to as many of them as possible.

Nursery School

Were the purpose of the nursery school solely to give twenty-four children and their parents the best education of which we—and they—are capable, I think it highly probable, in view of the spiraling costs of this service, that ere this we would have discontinued it and have found another means of spreading some lesser amount of service among more parents and children. However, the primary purpose of the nursery school is to provide opportunities for demonstration, observation and research. It continues to furnish that "one picture that is worth a thousand words" to visitors, students, and all parents whether or not they are enrolled in the nursery school. It is our laboratory, where we are able to try out and assess new ideas and teaching methods over continuous periods of time.

The program itself is such as one might find in any good nursery school for hearing children, plus special tutoring. It is open to a limited number of children and their parents. Each year we accept six new families and they are expected to remain in the program for four years. On entrance, the children usually range from two to two-and-a-half years of age. Acceptance depends principally on the considered ability of the parents to participate fully. Various considerations would be the distance of their home from the clinic and possible transportation problems; the number of children in the family and their care at the times, both day and evening, when the parents are scheduled to be at the clinic; the quality of the desire to participate as demonstrated by the parents in their participation in the clinic's program up to this point. Most of the families up for consideration have been seen initially a number of months, possibly even a year or more, previously, and in all instances have been taking part in two or more phases of the program. As for the child himself, he must be thought ready to enter such a program, that is, to be a good solid two, in good health and able to profit from such experience and training.

All of the teachers in the nursery school as well as the tutors are trained teachers of deaf children, which insures that each child is surrounded by "that constant flow of language" to which we so often refer. It enables those teachers in the playrooms and play yards at all times to carry on in natural situations much of what is done by the tutors during each child's planned lesson period. This is of tremendous value not only as far as the children themselves are concerned, but also because it continually demonstrates to the mothers how they can seize upon the countless, what one mother called "on-the-hoof," opportunities to build language and develop lipreading, and how to cultivate such opportunities.

Each child's individual lesson varies in length from five or ten minutes to forty-five minutes depending on his age and on his attention span both generally and on that particular day. Children are different one from another and they are different from themselves from day to day. Hearing aids are worn by all children regardless of the amount of hearing each is thought to have. Even with a minimal amount, it is our belief that auditory training when practiced from early childhood with understanding, patience and perseverance, will pay dividends. It is part of every tutoring period, not as a separate exercise but interwoven with language, lipreading and speech. Our approach is through sight, touch and hearing.

We start parents off on their first visit to the clinic with the advice to "talk, talk, talk," to their child. In the classes, in the Demonstration Home Program, in the open Friday Clinic, and now in the nursery school, they continue to learn *how* to talk, *when* to talk, and what to say. They also learn there is a time to listen, for communication depends not only on a desire to talk, something to talk about, but *someone to talk to.* They learn how concepts are developed, how a vocabulary and language are built, and they learn how to get evidence that a child actually is lipreading and not depending upon clues for his understanding. They learn how to make and present training material. They learn how to motivate.

Psychological Counseling

Psychological counseling is directed to the parents. This service is available to all parents requesting it. Here they are given help in understanding their fears and resolving their conflicts, many of which are of long standing, needing only the fright, the frustrations and turmoil of having a deaf child to bring on an emotional crisis. As their confidence in themselves increases they are better able to cope with the demands made upon them. At the same time, we find that as they discover their child is able to learn and that they are able to contribute to this learning, emotional pressures continue to lessen.

Summer Session

To those of us who greet the summer session parents and children as they arrive, and follow them through the next six weeks, this service often appears in many ways to be the most satisfying of all services. The differences between the before and after are so striking. Children are accepted between the ages of two-and-a-half and five. Although preference is given to those families living outside the Los Angeles area, its parents' classes are open to all parents regardless of their place of residence. It sometimes happens that parents living at quite a distance, and unable for some reason or other to bring their child, come themselves. During the intensive program with daily all-morning classes for the parents and a nursery school experience plus individual tutoring for the children, we try to cover as nearly as possible, insofar as the parents are concerned, the material presented during the first year of the regular nursery school. There is always a sprinkling of fathers present for the entire six weeks, and a large majority of families produce them for the closing "Fathers' Week."

In connection with this session, a course open to teachers is offered in association with the University of Southern California.

Demonstration Home

In 1964 the Clinic added another service for parents in the Los Angeles vicinity—the Demonstration Home. Financed by a research grant from the Office of Education, Department of Health, Education, and Welfare, the Demonstration Home is a pilot project designed to show what can be done wherever a family, a special teacher, and a deaf child come together, and particularly what can be done in the home as mothers and fathers go about the hundred and one things that make up their usual—and sometimes unusual—pattern of living.

From its beginning the clinic has always aimed at this kind of training—the casual and seemingly casual, even though planned, use of material and vocabulary at hand, rather than the carefully planned and more rigid training which usually takes place at a little table at a certain time of day with material which shouts "lessons." Both methods are valuable, but the Demonstration Home Program is planned to emphasize and to try to make the most of these informal always-at-hand opportunities to help very young children acquire, first, an understanding of words and language, and then possibly some speech—at least a speech readiness, which always precedes actual speech.

Previous to the inauguration of the home, teachers at the clinic, in a classroom or tutoring situation, had shown parents what to do. They *talked* about what they could do. Parents were given word lists—hundreds of words—with suggestions for how and when they could be used to good advantage. There was nothing wrong with this as far as it went, but it gave parents little or no opportunity to *do* the things suggested under observation and guidance. We all know that although something often seems clear when it is first explained, later, when we actually start to follow the directions we are lost. It does not seem to happen as they said it would. And I suspect often mothers have thought, "Well, that's all very well for them to say, but they don't have two children at their heels all day." There can be dozens of unusual circumstances that seem to change, to complicate and confuse.

In the Demonstration Home, complete—well, almost so!—with living room, bedroom, kitchen, dining room, etc., not only the parents and their deaf tot try it on for size but any other children in the family who are available; and we agree that perhaps teachers learn too. It is a new approach to helping parents to recognize and use the infinite number of opportunities which are to be found almost moment-to-moment in most homes. Here a mother may cook, make a bed, set a table, darn socks or mend, read, do almost anything she may do in her home, and the teacher helps to show her how she can carry on these activities and at the same time use them, and those in which her child happens to be involved, to develop language and lipreading.

It is a program which should have occurred to us much sooner, for it is one which cannot be demonstrated as easily or as well, even in the pleasantest kind of schoolroom, as it can be on "home ground." Since its inception, the clinic with the aid of two of its local support groups has opened two new demonstration homes, one in Long Beach and one in Costa Mesa.

I must not forget a service which, although for some reason it is not listed with those just described, at the time of its inception was thought important enough to rate a leaflet of its own.

This service consists of a series of nine ten-minute films, designed to show a number of attitudes common to many parents, along with nine twenty-minute recordings; and a like number of so-called information films and recordings which relate to deafness and the training of young deaf children in their homes; plus a twenty-minute film and recording serving as an introduction for both sets.

These films and recordings are available to parent groups, and their purpose is not only to present material but to stimulate discussion. They are most effective when the group has a leader who is adept at generating such discussion. Since 1962, 265 parent groups, with a total given enrollment of 7,536, have used this service.

Many people ask how the clinic manages to give all of these services to parents without any charge whatsoever. I sometimes wonder myself. This is made possible by the contributions of many interested people and groups of people, notably the auxiliaries, guilds and other support groups such as the two which are financing the two new demonstration homes. And, of course, although parents do not pay for any services for themselves and their child, they may and do contribute to the program as a whole. We say to parents, "What you do for your own child will help all deaf children, and what you do for all deaf children and their parents will help you and your child. What you get out of life you must give back." Our parents *do* give back.

Chapter 9

THE RESIDENTIAL SCHOOL FOR THE DEAF IN THE UNITED STATES

RICHARD G. BRILL

HISTORICAL BACKGROUND

THE father of the education of the deaf in the United States was Thomas Hopkins Gallaudet, who was graduated from Yale in 1805 at the age of eighteen. A few years after graduation from college, Gallaudet decided to enter the ministry, and so enrolled at the Andover Theological Seminary. Because of ill health he remained at home in Hartford during the winter of 1814-1815 and during this time became interested in Alice Cogswell, the little deaf daughter of his father's neighbor, Dr. Mason F. Cogswell. During the remainder of the winter and during subsequent vacations from the seminary Gallaudet tried to teach the little Cogswell girl.

In the meantime, a report of a committee of the General Association of Congregational Clergymen of Connecticut, in June 1812, stated that there were eighty-four deaf and dumb persons within the limits of the state; and if there were a like proportion in the other states, there were probably 400 in New England and 2,000 in the United States. This survey had been undertaken at the request of Dr. Cogswell who was anxious about the education of his daughter.

Dr. Cogswell interested a number of his influential friends in the possibility of establishing a school for the education of the deaf by bringing the statistics mentioned above to their attention. This group of men decided to raise funds by subscription and to send someone to Europe to study the art of educating the deaf. This meeting was held on April 13, 1815. The funds were raised in one day, and on April 15, Thomas Hopkins Gallaudet signified to the committee his willingness to take up the work; and on May 25, he sailed to England.[4]

The education of the deaf in England and Scotland was a monopoly of the Braidwood family, who placed so many obstacles in the way of Gallaudet that he proceeded to Paris. There he was welcomed by the Abbé Sicard who was head of the school for the deaf which had been founded by the Abbé de l'Epee. By August, 1816, Dr. Gallaudet believed that he had mastered the technique of teaching the deaf sufficiently well to initiate a program in the United States. One of the Abbé Sicard's best pupils, Laurent Clerc, offering his services as a teacher, came to this country with Gallaudet.

After returning to this country Gallaudet and Clerc spent eight months visiting prominent places throughout the country to obtain subscriptions for the new school and to interest the general public. On April 15, 1817, the first permanent school for the deaf was opened in this country at Hartford, Connecticut, under the name of "The Connecticut Asylum for the Education and Instruction of Deaf and Dumb Persons." The school opened with seven pupils and within a year it had grown to thirty-three pupils. In May, 1819, the name of the school was legally changed to "The American Asylum at Hartford, for the Education and Instruction of the Deaf and Dumb." Subsequently the name of this school was changed to the American School for the Deaf.[5]

EARLY RESIDENTIAL SCHOOLS

Only a year after the founding of the American School, the New York School for the Deaf, which was first known as the New York Institution for the Instruction of the Deaf and Dumb, was founded in 1818. The Pennsylvania Institution for the Deaf and Dumb, now known as the Pennsylvania School for the Deaf, was founded in 1820. All three of these first schools were founded under private auspices with a private board of directors and they have continued as such to this day. However, in each instance, as is true with many other residential schools for the deaf that were established as private schools, the major financial support comes from their respective state governments. In order to be eligible to receive this support, these schools admit all deaf children from their particular geographical area who meet their particular entrance requirements, and no charge is made to the parents for their board, room, laundry, tuition, or minor medical care.[5]

The fourth residential school established in this country was the Kentucky School for the Deaf established in 1823 by the legislature of the State of Kentucky. From the onset, this was a state public residential school with all support, both for capital outlay and operating expenses, coming by means of appropriation from the state legislature.[5]

Subsequently, other residential schools were established, but from the point of historical significance, note should be taken of the establishment of the Columbia Institution for the Deaf and Dumb in Washington, D. C. in 1857. The original part of this institution was the Kendall School for the Deaf established that year. This was a school to serve deaf children of the District of Columbia, established to educate deaf children on the elementary level, as was the case with the public residential schools in other states that had already been established. The founder was Edward Minor Gallaudet, a son of Thomas Hopkins Gallaudet, the father of the education of the deaf in this country. The original charter of the Columbia Institution contained no limit as to the time that pupils might remain under instruction at that school. As long as they could be benefitted they could remain in the school. Therefore, it was only necessary to add a college course of study to the curriculum and retain those pupils that were capable and desirous of a college education to begin a college program. This was done and a bill was passed by Congress in 1864 and signed by President Abraham Lincoln authorizing the institution to grant such degrees and diplomas as are usually conferred at colleges.

The collegiate department of the Columbia Institution for the Deaf was first known as the National Deaf Mute College and was later named Gallaudet College in honor of the father of education of the deaf, Thomas Hopkins Gallaudet.[1]

The establishment of the New York Institution for the Improved Instruction of Deaf Mutes in New York City and the Clarke School for the Deaf in Northampton, Massachusetts, both in 1867, are of historical significance because these two schools were the first exclusively oral residential schools established in this country. In these schools, not only were the students taught speech and lipreading, but all instruction was by means of speech and lipreading, with all manual communication, that is the sign language and manual fingerspelling, prohibited.[5]

DAY SCHOOL PROGRAMS

By 1900 there had been fifty-seven public residential schools established in this country. Beginning in 1869 with the establishment of the Horace Mann School for the Deaf in Boston, Massachusetts, various day school programs had also been established. These were classes or entire schools for deaf children within public school systems conducted on a day school basis so that the children could live at home. By 1900 there were forty public day schools in the United States and of these eleven were in the city of Chicago. Also by 1900, fifteen denominational and private schools had been established. As is shown in Table I, 90 per cent of the pupils being educated in schools for the deaf were receiving their education in fifty-seven public residential schools in 1900.[11]

TABLE I

EDUCATIONAL PROGRAMS IN 1900

Type of School	*No. of Schools*	*No. of Pupils*	*Per Cent of Pupils*
Public Residential Schools	57	10,760	90
Public Day Schools	40	740	6
Denominational and Private Schools	15	442	4
Total	112	11,942	100

TABLE II

EDUCATIONAL PROGRAMS IN 1965

Type of School	No. of Schools	No. of Pupils	Per Cent of Pupils
Public Residential Schools	69	17,643	55
Public Day Schools and Day Classes	296	11,660	36
Private—Residential and Private Day Schools	73	2,772	9
Total	438	32,075	100

Table II shows the educational programs in 1965. In comparing the programs in 1900 with those in 1965, the large increase in the number of children in day schools and day classes is due to the rapid expansion of public school programs in the field of special education.

It should be noted that in many cases children with some hearing loss attend programs in public schools that are established for deaf and hard of hearing children who would never attend programs in a residential school because their hearing loss is not severe enough to go away from home. At the same time, the special program is of great benefit to them. Thus it is probable that a much greater percentage of children with moderate as well as severe hearing loss are being served in 1965 than were being served in 1900.

COMPARATIVE CHARACTERISTICS OF DEAF POPULATIONS

Another important factor is that the typical population of a school for the deaf in 1965 is quite different from the typical population of schools before the early 1940's. Until the discovery of the antibiotics and their widespread use about 50 per cent of the enrollment in the typical school for the deaf was composed of children whose deafness was adventitious. They lost their hearing as a result of the many childhood diseases that have high fevers such as measles, mumps, whooping cough, scarlet fever and pneumonia. Many of these children did not lose their hearing until after speech and language was learned normally through hearing. As a result they are post-lingually deaf and posed a different kind of educational problem than the prelingually deaf child.[8]

The prelingually deaf child has no concept of language, no knowledge of the meaning of words and, in fact, is unable to think beyond the realm of the concrete or the things he himself has experienced until a language pattern is developed. In addition to the lack of language is the complete lack of any knowledge of speech.

Since the advent and widespread use of the sulfa drugs over 90 per cent of most children in residential schools for the deaf are prelingually deaf. The few adventitiously deaf are generally those losing their hearing as a result of meningitis.

Another factor that helps to account for the difference in type of child found in schools for the deaf currently has been the high stage of development of the hearing aid. Before the use of the hearing aid many children who had a rather severe hearing loss, but not total, did not really have the opportunity to make the best use of their residual hearing. Since the development of the vacuum tube hearing aid and more recently the transistor type hearing aid which can give powerful amplification with a very small aid that can be worn by a very young child, the training and use of residual hearing has been developed to a high degree. Thus, many of the severely hard of hearing can be taught as hard of hearing in special hard of hearing classes, and some of them can go into regular public school classes which was not true in earlier years before the development of good hearing aids.

PROGRAM AT A MODERN RESIDENTIAL SCHOOL FOR THE DEAF

In spite of the increase in percentage and the increase in numbers of pupils attending the public school programs, the public residential school for the deaf provides a complete program serving in many ways, many deaf children. The California School for the Deaf, Riverside is representative of one of the larger, modern residential schools with a complete program.[7] The State of California began educating deaf children in 1860 with the establishment of the California School for the Deaf, Berkeley. Until the opening of the second school in the southern part of the state in 1953, the school in Berkeley served the entire State of California. Since 1953 the California School for the Deaf in Riverside has served the southern part of the state. There is also an extensive program of day schools and day classes in the State of California. Both California residential schools are financed completely by direct appropriations by the legislature. This includes appropriations for capital outlay and for operating expenses. The total value of the buildings and grounds of this school at Riverside is $6,692,100. The average enrollment is 520 children with an operating budget in 1966 of $2,140,000 for an average per capita cost of $4,120. This enrollment of 520 students is composed of 465 pupils in residence and fifty-five day pupils. This number of day pupils is a larger number than would normally be found in the population of a city the size of Riverside. The reason for the large number is because families move to an area where there is a special school so that their children may attend.

The minimum age for admission is five and a half for regular enrollment although a preschool program is operated for children between the ages of three and five and a half if they live in the vicinity and can come to this as day pupils. The pupils in the preschool program are not included in the overall enrollment of 520. Pupils may remain at the school as long as they are continuing to benefit from the educational program until the age of twenty unless they attain graduation before that time. Most pupils graduate at eighteen or nineteen years of age.

This school has four academic departments with a lower school accommodating the children from the age of five and a half to approximately nine. They are classified into groups of eight on the basis of chronological age, physical, emotional and social maturity, and ability to respond to the educational program.

Nearly all instruction at this level is oral, which means that communication with these children is carried on through speech and speechreading. The curriculum is planned to include all subject matter and activities necessary for the total development of each child. The average class program includes reading, writing, language, arithmetic, speech, speechreading, physical education, rhythm, auditory training and creative activities.

Each classroom is equipped with the latest development in group hearing aids, which makes it possible for each child to learn to make use of any residual hearing he may have. Maximum use is made of these instruments.

Children, ages three to five-and-a-half, who live within commuting distance may attend a preschool class. In addition to the teacher of the deaf and a teaching assistant with each class of six, each mother is required to attend one day per week.

The elementary school is composed of children from approximately nine years old through twelve. Of the fourteen classes in this department generally seven are taught by the oral method. The other classes, always including the four oldest classes, are taught by the simultaneous method. The subject load becomes greater in the older classes and the added means of communication by fingerspelling is helpful.

All the children in elementary school receive instruction in speech and speechreading. Every room is equipped with a group hearing aid and auditory training is given to each class. The elementary school curriculum also includes language, reading, social studies, arithmetic and science. In addition, children have art and physical education. The four oldest classes have language arts with their homeroom teachers and rotate for the other subjects.

The junior high school is a three-year program. Students usually are at least thirteen years old when they enter junior high school although the placement of any pupil depends upon his physical maturity as well as his educational achievement.

The simultaneous method of instruction, which is the oral means of communication supplemented by manual fingerspelling, is used as the method of instruction for every student in the department.

In addition to curriculum areas offered in the preceding schools, health becomes a required subject for one semester each year. There are special speech and rhythm classes taught by teachers who have specialized in these areas. Departmentalized work, rotational schedules, homework, assembly programs, exploratory vocational training, a full extracurricular program including organizations and evening parties become an integral part of school life at this time.

The high school program has been accredited by the Western Schools and Colleges Association and offers programs on various levels to meet the needs of the deaf students enrolled. All instruction in the high school is using the simultaneous method of instruction as is used in the junior high school.

All students in the high school are also given vocational instruction, and the vocational department offers its students at the vocational level courses in the graphic arts, spotting and pressing, general electricity and appliance repair, electronic assembly, power sewing, upholstery, cabinet making, auto body repair, welding, sheetmetal, baking, commercial art, typing, bookkeeping and business machines operation and horticulture. On the elementary level it offers industrial arts, homemaking and art. It is the aim of the well-trained staff, through well-equipped shops, to give all students the best possible training within the scope of their abilities in order to prepare them to take their places in the industrial world.

THE RESIDENTIAL PROGRAM

The residential program plays an important part in the education of many deaf children. One basic reason for the prevalence of residential schools is the relatively low incidence of deafness. While estimates vary, there is some evidence that there are about seven children who should be educated in a school for the deaf for each ten thousand children in school. It must be remembered that these seven children would range in age from approximately five to eighteen or nineteen and thus it can be seen that a relatively large population must live in a concentrated area for there to be a sufficient number of deaf children to establish a school with the full range of classes and homogeneous grouping. Even though classes for the deaf must be small, with six to eight children to a teacher for the younger classes and approximately ten to a teacher in the older classes, it would still require approximately 70,000 children of school age to produce about fifty deaf children who might be grouped into six classes with eight children to a class. A school population of 70,000 children means a total population of roughly 350,000 population. There are not many school districts of this size. Frequently school districts have cooperating agreements so that they can establish special education classes, drawing children from neighboring districts, but the factor of transportation time and distance affects the feasibility of establishing day classes to serve distant areas.

This has been one of the basic reasons why residential schools for the deaf were established. Children had to be drawn from a wide geographical area to have a sufficient number of children in one school to provide homogeneous grouping, to provide adequate facilities including specialized teaching equipment such as special textbooks for the teaching of language to the deaf, and hearing aid equipment. Better educational programs also generally result when teachers can be given supervision by experts in their own field. Where there is a program for deaf children with only one or two classes, the teachers of these classes rarely have an opportunity to receive supervision by the professional person who knows more about the job than they do. A school of any size may have a supervising teacher for each eight to twelve teachers and thus each teacher receives the benefit of supervision by an expert in his own field.

The basic problem of deafness is the lack of communication. Frequently, parents and others are so concerned with the communication problem that they forget that deaf children are subject to all the psychological problems that anyone else may have and these in effect may be aggravated because of the frustrations resulting from little or no communication.

A benefit of the residential school to the large majority of its pupils is the fact that it provides a situation where there is the ease of communication between one child and another and between children and adult staff. Many of the constant frustrations resulting from deaf children living continually with hearing people are eliminated, and in consequence better mental health and thus better climate for learning is frequently the result.

The modern residential school takes seriously the responsibility of developing its students in many areas in addition to the strictly academic and the strictly communication field. Responsibility, self-respect, respect for others, honesty, initiative and many other traits are best developed through participation in many so-called extracurricular activities. These include such things as Boy Scouts, Girl Scouts, dramatic clubs, student body government, vocational interest clubs such as printing clubs, science clubs, as well as planning for parties, dances and participation in both intramural and interscholastic sports.

It is the rare deaf child who makes a bona fide place for himself in these activities that are organized by and for hearing boys and girls with their ease of communication. In the residential school, each child has the opportunity to develop his individual talents in one or many fields because he is competing against someone else with the same handicap that he has, and because he is able to communicate with the others on an understanding basis. All of this is to prepare the deaf child to take his place in our current society where he will be earning his living among hearing people.

Many individuals speak of "the deaf world" and "the hearing world" as though the individual deaf person must make a choice as to whether he is going to live in one of these worlds or in the other of these worlds. In actual practice, each deaf person lives in both "the deaf world" and "the hearing world" and the degree to which he enters each is dependent upon himself and also dependent upon the individual situation. Nearly all deaf people are employed with hearing people. They have hearing neighbors, the large majority have hearing children, the large majority have hearing parents and hearing relatives, and they shop in stores operated and patronized by hearing people.[6]

On the other hand, over 90 per cent of deaf people who marry are married to other deaf people. Most of their social life is with other deaf people because of the communication factor. Relying strictly on oral communication, a deaf person who is excellent at oral communication is still restricted generally to the one-to-one communication situation. There are few, if any, natural social situations where there are a group of people present, but everyone in the group is divided into pairs with strictly one-to-one communication. Therefore, the deaf person gets the most social enjoyment by finding his social life with other deaf people who are using manual communication which is conducive to group participation.

It is rare that a deaf person will get a great deal out of a church service that is strictly for hearing people. Church services for deaf people require that the sermon be given in manual communication which can be understood by a group of deaf people in the congregation. As a result most deaf people get their religious life with other deaf people. Therefore, it is not an all-or-none situation with the deaf person finding his entire life among the deaf or his entire life among hearing people.

The residential school has this as the basis of its philosophy when it brings deaf children together for their education. It is not trying to segregate them from the rest of society, but rather it is recognizing that each deaf person will determine for himself the extent and the areas in which he will find his place in a hearing society and the extent and the areas in which he will find his place in a so-called deaf society. The deaf person is being prepared to make the most of himself as a deaf person and the residential school is not trying to make him a pale imitation of a hearing person.

THE SCHOOL PSYCHOLOGIST

The position of school psychologist in a residential school for the deaf requires certain skills over and above those required of psychologists working with other kinds of people. The function of a school psychologist will include that of evaluation, counseling and therapy for students, and sometimes counseling of staff in the manner of understanding and handling students.

For evaluation purposes, the psychologist working with deaf children is restricted to using tests when he wants to measure intelligence that are non-language tests or performance type tests. Commonly used tests with deaf children include the Wechsler Intelligence Scale for Children, Wechsler Adult Intelligence Scale, Raven's Matrices, the Leiter, the Nebraska Test of Learning Ability, the Goodenough and others of a similar nature. The Bender Gestalt Test is frequently used to measure personality adjustment.

The successful psychologist working with prelingually deaf children must have a thorough understanding of the language handicap of deaf children, and must also have the facility to understand manual communication as used by deaf children. Many deaf children have never been able to communicate with their own parents and frequently have been unable to communicate very well with other adults they may have come in contact with. One of the reasons for this has been that most often their parents, and frequently other adults, not only have never learned and tried to understand the manual communication used by deaf people in general and by deaf children, but they have also tried to prohibit the children from using any kind of manual communication in the belief that if the child were not allowed to communicate manually he would develop speech skills. In actual practice, not only did the child not develop the speech skills, but he developed many psychological problems that he otherwise might never have developed because of the lack of opportunity to communicate with anybody. For the psychologist to be able to help this child, the psychologist must be as fluent as possible in his communication with the child and use any means or any combination of means.

The school psychologist, or someone with understanding, must be able to explain to other staff members the viewpoint of the child who has not been able to interpret his environment through the language structure used by most of the rest of society. The correct understanding of the cause of behavior is necessary before a person can bring about a change in behavior.

The residential school, by bringing many deaf children together for a twenty-four-hour per day program, should be able to assemble a staff large enough and competent enough to understand and to work with the children. When only a few deaf children are grouped together in a particular day class situation, it cannot be expected that teams of adults with these skills will be available.

THE RESIDENT HALL COUNSELOR

Another highly important part of the residential school team is the houseparent or the dormitory counselor. This must be a person who not only serves as a parent to see that the child learns and carries out the expected routines of daily living, but it should also be a person who is able to plan and carry out worthwhile activities; is able to understand the reasons behind children's behavior; is able to bring about changes for the better in the children's behavior because he understands the reasons and because he has knowledge of appropriate activities to bring about behavior change.

PHILOSOPHY OF A RESIDENTIAL SCHOOL FOR THE DEAF

The following is taken from The Educational Philosophy printed in the official handbook of The California School for the Deaf, Riverside:[2]

> The California School for the Deaf at Riverside has been established for one principal purpose. This is to give the best possible education to the children who attend this school. Our objectives in educating these children are the same objectives as those in the education of all children. As stated by the Educational Policies Commission of the National Education Association, they are the achievement of self-realization, the development of proper human relationships, the attainment of economic efficiency and the assumption of civic responsibility.
>
> The education of deaf children differs from the education of other children, even though we have the same objectives, because the necessity and difficulty of teaching deaf children is complicated by the fact that they do not have normal communication skills. This in turn affects their social, psychological and emotional development, as well as their general educational development.
>
> Education is going on during all of a person's waking hours. It is never restricted entirely to the classroom, and in a school such as this some of the most important education is going on in the dormitories, in the dining room, and on the playground. Everyone with whom a child comes in contact is influencing that child and thus, in one way or another, teaching him.
>
> Decisions in regard to everything from general policies to relatively minor items must be based on the fundamental principle of what is best for the educational development of the children as a group. We recognize the factors of individual differences and try to adjust to them as long as such adjustment does not work to the detriment of the majority.
>
> The ability to communicate orally is highly advantageous to all deaf people. To be successful, oral instruction must be carried on as a way of life and requires the complete cooperation of all individuals associating with the children who are being instructed orally. In this school the youngest children will be instructed orally, and all communication with those children, including the times they are on the playgrounds, and any place around the school is to be carried on orally. Oral communication is understood to include written communication, but excludes formal use of the sign language and fingerspelling.

The major special objective during the first years a child is in a school for the deaf is the development of communication skills. After a few years this major special objective changes to the objective of having something to communicate about. By the time a deaf child is eleven years of age his basic oral habits of communication should be fairly well established, although continuing work is necessary to maintain and improve these skills. As the children become older oral communication will be continued, but this will be supplemented by manual fingerspelling. This means the fingerspelling of complete words and complete sentences in English exactly as it is spoken. Deaf children will only learn to use the English language by seeing it used properly and by continually using it properly themselves. When children in these departments sign, always insist that they put into fingerspelling what they are signing about before you accept it. If necessary, you can give the child the proper English, but insist the child spell it himself after you have given it to him.

MODERN DEVELOPMENTS IN RESIDENTIAL SCHOOLS FOR THE DEAF

Recent Federal legislation, including the Elementary and Secondary Education Act which provided funds specifically for publicly supported residential schools for handicapped children, should result in the strengthening of educational programs in many schools for the deaf. After a period of many years when complete oralism held sway, many residential schools are now again utilizing manual fingerspelling combined with oral instruction as a means of teaching deaf children. The relatively low level of academic achievement of deaf students throughout the United States as exemplified by the report of the special committee to the Secretary of Health, Education, and Welfare, known as the Babbige Report, has pointed up the need to improve the academic level of deaf students.[3] This in turn has helped people to realize that communication with deaf students cannot be restricted to one means, but rather any and all means of communication might be used to bring about learning. Now more and more residential schools throughout the country are advertising the fact that they are using manual fingerspelling to supplement oral communication in their educational program. Some of the leading schools in this field in addition to both state residential schools in California are the New Mexico School for the Deaf, the Louisiana School for the Deaf, the Indiana School for the Deaf, the North Carolina School for the Deaf as well as the Rochester School for the Deaf which for years has been a leader in this field.

In the past, some people have predicted that public residential schools for the deaf would diminish and perhaps die out as day schools grew and took over the student body from the residential schools. This does not seem to be the case. While the increase in percentage of those attending day schools has been great, the increase seems to be due to a combination of increase in population in the country and the increase in numbers with a less severe hearing loss who are quite appropriately educated in day school programs. The total number being educated in public residential schools continues to increase, and school after school throughout the United States has been replacing, modernizing and expanding its physical plant.

Residential schools have developed tremendously in cooperating with the Vocational Rehabilitation Administration to work toward appropriate preparation for employment. More post-high-school education is being developed with the California School for the Deaf in Riverside being a pioneer in establishing a program and classes for deaf students in Riverside City College. This program's special instructors for the deaf work with deaf junior college students.[8]

Recent Federal legislation provides for the establishment of a National Technical Institute for the Deaf. This is envisaged as being an institute that will be attached to a college for hearing students and which will provide both advanced technical training for deaf students and technical training on a less advanced level.

There is a tremendous need for adult education services for deaf people. The pioneer in this field has been San Fernando Valley State College in California. It has had a graduate program sponsored by the Federal Vocational Rehabilitation Administration to prepare graduate students in what is called the Leadership Training Program for the Deaf. An off-shoot of this program has been the development of adult education services for deaf people in the Los Angeles area. The need has been shown and methods of meeting the need have been demonstrated. Schools for the deaf in other parts of the United States may well follow the leadership of the program at San Fernando State College in providing needed classes for adult deaf people, particularly where there are large groups in metropolitan areas.

The education of deaf people is the oldest form of special education in the United States. Teaching speech to the deaf is an important part of the education of deaf people, but it is a relatively small part of the total educational problem. The total problem has never been completely met by any educational program, but all special educational programs for the deaf are continually striving to meet their needs and the part of this program that is centered in public residential schools for the deaf throughout the United States continues to be a major part of the program nationwide, has contributed to the educational welfare of hundreds of thousands of deaf people for the past century and a half, and has a great deal more to offer in the years to come.

BIBLIOGRAPHY

1. Atwood, A. W.: *Gallaudet College, Its First One Hundred Years.* Lancaster, Intelligencer Printing, 1964.
2. *California School for the Deaf, Riverside, Staff Handbook,* 1963.
3. Education of the Deaf, A Report to the Secretary of Health, Education and Welfare

by his Advisory Committee on the Education of the Deaf, Washington, D. C., February, 1965.

4. Farrar, A.: *Arnold on the Education of the Deaf,* London, National College of Teachers of the Deaf, 1923.
5. Fay, E. A. (Ed.): *Histories of American Schools for the Deaf,* 1817-1893. Washington, Volta Bureau, 1893, vols. 1 and 2.
6. Lunde, A. S., and Bigman, S. K.: *Occupational Conditions Among the Deaf.* Washington, Gallaudet College, 1959.
7. Portrait of a School. Riverside, California School for the Deaf, 1963.
8. Brill, R. G.: Hereditary aspects of deafness. *Volta Rev, 63*:168-75, 1961.
9. Brill, R. G.: Junior College Program at Riverside. *Silent Worker, 14* (12):3-4, Aug. 1962.
10. Doctor, P. V.: Tabular Statement of American Schools and Classes for the Deaf, Oct. 31, 1964. *Amer Ann Deaf, 110*:278, 1965.
11. Fay, E. A.: Tabular Statement of Acerican Schools for the Deaf, 1899-1900. *Amer Ann Deaf, 45*:65, 1900.

Chapter 10

GALLAUDET COLLEGE

Albert W. Atwood

GALLAUDET COLLEGE has long been and is today the culmination, the national capstone of this country's system of educating the deaf. It was the outgrowth of a local school for the deaf and blind, and this school itself came into being more by accident than by plan or design. Fortunately first the school and then the college that grew out of it were dominated from the start by two men who seemed endowed by nature with sheer genius for the parts which they played.

Amos Kendall, the astute journalist and politician, who played a major role in Andrew Jackson's administration, and served as Postmaster General under Presidents Jackson and Van Buren, was the guiding spirit in organizing the Columbia Institution for the Instruction of the Deaf, Dumb and Blind in 1857. He was the first chairman of the board of directors of the National Deaf Mute College which became part of the institution in 1864.

Able, enthusiastic and zealously devoted to his task, twenty-year-old Edward Miner Gallaudet was employed by Kendall to head the school and the college. For more than half a century he was a towering figure in the world of the education of the deaf. It is doubtful if education of any kind has ever been served by a more wonderful team than by the mature, sophisticated and influential Kendall and the youthful, energetic and ambitious Gallaudet.

Kendall himself told the story of the school's beginning:

> An adventurer brought to this city (in 1856) five partially deaf mute children whom he had picked up in the state of New York, and commenced exhibiting them to our citizens in their houses and places of business. He professed a desire to set up an institution for the education of unfortunates of that class in the District of Columbia, raised considerable sums of money and gathered a school of about sixteen pupils.
>
> Apparently to give respectability and permanence to his school, he sought and obtained the consent of some of our leading citizens, to become its trustees. It soon appeared, however, that he had no idea of accountability to them, and only wanted their names to aid him in collecting money to be used at his discretion. On being informed by the trustees that such an irresponsible system was inadmissable he repudiated them altogether.
>
> In the meantime the impression had gone abroad that he mistreated the children, and it led to an investigation in court ending in the children being taken from him and restored to their parents, except the five from abroad, who having

no parents or none who seemed to care what became of them, were bound to me by the orphans' court and formed the nucleus of our institution.

When Amos Kendall found himself the guardian of five deaf children from New York, four boys and a girl, he at once took charge of them and made arrangements to start the new school. One of his first acts was to consult with the heads of several schools for the deaf to secure a superintendent for his own schools.

Soon he was in correspondence with Edward Miner Gallaudet, a twenty-year-old teacher at the Hartford, Connecticut school of which his father, Thomas Hopkins Gallaudet, was the head. Mr. Kendall had written H. P. Peet, head of the New York Institution for the Deaf, with the idea of securing Mr. Peet's son, Isaac Lewis Peet. But the younger Peet was not interested and his father suggested that Mr. Kendall contact young Gallaudet. When he was appointed superintendent, his mother was appointed matron, and she proved a great sustaining force to her son for years to come. Gallaudet's first work was to put in order for occupancy the house Mr. Kendall had given together with one belonging to his son-in-law, Mr. William Stickney, which the directors had rented. These two houses stood on adjoining lots of two acres, each facing on Boundary Street (now Florida Avenue) opposite the northern end of 8th Street. Both houses were loosely built and were not comfortable in cold weather. Years later Gallaudet spoke of the "frail, rustic cottage through whose slender walls winter winds whistled and summer sun scorched."

There were twelve deaf and six blind pupils the first year. The report for the second year showed fourteen deaf mutes and seven blind, "all but one supported by the United States." Mr. Kendall said that the institution had only three acres, two houses and a stable. "The site might be exchanged for a suitable tract farther from the city for teaching agriculture and horticulture." But the school and the college which grew out of it are still, more than a hundred years later, on the same site.

In his report Gallaudet said the deaf mutes had made commendable progress in language, arithmetic, geography, composition and penmanship. The blind in addition to the ordinary school exercises had instruction in vocal and instrumental music. The ladies in Georgetown raised $250 for a piano.

It was in the fifth annual report, the one for 1862, that Gallaudet first officially suggested that a college be started. He stated that, "the Columbian Institution needs to be more than a local school; it should exert a national influence and our labors are not complete until there is a college." Later Mr. Kendall, describing the incorporation of the Columbian Institution for the Deaf, said it allowed the college to receive pupils from the states and territories, leaving the details of subjects taught, arrangement of classes and length of time the pupils should stay to the discretion of the directors and enabled the institution "to expand should it ever become practicable and desirable into a great national institution in which all the higher branches of science, literature and art should be taught."

That President Gallaudet was grateful for the breadth of the incorporation was evident when he said:

> By a fortunate inadvertence on the part of Mr. Kendall who drew up the charter of the Columbian Institution, no limit was set to the time during which the beneficiaries of the Government might remain under instruction. So long as they could be benefited they might remain in school. To start a college, therefore, it would only be necessary to add a college course of study to the curriculum and carry forward such of its pupils as were capable and desirous of going further.

He felt, however, that the Columbian Institution needed the legal authority to grant diplomas and degrees. Gallaudet, therefore, early in 1864 drew up an act authorizing the institution to grant "such degrees and diplomas as are usually conferred in colleges." The bill was introduced in the Senate by Senator Grimes of Iowa, chairman of the District of Columbia Committee, and caused a spirited discussion, found on pages 1108 and 1109 of the *Congressional Globe* of March 15, 1864. The bill was passed without a dissenting vote. Nor were any votes cast against it in the House. President Lincoln signed the bill on April 8, 1864.

On June 28, 1864, at the First Presbyterian Church, a collegiate department, to be known as the National Deaf Mute College, was inaugurated. This was not the ambition of Edward Miner Gallaudet alone, for the idea of a college for the deaf had been suggested by his father in his boyhood and had been urged by various teachers of the deaf, especially in the Hartford School.

Mrs. Boatner writes:

> Abraham Lincoln did not attend the Inauguration of the College in 1864. But the presence of his spirit surely pervaded the campus that day. Again his mission on earth seemed to be the freeing of those in bondage. Through the admirable foresight and planning of Edward Miner Gallaudet, and his appeal to the United States Government, Lincoln took the time in the days of his greatest stress to lend his ears to those who could not hear—and put his name to a document that would forever advance their cause: an act of Congress granting the deaf the right to have a college of their own.

Gallaudet was twenty-seven years old at the time of the inauguration. He said it would not be proper to ask the state legislatures for funds for a college, but that it was entirely proper to ask Congress. One of the purposes of the college, he added, was to train teachers.

> My father gave to the world convincing evidence of his belief that through education the deaf could be made the social and intellectual equals of the hearing by marrying one of his pupils. He lived to see 22 schools for the deaf in success-

> ful operation. . . . He often spoke to me of a college. We have a West Point. Why not a national college for the deaf? . . . Our college will not compete with the state schools; none of them give degrees.
>
> If a higher education is important to a man with all his faculties, is it not of even more consequence to those who make their way through the world in the face of difficulties which a few years ago seemed almost insurmountable?

The eighth annual report dated November 6, 1865, showed a total of fifty-eight pupils, the blind having been transferred to the school for the blind in Maryland during the year. No blind were ever educated in the college department. During the year the word "blind" was taken from the name of the institution.

In his report President Gallaudet said that an intermediate or preparatory department was a necessity.

> The College is not in competition with any other organization for teaching the deaf but is a natural outgrowth of and supplement to other institutions; it would be impossible without them. We will till a field hitherto uncultivated and unappropriated. We hope to build an institution of which our united and free people shall be proud.

In 1867 the directors of the Columbia Institution learned that schools had been founded in Northampton, Massachusetts and New York City where speech was taught, and sent President Gallaudet to Europe to study especially schools which employed the oral method. He was gone six months, visited more than forty institutions and made a detailed and lengthy report upon his return. He reported that instruction in speech and lipreading should be entered upon as soon as possible. In fact he was one of the first educators of the deaf in the country to advocate that all deaf children should be instructed in speech and lipreading. He said:

> I have found not a few persons deaf from birth who have become fluent in speech and lip reading. Thus it would seem that attempts in articulation should be made with all deaf mutes, lest, unhappily, some possessing ability to acquire it by neglect fail to do so.
>
> The oral language can not be mastered by a majority of the deaf, an accomplishment attainable by a minority. To the mass of the deaf articulation is unattainable except to a degree that renders it comparable to sculptures and paintings that never find a purchaser, to books and poems that are never read, to music that is never sung, involving much labor by teacher and pupil but only limited success.

Gallaudet felt that if speech and lipreading were to be taught, more teachers would be needed and that all the teachers could not be deaf mutes. So he recommended to the directors the starting of a normal school, at which students with hearing should be admitted, young men and young women "who wish to fit themselves for deaf mute instruction." Late in

December, 1867, the directors voted to admit speaking persons to become teachers, but it was more than twenty years before this was actually done.

The graduation of the first class to take the entire college course was held in the First Congregational Church of Washington on June 23, 1869. The diplomas of the three graduates were signed by President U. S. Grant. They have been signed by the President of the United States, acting as Patron of the College, ever since that day.

At Presentation Day, May 5, 1880, an honorary degree of doctor of philosophy was given Alexander Graham Bell. A news account said that Bell gave an interesting exposition of visible speech at the close of which he was surprised with the honorary degree in recognition of the valuable services he had rendered to the art of articulation teaching. Gallaudet had seen quite a little of Bell, had dinner with him several times, and the two men became friendly enemies in respect to the methods of teaching the deaf. Each of them devoted a lifetime to that cause. However much they may have differed in their views, the fact remains that the first collegiate degree received by the famous inventor of the telephone came from the National Deaf Mute College.

In 1887 it was definitely decided to admit women, as an experiment, and six were admitted. There being no suitable accommodation, the president gave up the greater portion of his house to them. Gallaudet had written the superintendents and principals of the state school for the deaf in March of "our new departure to admit young women next September, but only of the highest personal character." Two years later President Gallaudet reported that eight young women could be accommodated without asking money for a dormitory, but there had not been as many applications as had been expected.

In 1894 the directors changed the name of the college department from the National Deaf Mute College to Gallaudet College, in honor of Thomas Hopkins Gallaudet, the parent corporation remaining the Columbia Institution for the Deaf. The change in the name of the college department was made in accordance with a petition from the alumni association. It was explained that the old title was long, cumbersome and inconvenient.

Presentation Day on May 2, 1906, was a particularly distinguished occasion. President Theodore Roosevelt spoke, the prayer was by Edward Everett Hale, Chaplain of the Senate, and the benediction by Henry Yates Satterlee, Episcopal Bishop of Washington. The *American Annals of the Deaf* called attention to the fact that this was the fiftieth anniversary of teaching the deaf on the part of President Gallaudet and James Denison, principal of the Kendall School.

A group of alumni wrote President Gallaudet on February 5, 1907, his seventieth birthday and the fiftieth anniversary of his labors on Kendall Green.

> The ability, courage and devotion you have shown in founding, upbuilding and sustaining the College command their admiration and respect. Your clear and cogent qualities as an instructor and lecturer, your mastery of the sign language and delight in using it in its place . . . and your uniform and considerate kindness to each and all of them awake their answering love and gratitude. So started the Edward Miner Gallaudet Fund, which in whatever way it may be used will forever be associated with your memory.

President Gallaudet spoke and wrote about retiring in 1908 but did not actually submit his resignation until March, 1910. The directors elected Professor Percival Hall as president, to assume office in September. It was freely stated at the time and later on that the directors would have elected Vice-president Fay as president but they knew he would not accept the position.

President Gallaudet's retirement was formalized and Professor Hall installed in June. Dr. Gallaudet received gifts from the faculty and students and an illuminated scroll from the alumni. One of the directors had remarked of the retiring president:

> He had threefold duties, educational, financial and social. I think this last part of the work was not the least difficult and has been the least appreciated; it was the part of the voyage in which the rocks were not in sight, but they were there and ready to make shipwreck of the craft. With skill and forbearance and self-sacrifice on his part all harm was safely averted.

When he was only thirty-two years old the *Deaf Mutes Friend* had this to say of him:

> With a kindly young man's face, a persistent set of the under jaw, buoyant of step and hearty in the hand, and of speech of frankness and persuasive eloquence. It was his steady, tireless labor that made this College; it was his ready intelligence that carried through all stages of Congressional contempt and opposition.

Percival Hall was President of Gallaudet College for thirty-five years, and they were mostly hard years, with two world wars to be lived through. The whole plant was inadequate and usually overcrowded, new buildings were badly needed, salaries were too low and the faculty were not covered by the Civil Service retirement system. Pleas for relief went unheeded.

"In 1922, we lost three of the most skillful instructors to positions paying 10 per cent to 100 per cent more salary than we could pay," reported President Hall. "The greatest need is for higher salaries and an Administration Building."

The seventy-fifth anniversary of the college was celebrated in 1939, and Dean Elizabeth Peet spoke on seventy-five years of the higher education of the deaf. She said that the college's modern curriculum combined the liberal arts with practical subjects. She continued:

> The story of the College falls into three natural periods, of twenty-five years each. The first from 1864 to 1889 was one of the founding and gradual development, the second from 1889 to 1914, a time of growth and transition, the third from 1914 to 1939, all under Dr. Hall, a period of modernization, diversification of curriculum, growth in the number of students and faculty members, and development of the normal and research departments.

At a conference of the deaf and hard of hearing at the Michigan School for the Deaf, in February, 1944, Dean Fusfeld said that at Gallaudet,

> We have in mind the development of character, education in the broad sense of tolerance and sympathy for fellow man, wholesome health, and leadership. We want our students to be adequate human beings . . . the aim is not that of a technical school, it doesn't provide the concentration of interest along highly specialized lines, but an opportunity to acquire basic training in chemistry, bacteriology and the graphic arts.
>
> College life for the deaf should have indirect but potent development in the practice of getting along with one's fellow . . . from the interplay of daily experience in residence halls, dining rooms, reading rooms, library, campus social activities, athletic events and chapel meetings.

Late in the year President Hall called the board's attention to the fact that in September, 1945, he would have completed fifty years of continuous service in the institution and suggested that the board consider finding a new president. Dr. Hall resigned as president on May 7, 1945, to take effect July 1. For two years he remained on the board, continuing as its chairman for that period of time, and he died November 8, 1953, at the age of 81.

On May 7, 1945, Leonard M. Elstad, a graduate of the college's normal department in 1923 and the head of the Minnesota School for the Deaf, was elected president.

President Elstad suggested to the directors late in 1945 that it might be necessary to sell the dairy herd because it was not possible to get farm help. The herd of thirty cattle had long supplied the students with fresh milk, and when the students were away in the summer the milk was sold at the Eighth Street gate to all who were interested.

But as far back as 1920, President Hall, in addressing a conference of educators of the deaf, said in regard to the college farm that young men were attracted to the big cities, and it had become increasingly evident that the students were not interested in agriculture.

Dr. Harry Best, who was engaged in 1945 to make the survey of the college for the Federal Security Agency, reported that the deaf are deterred from farming by the heavy capital outlay and the desire to be near their comrades in the city.

> Evidence is at hand that they (the deaf) are to a greater or less extent leaving agricultural pursuits in order to go into manufacturing and mechanical industries. At the same time there is a considerable degree of clannishness among the deaf or a natural desire on their part for companionship on equal terms, or with each other, which would further incline them to congregate in localities where their fellows are to be found.

The report of the institution for 1948 showed that systematic psychological testing of students was continuing. A series of standardized tests was used, with achievement and personality tests for all students entering the preparatory examinations for freshmen, and the National Cooperative College sophomore tests at the close of the sophomore year. Later a new series of tests was added, the Differential Aptitude Test, prepared by the Psychological Corporation.

Dean Fusfeld told the directors in May, 1948, that the curriculum had been revised by the establishment of a number of main areas of concentration of study: education, home economics, language and literature, science and mathematics and social studies, library science and printing. The two semester system in place of three term system was adopted.

At a special meeting on June 17, it was voted that the present location was not suitable for the development of new buildings because of the commercial and industrial development of adjacent properties, and a committee was appointed to find a new location.

At another meeting the board was told that appraisal of the institution's land showed the property to be worth $1,500,000. There was a discussion of the availability of purchasing the Glover property on Massachusetts Avenue as a site.

Bright hopes for the future of the institution came in a letter to President Elstad in May, 1950, from John L. Thurston, acting administrator of the Federal Security Agency:

> Many people in the Agency have commented on the very real advances that have been made at the Columbia Institution for the Deaf under your leadership. I want you to know that we are going to move ahead at this time and strongly recommend to the Bureau of the Budget and, I hope, to Congress, an expanded program for the Institution that will result in even greater progress in the coming years.

At the May 29 directors meeting, the board considered the many proposals in Dr. Gallagher's report and agreed that a large number of them be accepted in principle. Dr. Gallagher's study was entitled, "The Federal Government and the Higher Education of the Deaf, a progress report on the Columbia Institution for the Deaf, with proposals for action." In a summary he said there was a shocking discrepancy between the numbers (210) of the deaf who now go to college and the numbers (5,586) who would be in college if deaf persons were enrolled in the same proportions as hearing persons.

> Poverty and deafness are correlated and the public education of the deaf is a clear responsibility. While many persons in homes of higher incomes are deaf, one and a half times as many children in homes of low income are deaf. Not all deaf persons should attend hearing schools and colleges. In each case an individual decision should be based on the whole personality of the deaf person.
>
> The Federal Government must continue responsibility for providing higher education for the deaf (whose hearing is inadequate for usual school purposes and who can make normal progress only with special facilities and instruction). It is uneconomic for any state to establish a special college for the deaf. Realistic plans for a first-rate college for the deaf call for imagination and bold reconstruction of prevailing patterns and programs at Gallaudet College [Dr. Gallagher noted, and added that], legislation can provide a revised charter with new working relationships between Gallaudet College, the Federal Government, the states and the District of Columbia. Kendall School should be a continuing part of the teacher education program. The District of Columbia should be encouraged to meet more nearly its full share of the costs of the school. Research should be adequately promoted. The Master Plan for the future Gallaudet can and should be constructed.

Appearing before the House Appropriations Committee on February 8, 1955, President Elstad spoke of the three phases of the proposed building program: shop, laundry, heating plant and gymnasium under one roof; a girls' dormitory; a boys' dormitory; a speech and hearing center; a new Kendall School, "which would be a model school"; an auditorium; and lastly, athletic fields and stands. The buildings should be so designed that the students could more readily see all that was going on at all times.

The committee learned that the enrollment of the college was 280, made up of 150 boys and 130 girls, all the college students being boarders except for four married students living off campus. They also learned that like most Gallaudet graduates the thirty-six graduates of June, 1954 will probably show 40 per cent teaching in schools for the deaf, while others will be in the Commerce Department, Coast and Geodetic Survey Laboratory, work in libraries, become chemists, etc. Athletic facilities should be adequate not only for the regular activities but also because the college trains physical education instructors especially for the schools for the deaf. President Elstad was able to tell the board of directors that the committee gave favorable consideration to the construction budget of $2,225,000.

On June 4, 1955, ground was broken for the new library, a truly significant occasion because it marked the beginning of an extensive building program to give Gallaudet a plant to serve from 500 to 700 students. The year 1955 was also notable for the large number of new courses in the curriculum. Two new departments were added, psychology and business administration. The college now was able to offer special fields of study in art, biology, business administration, education, economics, English, home economics, library science, mathematics, philosophy, political science, physical education, physics, psychology and sociology. There were fourteen persons on the faculty holding Ph.D. degrees, and nineteen of the staff were taking graduate work at various universities, seven for doctors' degrees and the rest for masters'.

At the House Appropriations Committee early in the new year, President Elstad asked for money for the second stage of the construction program, a classroom and laboratory building and a hearing and speech clinic. While before the Senate Appropriations Committee, he said that if deaf students went to college in the same proportions as hearing students, enrollment of Gallaudet College would be doubled.

Early in 1956 John E. Fogarty, chairman of the subcommittee of the House Appropriations Committee, told representatives of the college, "We want to see this school accredited. I think we made that very plain, didn't we?" Fifteen months later the college was accredited by the Middle States Association of Colleges and Secondary Schools because of rapid development in teaching staff, curriculum, plant and facilities. This was a major and vitally essential forward step for the college, and the result of long and persistent effort to enlarge and/or enrich its physical facilities, faculty and curriculum.

Construction of the new classroom building and the hearing and speech clinic started late in the year of 1957. Enrollment was 381; 306 were in the college and seventy-five in the Kendall School.

Before the House Appropriations Committee on February 10, 1958, the president was asked how much the students pay for their education. The committee was told that they are asked to pay $800, but many cannot. They may go to the vocational rehabilitation offices in their states, which usually assist them up to $250, the tuition part of the $800. That leaves $550. The student who needs further help signs an application blank stating his financial condition. If the college feels he can pay $400, he pays that or $300 or whatever he can afford. No one is kept out for lack of funds; the average paid is $450.

> Day School graduates are hearing about Gallaudet. We are building for 700 to 1,000 students. The hearing and speech center should be equal to those at Walter Reed Hospital and Johns Hopkins University.

Professor D. Robert Frisina, director of the center, was called in and said the services would include comprehensive audiology and related psychology assessments, provision for procuring hearing aids, instruction in speech, speech reading, auditory and manual communication course work and clinical facilities for graduate students in training. Eventually students preparing to become audiologists and psychologists in programs for the deaf would be trained. Research efforts would be directed toward communication problems as well as educational, audiological and psychological aspects of hearing impairment. Before the Senate Appropriations Committee President Elstad said: "The hearing and speech center would be an institute for the study of deafness, functioning primarily to provide service to the deaf students, second to provide clinical training for the graduate students, and third for research."

President Elstad also called in Dean Detmold to acquaint the board with two research projects then being conducted in the college. He described the Central Index of Research on the Deaf, which abstracts and indexes all published research on the deaf, and the Structural Analysis of the Language of Signs, which studies this language through modern scientific approaches that have been developed for the study of other languages, in order to prepare a grammar, a lexicon and a notational system.

The fall of 1959 saw a continued expansion of the faculty with eleven additions, including four members of the staff of the Counseling Center. Also the college started the year with thirty-three graduate students, seventeen being the largest number ever before enrolled. Gallaudet had thus become the largest teacher training center for the deaf in the country, other leading centers being the New York and St. Louis schools and the Clarke School in Northampton, Massachusetts. Because of the increased size of the class it was necessary to send a number of students to the schools in West Virginia, Western Pennsylvania and Maryland for practice teaching.

Early in 1960 the Donner Foundation of Philadelphia gave the college $12,000 to build an anechoic chamber, that is, an echo proof chamber, to be used for research into hearing and speech. This gave Gallaudet an installation found in few colleges and Government research centers. The chamber's walls and ceiling are built of conical spun glass, the floor of woven steel. Besides hearing and speech research the chamber is available to the physics department.

In the fall of 1960 two new research projects were announced. One was concerned with new methods of language development in deaf children. The purpose of this two-year study was to find a method or methods by which deaf children could acquire language at an earlier age than they normally do. It would give initial emphasis to adapting to use with deaf children methods of using visual aids which have been employed with normal hearing children.

The other new research project was a study of how deafness affects the pattern of everyday living in metropolitan Washington, and in turn to determine how this pattern is related to vocational and social adjustment.

This study concerned the numbers and vital statistics of deaf persons in the area, family composition, occupations, population, movement, relation between the deaf and the hearing, social participation, and needs for counseling and other rehabilitation services.

At the 1961 hearing before the Senate Appropriations Committee Senator Allott of Colorado asked President Elstad, "Who is deaf for your institutions?" Dr. Elstad replied as follows:

> Perhaps some persons with 50 decibel loss are good subjects for us where others with 75 decibel loss would not need us because of good lipreading ability. Each case is a study in itself. The audiometric record is only part of the problem.

The catalogue says that Gallaudet College was founded "to provide a liberal, higher education for deaf persons who need special facilities to compensate for their loss of hearing," Dr. Gallagher in his study said it is for those whose hearing is inadequate for the usual school purposes and who can make normal progress only with special facilities and instruction.

Testifying before the House Appropriations Committee on February 22, 1962, President Elstad said, "We require an audiometer reading for each student. If there is any question about his hearing, we get in touch with his school. We don't want to become a college for the hard of hearing."

May, 1962, was a very busy month on the Gallaudet campus. There was a grant of $24,000 from the United States Office of Education for a study of high school mathematics programmed texts to be used by deaf students. The Charles E. Merril Trust gave the college a grant of $15,000 to start a national center for producing and distributing films and video tape for the deaf. Dean Elizabeth Benson was given an award for outstanding achievement by the alumni association of the State Teachers College at Towson, Maryland. Professor William C. Stokoe, Jr.'s book, *Sign Language Structure: An Outline of the Visual Communication Systems of the American Deaf,* was extensively reviewed. Andrew Jackson Foster, first deaf Negro graduate of Gallaudet, and founder of schools for the deaf in Ghana and Nigeria, was named "Man of the Year" by the Alpha Sigma Pi Fraternity.

Deafness, Speech and Hearing Publications, Incorporated, a joint enterprise of the American Speech and Hearing Association and Gallaudet College, received a grant from the United States Office of Vocational Rehabilitation to catalogue all past writings of scientific interest that deal with deafness, speech and hearing published before 1960 and to cross index the material extensively.

From June 22 to June 28, 1963, the college was host to the International Congress on Education of the Deaf, attended by some 2,200 educators from approximately fifty countries. Professor Powrie Vaux Doctor, chairman of the department of history and political science, acted as executive secretary of the congress, which first met in Vienna, Austria, in 1873. Its last previous meeting was at the University of Manchester, England, in 1958, and its only previous meeting in this country was at the New Jersey School for the Deaf, West Trenton, New Jersey, in 1933. Dr. Elstad served as co-chairman of the 1963 Congress with Dr. S. Richard Silverman, director of the Central Institute of the Deaf in St. Louis. The *Proceedings* of this World Congress are contained in Senate Document No. 106, 88th Congress, 2nd Session (U. S. Government Printing Office, Washington, 1964).

Saturday evening, June 22, the Conference of Executives of American Schools for the Deaf at a dinner at the Cosmos Club presented awards to Mrs. Spencer Tracy, director of the John Tracy Clinic of Los Angeles and to Dr. Eric S. Greenaway, headmaster of the Yorkshire Residential School for the Deaf, Doncaster, England.

In 1964 Gallaudet College celebrated its one hundredth anniversary which culminated in a banquet attended by President Lyndon B. Johnson.

Also in 1964 the International Games for the Deaf were held in Washington, D. C. Athletes from twenty-seven different nations were housed and fed on the campus. The actual games were held at the University of Maryland because of the more adequate facilities there. This gave interesting evidence of the competence of deaf persons who have had the full advantages of an education. The deaf population of the United States got behind these games and were signally successful in the entire endeavor. The culminating event was the banquet held on the last Saturday night at which more than 4,000 persons were seated in two hotels—2,700 in the Sheraton-Park and 1,500 in the Shoreham. Presentations were made by representatives from each of the twenty-seven nations. This again gave evidence of the effectiveness of the sign language, because most of those who attended were deaf and all of them understood the presentations because of the use of the sign language. Although this language is not international, it was possible to make the presentations through a sign language that was understood by most of those present. The International Games created a great interest among the foreign deaf athletes in Gallaudet College. As a result, we have had many requests for enrollments from other nations. Most of these have had to be denied because the candidates have not had an opportunity to prepare for a college education.

In 1966 we were again visited by the President of the United States at our graduation exercises. This was a surprise visit and, of course, was enthusiastically received by the Class of 1966 and all who were on the campus at that time. This visit gave added evidence of the real interest of the President of the United States in the deaf and their welfare.

During 1966 a new position was established at Gallaudet College, Vice-president for Long Range Planning. Dr. Orin Cornett was selected to hold this position. It is his responsibility to study the history of the college and predict through various studies what the future trend should be in higher education on the Gallaudet College campus. His work has gone ahead very rapidly, and the college is pleased with the outlook for its second one hundred years.

In 1967 the college will complete ten years of history as an accredited college. Gallaudet College received accreditation by the Middle States Association of Colleges and Secondary Schools in 1957. It is customary to seek reevaluation each ten-year period. The faculty and staff have been very active during the closing months of 1966 in preparing the self-evaluation report which will be the basis for reaccreditation when the committee comes to the campus in March of 1967.

Congress has passed legislation to establish a model high school for the deaf on the Gallaudet College campus. No funds have been provided. This will be a part of the 1967-1968 budget. This high school will provide a full academic program, with all the fringe benefits that help stimulate growing youth to maintain the interest necessary to complete the courses provided.

Chapter 11

A HISTORY OF THE CLEVELAND HEARING AND SPEECH CENTER

Ruth E. Bender

THE Cleveland Hearing and Speech Center has been, for a good many years and in an evolution of varied forms, a respected member of the service and educational community of Cleveland, Ohio. The institution is situated, at the present time and in the foreseeable future, within the University Circle area of the city. It is an integral part of the educational, medical and social service institutions that make up the complex of Western Reserve University and the University Hospitals. A circle of teamwork links all these institutions together in their service to people and in the education and training programs. Within this circle, the major responsibility for nonmedical rehabilitation of hearing and speech problems falls on the Hearing and Speech Center.

The center is now a rather complicated organization with some seventy-five employees and an equal number of students and trainees. Its beginnings were small and the patterns of the structure were very different.

Early history in Cleveland of work with hearing problems may be traced back to an old yellowed clipping from a Cleveland newspaper showing the valiant "coat of arms" reproduced above, with its defiant legend, "EARS BE DARNED."

The crumbling piece of paper is dated "Sunday, September 18, 1921, Woman's Magazine Section." The banner at the top titles it "News of Cleveland Women." The handsome, clear-eyed Cleveland woman in the accompanying photograph is Miss Louise Howell.

Miss Howell is credited, in the text of the article, with the formation of the Cleveland Lip Readers' Club. It was also through her efforts that the public schools of Cleveland became interested in offering free evening classes in speech reading. Lessons were offered, according to this article, under the direction of the Cleveland Board of Education, meeting at the Normal School Building on Stearns Road, S.E. For this season, the classes were held at 7:00 P.M. on Thursday evening. They were open to all members of the community over twenty-one years of age, who were hard of hearing, with a good command of English. High school students were also admitted.

As an outgrowth of these classes, the Lip Readers' Club was established,

REPRODUCED BY

LILLA DALE SAMSON

with Miss Louise Howell as president. There was "a large board of trustees and an advisory board of prominent physicians." The club rooms were at 859 Rose Building, 2060 East Ninth Street. The club was to be "a center where opportunities for self-expression and social enjoyment may be encouraged and provided."

Also mentioned in connection with the local organization was "a new National Federation of Organizations for the Hard of Hearing." The convention of the National Federation, held in Boston about this time, brought together officers of local organizations and teachers of speech reading from various parts of the country. One joint meeting was held with the otological section of the American Medical Association, where the "aurists" of the country "strongly advocated the forming of these organizations in every town." This was the foundation for the American Hearing Society.

In June 1966, this agency was reorganized, with an enlarged focus for its work, and is now called the National Association for Hearing and Speech Agencies.

Miss Howell, herself, was deaf and depended upon lipreading for communication. She insisted that lipreading was no miracle, but a "wholesome mental exercise" requiring study and practice. Then she added, wistfully, "There will always be some necessity for it, I suppose. But how much better it would be if we could start with the children and prevent all deafness."

Miss Howell was, at that writing, apparently an old hand at the profession, having established her own "Cleveland School of Lipreading" at 952 Rose Building in 1914, using methods brought from Europe. From all accounts, this school was apparently in continuous operation for years, until it eventually merged with other organizations in the city that had similar goals.

The next report we find of work in this area was in 1924, when a major expansion of these services took place under the guidance of Helen Newell Garfield. Mrs. Garfield was the wife of James R. Garfield, who was the son of the late President Garfield, and former Secretary of the Interior in the cabinet of President Theodore Roosevelt. Deafened herself, Mrs. Garfield "opened a small lipreading class in 1920. When the work prospered, she organized the Speech Readers' Guild. It grew, year by year, until in May, 1924, the Cleveland Association for the Hard of Hearing, named by the founder, established permanent headquarters at Hall House on Euclid Avenue, near the business center of the city."*

This building was on the Orlando Hall Estate, at 2636 Euclid Avenue, and was occupied by the association for nine years. Mrs. Garfield directed the work of the association for six years. After her death, the name Hall House was changed to Garfield House, in her honor.

Dr. Chamberlain was president of the board of directors and Arthur C. Palm executive director of the first organization of the association. As early as 1931, repairs were necessary for the building, which the Hall Estate Trustees did not seem to find within their responsibility. There was discussion then of moving to another place, but none could be found at the time that was suitable.

There was a two dollar fee for membership in the organization. Expenses were also paid in part by income from the rental of rooms on the upper floors of the building as dormitory rooms. As a charitable organization, the association was granted tax-free status. It was accepted as an

---

* Quoted from *Garfield House Life,* May 24, 1938.

agency of the Community Fund, from which it derived another portion of its budget. The association was a member of the Health Council and of the Welfare Federation, and operated under the principles and regulations of these organizations. Since lessons were offered without fee to the public, the governing board resorted to various devices for fund-raising. Once, an amethyst necklace was donated to the association for the purpose of raising money. Some members of the board were opposed to the use of a raffle to dispose of the necklace, so it was decided to have a benefit bridge, at which time it was given as a door prize to the holder of the lucky number. St. Patrick's Day suppers, white elephant sales, bake sales and similar devices were also used to raise money. For years, many Ohio sales tax stamps were collected in volume, sorted and counted by volunteers, and returned to the state for refund. It was with some relief that these workers heard of the discontinuation of the sales tax stamp.

By January of 1933, it was found necessary to dissolve the old organization in order to reorganize as a corporation. This was accomplished and plans were immediately underway for a move to a new location. A house was obtained at 8917 Euclid Avenue. Minutes of the board of director's meeting for April, 1933, record that "title of the Garfield House property has been transferred from Mrs. Treadway to the Association." There is also a story that the association paid a fee of a dollar a year for use of the mansion. This location was to be the headquarters of the association for twelve more years of strenuous work.

The policies of the association were carried intact into the new quarters. The name Garfield House was again applied and a large portrait of Mrs. Garfield hung in one of the classrooms. The upper floors were, again, used as dormitories, occupied by women who were in some way connected with the work. Some were hard of hearing themselves, and some were teachers in the profession. Among the latter was Miss Clara E. Vandersall, who taught lipreading and speech correction at Garfield House and also in the public schools of Shaker Heights.

There were kitchen facilities for the dwellers at Garfield House, and the custodian, George Hacker, who also lived there, was much more than a janitor in his interest in the hearing-handicapped people who came to Garfield House, and his devotion to their service. He was particularly attentive to the children who came for Saturday morning classes. He thought they looked in need of more substantial help than lessons, and took to inviting them to his basement quarters after class for hot cocoa and sandwiches or cookies. It was some time before someone realized that George was providing these treats out of his own meager income, and the Junior League volunteer women took over this responsibility.

The schedules of the organization, printed in their monthly newsletter,

Garfield House Life, show a tremendous amount of constructive activity. It is certainly not possible that all the dedicated people involved in all this activity were adequately paid—or, at times paid at all—for the services they gave to the hearing handicapped of Cleveland.

Adult lipreading classes were scheduled at Garfield House, two and three evenings a week. Practice classes for advanced lipreaders met at 10:00 A.M. once a week. Twice a week, also, adult classes were scheduled at 2:30 in Lakewood and East Cleveland. Voice training classes were offered at Garfield House at 8:15 P.M. twice a week. There was also a dramatic club, for those interested in such activities.

Saturday mornings from 9:00 to 12:00 were devoted to children's classes. They were offered lipreading, voice training and singing (in addition to Mr. Hacker's cookies).

A pure tone audiometer, then a relatively new device, was acquired and hearing tests were given in a "silent" room in the basement of Garfield House. Efforts were also made at a wider range of meeting and educating the public by periodic forays into outlying communities with a mobile trailer equipped with an audiometer for testing hearing.

Every effort was made to have all this work as valid and professional as possible, but the progress in philosophy from that day to this is illustrated in a newspaper account of one such test in the mobile trailer. The young man having his ears tested was discovered to have considerable loss in one ear, but only a 4 per cent loss in the other ear. The examiner told him that this was to be expected because it was a rule of nature that as one ear became worse the other ear became better to compensate for the loss in the deafened ear.

Along with hearing tests, the association gave demonstrations of hearing aids. The use of these amplifying devices was strongly encouraged by the association. At that time there was still a great deal of resistance to the acceptance of hearing aids by deafened persons, who seemed to consider them something of a disgrace, in spite of the fact that prominent persons were beginning to use them openly and effectively.

Social activities for the hard of hearing were provided at Garfield House by club organizations that served a very real function in the lives of its members. There was a men's club and a women's club. There were mixed groups, one called the Garfielders and another the Panthers (the latter club composed, understandably, of younger people). Club activities were frequently linked with public school classes for deaf children. The Panther Club was an outgrowth of such an organization of graduates from the Alexander Graham Bell School for the Deaf under the Cleveland Board of Education. There were other clubs, whose names indicate their major interest, such as Social Club, Wednesday Bridge Club, Contract Bridge Club,

Ping Pong Club, etc. Each of these had their own officers and conducted their own events. These clubs held parties, went on skating trips, had annual picnics and dinners, and in many ways contributed to the happiness and enrichment of the lives of people who often felt themselves outsiders and onlookers in the social life of the normally hearing world.

National Hearing Week was always an important celebration at Garfield House. This included a professional convention with important guest speakers in the fields of hearing conservation, hearing aids, and allied subjects. It included an open house for visitors at Garfield House, and an increased campaign for hearing tests for the general public. National Hearing Week was always made an opportunity for wider advertisement of the services offered to the hard of hearing by the Cleveland Association for the Hard of Hearing.

Members of the lipreading classes took part in contest tournaments in lipreading. More than once a Cleveland lipreader carried off the prize of first place in the National Lipreading Tournament. This was conducted under the auspices of the American Society for the Hard of Hearing and in 1938 was held in Cleveland, as part of the program for National Hearing Week.

A letter contest was held as a feature of National Hearing Week in 1936. The subject was "If I Had Three Days of Normal Hearing." The first prize was a hearing aid, donated by a hearing aid company. It was won by a Lakewood woman.

A little monthly magazine, called *Garfield House Life,* was published by the Association for the Hard of Hearing. It contained schedules of the month's activities, special notices to members, and inspiring articles. Lowell C. Ruch (who had been appointed executive director in 1936) contributed an article for the issue of October, 1938. In this column, he announced that, after several years of study of the problem, instruction would be offered on Saturday mornings to pre-school children with defective hearing. These children were to be three years of age and to have a statement from an otologist that their hearing was permanently defective, to be eligible for the classes. They were to be offered instruction in lipreading, speech correction and singing. There followed a sympathetic paragraph by Mr. Ruch on the danger of a trend toward personality isolation at this important stage in a child's development unless these children were given special help. To augment the more formal instruction at Garfield House, each child was also to be placed in a day nursery as close as possible to his home.

There is no disputing the excellence of this philosophy. Unfortunately, nothing further appears in the literature of the organization to indicate the progress of these preschool classes.

It is obviously impossible to acknowledge even a handful of the dedicated people, who gave so freely of their time, energy and means to improving the lot of hearing handicapped people in Cleveland. There is, however, one individual whose personality begins to run, as vivid as a flame, through the fabric of all that was being done in this field, at this time and for years to come. Everyone familiar in even a small degree with this work in Cleveland knows the name of Marie Hays Heiner.

She had been giving of her services to Garfield House for at least a year when her name first appeared on the minutes of the board meetings as a member of the board of directors of the association on September 16, 1935. With the characteristic drive and enthusiasm with which she tackled any project she undertook, it is not surprising that she soon appeared as vice-president in 1938, a post she was to hold for many years. James R. Garfield was elected president of the board at the same time, following Dr. Chamberlain.

At the age of almost nineteen, a sophomore in college, Marie Hays awoke one morning in response to her roommate's shaking, to find herself frighteningly deaf. Her family followed every possible avenue in the search for a cure. Marie tried hard to believe, as time went on, that her hearing was not seriously impaired, but finally took lipreading lessons, almost secretly. She became a very proficient lipreader. When a Chicago otologist finally persuaded her that her hearing would never be any better and that she must simply learn to live with her handicap, Mrs. Heiner returned to Cleveland and plunged whole-heartedly into doing just that.

In Chicago, she had seen, for the first time, classes for deaf children. She was never to lose her interest in this vital phase of the work with the hearing handicapped.

Another thing she saw in Chicago was the wiring of theater and church seats with amplifiers and earphones, so that the hard of hearing might understand what they heard. Fired with enthusiasm, she campaigned for such hearing aid devices in Cleveland. Many churches were glad to install these amplifiers, but the theaters were harder to persuade. For a number of years, this was a militant campaign in Cleveland. Popular newspaper columnists joined the battle, with frequent references to the lag in the development of such services. By 1938, announcements began to appear in the newspapers, describing theater parties for the hard of hearing in theaters with wired seats. The roll of theaters with such equipment became gradually longer as time went on. There was also an announcement of a party of special guests of the Cleveland Association for the Hard of Hearing at Severance Hall, to mark the installation of specially wired seats in the concert auditorium.

Another project that was vigorously pursued by the association was the policing of local advertisers who offered dubious cures for hearing loss.

Under investigations and pressures from this group, local newspapers withdrew advertising space from such people, in cooperation for the protection of the hard of hearing.

In these days, a minority group or an affliction was still considered fair game as humor on radio programs. Mrs. Heiner personally wrote letters to the heads of radio networks, protesting the portraying of hearing loss in such a fashion as to hold up the handicapped to ridicule. She exerted a real influence in the change of philosophy along these lines.

Interviews were held at Garfield House for hearing handicapped persons who were seeking work. According to the figures in the association reports, they were not too successful in filling this need. A typical report read "Employment applications, 21; positions found, 2." At least, they tried. Finding that some other states were more successful in this project by means of a state bureau for the deaf, some attention was given to advocating the formation of such a bureau in Ohio.

During World War II, the association threw its resources heartily into the defense effort, led by Mrs. Heiner. A phosphorescent insignia was planned, to be worn by the deaf during blackouts, so that they might be recognized if they failed to hear a warden's command. The hard of hearing were urged to offer themselves, whenever possible, to industry and defense, in substitution for the men who had gone into the armed forces. First aid and Red Cross classes were conducted at Garfield House.

As veterans began to return from the wars, with hearing and speech impaired by their war experiences, a new type of need began to develop in the field of hearing.

But first we must take into account the contribution which was being made by the speech clinic at Western Reserve University.

In 1938, Amy Bishop (later Mrs. Chapin and now Mrs. Foster) was brought from New York to "introduce speech sciences to Mather." Flora Stone Mather College was a college for women. It was, and still is, a division of Western Reserve University. Amy Bishop was a graduate of Columbia University with a degree in speech. She was asked, among other things to "do something exciting" with the Tower Theater of the College and to set up a speech clinic for those of the girls at Mather who had "dreadful speech." This she did, with such success that very soon the speech clinic was expanded to include young men from adjoining Adelbert College for Men and Case Institute of Technology.

With the Red Cross and the Veterans Administration needing some outlet for speech rehabilitation and with Air Corps Cadets on the campus needing speech training as officers, Western Reserve University (of which Adelbert and Mather Colleges were a part) was approached on the subject of expanding the speech clinic to include much-needed community service.

Other organizations in the community offered to share specialists and to contribute to the new venture such guidance and assistance as they could offer from their services. Among these was Belle Greve, who was in charge of the Cleveland Rehabilitation Center situated on 55th Street. This was a center that offered speech correction, job training and a sheltered work-shop to handicapped persons. It included a program of speech training for crippled children. Another strong supporter was Dr. Henry Schumacher of the Cleveland Guidance Center. With the addition of a small staff, financed at the beginning by the Cleveland Foundation, the Speech Clinic began to take on an expanded role in speech services to the community. The univer-sity contributed further by offering courses leading to a teacher's certificate in basic speech correction.

On June 6, 1943, the *Cleveland Plain Dealer* had a photographic section dealing with the work of the speech clinic in the training of the young Air Corps Cadets. Two instructors appeared on the photographs with the trainees. One was Amy Bishop. The other was George J. Fortune, demon-strating "the transmission and reception of the human voice." For George Fortune, this was the beginning of a long association with the work that was about to be organized as a combined effort in speech and hearing re-habilitation, for by this time, the speech clinic was feeling the need of more help in the field of hearing. Suggestions came from several directions. Wal-lace Finch, principal of Alexander Graham Bell School for the Deaf, offered to help. So did Lowell Ruch, who was still director of the Cleveland Hear-ing Center (the name was changed in 1943). At this point, a still more useful idea was put forward. Dr. Charles E. Kinney, a noted Cleveland otologist and long a member of the board of the Hearing Center, along with Marie Heiner, still vice-president of the board, suggested that the two organizations, the Speech Clinic and the Hearing Center, merge into one united effort for their allied fields of service. There must have been many details and problems along the way, and the war was certainly some inter-ruption in terms of personnel available, but it was done. The Speech Clinic of Western Reserve University and the Hearing Center of Garfield House were combined into one organization.

A resolution to the Secretary of State, Columbus, Ohio dated March 27, 1946, made this statement, in part,

> Resolved, that the Cleveland Hearing Center shall consent to the use of the name the Cleveland Hearing and Speech Center as the name of a corporation proposed to be formed by Marie H. Heiner, James A. Doull and James R. Garfield as in-corporators.

Dr. James A. Doull, professor of public health at Western Reserve University and long a member of the board of the Hearing Center, was chosen the first president of the board of the new organization. Marie Heiner was vice-president. Lowell Ruch was executive director.

A house on the campus owned by the university at the corner of Abington and Euclid was remodelled by the university as quarters for the new, expanded facility. The name Garfield House was brought along from the old quarters of the Hearing Center. Some of the previous tenants of the Garfield House rooms were disturbed because they could not also come along and continue to live in its shelter. Mrs. Garfield's portrait was moved to the new home, and hung on the spacious stair landing. For years someone who loved her sent money every Christmas for a wreath to be placed at her portrait.

The new center began to gather a staff. Warren H. Gardner, a specialist in audiology and speech pathology, was called from California to be director of clinical services. Rachel Dawes Davies was hired for the training program for teachers of the deaf. Amy Bishop was still teaching voice and diction, among many other duties.

In May, 1946, Lowell Ruch left the Cleveland Center for a position in Los Angeles. George J. Fortune was chosen to succeed him as executive director. He was a former Army psychologist, a teacher in special education, and head of the pupil personnel and guidance department of Garfield Heights School.

In June, 1946, Marie Heiner became president of the board of trustees, with Dr. Charles E. Kinney as vice-president. Dr. Kinney was at all times most active in the organization. Not only was he a member of the board of trustees, but also the first chairman of the medical advisory committee. He was, and still is, the official otologist of the Cleveland Board of Education and directly connected with the Alexander Graham Bell School for the Deaf. The medical advisory committee has been from the beginning an important and influential body in determining policies and policing the medical aspects of the work at the center.

The work of the Cleveland Hearing and Speech Center rapidly became an expanding, many-faceted operation. Three major divisions were in continuous and simultaneous operation; clinical services to the community, academic teaching and research. Most staff members were involved in all three aspects of the program.

The services to the community began with the youngest. Hearing tests for babies were applied as young as parents and physicians requested them. These children were usually referred by the physicians, and always referred back to the physicians for a cooperative effort in parent counseling and treatment of the problem. A consultant otologist was an invaluable member of the staff. From about the age of eighteen months, a child could be accepted in the nursery class for hearing impaired children, and taught the beginnings of speech reading and speech. Auditory training was an important part of the program, using amplifying units with earphones. By about 1950, wearable hearing aids had become small and effective enough so that children could wear them comfortably. This immediately made a great difference to the deaf babies. Improvements continued until by 1960 they were wearing binaural aids, one behind each ear, fastened to a steel band over the head. This program included parent education and observation and the clinical training of students interested in the field. Some action research was carried on within the framework of the educational program.

During the summer months, classes of school-age children with hearing impairments were often brought in, both for the sake of the children's education, and as observation and training classes for the students.

Since the public schools of Greater Cleveland offered special classes for deaf children from the age of three, there was no need to duplicate services in that area. The center continued to serve, upon request of the schools and physicians, in testing hearing for older children, recommending hearing aids, and often in holding enough therapy sessions with the child to teach him the most effective use of his hearing aid.

Parallel to the program for children with impaired hearing was the language program. This took account of children whose speech and language development was delayed or distorted due to reasons other than auditory dysfunction. Many of these children presented multiple handicaps. They were given work in speech stimulation, language and speech correction, either in small groups or individually.

Another section of the clinical work gave assistance to children and adults with articulation defects, cleft palate speech problems and stuttering. In many cases corrective therapy was used directly with the client. In some cases, such as children with problems in stuttering, the work was conducted largely by means of counseling and training of the family.

In all these areas of work, techniques and methods have been expanded and refined in line with continuing knowledge and research. Nowhere is this type of progress more evident than in the diagnostic procedures. Time is made available for study of any child's problem, when the need is indicated, by specialists from the center staff in audiology, language and speech pathology. A medical social worker is an integral part of the total picture. Consultants on a regularly scheduled basis include an otologist, a psychologist and a pediatrician. These are frequently assisted by psychiatrists and neurologists from neighboring institutions. Every effort is made to reach a valid evaluation of each child's problem in order to recommend the most adequate therapy and educational placement for his assistance.

In the adult program are included victims of stroke or other cerebral accidents, who have paralysis or aphasia hindering their use of speech. Training for the clients in speech is in both group and individual sessions and counseling for the families is a major part of the services.

The Cleveland Hearing and Speech Center has developed an extensive program for laryngectomees. This area was always one of major interest to Warren Gardner and to Amy Bishop who taught, and trained others to teach, the use of esophageal speech.

Around this work at the Cleveland Center was organized a unique "Lost Chord Club," which has been copied in many places. This club is composed of members who have had the larynx removed, almost always because of cancer, and have learned to speak without vocal cords. When a new case for a laryngectomy is diagnosed by his physician, this group is contacted and requested to provide psychological support for the person facing this major crisis. Members of the club visit the patient before the operation, giving encouragement and a practical demonstration that life can continue with a fair degree of normalcy even without a larynx. When the patient has recovered, therapy lessons are instituted at the center and he is welcomed into the club to continue practice and assistance for his "new voice." The club has monthly meetings at the center for social and educational activities.

A training film, called "New Voices" was produced by the center in cooperation with University Hospitals and financed by United States Steel. This film shows the operation itself and also therapy sessions in teaching laryngectomees to speak again. The center was instrumental in founding the International Association of Laryngectomized Persons and organizing its first symposium, which was held in Cleveland, on the university campus, in July, 1952.

The audiology department of the center has continued all types of services originally offered by the previous Hearing Association, and continued to progress and expand with the advances of science and research in this area.

Hearing tests of increasing complexity and sophistication are given. In cooperation with the otologists, clients are advised concerning the nature of their hearing problems and the use of hearing aids. Trained audiologists are constantly available for assistance and counseling in the use of the hearing aids. A stock of representative aids is kept on hand, through the cooperation of the hearing aid dealers, for demonstration and testing purposes.

Classes and individual sessions in lipreading are offered in the rehabilitation program. When trained personnel is available, there are follow-up classes for adult deaf, graduated from schools for the deaf, who wish help in improving their speech and language for use in daily living. Many of these clients are sent to the center by the Bureau of Vocational Rehabilitation, in order that their speech and lipreading may be improved to the point that job training and finding of adequate employment can be made practical.

When the move was first made to the quarters on the university campus, the social activities of the association were carried over into the new Garfield House. A club-room was arranged in the basement where meetings were held. Gradually, these social groups found it pleasanter to meet in other surroundings and to merge with other community functions. Only a few of them still use the center facilities for social purposes.

One of the most dynamic aspects of the Cleveland Hearing and Speech Center has been its growth in the academic department. This growth has been an enlargement but also, more significantly, a development of philosophy and teaching that is keeping pace with the progress of the times. From the first merger with the university, the professionally trained staff of the center, which then numbered six, held academic rank and taught courses as members of the faculty of Western Reserve University. The program was a part of the speech department, headed by Warren Guthrie.

The relationship with the university has been an evolution in itself. In the early days of the affiliation the members of the center staff, who were also university faculty, still had the major portion of their time absorbed by clinical duties. As time went on, the need for more academic time became increasingly evident. Staff appointments by the university were largely on a clinical basis with university rank. Now there are full-time trustee appointments to the university for staff members whose major assignments are academic. The salary costs of center staff members are shared by the university and the center in proportion to the responsibility and time allotted in each area.

A similar relationship exists with the University Hospitals. Center staff members whose area of interest is particularly allied to the medical field have similar part-time appointments on the teaching staff of the Medical School. Students from the audiology department work with the physicians in the ear, nose and throat department of the hospital. Medical students are assigned to the Hearing and Speech Center for observation in the clinical and teaching aspects of hearing and speech problems.

The specialized nature of this work finally gave it a self-contained program within the general university curriculum, called Speech Pathology and Audiology. Students in this program are eligible for government grants to finance their special training and research. These grants are obtained from such agencies as the Vocational Rehabilitation Administration, the National Institute of Health, the National Institute of Neurological Diseases and Blindness and others. During the past year approximately

$180,000 has been received through such funds to support the work in one way or another.

Students at Western Reserve University who are part of the center program have a unique opportunity. It is seldom that trainees in this field are presented with a full spectrum of community services for observation and clinical practice under professional supervision. In addition to the cases they see at the center, students are scheduled to observe or participate in such areas as the divisions of otology and neurology at University Hospitals, acute neurological diseases at Benjamin Rose Hospital, and chronic diseases at Highland View Hospital. There have been opportunities for therapy and research in homes for the aged, such as Montefiore Home, McGregor Home and the Golden Age Center. Members of the staff have been asked by industries to research noise levels in their factories and assess the effects upon their workers.

In 1952, a request came to the Hearing and Speech Center for a complete evaluation of hearing and speech defects throughout the schools of Geauga County. Five thousand two hundred and twenty children were tested in eighteen schools. The survey showed the number of children with articulation defects, voice defects and hearing defects. The report was filed with the county health commissioner, with recommendations for remedial procedures.

The research division has become an important, full-sized department of the work of the center. Here students, under the guidance of competent professors, can add functional meaning to their studies by following a line of question to a conclusion. Staff members avail themselves of these opportunities, as well, to explore their own questions in this line of work. Staff seminars on these studies are stimulating sessions.

The center has won approval for its professional services from the American Board of Examiners of Speech Pathology and Audiology in 1965. The same board accredited the student training program in 1966.

Among the more colorful aspects of the work at the Cleveland Hearing and Speech Center are the foreign students who are attracted to the place. To name a few will show the breadth of the contacts which are made.

Sofia Battó, a speech and hearing therapist, came from Montevideo, Uraguay. Tom Okimoto was sent by the Rehabilitation Center of Honolulu, Hawaii, for help with his own hearing loss and advice concerning his career in social work. Maria Bienvenu spent a year in graduate study in hearing and speech therapy, and returned to Mexico City to work in that capacity at the Children's Hospital and the Mexico City Rehabilitation Center. Helen Varytimidou spent a year in study and training to teach deaf children, then returned to Athens, Greece, to teach in the Greek school for the deaf. In 1950, a staff member at the center was requested to spend a month in Caracas, Venezuela, as consultant to their school for deaf children. The trip was sponsored by a Cleveland business man, James L. Myers, but repaid later by the Venezuelan government. Later two teachers from the schools, Vincente Arnoriago and Dyana Chacin, were sent for a month's study of the schools and classes for the deaf in Cleveland. They were followed shortly by Carlota Landaeta, who was given a two-year scholarship by the Venezuelan government to study Cleveland methods for teaching deaf children. She returned to Caracas to teach in the school there. Dr. Helmuth Ormestad, a professor at the University of Oslo, came to Cleveland as an exchange professor at Case Institute. Part of his time was allotted to the Hearing and Speech Center, where he contributed greatly to research studies in hearing. When his wife and children joined him, they added much to the charm of the exchange.

Publication has always been a vital part of the work of the Hearing and Speech Center. There are always newspaper articles and radio and television shows, in an effort to reach the public and inform them of the services available to assist them with their handicaps. There was also a telecourse, for which credit could be earned at the university. This was conducted by Nancy E. Wood of the center staff.

There have been many articles contributed by almost all staff members to professional, semiprofessional and popular magazines, in order to communicate with colleagues in the field. It would be impractical to attempt to detail even a small part of the outpouring of this type of writing.

Another center project in the publication field was a series of pamphlets by members of the staff, published by the Hearing and Speech Center through the support of the Junior Chamber of Commerce of Cleveland. These were produced, one at a time, from 1947 to 1954. They covered the following subjects, *A Child Doesn't Talk, A Child Stutters, A Child Has a Cleft Palate, A Child Doesn't Hear, A Child Has Cerebral Palsy.* They were written to attract a reading audience of parents with handicapped children, and served this purpose excellently.

In 1960, *Language Disorders in Children,* by Nancy E. Wood, was published by the National Society for Crippled Children and Adults. In 1960, also, a history of the deaf and their education, written by Ruth E. Bender, was published by Western Reserve University Press under the title *The Conquest of Deafness.*

Marie Heiner was persuaded to write the story of her own hearing loss and her adjustment to the problem. *Hearing Is Believing,* published by the World Publishing Company in 1949, turned out to be a most inspiring and popular book. A radio program, called *The Wall of Silence,* made from the book, was also successful.

It was inevitable that the old mansion on Abington and Euclid should soon be entirely inadequate for all the activities undertaken by the Cleveland Hearing and Speech Center. A campaign was begun for a new and larger building to be added on Abington at the rear of and connected with Garfield House. The university gave the land, and money was acquired by grants and donations from many foundations and private sources. The first figure was set at $325,000, but was raised to $400,000 before the building was completed. Many of the friends of the center, who had been with it from the beginning, were most active in pushing the campaign. Marie Heiner donated all royalties from her book to the Cleveland Hearing and Speech Center. She had a private slogan of her own, "Every book a brick." In May, 1954, the building was dedicated, and the work of the center overflowed into it from Garfield House.

Next door was the beautiful old home of Nathan Dauby. This, the noted philanthropist donated to the Hearing and Speech Center. For some years, the center rented it and used the income. Finally, the pressure for more space became too heavy. Dauby House was taken over, largely for the academic work of the center, and its gracious rooms were converted for use as classrooms, offices and laboratories.

The financing of an institution as complex as this is never a simple project. There are many sources of income. In the clinical program, fees are set for services on a cost basis, but with a merciful eye on ability to pay, and adjustments can be made. No one is ever refused service because of inability to pay. The Hearing and Speech Center, from its beginning, has been an agent of the United Fund and received its due portion of income from this source. There have been many grants from foundations willing to underwrite the initiation of a new program until it could be proved and absorbed into the budget. The university pays its share of the salaries of its faculty members. Research projects are supported by Federal grants designed for such purposes. And there are always the private philanthropists who add their assistance to a worthy cause. The comptroller, Charles Barney, who has been with the center through all these vissicitudes since 1947 is still serving in that position.

Perhaps a small measure of the growth of the institution can be gained by a comparison of figures. In 1924, the total income for the year was quoted as $2,819. In 1964, the figure was $506,300.

In December 1957, the center staff was shocked by the sudden death of the director, George Fortune. Earl D. Schubart served as acting director until the summer of 1958, when Samuel Whitman was appointed to the position by the board. In the fall of 1962, he accepted a position with the hospitals of Cuyahoga County, but remained as consultant until January, 1963, when Irwin Brown came to take over as executive director.

Inevitably, the work of the Hearing and Speech Center again outgrew its quarters. In the fall of 1965, the old mansion called Garfield House was torn down. A well-designed new building, with room for expansion and refinement of all facilities, now stands in its place.

When the first "new building" was added to the rear of Garfield House, the entrance was moved to the side of the building on Abington Road, but the old Euclid Avenue address was never changed. The visionaries who saw this work going on in the future replied, when they were asked, that it would be needed again before long, when the next building would again front on Euclid Avenue.

This vision has now been realized. On September 20, 1967, in a dedication program, the Board of Trustees and officials of the organization formally accepted the new facilities for the Cleveland Hearing and Speech Center and Case Western Reserve University. The newly constructed building is called the Nathan L. Dauby Building. The previous one, which is integrally linked to it on all floors, is the Marie Hays Heiner Building.

The long familiar address 11206 Euclid Avenue is now again accurate!

BIBLIOGRAPHY

COMER, LUCRETIA GARFIELD: *Harry Garfield's First Forty Years.* New York, Vantage, 1965.
HEINER, MARIE HAYS: *Hearing Is Believing.* Cleveland, World, 1949.
ROSE, WILLIAM G.: *The Making of a City.* Cleveland, World, 1950.
WILSON, EDNA GRANT: *Famous Old Euclid Avenue of Cleveland.* 1932, vol. 1; 1937, vol. 2.

Chapter 12

THE BILL WILKERSON HEARING AND SPEECH CENTER

Freeman E. McConnell

Community Planning for Speech and Hearing Services

THE establishment and rapid development of the Bill Wilkerson Hearing and Speech Center in Nashville, Tennessee, which has attained widespread recognition for its comprehensive and specialized program for disorders of communication, has been noteworthy from a number of aspects, not the least of which is its excellent example of how community planning can provide high caliber professional service, together with the technical equipment needed, in a functional and attractive physical setting. In fact, not only this center, but the statewide Tennessee plan in speech and hearing has been often cited, particularly in the federal public health agencies, as an example of the effectiveness which may be gained by the willing cooperation of public and private agencies in achieving services needed for its handicapped citizens. The Wilkerson Center, inextricably linked with the total development of the state program in Tennessee, served as the original focus of this unified program and one of its chief implementing forces.

THE DEVELOPMENT OF A STATEWIDE PROGRAM

One cannot review the history and origins of this statewide movement without recognizing from the outset that dynamic and astute leadership was involved. Such a quality was indeed the catalyst which was required to muster the many forces in a cooperative endeavor in a specialty area which in 1950 was virtually unheard of in Tennessee. This catalyst was provided in the person of the late Dr. W. W. Wilkerson, Jr., a practicing otolaryngologist in Nashville. His vision and aspirations, together with his unusual facility for bringing together people from various walks of life in a concerted objective, was without doubt the noteworthy factor in the initial stages of the movement.

The name of the center was originally the Tennessee Hearing and Speech Foundation. As clinical centers developed in other areas of the state with stimulation of revenue from the state Crippled Children's Service,[1] the name, Tennessee Hearing and Speech Foundation, became inappropriate for the Nashville center, and reorganization under a new charter of incorporation became necessary. As a tribute to the pioneering effort and zealous perseverance in behalf of Tennessee's speech and hearing handicapped citizens, the board of directors announced at their June, 1951 monthly meeting that the Nashville center would henceforth be called the Bill Wilkerson Hearing and Speech Center in honor of the Wilkersons' only son, who lost his life in World War II. This young man was a Vanderbilt premedical student when he entered the armed services in 1944. His death occurred in February, 1945 during the Battle of the Bulge. These facts, which may seem irrelevant to the purpose of this chapter, are worthy of being noted for the sake of accuracy, for the center was not named *by* the family of this young soldier, but rather by a group of Nashville's outstanding civic leaders comprising the board at that time. The name, therefore, honors not only the young soldier but also Dr. Wilkerson and other members of the Wilkerson family whose support and unceasing energy in behalf of the program have been an excellent example of voluntary community effort.

The embryo concept of the center took shape in 1949 when Dr. Wilkerson established a steering committee. This committee (composed of Mr. Dan May, owner and president of May Hosiery Mills; Mr. Laurence B. Howard, an attorney; and Dr. Wilkerson) held its first meeting at the home of Mr. May. Several other civic leaders joined these three men in a pre-incorporation meeting on December 14, 1949, and a charter was drawn up and signed December 28, two weeks later. Soon after this incorporation, the group invited a professional consultant, Dr. Herbert Koepp-Baker, to come to Nashville to discuss the founding of a clinical center. His visit was followed by consultation with Dr. Stanley Ainsworth, then of Florida State University, who assisted the group in its preliminary planning for the establishment of a student training program to be affiliated with Vanderbilt University and Peabody College. Mr. William Geer, then of the State Education Office staff, gave continued and valued professional counsel in the early months before the center was staffed.

A significant event which occurred at about this time, and certainly not without some effective groundwork laid by the hearing and speech group, was an act of the General Assembly of the State of Tennessee in its 1951 session. The Assembly rewrote its legal definition of a crippled child which made it permissible for the Crippled Children's Service, Tennessee Department of Health, to consider those children with defects of speech and hearing as crippled or handicapped. The Assembly also appropriated to Crippled Children's Service an annual sum of $120,000 for special services in speech and hearing.[1] The Tennessee State Medical Association, through the Tennessee Academy of Ophthalmology and Otolaryngology, yielded their influence in the passage of this legislation.

In conformity with the appropriation, Crippled Children's Service put into operation on July 1, 1951 a statewide program designed to find, test, and refer for treatment children with speech and hearing disorders, and to provide prosthetic aids, clinical treatment and auxiliary services for all indigent children so handicapped. The health department program from the outset was planned in close coordination with the State Department of Education and with the Tennessee Hearing and Speech Foundation, which had become a statewide private, voluntary group with representatives from each area of the state. A major objective of the state public health and education agencies, in cooperation with the foundation, was the establishment of other clinical centers throughout the state. Following the incorporation of the Bill Wilkerson Center in Nashville in 1951, the next center to be established was the East Tennessee State College Speech and Hearing Center at Johnson City in 1952. In 1953 the Memphis Speech and Hearing Center, which had been in operation under Easter Seal sponsorship several years previously, elected to affiliate with the Tennessee Hearing and Speech Foundation program; in the same year the East Tennessee Hearing and Speech Center in Knoxville, the West Tennessee Hearing and Speech Center at Jackson, and the Chattanooga-Hamilton County Center, were organized and services established. Several years later the Bristol Speech and Hearing Center became the seventh and last center to become a member unit of the foundation program. By this time it was evident that Tennessee was committed to providing a diagnostic and treatment facility in every section of the state so that speech and hearing clinical services would be within commuter distance of every family.

ESTABLISHMENT OF THE BILL WILKERSON PROGRAM

The early years of the Bill Wilkerson Center were spent in an old residence owned by Vanderbilt University at 2109 Garland Avenue. A former Sigma Chi House and later a nurses' and dietitians' residence unit for the University Hospital, this building was adapted to accommodate a rapidly growing speech and hearing clinical service. Through the generous support of the city of Nashville, the Davidson County Health Department, the Davidson County Schools, and the United States Children's Bureau, a way was found within two months following the addition of a director-audiologist to begin services, and the first clinical case was seen on July 1, 1951. Upstairs bedrooms in the old house were partitioned into small therapy cubicles; excavation at the back of the building to extend the basement floor level afforded space for a double-room test suite for audiologic services. A $35,000 grant from the Children's Bureau made it possible to begin the service program with an excellent inventory of the specialized electronic and other types of equipment needed in the clinical management of communication disorders.

The staff of the center were imbued initially with a single purpose—the establishment of a high level of diagnostic and treatment service. In effect, this purpose required a public education program to convince a metropolitan population of 400,000 people that a speech and hearing clinical center is a necessary community resource. At the end of the first year, the staff consisted of one audiologist and one speech pathologist at the doctoral level, one each at the M.A. level, and one speech clinician at the bachelor's level, two secretaries and a maid.

Although service was, and is still, in important focus at the center, the center's governing board had insisted from the beginning that the best service to the public would be best insured by the development of a student training program. The influence of the medical center with its strong tradition of Vanderbilt as a teaching institution was undoubtedly a significant factor here. The Hearing and Speech Center was thus subject to these shaping concepts which dictated its direction, and at the same time forced center personnel to be an interpreter of their own professional role to other disciplines and to students.

Soon after the clinical program was underway, an agreement was reached whereby qualified members of the center staff were given faculty appointments both at Vanderbilt University and at Peabody College. Within two months after the center opened its doors to the public, it also launched its teaching program. Three courses were added to the curriculum in September 1951, and a division of audiology and speech was formed in the School of Medicine. The same courses were made available to students at Peabody College, although there was no special education department at that time. By the end of the first year, sufficient progress had occurred to warrant an application to the Children's Bureau for a training grant to help provide the cost of faculty salaries as well as stipends and tuition scholarships for graduate students. The first training grant at Vanderbilt was awarded in the summer of 1952, and five graduate students entered the program in September. The number of graduate students steadily increased each year, and more than one hundred master's degrees were awarded in the first ten years.

The third objective of the Bill Wilkerson Hearing and Speech Center, as defined by its own bylaws, is research in the areas of speech and hearing science, audiology and speech pathology. No attempt was made, however, to implement a research program until a firm foundation of clinical service and graduate education was well established. The graduate program contributed to the research training and experience of the staff, however, since each student receiving a master's degree from Vanderbilt was required to complete an experimental type thesis. The first grant-supported research project was initiated in 1957 with a study of the speech and language development of preschool deaf children. This project, which was supported by the National Institute of Neurological Diseases and Blindness extended over a five-year period, and was followed by numerous others from several Federal and private agencies.

In 1954 new plans for space became necessary for the Hearing and Speech Center when Vanderbilt announced their expansion program would require the land on which the old residence housing the center was located. The center subsequently purchased two large lots on 18th Avenue South, one of which included an old brick residence. Initial plans were in process to renovate this old home and make the necessary alterations required for a speech and hearing clinic when Dr. Wilkerson announced to the board of directors that he was expecting to ask for a $1,000,000 bond issue from the 1955 state legislature to build a comprehensive hearing and speech center.

Into this effort Dr. Wilkerson put himself wholeheartedly, determined not to fail. Although he had spent his life as a practicing physician in the region, he appeared to understand thoroughly the art of politics, for he left no stone unturned in his campaign to convince the entire body of legislators, each one individually, that Tennessee should provide this rehabilitation resource for its citizens with communicative disorders. He presented this program to them as an opportunity to place Tennessee in the ranks of those progressive states which were demonstrating their concern for the care of the disabled. In this effort, he solicited and obtained the support of Governor Frank Clement, State Health Commissioner R. H. Hutcheson, and Davidson County Health Director John J. Lentz. Governor Clement's active interest and innovations in the area of mental health was a timely factor, of course, and Dr. Wilkerson had always taken advantage of every opportunity to relate speech and hearing to public health.

By presenting a blueprint for the future in which hearing and speech centers could be built by the state in other regions if the Nashville model were successful, the support of all the Tennessee Hearing and Speech Foundation Clinics was obtained. Thus, legislators from each section of the state were influenced favorably for the plan, and so much so that every member of the lower house voted *aye,* and every member of the senate but one. The next biennial legislature in 1957 passed a bond issue for centers to be built at Jackson, Johnson City and Knoxville, while the 1959 General Assembly approved one for Memphis. The Chattanooga Center was built through private philanthropy while the Bristol Center was housed adequately at that time in Bristol Memorial Hospital.

Although Vanderbilt University offered a site on the campus for the center, the regulations governing state-owned buildings prohibited this arrangement. The board was required to deed the land it had purchased to the state. The state in turn rented the center back to the board at one dollar a year, and the lease is written to continue ninety-nine years. The only stipulation is that the center be used to further the work in speech and hearing. About one-third of the ultimate cost of the building ($1,200,000) was assumed by the Federal Government through the provisions of the Hill-Burton Act and the Vocational Rehabilitation Administration.

The ground-breaking ceremony for the construction of this facility was held on May 2, 1956. The building was completed in early January, 1958, and the staff removed its operation from its old quarters on Garland Avenue to the new structure at 19th Avenue South at Edgehill on January 27, 1958. The construction of this one-unit comprehensive speech and hearing facility was not only the first of its kind in the State of Tennessee, but actually the first speech and hearing center not part of a state college or university to be built by a state legislature appropriation anywhere in the United States.

The center is ideally located virtually in the heart of Nashville's university and medical center complex. Standing on a corner lot, the three-story structure presents an exterior finished in old English pink face brick. At the front entrance a Virginia greenstone facade with Indiana limestone trim breaks the monotony of the nearly windowless building. Cast aluminum sculpturing to represent the speech and hearing theme is placed above the main entrance. These sculptures, the work of the artist Julian Harris of Atlanta, depict the anatomical outline of the vocal folds and the ear, between which stand two youths, a boy and a girl, representing the agelessness characterizing speech and hearing problems which may occur in early childhood or in the senior years. Through all-glass doors at the main entrance light streams into the main lobby onto walls of Vermont marble and terrazzo flooring. Tennessee marble and terrazzo are carried through the main stairwells leading to the first and third floors off the lobby. All materials for the building were carefully chosen both from the standpoint of durability and for being as maintenance-free as possible. The area in square feet for each of the three floors is as follows: first floor, 14,658; second floor, 14,658; third floor, 6,712—making a total floor space of 36,028 square feet.[2]

Planning for six basic areas was incorporated into the floor plan design. Four of these areas are those used specifically for (1) clinical services; (2) teaching of students, and (3) research; (4) preschool education represents a special area, though as a function it may be thought of as a part of clinical services. Added to the four just mentioned are (5) public and administrative areas, and (6) general service areas, the latter for utility and maintenance. A mechanical shop, printing and duplicating room, and television monitoring room are also included in general service. Public and administrative areas include lobbies, rest rooms, reception rooms on each floor and the auditorium. Each reception room is partitioned to provide attractively for both children and adults, and each serves a particular service or function in the building, one being near the Hearing Clinic, one near the Speech Clinic, and one on the third floor, which is used primarily as a speech therapy area.

Administrative spaces include a main business office, central records room, departmental secretarial offices and an office for the building manager. Also, in this group are the offices of administrative and supervisory personnel of the clinic and faculty as well as a staff conference room for both the Speech and Hearing clinics.

FINANCIAL SUPPORT

It is the service program which distinguishes the center as a community agency with a wide base of community support. Foremost in local support from the beginning of the program has been the local Health Department. A substantial annual allocation of unrestricted funds is made through the Metropolitan Nashville and Davidson County Department of Health. In exchange for this valuable financial support the center makes any of its services available without charge to any resident within the county who has been certified as medically indigent by the health department. From one-third to one-half of the clinical population each year is comprised of such patients. The public health leadership and farsighted vision which was manifested in this recognition of communicative disorders as a public health problem at the local level is a great tribute to the man who served as Nashville's public health director for more than forty years, Dr. John J. Lentz.

Another public health agency which has supported speech and hearing clinical services is the Crippled Children's Service of the Tennessee State Health Department,[3] whose case-finding program was alluded to earlier. Their direct financial assistance in the form of salary costs to each of the seven clinical centers in the state, including the Bill Wilkerson Center, makes available the diagnostic and remedial services needed for any indigent child in the state from birth to twenty-one years of age.

A distinguishing characteristic of the Bill Wilkerson Center has always been the wide base of its financial support to include both public and private voluntary agencies. This feature of its developmental pattern has perhaps been the result of the philosophy of its board and staff, which has consistently refused to define its role in any narrowly restricted sense as it pertains to functions involved in the remediation of a communication disorder. Thus, preschool education has always been an integral part of the service program, not on the basis of subsuming public education responsibility, but rather to complement what the schools offer the handicapped child, and further, to encourage and stimulate the development of special education facilities in the local schools. It was in this light that the active cooperation and financial assistance of the local school system was sought and successfully obtained from the beginning of the program. The Metropolitan Government Board of Education makes an annual budget allocation to support the cost of two preschool teachers and a supervisor in the program for deaf and hard of hearing children at the center. The supervisor also has responsibility for the day classes in the local schools, thereby affording a sequence of consistent instruction for such children from infancy to high school age.

Other community support comes from United Givers Fund, which makes a combined budget appropriation to the Nashville League for the Hard of Hearing and the center. The center receives assistance from the UGF which is used mainly in its hearing aid program for indigent elderly persons. Center patients are referred to the league for social and recreational services, for help with transportation, and for other problems not actually cared for or alleviated by the clinical diagnostic and treatment program of the center. The Pi Beta Phi Sorority Alumnae of Vanderbilt University, the Society for the Preservation of Barbershop Quartet Singing in America, the Davidson County Society for Crippled Children and Adults, the Nashville Pan-Hellenic Council and the Civitan Club are other groups which have made major financial contributions to the center, the first three of these now on an annual basis. The Pi Phi's and the SPBQSA stage an annual benefit performance as the source of this revenue.

MAJOR FUNCTIONS OF THE CENTER

Clinical Services

There are three service departments within the center, the Audiology Clinic, the Speech Pathology Clinic and the Education Department, each headed by a master clinician or educator. All incoming patients are referred either to the Audiology or the Speech Pathology Clinic on the basis of whether or not the individual requesting service is considered or suspected to have a hearing impairment. The staffs of the two clinics coordinate their time and efforts on all children under six who are reported to have either delay in or absence of oral language development, and a jointly staffed Language Clinic is held three times a week for all infants and children six and under. Depending upon the findings from the Language Clinic, the child's treatment program is scheduled in the Audiology Clinic, or he will come under the management of the Speech Pathology Clinic. The Education Department is mainly responsible for the preschool education of hearing impaired children and those with severe language disorders from other causes.

All deaf infants seen in the first or second year of life are referred to the Home Teaching Project, which is a parent-centered program funded as a United States Office of Education project. Mothers with their children are scheduled for weekly or twice weekly sessions in a demonstration home located in the same block as the center. The house is furnished as an ordinary home, and the project is staffed by teachers of the deaf who work with the mother and her child to demonstrate how the daily activities of the home can be utilized to lay a foundation for the child's receptive language development through speechreading and through hearing. An audiologist is assigned to this project two days a week to counsel the parents on the use of hearing and hearing aids and to carry out the diagnostic tests and periodic checks on the children.

After the home program, children at about two and one-half years normally will enter the preschool at the center. Here they are seen daily five days a week from 8:30 to 12:00 noon. There are two major groups, one consisting of three and four-year-olds and the other of five and six-year-olds. At six the children leave this program for either the state residential school for the deaf, a private residential school of the parents' choosing, or the day class program for acoustically handicapped children in the metropolitan public schools. Some few children may go into regular first grade from the preschool program depending upon degree of hearing loss, age of onset and other factors. These children, as with those in the home teaching project, are closely monitored by the Audiology Clinic from the standpoint of hearing aid management and use of hearing and a staff audiologist is assigned two mornings a week to the preschool. Other children who live at a greater distance are scheduled for small group instruction two and three times a week in the afternoons, usually from one to two hours each, by a teacher of the deaf. Approximately fifty deaf and hard of hearing preschool children are carried in the instructional program of the Education Department. The Education Department also has responsibility for tutorial assistance and communication skills training for all school-age children.

The program for hearing impaired teen-agers and adults, in which diagnostic service and some ongoing treatment are required is a function of the Audiology Clinic, whose staff members provide this service with the assistance of graduate students. A special project of the Audiology Clinic is the Senior Citizens Program which has a different rationale and concept. Instead of beginning with the diagnostic examination at the center on request of the patient or his physician, the staff takes its services to the Senior

Citizens Center where these elderly people are already congregated. The premise of this program is first to demonstrate to the older person that he can be helped with specialized instruction in lipreading and listening training. After a period of such instruction, a number are gradually able to accept the diagnostic procedure at the clinic, as well as the hearing aid and other recommended audiologic handling. This group constitutes the only patients that are seen or treated without the medical referral prior to the diagnostic examination.

Other functions of the Audiology Clinic include diagnostic services, such as the children's hearing clinic, adult hearing clinics and hearing aid selection for all age groups. In most instances the hearing aid selection follows the hearing evaluation in a second visit, and a program of training with a loaner hearing aid to determine the usefulness of the instrument for a particular person may be recommended. Arrangements are also made with local hearing aid dealers to rent hearing aids for a trial period to those who are not ready to accept the permanent recommendation. The monthly rental fee is then applied to the cost of the hearing aid if the patient decides later to make the purchase.

In the Medical Center in which the Bill Wilkerson Center is located, it is often necessary to see individuals for audiologic testing on an immediate referral basis, particularly where special tests to determine site of lesion may be needed as part of the information needed by the otolaryngologist in making decisions regarding feasibility of surgery or other medical handling. One staff audiologist devotes one-half time to the immediate referral program so that any person may be seen on an immediate basis upon referral from the various hospital ENT clinics or from any of the private otolaryngologists in the city.

Another program of the Audiology Clinic is that of hearing aid orientation, a series of six hourly sessions for groups of two to six. A better understanding of the nature of the hearing problem is afforded the patient, together with a trial use of hearing aids, auditory training and initial lipreading instruction. For those with more difficult hearing problems, this program may be followed by individual work in lipreading or auditory training. In all cases, the philosophy of the Audiology Clinic is that the ongoing management of the communication needs of the hearing impaired individual is essential to adequate service, whether relating to the preschool child, the school-age child, the teen-ager or the adult. Every attempt is made to channel him into the proper educational setting and/or to assist him with vocational and social problems resulting from his hearing loss. In conjunction with the Hearing Clinic, the services of a staff psychologist one day a week may be used. A Vocational Rehabilitation Counselor from the local district visits the center once a week for conferences with audiology staff on those patients needing assistance with vocational placement or in how best to help him keep the job he has, and there is a full-time staff social worker to assist with these problems.

The Speech Pathology Clinic offers a wide variety of services for the various types of speech disorders not related to hearing impairment. At the preschool level, this staff offers educational programs for cerebral palsied children and for children with delayed language. The cerebral palsy children leave the preschool at six and are enrolled in the special cerebral palsy classes in the public schools. Through an arrangement with the schools, sequence of speech handling is made possible by having one center staff clinician offering therapy service two mornings a week in the special classes for those children.

One staff clinician is housed full-time at Vanderbilt University Hospital in the Physical Rehabilitation Unit, where she provides speech services and counselling for inpatients at the hospital, follows their progress immediately before and after surgery or other medical regimes and makes referrals to the Hearing and Speech Center for follow-up treatment after they leave the hospital. She also attends the various clinics in the hospital where she offers consultant assistance and screening evaluations. Her presence at the Cerebral Palsy Clinic, the Ear, Nose and Throat Clinic, and the Birth Defects Clinic insures referral on to the Hearing and Speech Center for more thorough diagnostic work-up for those patients appearing to require speech help.

Special group programs with adult stutterers, with laryngectomees, and with aphasics are scheduled in an effort to give the individual the supportive therapy needed. Individual service may precede, follow, or be concomitant with this program. The center sponsors a Lost Chord Club which serves the Middle Tennessee area for post-laryngectomy adults. Special classes for preschool children with language disorders have been found highly successful in alleviating some of the learning disorders related to speech and language functioning. Emphasis is on both comprehension and expression of language. The Initial Teaching Alphabet as a visual reenforcement is used to assist the child with articulation defects, and the Peabody Language Development Kit has been found valuable. Children at four and five years are referred to these programs, in which they are grouped on the basis of whether their problem is primarily a receptive or expressive one. Many of these youngsters develop a readiness for articulation therapy at five and one-half or six, at which time they are much better prepared to benefit from the more formalized instruction program in articulation therapy. Their ability to enter first grade is also enhanced by the previous experiences in this program.

Preparation of Students

In addition to the Clinical Services Program, the center from the beginning has had as one of its main objectives the training of students in remediation of speech, hearing and language disorders. Preparation of professional personnel in the areas of speech pathology, audiology and teaching the deaf has offered a continuing challenge to those in training institutions to provide the kinds of experiences necessary to their adequate performance upon leaving the university.

The Bill Wilkerson Hearing and Speech Center with its diversified facilities and functions has constituted a valuable resource for the instruction of specialist personnel. An annual case load of approximately 3,500 individuals a year, a monthly therapy program being offered to 300-400 persons, and a diagnostic schedule providing 200-300 examinations a month are at the disposal of the faculty. Beyond that, the center through its extension into the community, has added to its program a number of valuable resources for training outside the center. Included in these extramural programs are the Vanderbilt University Hospital with its various outpatient clinics, previously mentioned, the Ear, Nose and Throat Clinic of the Metropolitan General Hospital, the Metropolitan Public School Speech Correction Program, and the Metropolitan Public Schools Special Education Programs for cerebral palsied children and for acoustically handicapped children. Through a consultant arrangement with the State Hospital and School for Retarded Children, located in nearby Donelson, staff clinicians are supervised from the center and in turn the school is afforded therapy service of graduate students.

As medical and public health personnel have become aware of the impact upon rehabilitation that our professions offer, the opportunities for diversified placement have multiplied. Consequently, it behooves the training institution to insure that they offer sufficiently comprehensive service programs to include public and hospital clinics in which many of the more severe and unusual problems are handled in order that their graduates may be adequately prepared to meet these challenges later. The need for a wide range of clinic services oriented toward communicative disorders of any type and without exclusive and specific age groups is vital to the training institution. Consequently, the Bill Wilkerson Center has had as its philosophy the development of a program which would give two major advantages to their students—first, an appreciation for the large scope of the field of communication disorders and second, to help them develop flexibility and self-confidence in handling a variety of age groups as well as problems. While considerable emphasis is placed upon diagnostic skills, it is not to the exclusion of therapeutic ones, for the ability to observe with insight the communicative behavior of an individual in all its facets is considered an important teaching objective.

Clinical teaching is planned to help the student learn to interpret his impressions not only to co-workers, but also to counsel individual patients and their families in a way that properly combines the necessary degree of optimism with realism. Sympathy, not pity, and sincerity, not effusiveness, in the counseling sessions are sought. The relations the Hearing and Speech Center have developed include various extramural affiliations, including the hospital setting in which the clinician may be called upon to make a tentative evaluation and prognosis after a brief ward visit. The student apprentice must learn to see that such situations require a maximum ability to size up quickly all pertinent observations, history, findings and subjective impressions. When made aware of the importance of such observation power, the student then has the opportunity to develop sound professional relationships with others, which in turn will be reflected in a constant interchange of opinion and knowledge that make for a most ideal working environment. In therapy as in diagnostic procedures, keen observation powers and an inquiring mind and personal warmth are each important. High on the requirement list is the ability to adjust to a clinical situation which may deviate from methods learned as a student. The Hearing and Speech Center, therefore, welcomes innovation by its staff members on ways of handling problems. Rigid adherence to one particular method may prevent growth, although the student in his educational program is provided with certain techniques and experiences to support him with definite guideposts in the beginning. The educational program which is best is the one in which he learns he is free to depart from these techniques if necessary as he adjusts to the dynamic conditions of the field of audiology, speech pathology and special education.

Research

The research program at the center is the most recently initiated, since this aspect of functioning was planned to emerge and develop following the establishment of a sound clinical service and a high quality teaching program. Center personnel have, however, participated in a considerable number of research studies supported by the National Institutes of Health and the United States Office of Education. In addition, through a close affiliation with the Division of Otolaryngology at Vanderbilt, studies in Cochlear microphonics and vestibular functioning, and the operation of a Temporal Bone Bank Laboratory sponsored by the Deafness Research Foundation are carried on within the center.

The value of a research program is reflected in the stimulation afforded the clinical staff, who may be assisted to develop a greater degree of scientific inquiry into their own activities. The center is also able to attract a higher level of personnel, which in turn enhances the level of the total program within the community, and ultimately, the speech and hearing handicapped themselves derive the benefit from the integrated efforts of clinicians, teachers and researchers.

BIBLIOGRAPHY

1. Foote, R., and Hutcheson, R.: Private medicine and public health meet a challenge. *J Tenn Med Ass, 44*:352-354, 1951.
2. McConnell, F.: Planning of a multi-purpose speech and hearing facility. *ASHA, 2*:175-177, 1960.
3. McConnell, F., and Wilkerson, W.: A hearing and speech center is organized. *J Tenn Med Ass, 44*:395-398, 1951.

Chapter 13

INSTITUTE OF LOGOPEDICS, INCORPORATED

ETHEL M. UMPHREY

"COMMUNICATION is civilization's cornerstone," stated Marconi, yet communicative disorders constitute a tragic and frequently preventable economic state throughout our entire social structure. Among them are the problems of cerebral palsy, stuttering, cleft palate, retardation, aphasia, visual difficulties, hearing losses, dysphonia, mongolism, voice loss after laryngectomy and disorders of intelligibility.

It is difficult to arrive at an accurate estimate of the number of people with problems of communication in the United States alone. The commonly accepted figure of 5 per cent of the population would find some ten million persons with greater or lesser degrees of handicaps at the present time. This estimate is based on populations below the age of twenty-one, and is the result of many hundreds of surveys. The extent of adult conditions can only be guessed, but we do know that the number of persons with aphasia as the result of strokes and similar conditions, automobile accidents, etc., is steadily growing with no spontaneous recovery or no significant improvement with age. Losses of hearing which will happen to all of us from illness or aging, constitute a universal problem and are almost unanswered.

Just how handicapped *are* these individuals with problems of communication? First, the lack of understanding of their problems and depriving them of help causes them to be isolated and misused by our society. With faulty speech a child will be one to six grades behind the normal school level and, as an adult, his earning power will be reduced 25 per cent. The speech handicapped cannot be full members of society because man often judges others by their speech, their written word, and how much they *seem* to know. Second, this group constitutes a serious economic burden upon society. In more severe cases the individual may be shut away at home and thus deprived of his potential as a human being, or be institutionalized at great cost to family or state. Until recently the only state residential institutions for such children were those for the mentally deficient. Yet the cost of rehabilitation is less in dollars and infinitely more useful and rewarding to mankind. Third, this group constitutes a serious social weakness in time of great national stress. Modern industry, modern warfare, all of modern life increasingly depend on communication and communicative skills. (The loss of manpower in these endeavors from hearing disabilities alone is conceivably great.) Fourth, if all the varieties of speech and hearing disorders were gathered together they unquestionably would form the largest single handicapped group in our society today . . . and there is no reason to believe the ratio is any less in other nations. In short, this segment of the population that is or will be affected by speech and hearing problems does pose an overwhelming problem from the standpoints of simple humanitarian decency, self-interests of economics, strength of society and numbers.

Any problem as broad and as urgent as this must be attacked in a systematic and organized manner. The Institute of Logopedics was founded for this purpose with three basic areas that are integratively supported and utilized: (1) clinical services; (2) professional education of logopedists, and (3) research.

The field of habilitation of communicative disorders is relatively young in this country. The American Speech and Hearing Association was founded in 1925 by nineteen persons. They represented nearly all of the individuals interested at that time. In 1930, recognition of the problem was given when the White House Conference of that year attempted to develop some estimates of the prevalence of those handicaps. The reason for this long neglect was a general public attitude that disordered speech must reflect a disordered mind. Nothing could be further from the scientific truth. The problems of cerebral palsy, mental retardation, cleft palate, stuttering, aphasia, etc., all are intimately connected with disturbances of speech and hearing.

In 1934, when the Institute of Logopedics was born, habilitative programs for these distressing handicaps were limited to a few services for minor defects in some public school systems, and experimental research clinics in connection with some of the larger universities. There were no professional standards. An interested person could go to a university, take one course and start to learn how to teach by his own tragic errors with the troubled people who came to see him. Enough has been learned to know that we can increase the precision of our diagnostic skills. We not only can increase the number of persons who are being habilitated into useful citizens, but we can reduce the time it takes to manage such habilitation. Finally, we must not lose sight of the ultimate goal of prevention which by no means is out of sight or unattainable. Communication is not the simple thing it may seem to those of us who have no difficulty with it.

CLINICAL SERVICES

One unique feature of the Institute of Logopedics lies in the availability of a complete habilitative program in one plant, a multi-disciplined program for even the most severely handicapped individual. It is the most complex aspect of human behavior. Impairments in the processes of communication (speech, language and hearing) leave myriad problems in their wake. Children with disorders of communication may encounter overwhelming obstacles to learning and may find it difficult, even impossible, to establish relationships with others which are essential to growing up to healthy, stable adulthood. The adult who acquires a speech or hearing disorder may experience a variety of social problems. His livelihood may be endangered; he may withdraw from his family and friends and cease to be a participating member of his family and community.

The institute's philosophy of habilitating the child necessitated the availability of a program which would offer all the services that even the most severely handicapped child could need. To do this it was necessary to bring together under one roof all the disciplines. Services also exist for young adults and older people who have lost their speech through accidents, strokes, illness or from other causes.

Pre-examination and evaluation by the examining staff of the institute are required before a person may be accepted for habilitative training. Appointments are made (by parents or guardian of a minor) in advance to allow time for completion of the pre-examination medical reports. The medical director of the institute sends a letter outlining procedures for completion of these.

The only requirements for the evaluation are that a person have a speech, hearing, or communicative disorder; and that the medical reports be received before the appointment date. Adults as well as children receive training at the institute.

Speech training which is the basis of each individual's program is speech habilitation. Lessons are administered on a private basis in individual training rooms. Lessons learned in the speech room are carried over and integrated into every other area of the child's program.

Special education subjects include an area from prekindergarten to high school in classrooms. These are designed to meet the needs of children too handicapped to progress in public schools, such as the multiply handicapped child who may have cerebral palsy, a hearing loss and a visual problem; or one with cerebral palsy, aphasia and hearing or visual loss; or any combination of handicapping conditions. In addition to the three R's, regular subjects such as history, science, spelling, geography, typing, etc. are taught allowing each child to learn at his own rate of speed and according to his own capabilities.

Approximately one-fourth of the enrollment at the institute has cerebral palsy, and many of them are unable to walk. Physical therapy teaches these children step by step the same basic physical accomplishments and skills that normal children acquire during growth and development. Registered physical therapists, under the orthopedist's direction, teach sitting and standing balance, plus all forms of locomotion so that the children and adults will reach their highest level of physical accomplishments.

The integrated team approach can be clearly demonstrated in occupational therapy. For example, a child will be practicing the sitting balance learned in physical therapy while sitting on a chair attempting to tie his shoe, a skill learned in occupational therapy. At the same time, his therapist has been clued by the speech instructor to observe and correct any mistakes in his articulation in speech. Every facet of the child's habilitative training is integrated into the other, and tied together by an institute preceptor (supervisor) who guides and evaluates the child's program, and by frequent staffings of all professional people working with the child.

Occupational therapy includes teaching of eye-hand coordination, self-helps such as eating, dressing, personal grooming, typing, simple crafts, etc.

Adjuncts of occupational therapy are home arts involving cooking, sewing, grooming, simple home decorating, etiquette, typing and other skills for girls, and similar skills for boys.

Original research and practice at the institute demonstrated that all possible avenues of communication should be utilized for maximum results. The first experiences of the human beings were art, the first and pure forms of communication, and development of new roads into oral communication.

Fine arts utilized at the institute with communicatively handicapped children include the following:

1. Creative arts such as painting, ceramics, weaving, charcoal work, collage design, sculpture, etc., are self-expression through communication. In addition, the children develop their manual dexterity, learn about color, line and design, and explore their creative talent. Creative art has revealed that they can create abstract art under special circumstances. Thus the total abstracting concept is not a lost function, but it is present and can be developed.

2. Interactive musiatrics is a natural growth from observations made over a thirty-year period by Dr. Palmer that the musical areas of the brain are practically invulnerable to circulatory accidents. Music has always been used as another avenue to communication at the institute. In interactive musiatrics, the instructor who is a graduate logopedist and musician works individually with the children in order to bring interaction between himself and the child, which many times is the intervening wedge leading to speech. This response may be accomplished in many ways. One of the approaches is through music especially composed for each child. The child's

response may come from his knowledgeable use of a drum or other rhythm instruments, the piano, singing, or perhaps simply through rhythmic bodily movements in response to the music. This interaction of the child and instructor through music is proving clinically successful, especially with children who have neurological damage.

3. DRAMATICS participation has no less appeal for handicapped children than for normal ones. Most children enjoy "play acting" and dramatics offers an effective lead into oral communication. Many programs involving drama and music are presented by the children. They constantly amaze their audiences with their versatility and comprehension of dramatic implications.

4. CREATIVE DANCE. With many handicapped children the sensory pathways leading to bodily coordination are undamaged, as with the musical areas. With some such children, creative dance can be the wedge leading to a breakthrough in speech. In the joy and self-expression of creative dancing some children are stimulated to communicate their ideas to each other, and this may be their very first expression of true communication.

In keeping with the institute's complete philosophy of habilitation of the whole child, communication alone is not enough. Many children with multiple handicaps can be equipped to earn a living partially or completely. To this end there exist vocational habilitative services to those who can profit from them.

Complete residential care is offered so the communicative habilitation can be best done when under control twenty-four hours a day. The institute has a special residential plan that offers a different concept relative to the economics and progress of habilitating the handicapped. Children and adults are cared for in comfortable family type groups of not more than three to each housemother or house parents. They eat, sleep, play, study, have parties, journey back and forth to classes, attend religious services and enjoy other pleasures of home life in these surroundings. The houseparent's proximity to the children, regular observation of the actual lessons, and the personal care and mutual affection make the housemother or father an integral part of the child's life and training program; and assure that gains of the day will be carried over into every facet of the child's life around the clock. This type of residential living closely approximates a normal home life and the institutional or hospital atmospheres are avoided.

The institute medical director, a pediatrician, supervises the program of health of the institute community. He reviews pre-enrollment medical information on each trainee, and maintains a periodic check on each case to be sure that he is reporting for medical examination to his personal physician. Each case maintains his own medical relationship with medical physicians in Wichita. Two registered nurses are on call twenty-four hours a day.

The medical director for cerebral palsy, an orthopedist, makes recommendations and supervises the program for individuals with cerebral palsy and other motor problems. This includes physical and occupational therapies, bracing and corrective surgery with a surgeon of the family's choice. Consultant relationships are maintained in otolaryngology, neurology, psychiatry, internal medicine and other specialties.

Physical education classes give boys and girls an opportunity to learn body building exercises and care. They also participate in games and sports where they learn body coordination and realize the importance of teamwork and good sportsmanship. The program is under the direction of a logopedist with a degree in physical education. For some handicapped children this program offers the first opportunity they have had to participate in competitive sports, and the tournaments for some of the advanced students generate enthusiasm and competition that further equip them for life in a normal world.

Believing that one's complete personality and potential cannot be developed unless his experience includes the religious factor in life, religious education and counsel are available to all trainees. The Sigma Alpha Inter-Faith Chapel offers services for Protestant, Catholic and Hebrew faiths, and ministers in each faith are available for counsel. Sunday school lessons and church services, led by the institute chaplain, are designed to allow participation by all the children, and here again the child has an opportunity to utilize his newly found speech in singing, story telling and other responses.

Camp Logos is a day camp located about twenty miles from the institute. Sessions of two weeks each are held during the summer, and clinical activities continue at camp. The camp director and most of the staff are logopedists assisted by volunteers who are interested in working with handicapped children. In a different and healthful atmosphere, the boys and girls share new and broader experiences which help to develop new language skills, stimulate speech and add immeasurably to their mental, physical and spiritual growth.

All children have a desire to participate in group activities with others of their own age. Here again the institute's habilitative program considers the total needs of each child, such as Scouting for both boys and girls, Junior Optimist Club for boys, Camp Fire Girls groups, and various hobby clubs such as photography, stamp collecting, electronics, etc. Visits to historical and industrial places of interest, and participation in drives such as the March of Dimes also help to develop a child's sense of "belonging" to the community . . . and will help him adjust to his own community upon his return home.

Supervised recreation plays an important part in their lives. This includes use of special playground equipment accompanying each apartment unit; general equipment, basketball, baseball, picnics, parties, and attendance at plays, movies, circuses and other entertainments provided by Wichita friends and business men. These activities furnish new subjects for speech, and sometimes, under the joyous pressure of a particularly happy and exciting moment, a child may utter his very first word.

Children from outside Wichita with less severe handicaps are given speech habilitation at the twenty-three field centers in Kansas. Staff members of the centers are logopedists trained in the Department of Logopedics of the institute, who teach under the strict supervision of qualified institute preceptors. The first such center was established in 1936.

While all types of communicative disorders are represented in the enrollment at the field centers, disorders of intelligibility and stuttering are most prevalent. The centers also act as examining and referral centers for more severe cases who need to come to the institute for the complete habilitative program.

In spite of the need for their services and the potential value of their work, competent logopedists are woefully few according to the need—for each one now active in the profession, ten are needed.

Logopedics is a complex and multi-faceted profession; competence requires extensive study of numerous subject matter areas plus clinical experience. Since the beginning year of 1934, the institute and the Department of Logopedics have cooperated for the education and training of workers in this area. The institute, as training and remedial center, makes available to the department whatever of its facilities and extensive services may be needed for the development of clinical insight and competence by the students. The department, a subject-matter division of the Wichita State University and the Department in the College of Education, is responsible for the academic courses that form part of established university programs of study.

Preparation for service as a logopedist requires varied experience and supervised clinical work with a wide range of disabilities. It also demands extensive and precise knowledge of the structure and function of the human being and his communicative processes. Thus, by the time he receives his first academic degree, the student will have of necessity extended and enriched his work in logopedics by study in other departments of the university courses in the humanities, biological and social sciences and education to increase his understanding of the complexities of human communicative behavior, his knowledge of the deviation of structure or function that handicap or prevent normal performace, and—of equal importance—his information concerning reliable diagnostic and remedial procedures.

With the knowledge and his clinical experience under the supervision of the institute, the logopedist has completed the program for his bachelor's degree and acquired the foundations for his later work, either as a therapist under supervision, or more appropriately, as a graduate student.

Though research is listed as a separate activity, it is an integral part of all institute activities. Formally or informally defined, it's the seeking of new knowledge. Whoever asks a question and attempts to find a reliable answer is doing research. He may be working in a laboratory, or the classroom, with apparatus or without. Why? How often? How many? I wonder? What would happen if? These questions are asked many times at the institute.

From the original group of three, the institute staff now includes slightly over 350 people, offering a wide variety of training and preparation and carrying many responsibilities of this overall program of remedial and educational work.

At their invitation, Dr. Palmer has visited numerous foreign countries and consulted with their leaders pertaining to their nation's speech and hearing problems. For example, in 1960, the World Health Organization selected him to act as consultant to the Japanese Ministry of Health, Education and Welfare to analyze existing rehabilitative conditions for the communicatively handicapped of that country, and to make recommendations on the work done. As a result the government of Japan sent physicians, surgeons, nurses and lay people to study logopedics at the institute. In 1965, the Bell Welfare Clinic for Speech and Hearing was founded in Japan and staffed by people who received their professional education at the institute. The clinic also serves as a complement to the programs at the University of Tokyo School of Medicine and the University of Osaka, which also have graduate logopedists on their staffs.

In 1963, Dr. Palmer visited India to lay ground work for a model communication center patterned after the institute. Four days before his death on August 13, 1965, the All-India Institute of Logopedics at Mysore, India, was opened. It is staffed by Indian students trained at the institute, and personnel from the institute will journey to India for periodic supervision and recommendations for the infant All-India Institute of Logopedics.

During 1965, over 11,500 individual speech lessons were given to a total of 2,241 cases. Nine hundred and ninety-one of these cases were dismissed to return to their homes as communicating, contributing citizens. Other services included over 5,000 orthopedic and other examinations, approximately 35,000 agency and family contacts, almost 30,000 physical education lessons, 11,000 occupational therapy lessons (including creative arts), about 9,000 physical therapy lessons and numerous other services. The majority of children in training received charitable aid, with more requesting it, despite the fact that training costs at the institute are as low as any in the nation for comparable services.

The institute is a prime example of free enterprise. From the beginning it has been a not-for-profit, self-supporting venture. No individual is refused help because of lack of finances. Last year the institute depended on one million and a half of its current two million dollar operating budget to be raised through one charitable source or another. The clinical work is completely dependent upon fees of parents who are asked to pay whatever they can (which accounts for about 25 per cent of the clinical costs), limited state and county funds for specific children, United Funds which screen their own applications and gifts from individuals, foundations, civic, fraternal and social organizations. The professional education of logopedists requires considerable funds per year which must come from charitable sources, and funds for the support of the very important program of research must be raised.

Dr. Martin Palmer had planned to retire from active administration in October of 1965 in order to devote his time to research, clinical work and teaching. In preparation for that time he had worked out a detailed plan for the growth of the institute in the next thirty years. So complete and feasible are the plans that, despite his death, they are furnishing the blueprint for the future of the institute.

The institute's National Board of Trustees recently launched Phase I of a $15,000,000 program of expansion of services and physical facilities. Called "The Dr. Martin F. Palmer Logopedics Development Fund," in his memory, its purposes are varied. They include the following:

> Additional and improved clinical services and expansion of the case load. For example, work with victims of cardiovascular accidents (stroke cases) will be expanded and affiliation has been made with local hospitals to increase work in this area. A deeper evaluation program involving all of the sciences and medicines will be developed to make sure that all valuable information pertinent to the child's condition is at hand. Enlarged special academic facilities and opportunities will be made available to more children and adults with cerebral palsy, aphasia, hearing or visual losses, or a combination of these handicapping conditions.
>
> All research will be expanded and intensified. One problem which had concerned Dr. Palmer was the separation of individuals from the categorical classification of mental retardation. For years, children with various handicaps had been tossed into this category with little or no thought to the cause of their inability to learn. At the institute, work is being done in discovering the problem causing the condition. Once it is found and isolated, the condition in many cases can be alleviated with

astonishing results. For example, many children with cerebral palsy have been removed from this classification, and Dr. Palmer's work in aphasia has started to separate that group. Other conditions labeled as mental retardation need to be studied in this manner.

To meet the tremendous demand and fulfill the serious obligation to the field in the professional education of logopedists, the institute will enlarge its program of fellowships and scholarships, while continuing to offer the finest quality of professional education.

To reach these objectives, a 50 per cent expansion of physical facilities is required. This will take the form of west and north wing additions to the present administration building, which will provide additional space for special education for more children and adults. Another proposed building will be the Children's Theater for Speech Arts and Sciences.

The story of the institute, and the future of the institute, is the story of Martin Palmer's life, a life dedicated to the cause of equipping children and adults for better lives through communication. In a world where nations and men with industrial, military, civic and social responsibilities increasingly depend on communicative skills, it is the sole purpose of the institute to bring mankind's most important tool, speech, to as many people as possible.

Communication is the cornerstone on which the speechless can build new and better lives. It is only through the proven integrated three fold program of clinical services, research and professional education of logopedists that these tragedies can be alleviated. The results do not carry the dramatic impact of a spectacular new vaccine or drug, yet the end results in the lives of the rescued victims are just as spectacular and just as rewarding.

Viewed with impartial and clinical objectivity, after almost thirty-four years of living proof, it is a fact that most of the speech handicapped can be habilitated into communicating, contributing citizens. In the words of Dr. Palmer, scientist, pioneer in speech, teacher and humanitarian, *There are no hopeless speech handicapped individuals, but only those whom we have not yet learned how to teach.*

Chapter 14

THE SUTTER DIAGNOSTIC AND TREATMENT CENTER

EDWARD RUDIN

FOR a number of years the Community Welfare Council of the Greater Sacramento Area and the Sacramento Area Mental Health Association had urged the development of psychiatric services for children, with emphasis on outpatient services. Several studies throughout the 1950's and early 1960's had confirmed the need. Meanwhile, the Sacramento Hearing Society began to identify the need for a sophisticated resource for evaluation and treatment of hearing and speech problems. Local physicians complained of the difficulties in having to refer hearing, speech and psychiatric patients to facilities and services eighty miles or more away.

In the early 1960's Sutter Community Hospitals began to consider what it could contribute to meeting these community needs. Sutter Community Hospitals is the second largest private nonprofit hospital in California. It operates two general medical and surgical hospitals with a combined capacity of 550 beds for medicine, surgery, obstetrics, pediatrics and psychiatry. After careful consideration, it planned and developed a request for a Hill-Burton Hospital Construction Act which would pay for two-thirds of the costs of construction of a 9,120 square foot, one story building.

On June 3, 1965, the Sutter Diagnostic and Treatment Center was opened. Within six months the Child Guidance Service was operating at capacity and there were many more demands for service than it could meet. Within eight months the Sacramento Hearing and Speech Center, established as a part of this new complex and co-sponsored with the Sacramento Hearing Society, was also operating at capacity. For the first time the Sacramento Valley and northeastern California had child guidance, language development, speech and hearing services available within one agency. The frequently seen complex combinations of emotional, behavioral, language, speech and hearing problems could now be dealt with in a better coordinated way. With psychiatric, psychologic, audiologic, speech, social service and nursing professions working together within one agency and geographically, administratively and professionally in proximity with the facilities and personnel of a modern general medical and surgical hospital, a language development clinic and a cleft palate clinic soon evolved.

STAFF

The entire center is under the direction of a board-certified psychiatrist who is a Fellow of the American Psychiatric Association and of the American Public Health Association. He serves full time at the center. The remaining full-time professional staff consists of a psychologist who has a doctorate in clinical psychology, three social workers with their master's degrees and clinical experience in psychiatric social work, an audiologist with a master's degree and a Certificate of Clinical Competence, a speech clinician with a master's degree and a Certificate of Clinical Competence, and a registered nurse with a bachelor's degree and school nursing experience. During the first year of the center's operation the speech clinician did not have a Certificate of Clinical Competence. A member of the American Speech and Hearing Association with Certificates of Clinical Competence in both speech pathology and audiology, and with a doctorate in speech, during that year served as consultant to the center's director in the planning and administration of hearing and speech services and also served as consultant to the center's speech clinician. This was a part-time position.

There is also a staff psychiatrist at the center three days a week. An additional psychiatrist is being sought, and other staff will be added as service demands require and finances permit.

Pediatric consultants are available to the center on a volunteer basis, but arrangements have also been made permitting referral to specialists on a fee-for-service basis whenever the child guidance, hearing, or speech evaluation requires additional, specialized medical information. Electroencephalography, laboratory, x-ray and pharmacy are available at Sutter Memorial Hospital, one of the two Sutter Community Hospitals, on the grounds of which the Diagnostic and Treatment Center is located.

Over 900 volunteers work at Sutter Community Hospitals. They comprise Sutter Hospitals' Auxiliary, which also provides volunteers for the Diagnostic and Treatment Center. Not only do these volunteers work in reception and hospitality at the center, but selected volunteers also assist in the hearing evaluation of very young children and in the work with children in group activities of the Child Guidance Service and the Hearing and Speech Services.

REFERRAL PROCEDURES

Persons are eligible for the services of the center regardless of the place of their residence, their national origin, their race, or their creed. Child guidance services are limited to dealing with the problems of persons under nineteen years of age or still attending high school. Hearing and speech services are available to persons of all ages, except that the Language Development Clinic currently serves children only between the ages of three and ten.

Patients must be referred by a professional person or agency, medical or nonmedical. Persons applying directly, without adequate referral, are advised to consult an appropriate referral source. The Child Guidance Service, correctly anticipating that demand for service would be greater than could be met, has consistently required that the referring person have a professional relationship with the patient. This permits the Child Guidance Service to offer professional consultation to the referring person in lieu of direct psychiatric evaluation or treatment, when such an alternative seems appropriate to the referring person. Such consultation with the referring person permits the latter to extend his ability to evaluate and deal with emotional, mental, or behavioral problems as they arise in his work. However, the consultation does not intend to "convert" the referring person into a child guidance clinician or mental health specialist.

Physical examinations and medical histories are required of all patients seen in the Child Guidance Service. Medical clearance is required of most hearing cases and of many speech cases. Persons requiring such examinations or clearances are encouraged to see their personal physicians. However, if they cannot, efforts are made to help them obtain such examinations through an established medical service program such as Crippled Children's Services, Medicare, or Vocational Rehabilitation. If these routes are not available, the center can obtain pediatric, otologic, and/or ophthalmologic examinations by special arrangement with the attending staff of Sutter Hospitals.

CHILD GUIDANCE SERVICES

When a patient is referred for child guidance services, the admitting social worker attempts to determine how the presenting problem is seen by the referring person, the patient and the family. A preadmission conference is offered to the referring person. Subject to the consent of the parents of the patient, other professional persons working with the child may also be invited to the preadmission conference. The conference is intended to do the following:

1. Bring together multiple sources of pertinent information.
2. Establish a basis for future cooperative, collaborative efforts on the case.
3. Determine whether referral for child guidance services is really indicated, whether there are contraindications to such referral, or whether there are better alternatives than referral.
4. Determine the degrees of interest and availability to the family of other professional resources.

If the referring person or the center does not believe a preadmission conference is warranted, or if such a conference is held and establishes the need for an evaluation, the case is ready for admission. However, since there is likely to be a delay before the first appointment, the family is advised by letter of the center's evaluation procedures. Parental consents are obtained for releases of information from schools and physicians. During the wait this professional information is collected. Much of it is already in the case folder by the time of the first child guidance appointment with the family. At this first appointment the parents are interviewed by a social worker. The parents may be seen together and/or separately several times in order to get a description of the presenting problems, a history of such problems, a social and developmental history of the patient and a picture of the family relationships. Additional sources of professional information are identified, evaluation and professional collaboration procedures are clarified, and fees are discussed, with arrangements being made as necessary for part-pay or for third-party payments. If discussion with the referring person indicates an emergency evaluation is required and this cannot be readily and appropriately acquired elsewhere, the entire intake procedure is condensed and medical, school and other reports may not be required as of the time of the evaluation. Conclusions are promptly shared with involved professional persons.

Since the parents have been advised early that a medical report will be required before the child is seen for psychiatric examination, it is generally possible to schedule the psychiatric examination of the child within two weeks after the parents' first appointment at the center. Within a week or ten days after the psychiatric examination, there is a staff conference on the case. All child guidance personnel and a pediatric consultant are present at such staff conferences. If indicated, the audiologist or the speech clinician may participate. Other professional persons involved in the case may also be invited to participate in the staff conference. Graduate and undergraduate students in social work or nursing may also be present.

Following this staff conference the admitting social worker and/or the psychiatrist sees the parents to report the center's findings and conclusions. A written report is sent to the referring person and to others professionally involved in the case. If a post-evaluation conference has been requested by the referring person, and that person did not attend the staff conference, an appointment is now made to discuss the case with the referring person.

Psychological evaluation may be arranged by the psychiatrist after his evaluation of the child or may be arranged after the staff conference. If the former, psychological evaluation findings are discussed with the parents as a part of the total discussion of findings and conclusions. If the psychological evaluation is completed after the staff conference, special arrangements are made for sharing these findings with the family, the referring person and other involved professional people.

Although center personnel can see patients who are hospitalized at Sutter Memorial or Sutter General Hospitals, only outpatient services are offered at the center. A wide range of psychiatrically directed treatment approaches are available: individual or group psychotherapy with adolescents, children, or their parents, individual or group play therapy with children and young adolescents, conjoin family therapy, parent counseling, or drug therapy. These may be used alone or in combination. Frequency and duration of appointments vary according to the needs of the case. Although individual appointments are generally for three-quarters of an hour, group therapy may last for an hour and a half, and a group therapy activity program lasting three hours each day has been established for children from three to nine years of age.

As already mentioned, pediatric consultation is readily available to the center. Local physicians have offered their services to work with the center on problems of special interest. This is also true of the clinical laboratory at Sutter Memorial Hospital, which is also prepared to work with the Diagnostic and Treatment Center on special projects of research interest. At least one local pediatrician also serves as a pediatric consultant in the weekly child guidance staffing of new admissions. Frequent contact with schools, physicians and other referring persons is encouraged. Interagency case conferences are planned whenever it is felt that such conferences will help coordinate the several services which may be involved in a complicated family situation. Each case which continues at the center for more than four months is reviewed quarterly in a staff conference to which other involved professional persons may be invited. The center views itself as collaborating with these professional persons so that all may present a composite approach to complex family problems.

The Child Guidance Service also offers consultation to professional persons or agencies on a regular, planned basis. Such consultation may or may not involve registered patients of the center. The child guidance staff member meets with one or more persons from a school, health agency, social agency, or law enforcement agency to help deal more effectively with mental and emotional problems in *their* case loads. Some recipient agencies view this consultation as essential on-the-job or in-service training for their staff. It increases staff awareness of the mental and emotional problems which are inevitable in professional relationships with people and improves the ability of the professional person to use himself fully in his helping or teaching relationship. Other recipients view the consultation as an alternative to direct evaluation, a more readily available alternative which depends for its effectiveness on the observation powers of the consultees, thus often making longer term observation available than is likely to be provided by a child guidance evaluation.

From the perspective of the center, such consultation helps preserve scarce mental health manpower for the more serious problems. This would seem to be a more efficient use of manpower than direct evaluation of all cases which pose an emotional or behavioral problem for the health, education, welfare, recreational, or correctional worker, or for the minister, lawyer, or other persons working with troubled people in the community.

HEARING SERVICES

Because of the co-sponsorship of hearing and speech services, these services are organized within the Diagnostic and Treatment Center as the Sacramento Hearing and Speech Center. It is the only such center in California from the San Francisco Bay Area north to the Oregon border. The center is equipped with contemporary audiological instrumentation that enables the audiologist to conduct a wide range of measurements of auditory functioning. Consideration is also given to the patients' rehabilitation potential. Recommendations are made for hearing aid amplification, appropriate educational placement, or other medical and nonmedical evaluation or therapy. The center maintains a large stock of hearing aids which have been loaned by manufacturers and by local heading aid dealers. No commercial obligations or sales are associated with the center. The models on hand are used for clinical trials with the patient, who is then referred to a list of local dealers for purchase of the most effective model.

Hearing services are divided into five major categories:

1. Audiological evaluation (pre tone, air and bone conduction and speech audiometry).
2. Special diagnostic audiologic evaluation (differential tests as indicated, including pure tone and speech, SiSi, SAL, Bekesy, distorted speech and loudness balance audiometry).
3. Medicolegal audiological evaluation (tests as indicated to ascertain and evaluate organic hearing loss, including pure tone and speech, delayed feedback, galvanic audiometry, and Stenger and Lombard tests).
4. Hearing aid selection and consultation (including pure tone and speech audiometry, trial of new hearing aids, counselling regarding the hearing impairment and use of the aid, and other testing and counselling as indicated).
5. Hearing aid recheck and consultation (including pure tone and speech audiometry and evaluation of the effectiveness of the patient's own hearing aid).

The audiologist has almost immediate access to a psychiatrist, psychologist, psychiatric social worker, nurse, or speech clinician for consultation about a case being seen in audiologic evaluation, follow-up, or counselling. If direct evaluation or treatment for speech or psychiatric problems seems indicated, the audiologist reports this recommendation to the referring profession and indicates the availability of such services at the center. However, referral for this additional service is left for the referring person to make.

Although persons are seen for hearing evaluation only on professional referral, a continuing professional responsibility is not required of the referring person. The audiologist has phone contact with the referring person if there are gaps in referral information and the audiologist currently obtains all pertinent history himself. However, thanks to a United States Public Health Service Grant, effective January 1, 1967, a full-time medical social worker was expected to screen referrals and obtain such histories, as well as to counsel families and patients about the social, vocational, educational and emotional aspects of the hearing impairment.

The referring person need not be a physician, but if any equipment is to be inserted in the patient's ear, a medical clearance is first obtained. If the referring person was not a physician and medical diagnostic or therapeutic procedures are recommended, a list of qualified physicians is given the patient and the recommendation is explained to the patient, the referring person and the physician whom the patient chooses.

On completion of the audiologic evaluation a report of findings and recommendations is given to the referring person. If so requested by the referring person, the audiologist also reports to the patient or family and to such other professional persons as requested by the patient or parents of a minor patient. In the case of a school-age child, an effort is made to obtain consent to report to both the child's physician and the school.

In addition to performing these clinical services, the audiologist is engaged in industry education regarding noise problems and in education of school personnel working with hard of hearing children.

SPEECH SERVICES

Referrals for speech services also come from medical or nonmedical professional persons. Through most of the earliest history of the center, the staff nurse obtained referral information and saw the patient or the parent of a minor patient to obtain a history of previous services pertinent to the language or speech problem, as well as to obtain consent to get reports of previous evaluation and treatment. With the addition of a medical social worker these duties were transferred from the nurse to the social worker.

If the family cannot pay the full evaluation fee, a referral is made to a payment resource such as Crippled Children's Service or Aid to the Disabled or arrangements are made with the Sacramento Hearing Society or Sutter Hospitals for partial payment.

Medical reports are obtained whenever the speech clinician deems them necessary to complete the speech evaluation. Routine speech evaluation includes an extensive history of physical and language development, a detailed description of the speech symptoms, a pure tone hearing screening, the Templin-Darley Screening and Diagnostic Test of Articulation and the Peabody Picture Vocabulary Test. The speech clinician may also examine the peripheral speech mechanism and administer such diagnostic tests as the Wepman Auditory Discrimination Test, the Halstead Aphasia Test, the Ayres Space Test and the Illinois Test of Psycholinguistic Abilities. If needed, the speech clinician can discuss the case with a child guidance specialist. Language observation groups are available for children three to ten years of age whom the speech clinician needs to observe for further evaluation.

Following evaluation, speech therapy may be recommended. Therapy is conducted for all types of speech problems on an individual or on a group basis. Frequency of sessions is determined by the needs of the patient, and combinations and variations may be arranged as clinically indicated. Further speech observation can be arranged by the speech clinician, but if psychiatric, psychologic, or psychiatric social work evaluation or treatment is indicated, the speech clinician recommends this to the referring person and advises the referring person of the availability of these services at the Diagnostic and Treatment Center.

Group speech reading instruction is currently available at the center under the sponsorship of the Sacramento Hearing Society. The participants are generally adults. Individual speech reading, group and individual auditory training, and group counselling of parents of severely hard of hearing children are provided as services of the center. Many children who receive these services are of preschool age and are expected to enroll later in public school classes for the auditorially handicapped. Classes for deaf and hard of hearing preschool children are being developed under the aforementioned United States Public Health Service grant.

SPECIAL COMBINATION SERVICES

Occasionally a referral is made to the Diagnostic and Treatment Center, rather than to either of its major services. Generally this involves emotional, mental, or behavioral problems associated with problems of language expression, reception, or comprehension. When contact with the referring person confirms that a total center evaluation is required, the staff nurse or the medical social worker interviews the parents, explains the child guidance evaluation procedure, and begins the speech evaluation with history-taking and information gathering. If, in the course of evaluation by the speech clinician, hearing screening indicates the need for audiologic evaluation this is then arranged, even as the speech evaluation continues. When the speech and hearing evaluations are completed the case is discussed with the psychiatrist-director of the center, who determines whether psychiatric, psychologic, and/or social work evaluations are required and arranges for the indicated child guidance evaluation procedures.

Upon completion of the total center evaluation a report is sent to the referring person or the referring person is invited to attend a staff conference on the case.

The unique combination of hearing and speech, mental health and general hospital services available at the center has opened the door to evaluation of several especially complicated, overlapping conditions. Two clinics have already developed reflecting the unique interprofessional opportunity provided by this setting. These are the Language Development Clinic and the Cleft Palate Clinic.

To provide a coordinated approach to the diagnosis and treatment of problems of delayed speech and/or delayed general language development, children are enrolled in a two or three days a week, language-oriented, group program for observation and study. A speech clinician and a graduate student in speech therapy observe the children in a language stimulation-free play setting at each session, and a psychiatrist or a psychologist observe periodic sessions and discuss the children with the speech personnel. Individual diagnostic procedures including pediatric, neurologic, psychiatric and psychologic examinations; psychometric testing, and extensive speech, hearing and language evaluations are conducted concurrently as needed. At the end of the diagnostic period, a case conference is held to identify significant etiological factors and recommend a management program for the child. The conference is attended by the speech clinician, the audiologist, the speech pathology consultant, the nurse, and the psychiatrist-director of the center. Children who have completed this diagnostic work-up may be candidates for the following: (1) continuing in the Language Development Clinic for its group and language stimulation orientation; (2) individual or group speech therapy and/or auditory training; (3) child guidance services; or (4) combinations of these therapeutic approaches.

Currently children participate in the Language Development Clinic two or three days a week. As the case load increases and the group becomes available daily, each child may then be seen from two to five days a week, as needed. Each daily session lasts for three fourths of an hour and is geared to take no more than eight children, ranging in age from three to seven.

Cases are selected from referrals made for speech or child guidance evaluations since language development delays may be presented to either service for evaluation.

At the urging of several dentists, pediatricians and reconstructive (plastic) surgeons, the Diagnostic and Treatment Center also operates the Cleft

Palate Clinic. A panel of general dentists, orthodontists, pedodontists, prosthodontists, pediatricians, reconstructive surgeons and otolaryngologists examine two cases per month at the center. Personnel of the center obtain social and developmental histories, compile pertinent data from previous studies, conduct hearing and speech evaluations and arrange for radiologic and ciné-fluorographic studies at Sutter Memorial Hospital. Cleft palate cases are referred by their physicians. (This is the only service of the center requiring a medical referral.) The services are coordinated by the center's nurse. Cases are discussed by all examining personnel in a staff conference and a summarizing report is sent to the referring physician. If psychological or psychiatric evaluation or treatment is indicated, this recommendation is made as part of the report to the referring physician. The entire Cleft Palate Clinic procedure is approved by state and local Crippled Children's Services and referrals are frequently through these services.

In addition to its direct service value to the referring doctor, the Cleft Palate Clinic provides a unique postgraduate training opportunity for physicians in private practice in the community. It makes possible rare interprofessional conversations about the complex physical and emotional handicaps associated with cleft palate conditions.

RESEARCH AND TRAINING

Although essentially a service facility, the Diagnostic and Treatment Center has research and training interests. Discussions with the research arm of Sutter Community Hospitals has only just begun. Sutter Hospitals has no research funds, but it makes skilled research personnel available to help develop protocols and grant requests. Staff research interests have been identified. These include development of reliable test instruments for the earliest detection of intellectual retardation and of hearing deficit in infants, evaluation of the effectiveness of a variety of psychotherapeutic approaches in dealing with predelinquent young adolescents, and the effectiveness of psychotropic drugs in the management of children with cerebral dysfunctions.

Even though the center is too young to give time to the detailed planning of clinical research, it is not too young to invest in operational research. Statistical data are being collected depicting staff deployment and services rendered. Patients served are identified statistically along several axes, permitting an assessment of characteristics affecting prognosis. Ultimately this should help identify needs for staff strengthening or modification of administrative or clinical procedures. Inefficient approaches can then be discarded; efficient procedures can be used as a model for ourselves and others.

Training responsibilities were faced early. Recognizing the unique multiprofessional features of the center, the Sacramento State College sought the center as a field placement for several groups of students. In its first year of operation the center was a work-study placement for two graduate social work students, eight undergraduate social work students and twenty-two student nurses. A psychiatric resident from a nearby state hospital, speech therapy students and psychology internes may also be placed at the center next year.

Several social science, speech and nursing classes from nearby colleges attended case conferences and orientation lectures at the center. One-way viewing auditing of play therapy, speech therapy, group psychotherapy and conjoint family therapy is possible at the center and arrangements have been made for appropriate students to observe selected therapies with selected families.

Staff members have met with several departments of Sutter Community Hospitals to explain the center's functions and to discuss the problems with which it works. Speech and hearing staff and child guidance staff attend each other's case conferences occasionally for their mutual professional growth. Films and seminars and attendance at professional meetings are periodically arranged to promote staff development. Conferences about cases and about agency consultations are the most favored method of inservice training, though, and there are four such meetings a week at the center.

FEES AND FINANCES

The Diagnostic and Treatment Center was established by Sutter Hospitals to meet a community need. Just as was true of charges for hospital services, patients were to be charged the actual cost of the services rendered. However, recognizing the total community need for these specialized services the center initially promulgated a sliding fee scale and entered into discussions with payment agencies to arrange for contracts and agreements which would help meet the deficit between cost and what patients could pay. Originally, therefore, all referrals were accepted, regardless of the patient's or family's ability to pay the full fee.

A simple fee-setting approach was used which did not require a means test and which made a minimal invasion into the family's financial privacy. Based on the Minnesota plan for charging for mental health services, the center concluded that families could annually afford to pay for long term care a maximum amount equal to that paid in federal income taxes for the year. In actual practice, therefore, the center required the patient or the parents of a minor patient to meet with an admitting social worker at the first appointment. The patient was to bring information concerning his last Federal income tax paid, his current year's estimated income, and his current dependency and exemptions claim. On the basis of this information the income tax for the current year was estimated. The family charge for one week's services was set at not to exceed 2 per cent of the estimated Federal income tax to be paid during the current year, or the actual cost of the service if that was less than 2 per cent of the annual income tax to be paid.

A child guidance evaluation, exclusive of psychological testing, was expected to require about five weeks, so a maximum charge of 10 per cent of the annual income tax was set for the total evaluation, exclusive of psychological testing. Since two weekly visits of two hours each were likely to be required for most psychological examinations, a maximum of 5 per cent of the annual income tax was set for a total psychological evaluation. Otherwise, the simple maximum of 2 per cent of the annual income tax was the weekly charge for services.

However, the actual costs (and therefore, the maximum charges) for each service were early set as follows:

Child Guidance Evaluation (without psychological testing)	$130 total
Psychological Evaluation	90 total
Child Guidance Treatment	15 per visit
Mental Health Consultation	15 per visit
Cleft Palate Evaluation (with physician services volunteered)	75 total
Audiologic Evaluation	20-45
Medicolegal Audiologic Evaluation	40-65
Hearing Aid Selection and Orientation	20-35
Speech Evaluation	20
Speech Therapy, Individual*	5 per ½ hr.
Speech Therapy, Group*	2.50 per ½ hr.

Only a few families seeking speech evaluations had difficulty paying the full fee and, as the center was recognized by the State Department of Health and Rehabilitation, these families could generally arrange for payments to be made by public health or welfare agencies. Since audiologic services were of a short-term nature, the Minnesota plan for long-term care payments did not seem relevant. Therefore, the time invested in fee setting was considered wasteful. On the recommendation of the Joint Advisory Board to the Sacramento Hearing and Speech Center,† the sliding fee scale was not applied to fees for hearing and speech services. Instead, installment payments or referral to health, welfare, or rehabilitation payment agents could be arranged, or the philanthropic resources of the Hearing Society or Sutter Hospitals could be tapped.

Early in the planning of the Child Guidance Service there were discus-

* The same charges were applied to individual or group auditory training and speech reading.

† The Joint Advisory Board consists of three members of the Board of the Sacramento Hearing Society, appointed by that society, and three members of the Board of Trustees of Sutter Community Hospitals, appointed by that board. The director of Sutter Community Hospitals, the director of the Sutter Diagnostic and Treatment Center, the supervisor of the Sacramento Hearing and Speech Center, the executive director of the Sacramento Hearing Society, and the Joint Advisory Board meet every three months, or sooner, if necessary. The Joint Advisory Board concerns itself with the Sacramento Hearing and Speech Center, not with the remaining services of the Sutter Diagnostic and Treatment Center.

sions between Sutter Community Hospitals and Sacramento County regarding a contract under California's Community Health Services Act (the Short-Doyle Act) whereby the county could purchase child guidance services on behalf of patients eligible for county mental health services. It was anticipated that such a contract would enable the county to pay the difference between Sutter's costs and what the family could pay on about one third of the part-pay patients at the center. The remainder would continue to pay on the sliding fee scale, with private philanthropy enabling Sutter Hospitals to meet the deficit.

Unfortunate administrative delays prevented implementation of these contracts during the first year of the center's operation. Meanwhile demand for child guidance services soon far exceeded the center's ability to meet the demand. With a deficit of from $8,000 to $12,000 per month in the child guidance service alone (plus $2,000 to $4,000 per month in the hearing and speech service), the center could not commit itself to staff expansion to meet the child guidance service demand. Thus, as of May 2, 1966, the center moved to a full fee for service basis on all its services. A modified Minnesota plan is applied on selected cases in the child guidance service. This modification calls for patients to be charged for the full cost of service, but for the family to have a maximum monthly personal liability of 10 per cent of its annual income tax payment. Charges in excess of this 10 per cent figure are "written off" but require that the deficit be met by private philanthropy.

After six months, costs are reexamined. Our experience with insurance and other third party payors was examined. As a result, the following fee scale was adopted:

Child Guidance Evaluation	$25.00 per visit
Psychological Evaluation	90.00 total
Child Guidance Treatment	
Individual	20.00 per visit
Group	15.00 per visit
Mental Health Consultation	20.00 per hour
Cleft Palate Evaluation (with physician time volunteered)	75.00 total
Individual Speech Evaluation or Therapy, Speech Reading, or Auditory Training	5.00 per ½ hr.
Group Speech Evaluation or Therapy, Speech Reading, or Auditory Training	2.50 per ½ hr.
Audiologic Services	
Pure Tone	12.00
Speech Reception	5.00
Auditory Discrimination	5.00
SISI	5.00
Loudness Balancing	8.00
Bekesy Audiometry	10.00
Tone Decay	3.00
Suboptimal Auditory Discrimination	5.00
Stenger	3.00
Electrodermal Audiometry	15.00
Hearing Aid Selection	15.00
Hearing Follow-up	5.00 per ½ hr.

However, costs are periodically reexamined and charges are appropriately updated. Families not eligible for public payment for health or rehabilitation services continue to be seen, limited by the availability of Sutter's funds. However, the United States Public Health Service grant has permitted extension of hearing and speech services to more part-pay or no-pay patients, and additional mental health contracts, grants and agreements have been negotiated which continue to extend child guidance services to part-pay or no-pay patients. Medicare and California's Medicare programs pay for some mental health services. Application is being made for a Community Mental Health Center grant from the Federal government. Special approaches to special problems may lead to demonstration grants. For example, the center has seen many children with mental retardation or with "minimal cerebral dysfunctions." These two conditions clearly demonstrate the evaluative and management advantages of this combined approach. Although much of public health and welfare care is financed through categorical programs, it is hoped that contracts will enable the center to contribute the full variety of its professional resources to the evaluation and care of part-pay patients with these baffling, long-term, multifaceted handicaps.

SUMMARY

The need for child guidance, language, speech and hearing services in the Sacramento area has long been recognized. After years of planning, such services are now available within one agency: the Sutter Diagnostic and and Treatment Center. Mental health, speech and hearing specialists have been brought together to deal with a variety of complex, overlapping physical and emotional handicaps. The multi-professional clinic the center has created to evaluate and treat the problem of delayed language development exemplifies one approach the center has made possible.

The Cleft Palate Clinic exemplifies another feature of the center. Its professional and geographic proximity to Sutter Memorial Hospital makes possible effective collaboration with modern x-ray, EEG and laboratory resources. Thorough multi-professional perspectives are brought to bear on the evaluation of individuals and families struggling with complicated disabilities.

Utilization of this array of highly specialized talent as consultants to general practitioners, pediatricians, welfare workers, school guidance personnel, teachers and so forth is illustrated by the consultation-collaboration approach employed by the child guidance service.

The experience of the center since its opening on June 3, 1965, has confirmed the need for these services in the Sacramento Valley and northeastern California. Demand for evaluation, treatment and consultation services has exceeded supply. Professional persons in the community have utilized contacts with the center for their own professional development. Staff of the center, meanwhile, has benefited from the unique opportunity to work with professions otherwise only fleetingly contacted.

Evaluations are thorough, making full use of previous assessments and conclusions while also reassessing the current problems and arriving at independent, but informed, professional judgments. The patient is seen as a truly "psychosomatic" organism whose medical and social history, current physical, social and emotional environment, and intrinsic physical and psychological condition must be understood whether the problem presented is one of behavior, emotion, intellect, ideation, articulation, comprehension, verbalization, or sensory reception.

Further expansion of staff and physical plant is required in order to meet the service needs already identified. However, resolution of the problems concerning service to part-pay or no-pay patients requires development of additional contracts, agreements, grants, and endowments. Only then can staff and facilities be expanded to meet the needs now known to exist.

Chapter 15

THE ASSOCIATED CLINICS AT THE CALIFORNIA STATE COLLEGE AT LOS ANGELES*

RICHARD G. CANNICOTT AND DELWYN G. SCHUBERT

THE Associated Clinics is a unique organization that integrates the clinical training, services and facilities of five clinics, and in addition provides opportunity for research, demonstration and training projects. The five clinics—Guidance, Hearing, Psychology, Reading and Speech—are sponsored respectively by six academic departments: Guidance and Pupil Personnel Services, Special Education, Psychology, Elementary Education/Secondary Education and Speech and Drama. Each of the departments is responsible for personnel and training in the clinic that it sponsors. Interdisciplinary training, fee collection, space assignment, interclinic referral procedures, format and filing of case records, client application and intake procedure, equipment purchase and maintenance, procurement of supplies, parking, initial contacts with the public, etc., are a joint responsibility handled by the Associated Clinics organization.

The primary purposes of the Associated Clinics are instructional: they are to provide students with supervised clinical experience in one of several specific disciplines, and to give experience in working with representatives of other disciplines. By enrolling in a practicum-type course offered by a participating department, a student becomes a student clinician in one of the clinics. He then works directly with clients from the surrounding community who come to the college by appointment for the services they have requested.

Service to clients constitutes a secondary purpose of the clinics. Clients are chosen on the basis of their having problems that meet the training needs of the individual clinics. Client evaluation and therapy proceed in a manner that enables the student clinician to experience, recognize and strive for high quality professional service. In addition, the combined resources of the five clinics allow for a more comprehensive approach to the client as a person. Specific problem areas can be assessed and treated more meaningfully within this broader context of several disciplines.

Most clinic courses are open only to graduate students who are pursuing a particular degree or a school credential in one of the following profes-

* California State College at Los Angeles, a liberal arts college enrolling approximately 20,000 students, is the second largest of eighteen colleges in the California State College System.

sional areas: audiology, child welfare, clinical psychology, reading disability, school counseling, school psychology and speech pathology. Professional and academic objectives of training will be delineated in conjunction with a discussion of individual clinics.

Since the inception of California State College at Los Angeles in 1947, there had been discussion and planning for some kind of integrated clinic training facility. Speech and hearing clinics were established during the 1950's and functioned in a temporary building known as the Speech and Hearing Center. In the fall of 1962, these clinics moved into a new five-story classroom building, part of which had been specifically designed for the Associated Clinics. During that school year, the Psychology Clinic and the Reading Clinic began functioning and, in the fall of 1963, the Guidance Clinic opened its doors to complete the activation of the five-clinic organization.*

The Associated Clinics physically encompasses an indoor area of approximately 22,000 square feet plus a large outdoor fenced playground. In addition to clinic and faculty offices, wide hallways, comfortable waiting rooms and separate restrooms for children and adults, there is a variety of clinical-training facilities. Specialized rooms include the following: prefabricated, acoustically designed cubicles for audiometric testing; storage and preparation rooms; large laboratory-classrooms, two-room observation suites with one-way-vision windows; numerous smaller cubicles for individual or small group diagnostic and therapy sessions, and electronic master-control rooms for coordinating the sound and television network that connects most of the clinic spaces.

Both children and adults are accepted as clients, depending upon the instructional requirements of the particular clinics. However, students of the college ordinarily are not seen as clients, primarily to avoid duplication of other campus facilities specifically designed for them.

Although physicians, schools and other people or agencies may inform prospective clients about clinic services, all applications must be made directly by the individual desiring help, or in the case of children, by the family involved. This procedure results in the individual client, or his family, assuming responsibility for keeping appointments and paying fees.† It also tends to provide clients with high motivation levels and avoids the

---

* Recognition should be given to Francis E. Lord, Ph.D., who while chairman of the Department of Special Education provided a guiding force and continuity over the years that resulted in the Associated Clinics herein described.

† Although fees of the clinics vary, they average between one and two dollars per hour or appointment. They are charged on either a per-session or per-semester basis, depending on the type of service and therapy program involved. Clinical directors may reduce or waive fees under special circumstances.

involvement of a third party. In regard to the latter, this does not preclude subsequent professional communication when in the client's interest. Such communications are authorized by releases signed by the client or his parents.

Irrespective of the type of service desired, the prospective client's first contact (usually by telephone) is with the Associated Clinics Central Office, rather than with an individual clinic. During this contact, basic identifying information is obtained, together with a brief statement of the presenting problem. This information is given to a central intake group which makes preliminary evaluations of all clients.

The Intake Group,* made up of student clinicians under faculty supervisors from the Psychology Clinic, sends an application form to the client and calls him in for one or more appointments as necessary to accumulate sufficient information upon which to base an intake decision. Upon notification of the client's first appointment, the Central Office of the Associated Clinics assigns the client a permanent file number. It then initiates a client folder which serves as the repository of all reports, protocols and communications on the client. The client folder is filed in the central office and checked out as needed by personnel from any clinic concerned with the client. Material in the client folder is arranged in a standard format to facilitate filing and locating specific types of information.

The Intake Group collects relevant information from schools, physicians and other professional persons or agencies. It combines this with interview and psychological test findings to obtain a clear clinical picture of the client as a whole, as well as of the specific area or areas of presenting complaint. After being staffed by the Intake Group, the client is then either transferred to one of the five associated clinics, or in a terminal interview, is given a statement of findings and, if needed, is advised of a more appropriate source of help.

Clients transferred to one of the associated clinics from the Intake Group may be involved immediately in that clinic, or placed on a waiting list from which they may be selected in accordance with training needs. By means of an interclinic request, any of the clinics may refer their clients to one or more of the other clinics for concurrent evaluation or therapy.

In addition to interclinic referrals and reports, the organization of five clinics provides other opportunities for inter-disciplinary clinical experi-

---

* In order to increase the opportunity for students to obtain experience working with members of other clinical specialities, and at the same time create an intake group enriched by multi-disciplinary representation, it is planned to offer a new course which will be open to a limited number of advanced students from each of the departments participating in clinic training. Although listed simultaneously as a course offering by each department, instructors will be drawn from the various departments on a rotation basis.

ence. The Intake Group may invite personnel from one of the clinics to confer on a client who is being considered for transfer to that clinic. In other instances, representatives of two or more clinics may confer informally, or hold a formal staff meeting about a client they have in common. Also, all clinics have the same two-hour period set aside each week for scheduling inter-disciplinary clinic activities. Generally, three to four weeks of a school quarter are planned jointly by all clinics to present diagnostic and therapy demonstrations for one another. At times, the same client may be examined by each clinic and the examination followed by a inter-disciplinary staff conference, all open to observation.

Each clinic has a clinical director (or co-directors) with a dual administrative responsibility to the Associated Clinics on the one hand—to a sponsoring instructional department on the other. The clinical directors meet together with the administrative director of the Associated Clinics to form the clinical directors staff. This group has the responsibility for carrying out decisions made at a higher level of authority, and consonant with this, for devising policies and procedures for the functioning of the Associated Clinics.

The administrative director is the executive officer who is appointed by, and is responsible to, the administrative council of the associated clinics. This council is made up of the chairmen of each of the sponsoring academic departments and is responsible to the dean of the School of Education, under whom the associated clinics is administratively placed.

The Associated Clinics does not itself offer courses or sponsor academic programs toward degrees or credentials. However, it does sponsor professional conferences and conduct training, demonstration and research projects. For example, the Learning and Behavior Problems Demonstration Project conducts special classes for educationally handicapped children at three age levels. These classes are open to observation through one-way-vision windows by college students and professional personnel from outside the college. These classes are utilized in conjunction with a training program for teachers of educationally handicapped children. Another example is a combination training and research project using family therapy as an approach to dealing with an individual's speech problem.

GUIDANCE CLINIC

The Guidance Clinic is sponsored by the Department of Guidance. One faculty member from this department serves as clinical director. Other faculty members who teach courses that require clinic participation serve as clinical supervisors. These, along with the director who also assumes a supervisory role, total eight.

The Guidance Clinic is in operation four evenings a week between 4:30 and 8:30. Clinicians are drawn from two graduate courses—Practicum in School Counseling and/or Field Work. At the time of this writing, one section of the Practicum in School Counseling and four sections of Field Work are being offered. Class enrollment is limited and none of the sections of the above courses exceeds five.

Graduate students from several sections of an introductory course in the Practicum in School Counseling also visit the clinic. These students attend the clinic for the purpose of gaining an appreciation and understanding of counseling relationships. They do not, however, work directly with clients. Still other classes utilize the clinic for observational purposes. An abundance of taped interviews and the accessibility of observational rooms equipped with one-way-vision windows make this practical.

All clinic activities are closely supervised and directed by qualified and experienced faculty members (supervisors) of the Department of Guidance. Each faculty member has normally only five student clinicians for an evening. The student clinicians are personally supervised, instructed and counseled. Clinic activities are controlled so that each student and client receives personal and unhurried assistance. The background of the faculty, the selection of the clients and the organization of the clinic make it possible to emphasize practical and desirable activities within the framework of current thinking and theory.

Credential and Degrees

Work in the Guidance Clinic is required for a master's degree in counseling. Students pursuing this degree must complete ninety quarter units of work. Clinic participation also is an integral part of the alternate program for the Standard Designated Services Credential with a specialization in Pupil Personnel Services. Individuals pursuing this credential may choose from three areas of emphases—school counseling, school psychology and school psychometry.

Clinic Training and Operation

The Guidance Clinic serves clients from the surrounding community whose problems are such that student clinicians working with them will be better trained for a regular and normal assignment with the public schools. Two major types of activities are carried on in the clinic. These are career planning and educational problems. Clinicians work with typical students and their parents who want assistance in their career planning or are having minor learning or developmental problems affecting their schooling. Severely disturbed clients are not accepted in the clinic but are referred to appropriate agencies for assistance. All clients who need therapeutic counseling and/or remedial activities also are referred to other agencies.

The Guidance Clinic has a working relationship with several nearby public schools. These schools supply the clinic with clients for routine counseling work involving test interpretations, coordination with group guidance classes, potential dropouts and college planning. Other "walk in" and referred individuals who contact the college for services are screened by the general Associated Clinics' intake procedure. Those that can be handled appropriately by the Guidance Clinic, as determined by standards set up by the clinic, are referred to its clinical director.

The clinical director assigns all clients to the clinical supervisors who, in turn, assign specific clients to their clinicians in terms of pedagogical needs. At this point, clinicians take over and assume responsibility for selecting appropriate tests, data gathering, making recommendations, etc. Efforts are made to provide circumstances closely resembling a normal school setting, but with the supervision that is possible only through the facilities of a clinic.

If the reader were to visit the Guidance Clinic he would see a number of activities taking place. He would see clients being counseled individually and in groups, clients being tested, data being gathered, counseling and testing being observed through one-way windows, taped interviews being played, replayed and discussed; and case data being reviewed and analyzed.

HEARING CLINIC

The Department of Special Education sponsors what may be considered two interrelated clinics in connection with its training program in audiology. Two faculty members from this department serve as co-directors—one of the Hearing Evaluation Clinic, the other of the Aural Rehabilitation Clinic.

Hearing Evaluation Clinic

The Hearing Evaluation Clinic involves five sections of students, each of which meets for three-hour periods on a biweekly basis. An additional hour is scheduled for conferencing. Sections are small; membership does not exceed six.

As a part of their training, clinicians in each section have an opportunity to view experts in action. All hearing aid selection and hearing testing are done by professional audiologists. The clients involved include children and adults in the community who are in need of hearing testing and hearing aid selection. These individuals generally are seen in the clinic one to four times, depending upon whether service is limited to hearing testing or is supplemented by hearing aid selection. In a few instances, when problems arise, additional sessions may be scheduled.

During a demonstration, the audiologist is observed by half of the clinicians in a section—usually three. The remaining clinicians in the section spend their time learning how to operate speech audiometers and master speech and audiometric techniques. At about the midpoint of the three-hour period, clinicians shift assignments and the process is repeated. After all of the clinicians in a section have had an opportunity to observe the professional audiologist, a conferencing period follows. Provision is made for gradual involvement of the clinicians in the actual testing procedures. From the beginning they sterilize ear molds, ready hearing aids for testing, and keep records of the test procedures for the audiologist.

The Hearing Evaluation Clinic provides both observational and laboratory experience. The objectives of its operation center around preparing clinicians for the role of clinical audiologists.

Aural Rehabilitation Clinic

The Aural Rehabilitation Clinic extends services to clients in the age range of three to fifteen years. Clients accepted generally are categorized as hard of hearing or severely hard of hearing. Occasionally, a deaf child is seen, but this is an exception.

All clients require hearing evaluation or reevaluation and some require hearing aid selection. Many have speech or voice problems. Most of them have some deficit in the acquisition of language. The majority of the clients are educationally retarded and some can be expected to show emotional disturbances. A few of the clients are in need of instruction in lipreading. Because of the variation in type and extent of client needs, the period of time spent by a child in the clinic varies but, in all instances, involves at least one school semester. Fees are charged by the semester.

Each child receives individual instruction. The remedial program that is initiated evolves from a careful diagnostic investigation. Diagnostic procedures include the following: (1) audiometric evaluation; (2) articulatory index; (3) tests for perceptual defects; (4) language index; (5) school achievement; (6) speech reading; (7) voice evaluation. Additional diagnostic information is gained through referrals to the Psychology Clinic and the Reading Clinic.

Credentials and Master's Degree Programs

The Aural Rehabilitation Clinic is part of the course requirements leading to a California credential for the preparation of speech and hearing therapists. Students are urged to choose the Hearing Evaluation Clinic as an elective. At the master's degree level, both the Aural Rehabilitation Clinic and the Hearing Evaluation Clinic are required in the course sequence leading to a master's degree in audiology and speech pathology.

The advanced training in both hearing clinics that is required for the master's degree differs from the introductory courses to which candidates may have been exposed. The responsibility that the master's degree candidate is expected to assume is far greater, and the clinical problems he encounters are more complex and involved.

PSYCHOLOGY CLINIC

Organization and Structure

The Psychology Clinic is a training facility of the Department of Psychology in the School of Letters and Science. The clinic operates for three or more hours on each of several late afternoons a week. The number of days the clinic is open depends upon the number of graduate student groups formed in a particular school quarter. A clinic group consists of five to seven students (clinicians), and a clinical supervisor recruited from the clinical faculty of the department. The number of groups varies between four and six in any quarter. At least one of the groups is formed to participate exclusively in counseling.

A clinical director is selected by the faculty members of the Psychology Department who have a specialization in clinical psychology. The director becomes one of the clinical supervisors as well as having responsibility for the overall functioning of the clinic. In addition to being chairman of the Department Clinical Committee, he also supervises the Psychology Test Materials Office and graduate assistants assigned to the clinic.

The Psychology Test Materials Office is located in the clinic area. It procures, maintains and loans out psychological test, play therapy and printed reference material for all testing and counseling courses taught by the department. Since this includes the courses in which students enroll to participate in the clinic, the office also is open when the clinic is in operation.

In addition to a series of individual conference rooms, the clinic has pairs of observation rooms, with sound amplification and one-way-vision windows between them that allow the clinical supervisor and/or the student clinicians to observe during interview, testing and counseling sessions. This enables beginning clinicians to observe before actively participating. Also, many other variations of training experience can be arranged without the risk of observers disturbing the ongoing clinical interaction with the client.

The Training Program

Students become clinicians by enrolling in one of two courses: Field Experience in Psychology, or Practicum in Counseling. Enrollment, usually for two or three quarter units of credit, may be repeated to a maximum of nine units in each course. The courses are designed to provide the student with independent practical experience plus both individual and group supervision. He is required to be present the day his group has the clinic open, and the day reserved for the inter-disciplinary program (see page 266).

Clinicians are drawn from two categories of graduate students. One group is composed of students who have chosen a preclinical emphasis in their work toward a master's degree with the Department of Psychology. The other group is made up of students who are working toward a Standard Designated Services Credential with a specialization in Pupil Personnel Services (School Psychometry or School Psychology) with the Department of Guidance in the School of Education.

Acceptance of psychology students in a clinic course requires prior written application to the Department Clinical Committee. Students from the Guidance Department are accepted on the advisement decision of a faculty committee in that department. Admission to the Field Experience course requires completion of basic courses in personality, abnormal psychology, theory of measurement, psychological testing and case study techniques. Admission to the counseling practicum requires completion of the same basic courses, excluding those in measurement and testing.

The Department of Psychology offers both master of arts and master of science degrees. The former is more of a liberal arts degree, allowing two courses outside the major department. Students most commonly choose this degree when they plan additional work toward a doctorate in psychology at another institution of higher learning. The master of science degree is frequently used as a terminal degree. Courses are drawn exclusively from the field of psychology with emphasis on applied subjects. Eight credits in the field experience course are required for the degree. A portion of this requirement may be met with units from the practicum in counseling course. Thus, all students working toward a M.S. degree in psychology spend at least two or three quarters in the Psychology Clinic.

Clinic Operation

Clients are seen in the Psychology Clinic for three basic purposes: (1) for preliminary evaluation when the clinic is serving the function of Central Intake Group for the Associated Clinics as a whole (see page 265); (2) for intensive clinical study to answer significant diagnostic questions and assist the clinic, and/or the client, in making decisions about treatment or referral, and (3) for individual counseling, family counseling, or play therapy.

Because of its intake evaluation function, the clinic sees many children who present problems in reading, speaking and hearing. Other children are seen with presenting complaints of school retardation and emotional or behavior problems. The adults seen are primarily parents of child clients. They are always interviewed in the intake evaluation procedure, and frequently they are referred for personal or family counseling by one of the other clinics. The student's task is one of gathering information by utilizing a variety of appraisal techniques. Techniques are chosen in terms of questions raised regarding a client's personality, intellectual functioning, social adjustment, specific skills, etc. In addition to observing, interviewing and studying biographical data, the clinician chooses and administers psychological tests appropriate to the particular client.

Some of the tests most commonly used with children in this clinic are the following: Wechsler Intelligence Scale for Children, Stanford Binet Intelligence Scale, Peabody Picture Vocabulary Test, Wide Range Achievement Test, Fehrenbach Sentence-completion Test, Bender Visual-Motor Gestalt Test, and Draw-a-Person Test. Most commonly used adult tests are the following: Wechsler Adult Intelligence Scale, Rorschach, Thematic Apperception Test, Forer Sentence-completion Test, Bender Visual-Motor Gestalt Test and Minnesota Multiphasic Personality Inventory. Approximately 485 different tests are available in the Psychology Materials Test Office (this includes different forms of the same test).

A client is initially assigned to one of the clinical supervisors. The supervisor meets with his group of clinicians and, together, they decide on the questions to be answered about the client, and a plan of action. The questions asked and the action taken are based upon sound clinical procedure as well as upon the training experiences needed by the individual student clinician. In some cases, a client will be tested or interviewed by one clinician while his parent, or parents, are being interviewed by another clinician. In other instances, a client will be seen by two or three clinicians in turn, each using a different technique. Frequently, a pair of clinicians will be assigned to make an evaluation together. They will divide the responsibilities involved, and then integrate their findings in one written report. A clinician may be given sole responsibility for working with a client; this is almost always the case in counseling assignments. At all times, clinicians are required to behave in accordance with ethical standards prescribed by the psychology profession.[1, 2, 3] Their training involves learning by personal experience and exposure to a wide range of clients, theoretical approaches and clinical techniques.

The clinical supervisor and his group meet together each week to "staff" clients, thoroughly evaluate the procedures used, and check the validity of the reported findings. Only when the supervisor finds the written report satisfactory does he countersign and place it in the client's folder. The report becomes an official record that may be used for professional communications—within the Associated Clinics, or outside.

Organization and Structure

READING CLINIC

The Reading Clinic is sponsored jointly by the departments of elementary and secondary education. One faculty member from each of these departments serves as a co-director and is responsible for the operation of one section of the clinic.

Each director has twelve graduate students (clinicians) working under his supervision. Each of the twelve clinicians sees an individual child for seventy-five minutes, once a week, for a full quarter. Clients are selected from the nine to seventeen years age group. Since each session of the clinic operates over a four-hour period, a division of cases into two time blocks of one and one-half hours in length makes it possible for the director to provide all clinicians with weekly on-the-spot supervision.

During each session of the Reading Clinic, two clinicians have an opportunity to view each other and to profit from constructive criticism provided by their own colleagues as well as from that offered by the clinical director. At the close of each session, one hour of time is devoted to individual evaluative conferences between the director and the clinicians. Additional individual conferencing takes place during the week.

Master's Degree Program

Experience in the Reading Clinic is an integral part of a special program in education that is offered at California State College. Students completing a core of courses in reading along with related electives, totaling forty-five quarter units, are awarded a master's degree in education with a specialty in the field of reading. The degree qualifies students for positions as special reading teachers, reading supervisors, or reading consultants in the public schools.

Candidates for the master's degree with a specialization in reading are chosen very carefully. Emphasis is on quality and not quantity. Students are not admitted to the program unless they have a background of successful teaching experience and a grade point average of B or better in their graduate work. A grade of A in a prerequisite course pertaining to the analysis of reading difficulties almost always is demanded. For most students, work in the Reading Clinic is the culminating experience leading to the master's degree.

Since the Reading Clinic is operated chiefly for the purpose of training clinicians and not for serving the community, many children who could profit from its services are never seen. Interesting and challenging clients always are sought, while children with reading problems amenable to corrective or remedial work in school often are not accepted.

Clinic Operation

After enrollment in the Reading Clinic, data in addition to that acquired by central intake procedures are obtained. Cooperation is sought from all agencies and persons—parents, teachers, psychologists, medical specialists, other clinics, etc.—who can provide information relative to the activities, accomplishments and difficulties the child is experiencing or has experienced. Such information is gathered through conferences or by use of questionnaires sent through the mail.

In addition to the foregoing, other information is made available to the Reading Clinic by the other clinics at California State College. The Hearing Clinic and the Speech Clinic assess the auditory and speech status of clients; the Psychology Clinic provides verbal and performance test scores that constitute one criterion of reading capacity, makes assessments of personality patterns by means of projective techniques, and employs tests designed to ascertain the client's neurological status. Both the Psychology Clinic and the Guidance Clinic provide parent counseling and, on occasions, counseling for Reading Clinic clients as well.

Detailed visual screening is carried on by the Reading Clinic. Included in the visual testing repertoire are the following: Keystone Visual Survey Tests, Orth-O-Rater, Bar Reader, Snellen Chart with plus lens test, ocular motility test, near-point of convergence test, cover test and near-point accommodation testing.

Specific recommendations are made for further examinations and study when there are indications of difficulty in hearing, vision, general health, neurological status and emotional status.

Two oral reading tests—the Gilmore and the revised Gray—and a variety of silent reading tests are employed in the analysis of the reading disability cases. Silent reading tests are chosen so that clients do not achieve at the upper or lower level of the tests. Retesting with duplicate forms of the same test is employed for evaluative purposes.

Philosophy

Therapeutic programs for each child are carefully planned and tailored to individual needs. Because this is true, no two programs are exactly alike. With all clients, however, the director impresses his clinicians with the importance of their instilling confidence in the children with whom they work. The clinicians are made to realize that their relationship with children is a therapeutic one and that warmth, understanding, patience and enthusiasm on their part often is an "open sesame" to reading improvement.

During the course of a quarter, a visitor at the Reading Clinic would see a wide variety of equipment and clinical procedures in action. SRA Laboratories, language masters, tachistoscopes, pacers, controlled readers, games and workbooks, etc. are found in abundance. The clinic has its own library of books which clients check out for outside reading. Various sight, phonics and kinesthetic procedures are used to develop reading vocabularies. Often a language experience approach is introduced for a number of weeks. In a few instances, a program in neurological and developmental training as promulgated by Delacatto[4] may be initiated. Youngsters who appear to be deficient in their perceptual motor skills are given exercises in improving ocular control and sensory-motor training as suggested by Getman[5] and Kephart.[6] The clinic has a walking board, a balancing board, and several School Skill Tracing Boards. Study of the lesson plans evolved weekly by clinicians shows a tremendous variety and flexibility in the use of materials and methods employed. In short, the reading improvement program in operation at California State College is an eclectic one.

SPEECH CLINIC

Organization and Structure

The Speech Clinic is operated as a clinical laboratory by the Department of Speech and Drama in the School of Letters and Science. Each school quarter, the clinic is in operation for three hours on two late afternoons a week. Ten to twenty student clinicians work on these days with individual clients under the supervision of the clinical director and a technical assistant. On a third late afternoon each week, a second faculty member serves as clinical supervisor for student clinicians working with clients in small group speech therapy. Some clients are seen concurrently for both individual and group therapy. Other clients continue with group therapy following a period of more intense individual therapy.

In addition to the speech diagnoses performed in the clinic operation specified above, a course is offered by a third faculty member. This course is scheduled on a fourth late afternoon of the week, and it specifically emphasizes training in the diagnosis of speech disorders. Diagnostic techniques and procedures are demonstrated to student groups through a one-way-vision window. These demonstrations are conducted by a faculty expert or a visiting consultant who evaluate persons with speech problems referred from the community. Many of the clients are accepted in the clinic for speech therapy.

Although clients from a variety of age levels are seen in the clinic, a larger number of children in elementary schools are selected because most of the student clinicians will be working in the elementary school setting upon completion of their training. Some secondary school clients with severe problems are seen. In addition, the clinic accommodates a limited number of mentally retarded and cerebral palsied clients. Students also have an opportunity to observe children with a variety of neurological involvements at a state school for the cerebral palsied adjacent to the college campus.

The Speech Clinic works closely with the Hearing and Psychology clinics within the Associated Clinics. The Psychology Clinic, in addition to psychological evaluations, provides counselors who work with groups of parents while their children are being seen as clients in the Speech Clinic. Since credential and degree programs in speech correction require that students also take training in the Hearing Clinic, clients needing hearing evaluation are usually referred to the Hearing Clinic for that service.

The facilities of the Speech Clinic include a number of individual conference rooms, four large observation suites, each divided by a one-way-vision window, and a special staff/preparation room. In the staff/preparation room, student clinicians can prepare needed materials, write reports, and leave personal articles while working with clients elsewhere. The largest observation room has multi-leveled seating for forty persons. This room is scheduled for two hours on each of two clinic afternoons a week. This arrangement provides observation of ongoing speech therapy and diagnosis for students from introductory and other speech correction courses requiring such observation.

Credentials and Degree Programs

Students may obtain both bachelor and master of arts degrees with a specialization in speech and hearing. The curricula for these degrees are correlated with the training required for a California school credential as a speech and hearing therapist. The foregoing credentials and degrees are offered jointly with the Department of Special Education. At least two quarters of clinic experience are required for both the undergraduate and graduate programs.

Clinic Operation

The student speech clinician generally carries a case load of two clients. Each therapy client is seen twice a week for a school quarter. Students enrolled in the graduate clinic course will see a number of clients for diagnosis in addition to their therapy load. The graduate student may also be called upon to do audiological testing and to give demonstrations. He may also be assigned as an assistant to help an inexperienced undergraduate student with a client. The clinical director periodically gives demonstrations in addition to supervising the students and meeting with them two hours a week for staff conferences. Since clients frequently are carried over for a second quarter of therapy, the student clinician generally is assigned one continuing client.

The student clinician turns in a weekly written progress report, initiates requests for service from a sister clinic, makes a master plan for the semester's work with his client, keeps the client folder up to date and submits a written case summary for each client at the end of each quarter.

In order to provide each student clinician with a wide range of clinical experience, a variety of clients is selected from a pool of available applicants. Some of these clients have organically based speech problems. These include persons with cleft palate, cerebral palsy and aphasia. Other clients present functional disorders such as delayed speech, articulation difficulties, stuttering and voice problems. The theoretical orientations and practical approaches of the five professional speech correctionists on the staff differ considerably. These differences—those of faculty and clients—provide a rich clinical training experience for college students working in the Speech Clinic.

ACKNOWLEDGMENTS

The authors wish to extend their appreciation to the clinical directors of the clinics: Guidance Clinic, Robert B. Benoit, Ed.D.; Hearing Clinic Co-directors, Janet Jeffers, Ph.D. and Donald B. Kinstler, Ph.D.; Psychology Clinic, Bernard J. Sommers, Ph.D.; Reading Clinic Co-director, Florence B. Sperry, Ed.D.; and Speech Clinic, Mary W. Huber, Ph.D.

REFERENCES

1. American Psychological Association: *Ethical Standards of Psychologists.* Washington, American Psychological Association, 1953 (a).
2. American Psychological Association: *Ethical Standards of Psychologists, a summary of ethical principles.* Washington, American Psychological Association, 1953 (b).
3. American Psychological Association: Ethical Standards of Psychologists. *Amer Psychol, 14*:279-282, 1959.
4. Delacato, C. H.: *The Diagnosis and Treatment of Speech and Reading Problems.* Springfield, Thomas, 1963.
5. Getman, G. N.: *How to Develop Your Child's Intelligence.* Luverne, The Author, 1962.
6. Kephart, N. C.: *The Slow Learner in the Classroom.* Columbus, Merrill, 1960.

Chapter 16

EASTER SEAL SOCIETY FOR CRIPPLED CHILDREN AND ADULTS

MORRIS VAL JONES
WITH ASSISTANCE FROM
DUANE HOLIDAY, ESTHER ELDER SMITH AND EARL C. GRAHAM

THE NATIONAL ORGANIZATION

ON Memorial Day in 1907, in the small town of Elyria, Ohio, there was a bad streetcar accident involving a group of boys and girls who were returning in a party from a holiday excursion. Many died of injuries which could not be properly treated on an emergency basis in the community's single hospital facility. Others were maimed for life. The effect of this tragic accident might have been confined to one rather remote community, in terms of the grief and shock of families and altered lives for the youngsters who were permanently crippled. Instead, the event was destined to have repercussions on the lives of hundreds of thousands of people throughout the world. The forces which it set in motion led, fourteen years later, to the founding of the National Society for Crippled Children and Adults, an organization of volunteers dedicated to a program of enlightening the public on what can be done for the crippled, and of mobilizing public and private resources to develop needed services.

The story of the society begins with what happened after the accident. One of the boys who died was eighteen-year-old Homer Allen. The death of his son brought out great qualities of devotion and drive in Edgar F. Allen, a prominent Elyria business man. Spurred by a new and personal awareness of the inadequacy of local hospital facilities in the community, Mr. Allen first directed his energies toward bringing about the construction, equipping and staffing of a new general hospital. His observation and sympathetic interest in a crippled boy who was brought to the hospital opened his eyes to a different need—that of crippled children for special medical care and treatment. He saw that proper care had brought this child from a hopeless condition to one of optimism and expectations for a normal life and began to visualize what it would mean to countless others to have similar care. Through his contact with the boy, who dubbed him affectionately, "Daddy," Edgar Allen was led into the activity which was to be a lifelong career of service.

Once his interest was aroused, the first logical steps for "Daddy" Allen were to conduct a survey to find out how many crippled children there were in his home county, and to organize community support to build the Gates Memorial Hospital for Crippled Children. He then entered upon an even more ambitious program of seeing to it that crippled children in Ohio were found and brought to the hospital, and that their care and treatment were paid for. To do this and to spread the word on what such help meant to crippled children, he enlisted the interest and support of Rotarians. It was Rotarians, in turn, who spearheaded the founding in Ohio in 1919 of the first state crippled children's society, an organization of volunteers dedicated to a program which provided privately supported services, while it sought extension and increased support for public services for the crippled. The program of the Ohio society flourished, and by 1921, "Daddy" Allen saw sufficient evidence of similar interest on the part of Rotarians in Michigan, New York and Illinois to cause him to feel that the time had come for national action. He sought official endorsement of expansion of the "Ohio Plan" through Rotary International.

Meanwhile a dedicated group of volunteers headed by "Daddy" Allen in 1921 launched the National Society for Crippled Children with headquarters in Elyria, Ohio. The first president was "Daddy" Allen, who served devotedly until three years before his death in 1937. In the early years, "Daddy" Allen alone stimulated much of the Rotary interest which led to the organization of state societies for crippled children. Later, he was aided in this activity by a small staff. Once the national society was launched, the movement spread quickly. Michigan and New York societies were organized in 1922. Kentucky, Pennsylvania, Tennessee, West Virginia and Illinois followed in 1923. By the end of 1929 there were twenty-three state societies for crippled children.

The national society exercised growing responsibilities for coordinating and disseminating information on the needs of the crippled, on existing services, facilities, and on rapidly expanding medical and professional knowledge. *The Crippled Child* magazine was established in 1923. A bureau of information and library began operation in 1924. One of the greatest tasks of the national society in the early years was to encourage and aid in the drafting of special state legislation to meet the medical, educational and vocational needs of the crippled. In 1922 the name of the society was changed to International Society for Crippled Children in order to encourage the development of similar voluntary organizations in other countries. By 1939 it had become clear that the national and international organizations should be separate, and there emerged the International Society for the Welfare of Cripples (name changed in 1963 to International Society for Rehabilitation of the Disabled) and the National Society for Crippled Children of the United States of America. In 1944 the phrase "of the United States of America" was dropped and the words "and adults" added.

The young organization first adopted Easter Seals as a fund raising device in 1934. The public has responded each year more generously to this appeal and "Easter Seals" have come to be synonymous with care for the crippled. The stylized Easter Lily, adopted in 1952 as the symbol of the organization is now well known; and the societies for crippled children and adults are called informally, "The Easter Seal Societies." Headquarters of the national society were moved to Chicago in 1945, a move which ushered in an era of expansion. In 1958 the national headquarters built and occupied its own building in the West Side Medical Center in Chicago.

The National Society for Crippled Children and Adults was forty-four years old in 1965. Through those years the society has steadfastly elected to take the pragmatic approach in its attack on the age-old problems of human crippling. As long as there were crippled children needing help, the society saw provision of treatment as its mission and the expression of its dedication to service to others.

In its early years it paid for surgery and hospital and convalescent care for individual children as they came to its attention. Then it instituted a few of its own services to demonstrate that many crippling conditions could be improved by appropriate treatment outside the hospital. It went to state and Federal governments for legislation to make treatment and education available to large numbers of children it could not reach.

Finally, in recent decades, it has established in fifty states a broad network of facilities and programs designed to meet specific community needs.

For example, rehabilitation centers are operated for the primary purpose of assisting in the rehabilitation of disabled persons through a coordinated program of medical evaluation and services, psychological, social or vocational evaluation and if it is designed only for children, a preschool or educational program.

In a center one finds a dazzling and expensive array of electrical and electronic equipment both for measuring muscle response and for nerve stimulation; heat treatment devices; tanks where patients can be totally immersed in water to facilitate exercise; whirlpool baths for stimulation of circulation in arthritic and other painfully afflicted arms and legs; equipment resembling that of a gymnasium but adapted to other purposes than athletics, specially designed kitchens and a host of other devices for testing, training and teaching.

The Easter Seal Society is today one of the country's foremost operators of such centers, with forty-nine directly under its aegis and others jointly administered or financed. As of 1965, more than 23,000 persons found in these centers the comprehensive treatment and training they required to restore them to maximum activity and usefulness.

In 102 communities throughout the United States, in Easter Seal treatment centers more than 28,000 children and adults are working to overcome appreciable handicaps. The treatment, always under medical prescription or professional supervision, although not so broadly inclusive as that to be found in the rehabilitation center, is nevertheless as indispensable in the pattern of community services and certainly in the restoration of function in the damaged limbs of the disabled. The treatment center usually offers one or more of the medically related specialties of physical, occupational, or speech therapy. However, when speech therapy is the exclusive service, under the Easter Seal definition, the center is designated as a speech and hearing center. There are another sixty-three such centers, caring for more than 6,917 persons in fifteen states.

In 1965, 239,037 children and adults were cared for at some 1,111 major Easter Seal clinics, treatment and rehabilitation centers, hospitals, camps, itinerant therapy programs, workshops and preschool classes and other programs, by Easter Seal staffs. This supremely important job of rehabilitation is entrusted only to persons whose education, experience, ingenuity and dedication to serving others entitle them to recognition by their own professional organizations and who meet the exacting standards of the Easter Seal Society. Searching them out from the all too limited number of such persons is a difficult task.

However, in 1965, the society maintained its leadership as one of the foremost employers of rehabilitation personnel, with nearly 3,000 social workers, physical, occupational and speech therapists, camping and recreation specialists and administrators. The effectiveness of these staff members was furthered by the supportive work of additional hundreds of clerical and maintenance personnel.

Education is one of the major points in the Easter Seal Society's nationwide program. To implement its professional education efforts, it publishes *Rehabilitation Literature,* a professional monthly which enjoyed continued growth in 1965 and its circulation to individuals and institutions and from which a number of articles were reprinted for professional use. Library services including bibliographies and "package libraries" were distributed to persons and institutions. Other papers, pamphlets, seminars, inservice training at the nationwide staff meeting and professional exhibits displayed at national professional conferences added impact to the effort. Such timely subjects as treatment of stroke, minimal brain damage, designing for the mentally handicapped, dental care for the handicapped child, occupational therapy, the workshop as a clinical rehabilitation tool were subjects for special treatment.

In recent decades the adult disabled have become of increasing concern to the Easter Seal Society. Hence, wherever the case load permitted, adult patients have been included in treatment programs. The number grows although it still comprises only 27.2 per cent of the total.

But after treatment has achieved its optimum level and as children grow into adults, employment becomes a problem of deep distress, particularly when total rehabilitation is not possible. Federal agencies estimate that there are 5.3 million persons with long-term disabilities of all kinds who are unable to work on a regular basis.

Hence, in order to help those whose handicaps fall within the scope of the Easter Seal Society's programs, the society has in twelve states established over the years twenty-one workshops that provide 1,300 young adults and mature men and women whose earning capacity is impaired by physical, mental, or social handicaps with remunerative employment, or other occupational activities. Workshops may, for example, provide job training, vocational evaluation, sheltered employment or work adjustment services. The equipment, instead of the devices for light therapy, hydrotherapy and electrotherapy, may be punch presses, die-cutting machinery, sorting and assembling machinery, office equipment and other workaday tools such as hammers, saws, wrenches, electric welding equipment and chisels.

Ambitious and determined young adults, not satisfied to accept "no's" from business and industry, come here to work at jobs that may require meticulous and tedious assembly or packaging. They may engage in highly creative and artistic production of articles that can be sold through retail channels. They may become skilled artisans, or they may find themselves ready to enter new fields previously not known to them—or not even possible for them.

Whatever they find to do, they are learning—and earning—independence.

At the same time that the society has been using every available practical means to correct existing handicaps, its Easter Seal Research Foundation has for the past ten years looked for ways to improve treatment, equipment and appliances, and to prevent crippling in those still unborn. It has supported scientific inquiry into the causes of crippling and measures for enhancing the effectiveness of the rehabilitation process. In some instances it has underwritten the costs of projects that in themselves are productive of answers to some of the many questions surrounding crippling and rehabilitation. In other cases, the foundations' grants have been intended as seed money to develop the basic rationale for broad-scale scientific research far beyond its own resources. Both basic and clinical research in some seventy-five major institutions such as universities, medical schools and rehabilitation facilities has been productive of significant clues to the reasons for prenatal malformations for improper growth or deterioration of bone and for other factors contributing to crippling conditions. It has also produced important knowledge bearing on the ways to accelerate rehabilitation processes and to release the captive potentialities of the handicapped through new educational and treatment techniques.

CALIFORNIA SOCIETY FOR CRIPPLED CHILDREN AND ADULTS

As early as 1860, the California legislature recognized a responsibility for helping the physically handicapped. In that year appropriations were made for the establishment of a resident school for the deaf in San Francisco. In 1865 this program was expanded when the state developed an institution to serve both the deaf and the blind in Berkeley. During the years from 1897 to 1900 day classes for deaf children were begun in Los Angeles, San Francisco and Oakland. As early as 1907, legislative permission was given to local school districts to accept children aged three to twenty-one in these special facilities.

While there was sporadic recognition of responsibility for rehabilitation for the blind and deaf, there were no extended services for the orthopedically handicapped from either private or public sources. For some years prior to this period Rotary clubs had interested themselves in the problems of crippled children, had organized the National Society for Crippled Children, and most of them were taking an active interest in individual cases through the work of Crippled Children Committees. For this reason the Parent-Teacher Association and California Federation of Women's Clubs brought the problem of California's children to a meeting of the second district of Rotary in San Diego in May of 1926. As a result of this action, Rotary undertook the organization of the California Society for Crippled Children.

The newly formed society was charged with the responsibility of informing local communities about the problem with specific reference to their own needs. These needs were demonstrated by diagnostic clinics which were held around the state and which brought to light hundreds of crippled children who needed care and whose parents were unable to provide it. As these needs became so readily apparent, local interest focused upon legislation which might make tax funds available for the physical rehabilitation and education of these future citizens.

Serving as consultant to the legislature in 1927, the society assisted in drafting four bills which were passed almost by acclamation because local interest in the matter had become so great. The measures, which were promptly passed by the governor, contained the following provisions:

Education

The first appropriation of funds was made to help local school districts meet the excess costs involved in the education of physically handicapped children. The measure provided for reimbursement to the local school district up to $100 for one-half of the excess cost. If matched by the local school district, $75 per month was allowed for employment of teachers for speech correction.

Medical Care

The Crippled Children's Act directed that the State Department of Public Health should seek out needy physically defective or handicapped persons under the age of eighteen, and made available such medical care as they might need if the parents or guardians were, in whole or in part, unable to furnish such care. The act set up machinery by which funds could be collected from the county in which the child resided. The counties were empowered to assess up to three mills on each dollar of assessed valuation and to use this money to meet expense of care for crippled children. A revolving fund was provided to the State Department of Health to permit the program to go into immediate operation.

In 1928 careful consideration was given to the function and purposes of the California society. A five-point plan was adopted to define the objectives of the society in the overall state program for the handicapped. This plan, known as the "California Plan," included these points:

1. Find the child who needs help and set up a registry of physically handicapped children.
2. See that the child receives physical rehabilitation.
3. Cooperate with the State Department of Public Instruction to the end that all educable handicapped children will receive an education.
4. Work with the State Bureau of Vocational Rehabilitation and other agencies to give to the child vocational training and guidance.
5. Find opportunities for employment of handicapped young people and do everything possible to assist in placing the handicapped person in a position which he can fill.

As communities struggled with economic depression, little thought and action were directed toward special needs of any kinds. Emphasis was on the provision of food and shelter; but, even before the country had returned to a better economic state, attention was again directed toward provision of services for California's handicapped. In 1934, the California Society for Crippled Children joined the national society in adopting the Easter Seal campaign as its basic fund raising method. Up until this time, the Rotary clubs had continued to finance the society. There was now recognition of the principle that the welfare of the handicapped is a matter of interest to all citizens and that all should be invited to participate in the society's activities.

Organization of the Spastic Children's Society of Alameda County represented the first formal recognition of the role which organized parent groups play in cooperation with citizen groups in the development of services for the handicapped. This group was formed for the specific purpose of co-operative effort to obtain special education for the children of its members. However, the parents soon saw the benefits of problem sharing, educational programs and social outlets which such organizations can provide. The first project undertaken by the Spastic Children's Society was to encourage the establishment of a pilot program of education and therapy for cerebral palsied children from preschool age through high school.

The year 1939 marked the beginning of California's recognition of the special needs of children who suffer from cerebral palsy. The legislature made legal provision which permitted school districts to accept cerebral palsied children in special classes at the age of three and receive reimbursement for the excess costs of their education. The 1940 Annual Meeting of the California Society for Crippled Children was devoted entirely to consideration of the needs of the cerebral palsied. The most important contribution to that meeting was an address delivered by the president of the Spastic Children's Society of Alameda County. Entitled, "A Program for Spastics in California," the address pointed out four areas of basic need: (1) special classes; (2) vocational training and guidance; (3) parent cooperation, and (4) public education.

The first preschool class for the cerebral palsied in California was established in 1940. As a result of the efforts of the Spastic Children's Society of Alameda County, and under the legislation passed in 1939, the Oakland Public Schools and the Children's Hospital of the East Bay established the Cottage School for Spastics on the hospital grounds. This school included, in a coordinated program, physical therapy under medical supervision, speech training, academic education and adjustment to group living.

The first resident camping program for handicapped children was started in California. The Los Angeles County Society for Crippled Children established Camp Paivika in rented facilities in the San Bernardino Mountains in 1940.

The California Society for Crippled Children, with its sixteen chapters and the then existing parent groups, brought information about the cerebral palsy problem to the legislature. As a result, the State Departments of Health and Education were instructed by the legislature to investigate the problem and make recommendations as to methods of meeting demonstrated needs.

Members of the society joined other interested groups, particularly the Spastic Children's Society of Alameda County, in presenting testimony before legislative committees relative to the need for services.

As a result of combined parent and citizen effort, the following program for cerebral palsied children was adopted by the legislature:

1. The State Department of Education was provided with two consultants

to assist local schools in developing special classes and to coordinate the activities of local and state centers. An appropriation of $40,000 was authorized for this purpose.

2. The State Department of Health was given an appropriation of $80,000 for field services and empowered to provide physical and occupational therapy in special classes in local schools—clinical supervision of the therapies to be provided through existing Crippled Children Services facilities; and medical and surgical treatment, bracing, etc., to continue through the same channels.

3. Two residential schools were established. These schools were to provide twenty-four-hour intensive programs of highly individualized observation, treatment and educational services. An appropriation of $280,000 was made to implement the resident schools and two diagnostic centers. These centers, one in the north and one in the south, were provided to supplement clinical and treatment services in local areas and to screen admissions to the two residential schools.

4. Local schools were encouraged to set up special day classes for cerebral palsied children and excess cost for their education up to $200 per unit of average daily attendance was declared reimbursable from state funds.

As the statewide cerebral palsy program got under way, it became evident that there was a pressing need for information on the medical and educational aspects of the care and training of cerebral palsied children. In April, 1946, the California Society for Crippled Children and its affiliated chapter in Los Angeles County jointly financed and presented the first statewide professional conference on the cerebral palsied child. Over 600 persons, coming from all parts of the state and representing all phases of the care and treatment program, attended the meeting which was held in Los Angeles. Leading national figures participating in the conference were Dr. Elise H. Martens of the United States Office of Education; Dr. Jay B. Nash of New York University; Dr. Meyer A. Perlstein, pediatrician, of Chicago, and Dr. Winthrop M. Phelps, orthopedist, of Baltimore.

An epilepsy division was set up in the California Society through a grant from Mr. and Mrs. Fred Markham. A coordinator was added to the society's staff to work with local communities in attacking the epilepsy problem. A medical advisory committee, members of which were leaders in this field, was found and began to work.

The California Society for Crippled Children, out of its almost twenty-five years of service to the handicapped, had recognized the need for a facility to give residential care to the severely handicapped, mentally normal person unable to care for himself and with no one to care for him. In 1949, the society joined with other groups in bringing this need to the attention of the Legislature with a specific request that four million dollars be appropriated for a residential center. This request led directly to the appointment by the State Senate of a special interim committee to study the education and rehabilitation of physically handicapped children and adults. This committee has continued in operation. The California Society for Crippled Children has served in an advisory capacity to the committee, assisting in compilation of data, in presentation of testimony, and in other ways as requested.

The year 1951 marked publication of "Opportunities Limited," a study of the employment problems of the severely handicapped cerebral palsied and epileptics. The necessary research work, financed by a grant from the Rosenberg Foundation, extended over a period of two and one-half years and explored the many facets of this serious and complicated problem. The results of the research were published through a grant from the San Francisco Foundation. Esther Elder Smith, associate director of the California Society for Crippled Children, and Carolyn Brinn, O.T.R., of the society's staff, collaborated in the research and the writing.

At its 1952 annual meeting, the California Society for Crippled Children changed its name to the California Society for Crippled Children and Adults. This change was made because the society had been serving handicapped adults as well as children for many years. Then, the recent years had brought the society's attention more and more to such matters as residential care and employment of the handicapped adults. Another milestone in the growth of the California Society for Crippled Children and Adults was reached when the delegates to its 1952 annual meeting approved certain minimum standards for affiliation of local chapters with the California society. These standards were designed to encourage a high level of operation and to insure maximum service to the handicapped as well as the most meticulous use of Easter Seal funds.

In practice, the Cerebral Palsy Division of the California society had for many years, placed emphasis on the problems of parents of all handicapped children. At its annual business meeting in 1952, the Cerebral Palsy Division changed its name to the Parents Division. A parents council was created to supersede the executive committee of the Cerebral Palsy Division. This council was made up of representatives from all affiliated parent groups in the state and served in an advisory capacity to the California Society for Crippled Children and Adults.

After several years of effort by the California Society for Crippled Children and Adults and great local interest, an appropriation of $868,920 was made by the 1953 session of the legislature for a building on the campus of San Francisco State College to house permanently the Northern California Training School for Cerebral Palsied Children. This school is a training facility for teachers and therapists and offers intensive education and therapy to severely handicapped cerebral palsied and multi-handicapped children who cannot be cared for in their own local schools. Again, several years of effort by the California Society for Crippled Children and Adults and other organizations resulted in the 1953 legislature's appropriating, after careful study, $80,000 for the planning of a complete rehabilitation center to be located on the grounds of the new medical school at the University of California at Los Angeles. Appropriations were made and the rehabilitation center opened in 1965. The training of personnel and the research which such a facility provides should prove of immeasurable benefit to the State of California.

In 1959 a group of California parents of aphasic children accepted an invitation to serve as a special subcommittee on aphasia for the Parents Advisory Committee of the California Society for Crippled Children and Adults. Then, as now, a major concern of parents and society alike was the establishing of guidelines for the development of services for aphasic children—through creating opportunity for the study and discussion of their diagnosis, treatment and education. To secure the professional guidance and advice sought by those working with the problems of aphasia, the society called upon its own Professional Advisory Committee, which includes specialists from a broad range of rehabilitative and medical services.

Aware of the wide divergence of practice in diagnosis and treatment of childhood aphasia, the Professional Advisory Committee recommended an exploration of professional opinion and practice on the broadest possible basis. To this end, it proposed a nationwide interdisciplinary Institute on Childhood Aphasia, at which every aspect of the existing body of knowledge of aphasia might be examined and charted, and from which the long-sought guidelines might be drawn. The Easter Seal Research Foundation made available a grant of $10,000 to finance the project. This fund was supplemented by a $1,500 grant by the Association for the Aid of Crippled Children and by the National Institute of Neurological Diseases and Blindness, which made possible the participation of four of the invited consultants. A subsequent grant from the Easter Seal Research Foundation made possible the publication of the proceedings.

The institute convened at Stanford Medical Center on September 19-20-21, 1960 in six sessions, each with its own chairman, keynote speaker and discussion panel. Twenty-eight specialists, representing as many institutions and agencies, participated. All administrative aspects of the Institute were assumed by the California society. Consultative assistance was given by Jayne Shover, associate director of the National Society for Crippled Children and Adults. The arduous task of coordinating every phase of preparation was in the capable hands of Runo Arne, consultant on the staff of the California society.

The number of affiliated area societies is now fifty. The decade of 1956-1966 was a "Golden Age" as far as new Easter Seal facilities in California were concerned. In August, 1952, the San Diego Easter Seal Society opened its new $1,250,000 Children's Hospital and in 1958 a new wing was built. In 1956, the Sacramento County Society for Crippled Children opened the doors of a new Rehabilitation and Pre-School Program for the Handicapped and Multi-handicapped Child. The building, valued at more than $225,000 was the gift of Sacramento's County organized labor, building industry and building supply firms. The summer of 1957 saw the opening of Easter Seal Camp by the Society for Crippled Children and Adults of Santa Clara County. The same summer the Crippled Children's Society of San Bernardino County opened a new recreation center, the gift of Junior Women's Clubs, labor and industry. The year 1959 also saw a procession of new Easter Seal facilities. First came the dedication of Covell Memorial Hall, a sheltered workshop building, by the Stanislaus County Society for Crippled Children and Adults. Next came the opening of a sheltered workshop in Richmond by the Easter Seal Society of Contra Costa County. Climaxing the procession was the new model rehabilitation and research center of the San Mateo County Society for Crippled Children and Adults. Still to come, in 1961, was the low altitude resident camp built near Malibu by the Crippled Children's Society of Los Angeles County.

Last year, one Californian in five faced the future with a crippling condition that in some way limited his activities; thus, three and one-half million children and adults in the state needed help of one or several kinds to attain—or to reattain—lives of dignity and full usefulness in their communities.

They were the baby born with cerebral palsy, the child who could not walk, the school boy who stuttered, the teen-ager who lost a leg in a highway accident, the factory worker with an injured hand, the business executive paralyzed by stroke, the senior citizen periled by "brittle bones."

They were people of all ages, in all communities, from all walks of life—some 23,000 of whom individually constituted the day-in, day-out "business" of the Easter Seal Society in its thirty-ninth year.

Easter Seal societies on a state-level basis and in fifty California counties in 1965 directed full-time operations to giving help or getting help for these thousands of California citizens.

Services the societies gave included the following:

Rehabilitation and treatment center programs established and operated by big-city units, providing a complexity of rehabilitation services for physically disabled persons who lived not only in metropolitan areas, but also in outlying communities.

Rehabilitation workshop programs, offering job training or employment for adults whose disabilities prevented a return to previous occupations or participation in the regular workaday world.

Physical therapy and occupational therapy programs, bringing the means for developing or restoring function to bodies and limbs crippled by accident, disease, or illness.

Speech therapy programs, helping children and adults to learn or to regain the skills of oral communication, which are sometimes latent or damaged by physical or psychological disorders.

Equipment loan services, standing ready as emergency sources for families requiring temporary use of hospital beds, wheelchairs, crutches, or other special appliances.

Transportation services, providing either the vehicles and drivers or the fares needed for getting patients, young and old, to treatment sources or to special social activities that divert them from daily routines.

Resident camps, affording two-week shifts of summer vacation, leisure and modified activity to crippled children and adults from every county in the state.

A special Krauss Memorial Speech Camp program, providing six weeks of intensive speech therapy and recreation for thirty children with cleft palate handicaps from twenty California communities.

Day camps and recreation programs, offering special summertime activities and year-round schedules of swimming, arts and crafts, outings and entertainment.

Other programs, meeting specific needs as indicated by individual cases and by the resources and services available in individual localities.

In addition to giving help, Easter Seal societies directed their efforts to getting help for the physically disabled. Some 10,000 persons who applied for help could be given necessary information or directed to other welfare organizations established within the community. Thus did the Easter Seal Society of California fulfill a measure of its role as the advocate for the physically handicapped in 1965.

CALIFORNIA EASTER SEAL SOCIETIES SERVED THESE PEOPLE

With these crippling conditions	*Adults*	*Children*	*Total*
Arthritis	357	104	461
Cardiac Ailments	333	557	890
Cerebral Palsy	1,394	4,052	5,446
Epilepsy	215	606	821
Hearing Disorders	169	745	914
Multiple Sclerosis	182	18	200

Muscular Dystrophy	135	535	670
Poliomyelitis	308	632	940
Other Orthopedic-Neurological	1,331	2,147	3,478
Sight Impairment	136	603	739
Speech Problems	335	3,268	3,603
Other Conditions	2,776	1,980	4,756
Served in 1965	7,671	15,247	22,918

A Direct Service Program

The operational pattern of the Easter Seal Society for Crippled Children and Adults of Sacramento Physical Rehabilitation Center as it exists today involves the following major services. These are speech and hearing therapy, physical therapy, occupational therapy, a vocational training workshop and social service. Each of these services is provided at the Easter Seal Rehabilitation Center.

The services of the Speech and Hearing Department are planned and operated to adhere to the standards of the American Speech and Hearing Association. During the past year more than 125 children and adults received diagnostic services, therapy for speech and hearing disorders. The newest program of the society is a demonstration project using rehabilitation services for adult aphasic stroke patients.

The physical therapy service is closely interrelated with the discipline of occupational therapy. The department is completely equipped including a Hubbard tank and therapy pool. The medical profession and its related disciplines, as well as the community as a whole, understand the meaning of the comprehensive program found in the physical rehabilitation center. This is demonstrated by the referrals received from the increasing number of physicians in the community. Eighty-three physicians referred patients to the center for physical therapy in 1965.

The workshop offers the client opportunities for work adjustment, work experience, vocational counseling and placement. These services are also closely interrelated with occupational therapy and the Vocational Rehabilitation Services of the State Department of Education. Some patients receive physical, occupational and speech therapy simultaneously in a "total push" effort. When a patient is ready for workshop services and receives further vocational training, or to be returned to his job, a milestone is reached. Contracts with industry and private work provide funds to pay the workshop trainees an incentive wage or wages. Additional services include preschool program for handicapped children with an enrollment of sixty, loan equipment, pool, recreation, year around swim program, resident summer camping and assistive devices.

A fee schedule has been established for each of the therapeutic services. Fees are set in relation to direct costs of staff salaries. Since services are rendered without regard to financial ability to pay, fees are modified after confidential review of the applicants' finances. Total "free" service last year exceeded the total paid service. The center's patient case load is comprised of 52 per cent children and 48 per cent adults. Patients are admitted to the center on a physician's prescription, official agency's referral, or by parents' request. The only means of financial support for this countywide program is from private contributions, memorials, bequests and the annual Easter Seal appeal.

THE YEARS TO COME

The legislators, public officials, parents, professional workers and private citizens who have built California's program of aid for the handicapped continue to look ahead. Maintenance and improvement of good services are always their goal. In 1966, they also have unfinished business ahead of them: the business of a rehabilitation and residential center for the severely handicapped, definitely a need; the business of study of financing of crippled children services and special education; the business of study of physical disabilities now excluded from some of the treatment, educational and rehabilitation services; the business of the employment problems of the severely handicapped young adults.

Part III

CITY, COUNTY, AND STATE PROGRAMS IN SPECIAL EDUCATION

FIGURE III-1. Leaders in establishing the Cleveland Speech and Hearing Center included Marie Hays Heiner, Nathan Danby and George Fortune.

FIGURE III-2. Dr. Martin F. Palmer, founder and late director of the Institute of Logopedics.

FIGURE III-3. Dr. Edward J. Waterhouse, fifth director of the Perkins School for the Blind. Behind him is a picture of Anne Sullivan with Helen Keller who attended Perkins School.

FIGURE III-4. The blind can often excel in sewing. This girl at Perkins School is pinning up a hem.

FIGURE III-5. A deaf-blind child uses a Perkins braille writer, developed by Howe Press, Perkins School for the Blind, which enables blind and deaf-blind people to write braille as easily as using a typewriter. Over 30,000 braille writers are in use around the world.

FIGURE III-6. With the sympathetic understanding and help of an instructor, a boy is learning how to use a vise in an industrial arts class at the Perkins School for the Blind.

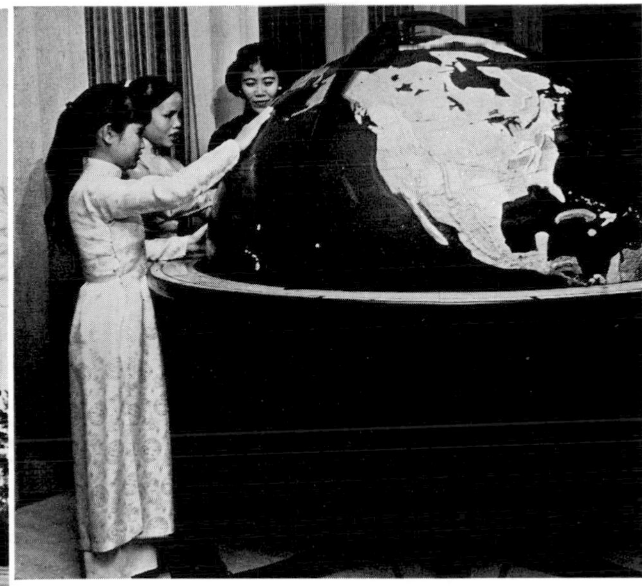

FIGURE III-8. Two blind girls from Viet Nam, students at Perkins School, find their homeland on the Howe globe in the lobby. Looking on is a teacher-trainee from China.

FIGURE III-7. Learning travel techniques using a cane under the watchful eye of an instructor at the Perkins for the Blind.

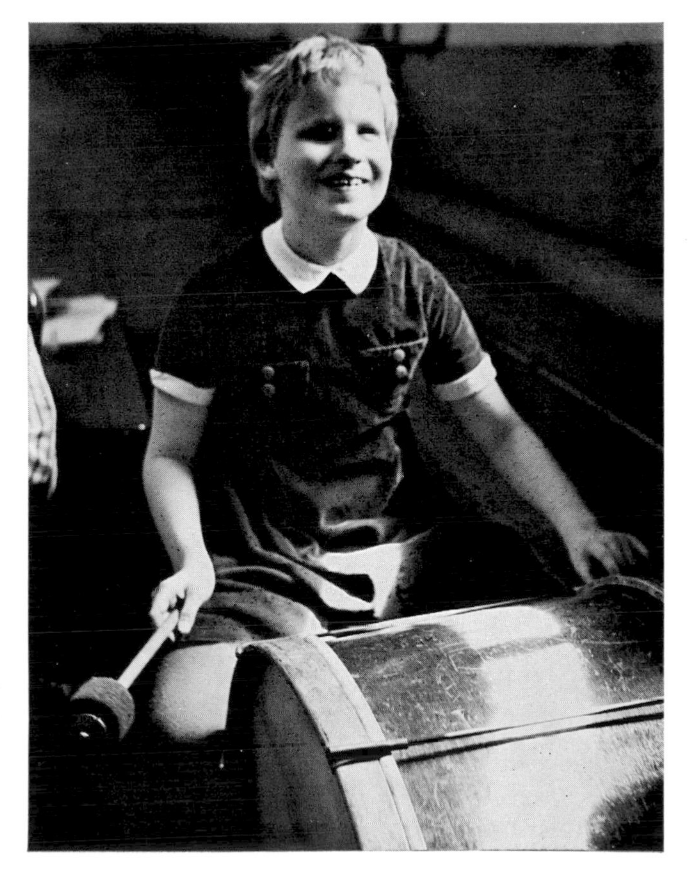

FIGURE III-9. This little girl at the Perkins School for the Blind is finding great delight in beating the drum. Music and all activities involving sound have great meaning for the blind.

Chapter 17

SPECIAL EDUCATION PROGRAMS IN THE NEW YORK CITY PUBLIC SCHOOL SYSTEM

EDMUND M. HORAN

THE Office of Special Services consists of eleven bureaus in the New York City Public School System. Mr. Richard M. Lubell is the assistant superintendent in charge of the Office of Special Services. These bureaus constitute two distinct branches: (1) those that are concerned mainly with special education, and (2) those concerned mainly with pupil-personnel services. The bureaus are distributed as follows:

Special Education

Bureau for Children with Retarded Mental Development
Bureau for the Education of the Physically Handicapped
Bureau for the Education of the Visually Handicapped
Schools for the Deaf (Junior High School 47 and Public School 158 both in Manhattan)
Bureau for the Education of Socially Maladjusted Children
"400" Schools (Hospitals, Convalescent Homes, Shelters and Institutions)

Pupil-Personnel Services

Bureau of Attendance
Bureau of Child Guidance
Bureau of Educational and Vocational Guidance
Bureau for Health Education
Bureau for Speech Improvement

Presented in this chapter are statements about the specialized functions of the bureaus in the Office of Special Services. In this presentation, use has been made of the current annual reports which the directors of the respective bureaus have graciously made available. In some instances, however, material has been obtained from an earlier overview of the bureaus made available by the Office of Special Services.

BUREAU FOR CHILDREN WITH RETARDED MENTAL DEVELOPMENT

(Miss Katherine D. Lynch, Director)

The Bureau for Children with Retarded Mental Development (BCRMD), a part of the Office of Special Services, is responsible for the education and training of mentally retarded children between the ages of five and twenty-one as mandated by state law. It is the largest agency in the world specifically concerned with the education of mentally retarded children and young adults. It is a bureau which consists of a director, five assistant directors, twenty-one field supervisors and six guidance counselors who project and implement a program of special education for over 12,000 children and young adults in nearly 1,000 classes in the New York City Public School System.

Under the mandate of state law classes are established in regular elementary, junior and senior high schools throughout the city. Specially trained and licensed teachers under Bureau CRMD supervision implement a carefully constructed developmental program with a curriculum that leads to attainable life goals for educable and trainable mental retardates.

Initial identification and recommendation of pupils for special class placement is made by the Bureau of Child Guidance after individual testing and evaluation requested by the parents or school principal.

All pupil placements—admission, discharge, transfer, or promotion—are authorized by the Bureau CRMD Director through the central office staff of assistant directors and supervisors. Pupils are assigned to appropriate special classes on the basis of chronological age, social and emotional maturity, psychological evaluation and indicated potential for independent functioning with limited supervision or semidependent or dependent citizenship roles.

Bureau philosophy, based on sound educational and administrative principles, strives to foster the establishment of clusters of BCRMD classes in the elementary schools rather than single classes where the age range between the youngest and oldest child generally tends to exceed four years. These clusters include the preprimary, primary and intermediate classes for the educable mentally retarded (EMR) in two educational tracks, with the students requiring less supervision and possessing a higher level of social and emotional maturity as well as better educational and vocational ability tracked into high school BCRMD classes with work-study programs. Other EMR pupils who require additional training in skills for independent living are tracked into the Occupational Training Center program. A third educational track provides a program for the trainable mentally retarded (TMR) child and young adult from age five through twenty-one. Educational and vocational guidance and all placement and follow-up services are a part of the total BCRMD program which accepts the responsibility for the mentally retarded child from his initial placement until his eventual adjustment in the life of the community.

The special class program for Track I educable mentally retarded pupils is based on a core curriculum which serves to integrate the eight curriculum areas: social living, health and hygiene, social studies, language arts, mathematics, science, fine arts and practical arts.

The core program builds on the child's known environment from the limited circle of his home and family to his eventual adjustment in the community as a productive contributing citizen. There are eight cores:

Core I Home and Family
II The Neighborhood
III The Larger Community
IV The City
V Study of Job Areas
VI Choosing, Getting and Holding a Job
VII Spending One's Income
VIII The Worker as a Citizen and Social Being

Track II pupils progress more slowly than the Track I pupils and achieve a more limited competency. The Track II program, while utilizing the core approach, follows the maturational development of the child in five major areas with a descending order of emphasis. These areas are the following:

Health and Physical Development
Personal Competency
Social Competency
Avocational and Vocational Skills
Academic Skills

The curriculum for Track III trainable mentally retarded children is designed primarily to develop the self-help skills of the child, and train him to operate more effectively, with direction and supervision, in his home and immediate neighborhood or possibly in a sheltered workshop or in a public or private residential school.

In discharging this total responsibility to the mentally retarded the Bureau CRMD works with and through many divisions, bureaus, institutions and agencies both within and apart from the Board of Education. To carry out this extensive and comprehensive total program for nearly 13,000 mentally retarded pupils the Bureau CRMD functions within broad areas of responsibility through its director, assistant directors, supervisors and teachers.

Services Available

	5 Boroughs—975 Classes					
Level—Type	*M*	*X*	*K*	*Q*	*R*	*Total*
Elementary	95	106	185	84	18	488
Doubly Handicapped	14	1	4	4	2	25
Trainable Mentally Retarded	26	27	42	29	5	129
Junior High School	63	49	92	33	5	242
Senior High School	16	12	15	11	2	56
Occupational Training Center						
EMR	18			10		28
TMR	3			4		7
	235	195	338	175	32	975

Although the first day-class for retarded pupils was established in Providence, Rhode Island, in 1896 and Elizabeth Farrell organized the first day-class for mentally retarded children in New York City in 1902, the beginning of special education for the mentally retarded must be placed a century prior to this date in the work of the French physician, Jean Itard.

They were years of enthusiasm, hope and experiment following the French Revolution. A door had been flung open and men were marching through it anxious to breathe the fresh air of change. The possibilities of science and the ideas of philosophy had ushered in a new age of optimism. Sensationalists pitted their philosophy against the naturalists. It was at this time that Victor, a wild boy, was captured in the woods of the Department of Aveyron in France. Taken to Paris he was exhibited to the people who, perhaps, had come to see the "noble savage." But what they saw was a frightened, dirty, grunting creature who was human only in shape. Itard also saw the child and, believing that his subnormality was caused by a deprivation of social intercourse and general experience in a social environment, set out to treat Victor at the institution for deaf-mutes where he was physician.

Itard's initial optimism, particularly after his initial success in his first two years' experimentation in treating Victor, was later tempered by reality. He had learned that not experience alone was necessary for success, but, also, a mind that could make adequate use of experience. Itard had made a considerable contribution to the training and education of a boy with subnormal mental capacity. He had demonstrated surely and definitely that a child with mental retardation could be helped and could be taught. His recommendations for Victor were, in effect, recommendations for the initiation of special education for the mentally retarded. Itard left his recommendation in these words:

> . . . looking at this long experiment from any point of view, whether it be considered as the methodical education of a savage or as no more than the physical and moral treatment of one of those creatures ill-favored by nature, rejected by society and abandoned by medicine, the care that has been taken of him, the changes that have taken place and those which can be hoped for, the voice of humanity, the interest inspired by such a complete desertion and a destiny so strange—all these things recommend this extraordinary young man to the attention of scientists, to the solicitude of our administrators, and to the protection of the Government.

As mentioned above, Elizabeth Farrell organized the first day-class for mentally retarded children in New York City in 1902. Added impetus was given to the day-class movement with the advent of efficient psychometric instruments, especially the original Stanford-Binet Test of Intelligence in

1916. The following figures graphically illustrate the expansion of the Bureau CRMD since 1906:

1906— 14 classes
1910—103 classes
1943—600 classes
1962—805 classes
1966—975 classes (991 classes as of September, 1966)

The worthwhileness of the child and the possibility that he can become a contributing member to society is emphasized in the modern educational approach to the retarded. Through education an evaluation of the specific abilities of each child can be made in order to assist him to develop to his maximum potential. Its dual aim is focused on the achievement of vocational and social competence for the retarded. This program of occupational education provides occupational and social skills which lead to social and occupational adjustment in society.

The Bureau CRMD functions on a decentralized borough basis under the leadership of its director. The director and professional staff have responsibilities in curriculum development and implementation, public relations, liaison with cooperative services and community agencies, guidance and placement, work-study and employment, returnees from state schools and institutions, transportation, budget, equipment and supplies, and an internship graduate training program, to mention some of their assignments.

Staff members are assigned to serve in a liaison capacity and as consultants to agencies that work directly and cooperatively with mentally retarded children and adults. These agencies include the following:

Association for the Help of Retarded Children
Child Development Center, Albert Einstein College of Medicine, Yeshiva University
Clinic for the Mentally Retarded, New York Medical College, Flower-5th Avenue Hospitals
Community Council of Greater New York
Departments of Special Education, local colleges and universities
Division of Vocational Rehabilitation, New York State
Federation Employment and Guidance Service
Kennedy Child Study Center
Mental Retardation Project, Teachers College, Columbia University
Morris J. Solomon Clinic, Brooklyn Jewish Hospital
New York State Employment Service
New York State Joint Legislative Committee on Mental Retardation
Association for CRMD, Inc.
Shield of David
State Schools, Hospitals and Training Schools of New York State
United Cerebral Palsy Association

In looking to the immediate future, the Bureau for Children with Retarded Mental Development is actively preparing the following plans:

1. The opening of an Occupational Training Center in the borough of Queens for both educable and trainable mentally retarded young adults.
2. A revision of the present BCRMD High School Curriculum.
3. An evaluation of the present BCRMD Tentative Curriculum for Trainable Mentally Retarded Pupils.
4. The organization of sufficient classes to eliminate waiting lists of children recommended for BCRMD classes.

5. The extension of the High School Work-Study Program.
6. The expansion of BCRMD classes to service the needs of mentally retarded children in each school district.
7. The extension of the BCRMD school program for emotionally disturbed mentally retarded children.
8. Projections for the opening of Occupational Training Centers in Brooklyn, Bronx, and Richmond.
9. The expansion of facilities for five to seven year old mentally retarded children.
10. The expansion of facilities for multiply-handicapped mentally retarded children.
11. An expansion in the field of parent education.

BUREAU FOR THE EDUCATION OF THE PHYSICALLY HANDICAPPED

(Mr. Marcus S. Arnold, Director)

The Bureau for the Education of the Physically Handicapped is charged with the responsibility of educating physically handicapped children other than visually and acoustically handicapped. Under state law a physically handicapped child is "a person under twenty-one years of age who by reason of a physical defect or infirmity, whether congenital or acquired by accident, injury or disease, is or may be expected to be totally or partially incapacitated for education or for remunerative occupation."

Among the physically handicapped children served by this bureau are those with the following conditions:

1. Orthopedic conditions.
2. Cardiac involvement.
3. Neurological impairment.
4. Lowered vitality and/or nutritional deficiencies.
5. Other conditions, such as diabetes, hepatitis, convulsive disorders, arrested tuberculosis, skin disorders, allergies, and postoperative.

Special classes for the physically handicapped are located in regular schools (Health Conservation Classes) and in hospitals and convalescent homes ("400") schools. When the handicap does not allow for attendance in a school facility, either temporarily or permanently, the school is brought to the home through the services of a specially licensed teacher of homebound children.

Health Conservation Classes are maintained in regular elementary, junior high and senior high schools. Children are placed in these classes on the basis of medical certification approved by the New York City Department of Health. The medical findings, with the accompanying recommendations for educational placement, are then reviewed periodically. Bus transportation is provided, where feasible, according to medical recommendation.

Health Conservation Classes No. 20 are units of two or more classes housed in regular schools and designed for severely physically handicapped pupils. Occupational, physical and speech therapists work with the children. Training is provided in rooms specially equipped for the specific therapies. The daily program for each child is worked out by a teacher-coordinator following consultation with the team—medical director, therapists, psychologist, social workers and teachers. This cooperation facilitates the training of the child in the other disciplines in the classroom situation.

Health Conservation Classes No. 30 are for children diagnosed as brain-injured. Registers are limited and emphasis is placed on perceptual training and in meeting special learning problems resulting from neurological impairment.

Home Instruction provides for continuity of education for children who must remain at home for brief or extended periods. The instruction, averaging four one-hour lessons each week, is individual. The teacher maintains contact with the child's home school and tailors her instruction to the physical, academic, emotional and social needs of the child. Home instruction is offered for grades 1-12.

The education of the physically handicapped is similar to that of normal children with modifications to meet individual needs. Health Conservation classes for the physically handicapped are located within the regular schools in special facilities. Activities are integrated with the regular school program as much as possible. Such activities include assembly programs, audio-visual programs, excursions, shop work, special events, and lunch period. Wherever possible, Health Conservation classes are grouped in clusters in a particular school. Integration of the homebound child with other children is encouraged by pupil affiliation with the neighborhood school and by an extensive program of socialization which includes visits to school, audio-visual programs, parties, picnics and theater parties. Further socialization and recreation are provided for some children through the cooperation of private agencies.

Pupils

Educational Facility	*Number of Pupils*
Health Conservation Classes	1965-1966
Enrollment	(Approximately) 4,200
Register	(Approximately) 2,800
Home Instruction	
Enrollment	(Approximately) 5,200
Register	(Approximately) 3,200

Number of Classes or Teaching Positions

Type of Class or Position	*1962-63*	*1963-64*	*1964-65*	*1965-66*
Health Conservation Classes (Grades 1-12)	190	185	177	173
Health Conservation No. 20 Classes (Severely Handicapped)	30	32	34	37
Health Conservation No. 30 Classes (Brain Injured)	36	47	57	78
Health Conservation Hospital and "400" Schools	88	84	80	81
Health Conservation Classes—Total	*344*	*348*	*348*	*369*
Home Instruction	*328*	*328*	*328*	*361*
Additional Temporary Substitutes (59)				
Total	672	676	676	730

The story of the program for classes for brain-injured children in New York City has not been one of gradual growth but rather one of remarkable spurts within a period of a few years. A pilot study of one class was begun in Public School 85, Bronx, in 1955. This was the unique facility for all of New York City. In 1959 additional classes were organized and the services have been extended to all boroughs. Presently there are seventy-eight classes.

A brain-injured child is a child who before, during or after birth has received an injury to or suffered an infection of the brain. As a result of such organic impairment, defects of the neuromotor system may be present or absent; however, such a child may show disturbances in perception, thinking and emotional behavior, either separately or in combination.

The brain-injured child was identified by research carried on by Warner and Strauss. They found that while generalization could be made about several psychological characteristics of these children there was also considerable variability among them. Whenever educational placement is planned, individual appraisal must be made of each child.

The psychological characteristics usually found among these children are as follows:

1. Distractibility.
2. Motor disinhibition.
3. Dissociation.
4. Perseveration.
5. Disturbance of figure-background relationship.
6. Absence of well-developed self-image and body-image concepts.
7. Bizarre behavior.

Some educators and psychologists feel that of all the characteristics distractibility is the most prevalent among these children. The attention span of these children is exceedingly short. They are distracted by minute details. Motor disinhibition is the failure of the child to avoid responding to any stimulus that produces motor activity. Dissociation is the inability of a child to see things as a whole or as a gestalt. The child sees the various parts and has difficulty in bringing the parts together. Perseveration is the meaningless and persistent repetition or continuance of an activity once begun. Disturbance of figure-background is noticed in children who confuse the figures and the background. Absence of self-concept and body image concept are often inadequately developed among these children.

The brain-injured child by virtue of the organicity of his condition and his problems in learning is best served by special education. In the classes for brain-injured children the child's special needs are met in a structured environment with methodology adapted to his perceptual difficulties.

Early identification of the child's needs and placement in the special class at an early age is advisable. In a successful program the child's learning problems are minimized, and his personality difficulties are resolved. Placement in the regular stream of education is the ultimate goal. In some cases the child may be better placed in other special education services.

Special Services Available to the Bureau for the Education of the Physically Handicapped

1. Board of Education
   a. Instruction by specially licensed teachers.
   b. Itinerant teachers for the visually handicapped.
   c. Speech and lipreading.
   d. Audio-Visual materials.
   e. Radio and television (High School of the Air).
   f. Provision of typewriters and radios to the homebound pupils.
   g. Curriculum coordination and materials.
   h. Educational and vocational guidance services.
   i. Bureau of Child Guidance clinical services.
   j. Research and Evaluation.
   k. Bus Transportation.
   l. Teacher training program.
2. Department of Health
   a. Processing of recommendations for educational placement (Health Conservation classes, Home Instruction) based on physical needs.
   b. Providing dental care.
   c. Providing medical director, physical and occupational therapists, attendants, secretary for the HC 20 classes, as well as some special equipment for therapy rooms.
3. State Department of Education
   a. Providing bulletins and curriculum materials.
   b. Consultation with specialized personnel.
   c. Providing services of Division of Vocational Rehabilitation—testing, counseling, training, placement.
   d. Teacher training through grants and workshops.

Parent Orientation and Guidance

The cooperation of each individual parent is enlisted as an integral part of the program for the handicapped. Parent groups are encouraged to participate in the program of the Health Conservation classes and participation by bureau personnel in the activities of local parents' association is encouraged.

In planning for the future the Bureau for the Education of the Physically Handicapped is currently working on plans for the attainment of the following:

1. Additional health conservation and brain-injured classes at the elementary and junior high school level.
2. Two special high school classes for the cerebral palsied and brain-injured annexed to cerebral palsied centers for prevocational and academic training.
3. An early childhood class annexed to a cerebral palsy center.
4. A Manual for teachers of brain-injured children.
5. Revision of bulletin, "Helping the Physically Limited Child."
6. Use of a greater number of auxiliary team teachers in B.I. classes.
7. Expansion of cyesis program to four new centers.
8. Teacher training Home Instruction workshops in mathematics and reading.
9. Wider use of Frostig and Stern materials.
10. B.I. team with clinical teaching on an experimental basis.
11. Use of ITPA diagnostic teaching for B.I.
12. Orientation of clinics, hospitals and agencies on B.I. program.
13. A team teacher assigned at a special orthopedic unit.

SCHOOLS FOR THE DEAF—J-47-M AND P-158-M

School for the Deaf—Junior High School 47, Manhattan
Principal, Miss Alice G. Rooney

School for the Deaf—P.S. 158, Manhattan
Principal, Mr. John D. Harrington

Services for children in the City of New York with hearing and other communications disorders are centered at two schools: The School for the Deaf at Junior High School 47, Manhattan and the School for the Deaf at P.S. 158, Manhattan.

The School for the Deaf at J.H.S. 47 provides for the education of approximately 500 deaf children from preschool through the junior high school. Included in this program are a nursery school, an elementary level, a junior high school, special classes for mentally retarded deaf children, and classes for aphasics. Admission to this school for the deaf is based upon the general criterion of an average hearing loss in the speech frequencies of over 60 decibels. However, each case is decided individually after careful review of audiological records, an examination by an otologist and a study of the information provided by schools, clinics and other cooperating agencies. Essentially, J.H.S. 47 is designed to meet the needs of children whose hearing disability makes education in a regular classroom impossible.

At J.H.S. 47 highly trained teachers use the oral method stressing the communication and speech arts in all phases of learning. All regular school subjects are taught, and courses of study and curriculum bulletins prepared and issued by the Board of Education of the City of New York followed with proper adaptations. In addition speech, language, auditory training and lip-reading are taught as provided for in official bulletins. Special features of the School for the Deaf at J.H.S. 47 include the integration of deaf and hearing children at the early levels of preschool training, the operation of a prevocational department consisting of seven shops and the use of group hearing aids in every classroom. The school serves as the center of education for deaf children in the Public School System of New York City.

The School for the Deaf at P.S. 158 is the home of a program for the education of aphasic children whose primary disability is lack of speech caused by brain lesion. The three major categories are the *receptive*—inability to understand, the *conceptual*—inability to synthesize inner language and *expressive*—inability to initiate the motor functions for speech. These difficulties may exist in varying degrees and combinations. Children are admitted to these classes after careful examination by and upon recommendation of a special Bureau of Child Guidance psychiatrist.

Also directed and supervised by this School for the Deaf are the following outlying programs:

1. A lipreading program for hard of hearing children. Children remain in their regular schools but attend weekly sessions with an itinerant teacher at one of more than 100 centers. Admission is based upon a hearing loss of at least 20 decibels, and upon the recommendation of the school otologist.
2. A program of itinerant service to 110 integrated deaf children. Itinerant teachers visit each child's school regularly to give whatever type of help is needed by the deaf child or the school. Deaf pupils are integrated by both schools for the deaf after careful consideration of the capacity of the child to adjust. The program extends from elementary through high school.
3. Provision for deaf students on the high school level. New York City educators of the deaf believe that deaf children should be integrated at least by the high school years. While many deaf children are integrated individually into their neighborhood high schools, or into high schools meeting their particular vocational needs, there are others who have a continued need for a special program in the setting of a regular high school. The programs take the form of either the homeroom-tutorial plan or the resource room plan.
4. Preschool Auditory Training Program. Auditory impressions are developed through play with the use of individual hearing aids. Audiological evaluation and parent guidance are major goals.
5. Evening Classes for deaf and hard of hearing adults. Instruction in lipreading, language and speech is provided.

Other operations of the schools for the deaf are shared responsibilities for which personnel from both schools contribute services essential to the total board of education program for children with hearing and language disorders.

A fleet of school buses transports the children from their homes in the five boroughs to the Schools for the Deaf.

A hearing conservation clinic is located at J.H.S. 47. This clinic not only serves as the audiological center for both schools but it is the central agency for complete audiometric testing of over 6,000 school children annually. Trained audiometricians, teachers of the deaf who are specialists in hearing aids and audiology, an otologist, and an assistant principal serve on the team which evaluates the needs of children seen at the clinic. For children found to have a hearing loss, appropriate recommendations and referrals are made.

The schools for the deaf conduct their own research in the development of curriculum. Recent publications in the areas of lipreading, speech auditory training and readiness have already achieved nationwide acclaim.

Teacher training is accomplished through pre-service training in cooperation with Hunter College of the City of New York, through in-service training done both within the schools for the deaf and in courses provided by the board of education, and through a special program in which experienced teachers of common branches are given the opportunity to receive a period of full-time training on salary as teachers of the deaf at J.H.S. 47 or P.S.158.

Guidance and psychological and social services for both schools are provided by a licensed guidance counselor and a Bureau of Child Guidance team consisting of a psychologist, psychiatrist and social worker.

Services Available at the School for the Deaf at Junior High School 47, Manhattan

1. Program for deaf children from preschool (two years and eight months) through junior high school.
2. Seven classes of mentally retarded deaf children.
3. Prevocational training provided on all levels from first through ninth grades.
4. Provisions made for deaf children with secondary handicaps such as deaf-aphasic, deaf-emotionally disturbed, deaf-cerebral dysfunctioning.
5. Bus transportation including matron services utilizing 25 vehicles.
6. Carefully planned and continuous parent education program.
7. Limited program of guidance.
9. Hearing Conservation Clinic administering tests to over 6,000 children annually.
10. Hearing Aid Clinic providing service to over one thousand pupils in the city who are in need of amplification of sound.
11. Teacher training program which includes training of teachers in service and of student teachers on the undergraduate level.

12. Laboratory school for graduate students from Hunter College and under the Federal Grant-In-Aid Program from New York University.
13. Part-time services of a Bureau of Child Guidance team which includes a psychiatrist, psychologist and psychiatric social worker.
14. Serves as the educational resource in demonstrating techniques of teaching the deaf to medical students and to visitors from all over the world.

Statistics

J-47-M	*1963-64*	*1965-66*
Preschool Children (under 5.8)	88	86
Elementary Classes (1 through 6)	209	218
Junior High School (7, 8 and 9)	98	99
Mentally Retarded Deaf	48	52
Total Register	443	455
Pupils screened for admission	220	232
Pupils admitted	107	106
Pupils graduated	34	32
Pupils promoted into high school	28	22
Deaf pupils being graduated from H.S.	23	25
Hearing Conservation Clinic		
Pupils receiving hearing tests	6,621	7,155
Pupils seen by the otologist	2,350	2,529
Hearing Aid Clinic		
Pupils received at Hearing Aid Clinic	676	1,155
Pupils referred to Speech and Hearing Centers*	615	951
Pupils referred to Division of Vocational Rehabilitation	54	92

Plans for the immediate future include the following points of emphasis:

1. Introduction of a new course of study in language, "Language Development for the Deaf Child, Design for Growth."
2. Work with the Bureau of Child Guidance team on the study of the hyperactive child.
3. A follow-up on loop induction and tape recording research projects now in process.
4. An upgrading of goals for oral communication.
5. Continued work on analysis of effectiveness of group hearing aids under laboratory conditions as set up in recently completed classrooms.
6. An emphasis on improvement of standards for living and learning in and out of school.
7. The continuance of parent education meetings oriented toward specific school levels and related to specific areas of learning as lipreading and auditory training.
8. Experiment with acoustically handicapped students in teacher training program.
9. An exploration of the possibility of an after-school tutorial program.
10. The publication of the Program for Young Deaf Children in Volta Review.
11. A workshop in Language for the Deaf Child. The purpose will be to have teaching staff and supervisory staff explore recent proposals in the teaching of language.
12. Continuous tape experiment with four-year-olds in order to reinforce auditory impressions of learned language.

---

* Initial referrals plus reevaluations

PROGRAMS OFFERED BY THE SCHOOL FOR THE DEAF AT P.S. 158, MANHATTAN

1. *Located at P.S. 158-M*
   Classes for children with language learning disorders (aphasia)
2. *Outlying Programs*
   a. Itinerant Teacher Program for Hard of Hearing and Integrated Deaf Centers in schools in the five boroughs.
   b. Special Integration Center at P.S. 40-M and J.H.S. 104-M.
   c. Classes for the Deaf in High Schools: Charles Evans Hughes H.S. (M); N. Y. School of Printing (M); Bryant H.S. (Q); Eli Whitney V.H.S. (K); Canarsie H.S. (K).
   d. Preschool Auditory Training Program at Speech and Hearing Centers: Bellevue; Bronx Municipal; Kings County; Hunter College.
   e. Classes for Deaf and Aphasic Children in Richmond: P.S. 40-R and McKee V.H.S. (R).
   f. Evening Classes for Deaf and Hard of Hearing Adults: Washington Irving E.H.S. (M).
   g. Itinerant Audiometric Screening Program.

Services	*Children Served*		
	1963-64	*1964-65*	*1965-66*
1. Children with language learning disorders (aphasia)	138	154	180
2. *Itinerant Services*			
Integrated deaf	55	51	51
Special hard of hearing	60	65	80
Lipreading pupils	650	700	712
3. Classes for deaf in regular high schools	89	80	83
4. Preschool auditory training at Hearing-Speech Centers	25	26	68
5. *Program at P.S. 40-R, McKee V.H.S.*			
Classes for deaf	20	16	10
Classes for aphasics			6
(Resource Service)		10	11
6. Evening classes for deaf adults	—	—	—
Totals	1,037	1,102	1,201

BUREAU FOR THE EDUCATION OF SOCIALLY MALADJUSTED CHILDREN

(Mr. Sidney I. Lipsyte, Director)

The Bureau of S.M.C. Schools seek to set up a planned psycho-educational program where emotionally disturbed and socially maladjusted preadolescent and adolescent boys and girls may be helped to develop a level of integrated personality, by means of which they may function more adequately emotionally, academically, vocationally, physically, culturally and socially. These special schools maintain the basic philosophy that disturbed youth can be rehabilitated, given an environment rich in guidance, nonpunitive, where behavior may be modified through self-knowledge and self-evaluation, where the achievement of this insight may be stimulated as well as motivated, where personality and character may be molded through participation in significantly worthwhile activities, and where preadolescents and adolescents may discover their places in the community through the broadening of educational, vocational, cultural, and social horizons. Specifically, the goals are to teach each child the following:

1. To believe in and accept himself and his own self-worth.
2. How to handle his impulses in a personally and socially acceptable way.

3. How to make wholesome and meaningful personal relationships.
4. How to make a positive emotional investment in his environment.
5. Good habits, healthful attitudes and necessary knowledges and skills in consonance with his emotional and intellectual potential.

The Bureau of S.M.C. Schools are to be found in several settings:

Day Schools
Psychiatric Hospitals
Treatment Centers
Remand Centers
Institutions

The students found in the day schools are in the great majority of the acting-out type whose primary behavior disorder manifests itself in repeated disruptive and aggressive behavior extensive in scope and serious in nature. These students have not responded to the intensive efforts of the home school to help them. Cultural deprivation, low socioeconomic family living levels with their environmental handicaps, disorganized family life, among other factors, have been basic contributors to the emotional instability and poorly motivated goals of this group. The aggressive behavior patterns not only blocked their own learning but, also, interfered with the education of other children, thus necessitating their withdrawal from the normal school.

Rehabilitation is the focus of the work of the day school. Assisted by guidance counselors, psychological and medical teams, the teaching staff through the use of small class registers (ten to fourteen), curricula adapted to needs, intensified remediation in the areas of reading and mathematics and the development of a positive mental hygiene approach, seek to give the youngsters well-motivated goals.

The aim of the day school is to return the children to the main stream as quickly as practicable or to provide guidance and terminal education training, whose rehabilitative value will make itself evident in preparing an adolescent for wholesome living, law-abiding citizenship and job adjustment.

There are Bureau of S.M.C. schools located in psychiatric hospitals. These schools serve to provide an educational program for preadolescents who have been admitted to a psychiatric hospital for observation and diagnostic evaluation. Since many of these children are diagnosed as severely neurotic or pre-psychotic, teachers for these schools must have special training and techniques used in the educational program must be adjusted to meet the needs of the individual. For many of the children, the schools provide a valuable therapy. The reports of the teaching staffs' observations are carefully weighed by the hospital staff in the development of the diagnostic picture of the child.

The Bureau of S.M.C. Schools are responsible for the educational program in several treatment centers (Henry Ittleson Center, Childville, Inc., Godmothers' League, Inc., etc.) which are involved in basic research in the areas of autism, schizophrenia, neurological impairments, organic damage and poor maturational development. Each of these treatment centers has designed its own research; the treatment plan is carried on by psychiatric and clinical staffs, usually working under the overall supervision of a psychiatrist.

There is a close relationship at the treatment centers between clinical and teaching staffs. The Bureau of S.M.C. school teachers participate in the case study conferences and become an integral part of the treatment program. The techniques and approaches used in the schools parallel the treatment centers' programs, complementing the plan for treatment and rehabilitation and contributing to the research findings. A closely knit joint effort by clinical and school staffs leading to maximum cooperation supportive of the growth and development of the child, is considered basic to any good approach in total treatment.

Thus, research design of the treatment centers is a maximum concern to the school and becomes a frame of reference in the educational planning. The school seeks to carry its share in meeting the needs of the child through the use of techniques that fall within the clinical design.

Children at remand centers are being held pending adjudication of their cases by the justices of the Children's Part of the Domestic Relations Court. Some of the children are awaiting admission to the New York State Training Schools. The average remand period is approximately forty-five days.

The school provides a continuous educational program for the children and does not materially differ from that of the regular program, except in its adaptation to the needs of children with many emotional and educational problems. The school, like the institution, is nonpunitive and its teachers are receptive, supportive and understanding.

Bureau of S.M.C. schools have been placed in a variety of residential institutional settings some of which are maintained by the three major religious faiths, others as mandated services of other city departments, i.e., Department of Welfare, Department of Correction. Children from ages six to twenty-one are placed in the institutional settings by court order or social agency referral. The majority of these children and young adults fall into the categories of delinquent or emotionally disturbed. A smaller group has been assigned by reason of need to remove them from disorganized family life which was proving destructive.

The institutions provide counselor, guidance, psychiatric and clinical services. The Bureau of S.M.C. school staff works very closely with the institutional staff in somewhat the same manner as previously described under treatment centers. The sharing of problems, the cooperative planning and the team approach characterize the relationship of school and institution. In the school, class size is small and a maximum of individual attention with an emphasis upon remediation is given the child to meet his educational needs. Recognizing the fact that children in institutions are in need of a warm, sympathetic and supportive climate, teachers for institutional schools are carefully screened.

The program of an institutional school varies in terms of the type of child assigned. Basically, there is a functional integration with all phases of institutional living, an effective coordination with the special services available and a plan to develop a curriculum implementation that seeks to achieve the objectives of any regular school.

Services Provided (1964 Statistics)

Facility	*Number*	*Age Group*	*No. of Pupils*	*No. of Teachers*	*Supportive Services*
Day Schools	14	10-17	2,045	240	15 Guidance Counselors; 14 B.C.G. Teams
Psychiatric Hospitals	2	5-16	181	24	Provided by Hospitals
Treatment Centers	12	5-20	339	56	Provided by Treatment Centers
Remand Centers	4	7-18	616	66	Provided by Youth House, Inc.
Institutions	9	6-21	1,333	130	Provided by Social Agencies
Totals	41		4,514	516	

By the very nature of the task, the guidance and rehabilitation of emotionally disturbed and socially maladjusted youth is time consuming and costly. The following goals for the future are suggested:

1. A reduction of class size so that the child may be worked with more effectively.
2. Increased services in the areas of clinical assistance (medical and psychological), speech, attendance, art, music, guidance and industrial arts.
3. The setting up of an advisory committee of representatives of many fields (pediatrics, psychiatry, social work, colleges, public relations, etc.) to serve as a consultative board to the assistant superintendent in the exploration of activities of the bureau.
4. A richer relationship with social agencies, courts, guidance clinics, colleges, public and private agencies, parent groups, unions, cultural, recreational groups and employment services.
5. A planned summer and winter camping program for the Bureau of S.M.C. school students.
6. Formation of a research team that would perform valid and reliable research in the area of emotional disturbance and social maladjustment.
7. The establishment of a halfway house type of school to be used for pupils returning from state mental hospitals and psychiatric hospitals, who are in need of intensive supportive assistance.

THE "400" SCHOOLS

(Solomon Prigohzy, Principal)

The "400" Schools were organized, and have been expanded, to provide public education for those children confined to hospitals and convalescent homes, or living in public, private and parochial institutions and shelters. The instructional program is carried on by licensed New York City teachers. The principal objective of these schools is to maintain, without undue interruption, these children's educational activities, taking into consideration their scholastic capabilities and/or the limitations imposed upon them by their physical handicaps. Emphasis is necessarily placed on small-group and individual instruction, with curriculum adaptations made to best meet the specific, and sometimes unique, needs of each child.

The "400" schools are, therefore, comprised of two groups:

1. Hospitals or convalescent homes to which children are confined for two weeks or more.
2. Institutions and shelters for neglected and/or dependent children.

The children in these schools may be placed in four categories:

1. Children with illnesses that may be chronic or temporary.
2. Children in convalescent homes who are recuperating from illnesses and are confined because of residual disabilities.
3. Neglected and/or dependent children who are in children's shelters.
4. Children needing rehabilitation because of physical handicap.

Teachers holding the Health Conservation license are appointed to classes in hospitals and convalescent homes. The special needs of these children require teachers whose personality and training equip them for working with children with special health and related emotional problems.

Teachers with the common branch license are eligible for appointment in child care centers. The special needs of these children require teachers who understand the problems of children who are institutionalized and have the desire and ability to participate in a cooperative endeavor with the institutional staff. Supervisors holding the Junior Principal license are eligible for assignment as heads of "400" schools.

Much of the professional growth of teachers in hospitals and institutions is achieved through close association and cooperation with the administrators, specialists in other professions, social workers and parents. Practice in interpreting records and reports and understanding their implications for curriculum and guidance is fostered through the team approach in most institutions. In-service courses, workshops and conferences are arranged by the local supervisors and by the Office of Special Services. A coordinator is assigned to work with teachers to strengthen programs, conduct workshops and demonstrations and develop materials.

Number of schools—9, with classes in 58 different institutions
Number of hospitals and convalescent homes with "400" classes in New York City—38
Number of hospitals and convalescent homes with "400" classes outside the city limits—7
Number of shelters and institutions with "400" classes in New York City—6
Number of shelters and institutions with "400" classes outside the city limits—7

Students

Number on register at any one time	2,132
In hospitals and convalescent homes	1,004
In institutions and shelters	1,128

Total number of pupils registered during the course of the school year—5,850

The board of education provides teachers, supervisory staff, a coordinator, clerical assistance and materials of instruction. Additional services, such as medical, psychiatric, nursing and social services are usually provided to the "400" school pupils by other agencies. Many volunteer organizations provide other services to some of the hospitals and institutions. The Play Schools Association operates a play school program in several of the hospitals.

The "400" schools provide education for children while under medical treatment, convalescent and residential care. The curriculum is basically that of the regular schools. However, because of the many problems, physical, emotional and social, and the limitations of the hospital and institutional situations, curriculum adaptations and adjustments must be made.

Since illness, physical limitations, neglect and other disturbing factors may cause gaps in education and deprivation of the usual childhood experiences, remedial instruction and an enriched program are essential. The teachers work closely with other members of the team so that clinical findings, recommendations, and services may become an integral part of the program.

Teachers consult with the residential staff so that conferences can be arranged with the parents. The social worker often acts as the intermediary, interpreting the social problems to the teacher so that parent-teacher interviews can be child and problem centered. Parents are invited to visit the child's classroom at their convenience. The same principles apply to parent education as in other schools. Periodic appraisals and case conferences preferably with the referral agency and the parents are arranged in order to make plans for the child's continued education and care.

Information concerning the child's ability, stage of development, strengths and limitations determines the recommendation concerning school and grade placement, guidance measures and other services. Follow-up is arranged by guidance personnel of the Office of Special Services working with the receiving school and other interested agencies.

Services Available (1963 Statistics)

School	*Hospitals*	*Convalescent Homes*	*Institutions and Shelters*	*Total Number of Classes*
P.S. 401 M	13	0	0	24
P.S. 403 M	0	1	1	6
P.S. 405 M	0	0	1	11
P.S. 406 M	0	0	4	25
P.S. 408 M	0	0	1	6
P.S. 401 X	11	0	1	23
P.S. 402 X	2	3	1	21
P.S. 401 K	11	0	1	21
P.S. 401 Q	4	0	3	17
Totals	41	4	13	154

THE BUREAU OF CHILD GUIDANCE

(Dr. Simon S. Silverman, Director)

The Bureau of Child Guidance was organized in 1931 in response to public concern about maladjustment and delinquency. From a staff of fourteen psychiatrists, psychologists and social workers, it has grown so that it now has a staff of over 300 professional workers. It functions within the Office of Special Services of the Board of Education of New York City. Heading this bureau is a director, who is aided by three assistant directors, a chief school psychiatric social worker and a chief school social worker.

Even with its large staff, the bureau cannot serve all the children who need help since New York City has approximately one million children in its public schools. For years, therefore, the bureau has operated on the philosophy that by clinical study and treatment of the few and by inclusion of school personnel as part of the team which seeks to help the child, mental hygiene knowledge spreads in a school and so benefits other children.

The children are referred by the school principals and their problems run the gamut of problems seen in a child guidance clinic—from mild and incipient educational difficulties to severe behavior problems.

Teams, each consisting of a social worker and a psychologist and psychiatric consultant, are assigned to certain schools where they screen the referrals made by the principal, accepting some for service from the bureau and referring others to community agencies which, in many cases, are or have been active on these particular cases.

The bureau gives service to the schools to which teams are not assigned through what is called the "area service." Staff in each of the bureau's district offices are assigned to intake from these schools. The intake process involves careful screening in which all three disciplines may participate. It usually includes interviewing of the child's parent in addition to the gathering of information from the school. The intake service accepts certain cases for bureau service and refers them to staff who are assigned to carry forward the study of the cases from the area service schools. In order to keep an encompassable caseload, it has been necessary to limit the referrals from area service schools to mandated and emergency cases.

Certain types of service are mandated to the bureau. The state mandates the psychological study by the bureau psychologists of children who seem to need placement in the special classes for the retarded. The superintendent of schools has designated the psychiatrist and the psychologists of the bureau as qualified examiners when there is a question of exempting a child from attendance.

The amount of service given to individual cases varies. About 10 per cent of the cases closed in any one year have received full study involving a social study, a psychological evaluation and a psychiatric examination; about 10 per cent have been continued in treatment at the bureau after the initial study; other cases may have only psychological evaluation and advice to the school; in still other cases the bureau acts as consultant to the school. All three disciplines engage in treatment with psychiatric supervision.

The bureau works closely with teachers and school administrators so that the school becomes part of the therapy in any given case.

In addition, bureau staff give in-service courses for teachers and other school personnel on such subjects as Mental Hygiene in the Classroom, The Psychology of Adolescence, and other appropriate areas.

THE BUREAU FOR SPEECH IMPROVEMENT

(Dr. Helen M. Donovan, Director)

In the elementary and junior high schools the teachers of speech improvement screen, diagnose and provide therapy for all children who have speech disorders. These teachers also consult with principals and classroom teachers in the developmental speech program as part of the language arts curriculum.

The Bureau for Speech Improvement in cooperation with the Bureau for Children with Retarded Mental Development and the Bureau for the Physically Handicapped conducts a training program for classroom teachers of intellectually handicapped and physically handicapped children. Teachers assigned to the project give demonstration lessons, workshops and in-service courses in methods and materials in speech. Children in these classes who have speech defects are given individual help by the teacher of speech improvement.

Another special program is that for the cerebral palsied children who attend special units in the public schools. A teacher of speech improvement is assigned full time to these units where children receive intensive speech therapy.

A third special service is that given in speech centers for children who are severely handicapped in speech. If the parent consents to the transfer of the child to the speech center, the pupil then is enrolled in the school that houses it. In the center pupils receive individual speech instruction every day. Often they have a second lesson a day in group work.

On the senior high school level, the teachers of speech are also responsible for the discovery, diagnosis and therapy of all speech handicapped students. In addition, they are concerned with the improvement of the speech of all pupils, preferably in a speech centered term or year. Elective courses in the speech arts (public speaking, group discussion, choral speaking, oral interpretation of literature, dramatics and radio and television) are provided for the gifted in speech, for student leaders and for students who are interested in the speech arts.

Teachers of speech in the high school also provide services to the school at large by acting as coordinators of assemblies and as faculty advisers to groups and clubs. They direct and produce one act assembly plays, the three act varsity show, radio programs and other public performances. They serve as general advisers to all other teachers who produce plays in the high school. Special coaching is also provided for graduation speakers and for speakers in oratorical contests.

The central office offers consultation service to all citizens on problems of speech improvement and speech correction.

During office hours, diagnosis and referral are provided for preschool children, children in public schools not serviced by speech improvement teachers, children enrolled in private schools and children referred for speech diagnosis by speech improvement teachers.

The bureau also replies to inquiries from graduate students and school administrators on organization, methodology, recruitment, equipment, preparation of teachers, teaching materials and many other phases of the work.

The Bureau for Speech Improvement offers special conferences to assistant superintendents, principals and P.T.A. meetings on the child with a speech handicap, speech in the Language Arts Program, and speech problems of the Puerto Rican.

In-service training courses serve many purposes. A series of monthly conferences with at least two demonstration lessons are given to new speech teachers. For all teachers there are courses in speech in the language arts, voice training and choral speaking.

BUREAU FOR EDUCATION OF VISUALLY HANDICAPPED CHILDREN

(Mrs. Helen W. Fields, Director)

New York City maintains the Bureau for Education of Visually Handicapped Children as a unit of the Office of Special Services. A director and five supervisors administer the educational services for blind and partially seeing children within the public school system. Approximately 1400 children from kindergarten through senior high school are given services for the blind and partially seeing. Bus service is provided for most of these children. Others live close enough to their schools to walk or use public transportation.

The classes are organized as resource rooms, and are staffed by over one hundred teachers trained in the education of the visually handicapped. Children cover the same course of study as the regular grade pupils and at the end of each year progress to the next grade. Both partially sighted and blind children of all ages receive instruction in the regular grade classes as well as in the sight conservation and braille classes. The special teacher is available to teach, reinforce, or reteach necessary skills and to provide the child with those materials or devices which will enable him to maintain himself on a par with his sighted peers.

Sight Conservation classes are maintained to prevent the failure of children who because of poor eyesight cannot keep up with the work in the regular grades. Many children cannot read the fine print in the school textbooks and they cannot see the blackboard unless given special seat placement in the classroom.

Lighting is made suitable. Desks are adjustable. Large print books and audio aids are supplied. Typewriters with enlarged type are also part of the classroom equipment.

For the braille classes, braille books, machines, slates and other equipment are essential to meet the reading and writing needs of children who are blind and require instruction through tactual methods.

Placement in these classes is made only with the approval of the supervising ophthalmologist of the New York City Department of Health, and the criterion for placement in Sight Conservation Class is, generally speaking, 20/70 in the better eye after correction.

Braille placement is indicated when the child is legally blind and cannot function with printed material. It is interesting to note that in New York City nearly 300 children who are legally blind are functioning in the Sight Conservation Program.

The special class placement is augmented by an itinerant teaching program which serves about one hundred children for whom placement in existing classes is not feasible. Placement in a Sight Conservation or Braille Class presupposes normal mentality plus mobility. Therefore, the bureau provides this itinerant service for those children, who although visually limited, are placed in classes for the mentally retarded or the physically handicapped. Itinerant teachers are also provided for those children whose aptitudes warrant placement in either the special high schools such as music and art, or in the vocational high schools.

Special pilot study classes have been established in order to provide educational facilities for emotionally disturbed, and/or mentally retarded blind children.

An educational and vocational guidance counselor is assigned to the bureau, and close liaison is maintained through the counselor with the various service agencies involved with the visually handicapped.

BUREAU OF ATTENDANCE

(Mr. Arthur Clinton, Director)

> The Bureau of Attendance is concerned with what in this country is the keystone of all education. This is universal opportunity—all children in school with the best use of the capacities possessed. It is the philosophy of this bureau that this kind of service must be implemented through aggressive, reaching-out techniques and methods and must be centered in the home and in the community. There is a job of course for an attendance teacher in a school. He can interview both parents and children and maintain close contact and cooperation with classroom teachers, supervisors and other pupil personnel workers assigned in the school. But his major thrust and the unique characteristic of attendance service is the fact that the attendance teacher carries the school to the home and to parents who know very little about it. In other words, universal education and opportunity—all parents and children. (Mr. Arthur Clinton)

The Bureau of Attendance maintains a number of programs which are geared to the problems presented by absentee pupils, their parents and the schools of register and which also reflect the available manpower granted to the bureau. The more widely used programs in the bureau are these:

1. *Short-term.* Under the regulations of the superintendent of schools, principals refer absentee pupils after such help as is possible is given in the school. For a large number of these children a short, intensive, need-identification inquiry and offer of service is usually enough. Service may include specifying the area of problem, interpretation of school policies, counselling, referral to in-school personnel or community agencies. Objectives are necessarily limited. The short-term program is also preventive and casefinding.

2. *Continued Service.* A number of families already identified as in need of more intensive attendance service and those identified in the short-term

program comprise the continued service caseload. A number of factors are considered at Intake and these include school absence, school relationships, parental supervision and motivation, in and out-of-school behavior and availability of resources. The attendance teacher provides a continuous and more intensive service which aims at not only the return to school but, through counselling, a change in pupil and parental behavior.

3. *Casework Program.* This program is provided for the families with more serious presenting problems and less strengths. This case load is made up of families not acceptable to community agencies for specialized service and not reached by the in-school services. The pupils in this caseload are not only absentees but often live in disorganized, resistive and problem-ridden families. The family focus is necessary because often there is a familial pathology and the need for considerable reaching-out help to parents and siblings.

4. *The Mobile Group.* On an average school day there are 4,000 to 5,000 pupils, who should be in school, on the streets in various sections of the city. The identification and on-the-spot help of these pupils are provided by the attendance teachers in this group. Follow-through, as is required, is also provided within the group or by referral to one of the other Bureau programs or community agencies.

5. *Attendance Program in the Family Court.* As the bureau refers about 1,200 pupils a year to the family court and as the processes of intake and courtroom hearing are involved and lengthy, the bureau maintains a program in the family courts in Brooklyn, Manhattan and the Bronx. Relationships with the justices and probation staff are established, procedures have been developed, and professional guidance and supervision are given to the attendance teacher presenting the case in order to provide maximum service for the pupil and his parents.

6. *Unwed Parents.* Since 1953 the bureau has provided for thousands of pupils, not otherwise helped, a comprehensive service in the provision of medical help, referral for specialized services and supervised return to school. This program, which has increased steadily over the years, serves both the unwed mother and the putative father and the families of both adolescents.

7. *Attendance Teachers Assigned to More Effective Schools.* An attendance teacher is assigned to each More Effective School as part of the existing experiment. He works both in the school with parents, pupils and school personnel and in the homes and in the community with pupils, parents, relatives and other adults in the pupil's educational and social life.

8. *Consultants.* Attendance teacher consultants are assigned to district superintendents and to the nonpublic school systems in order to prevent school absence and to help supervisors and teachers install attendance sys-

tems and provide attendance help to school absentees and their parents. As consultants to the district superintendents, they participate in planning, training and evaluation.

9. *Attendance Teachers Assigned to Mobilization for Youth Project.* Attendance teachers are assigned to participating schools as part of the experiments conducted in this project. Several concepts have been evolved and experience gathered in evaluated implementation.

10. *Interdepartmental Neighborhood Service Center.* This project, from which attendance teachers were withdrawn at the end of the 1965-1966 school year, had been operative for about eight years. Attendance teachers gave considerable service to multi-problem families and tested a number of techniques in attempts to reach withdrawn, hostile and resistive families. Many successes in service were achieved and a number of advanced techniques were incorporated in bureau operation.

11. *Pupil Accounting Program.* During the past several years this program has been widely extended as the result of a number of bureau studies and considerable planning. First phase attendance service—identification and school placement—has been systematized and routinized so that a huge volume of transfers, admissions and discharges are served through this program at a considerable saving of professional field time. Effectiveness has been increased tremendously and a further expansion, within budget limitations, is being undertaken. The identification and movement control of pupils transferred inter- and intra-systems as well as returns from custodial and mental health institutions comprise a large part of this case load. In addition, there are labor violations, department of welfare referrals, movement into New York City and a number of miscellaneous categories.

12. *Employment Certification.* Employment certification is a year-round program with a septuple increase during June and July. In addition, there are a number of special employment programs of endless variety which must be understood and utilized properly and for which consultative and staff supervisory service is a daily necessity. In the last two to three years this program has evolved into a complex conglomerate which involves a process of constant surveillance, frequent organizational change and numerous problems.

During the 1965-1966 school year the Bureau of Attendance accepted the referral of 162,999 children. Of these, close to 6,000 children were carried in the Continued Service program and Casework programs. Nearly 800 children were referred to the family court.

Chapter 18

SPECIAL EDUCATION PROGRAMS IN SAN MATEO COUNTY

WILLIAM S. HERBIG, ELLA T. ALLAN, AND JOSEPH C. MARX

BACKGROUND INFORMATION

THE County of San Mateo is the second smallest in California. It contains an area of 477 square miles located between the Pacific Ocean and the San Francisco Bay. The city of San Francisco is the northern tip of a peninsula which includes San Mateo County in the middle and Santa Clara County on the south.

In 1856 San Mateo County, originally a part of San Francisco County, was established. In 1868 the territory south of San Gregorio was added to the original area and the resulting boundary remains the same today. The county is an integral part of the San Francisco Bay Region metropolitan area.

The March 1966 estimated population in San Mateo County is 545,000. The 1970 population projection is 644,000; 1980 is 765,000. The 1965-1966 assessed valuation of property in San Mateo County is $1,422,000,000.

ADMINISTRATIVE PATTERN OF SCHOOLS

The educational organization of the schools in San Mateo County is as follows: seventeen elementary (K-8) districts; three unified (K-12) districts; three secondary (9-12) districts; a junior college (13-14) district; and a county superintendent of schools office. The 1964-1965 average daily attendance in the public schools was 123,622. This A.D.A. consisted of 81,034 at the elementary (K-8) level, and varied from 426 in the smallest district to 11,967 in the largest district; 33,600 at the secondary (9-12) level, and varied from 6183 to 11,817; 8988 at the junior college level. In addition, the private and parochial schools (Catholic) had an A.D.A. of 9812. Other private schools had an A.D.A. of 1137.

The above figures include attendance of exceptional children in various programs available in San Mateo County. It would be well to take a look at current enrollments in these programs as of November 1965. The following programs in San Mateo County were available to and enrolled the number of exceptional children as indicated:

1. District operated programs for physically handicapped (elementary level)
   a. Deaf and severely hard of hearing (countywide)

1 district; 8 classes; 55 students
   b. Hard of hearing (multi-district)
      2 districts; 2 classes; 17 students
   c. Educationally blind (multi-district)
      3 districts; 4 resource rooms with 32 students
2. District operated programs for physically handicapped (secondary level)
   a. Deaf and severely hard of hearing (countywide)
      1 district; 2 classes with 11 students
3. County office operated programs for physically handicapped (elementary level)
   a. Orthopedically handicapped including cerebral palsied; 8 classes with 112 students
   b. Dysphasic; 2½ classes with 20 students
4. County office operated programs for physically handicapped (secondary level)
   a. Orthopedically handicapped including cerebral palsied; 1 class with 8 students
   b. Dysphasic; ½ class with 4 students (combined with one-half class of elementary students)
5. District operated programs for educable mentally retarded (50-75 IQ) (elementary level)
   a. 13 districts; 38 classes; 468 students
6. District operated programs for educable mentally retarded (secondary level)
   a. 4 districts; 16 classes; 244 students
7. County Office operated programs for trainable mentally retarded (25-50 IQ)
   a. 10 classes with 96 students in two schools (elementary)
   b. 3 classes with 30 students in two schools (secondary)
8. District operated programs for educationally handicapped (elementary level)
   a. 13 districts; 25 classes; 177 students
9. District operated programs for educationally handicapped (secondary level)
   a. 3 districts; 3 classes; 30 students
10. Districts and the county office provide 35 speech correctionists working with approximately 3,150 pupils with remedial speech defects
11. Districts and the county office provide 69 school nurses: 50 elementary level; 19 secondary level
12. Districts and the county office provide 44 school psychologists; 2 psychometrists; and 3 interns
13. Day care center for severely handicapped children. The San Mateo County Board of Supervisors through the San Mateo County Board of Eduation provides a program for thirty-six children in three groups. These are severely physically handicapped and/or mentally retarded youngsters who are not eligible for any other local program in San Mateo County.

The special education programs in San Mateo County involve approximately 125 classes and/or groups with a total enrollment of 1340 students.

Since this chapter is being written by county office personnel and deals largely with county office operated programs, it would be well to take a look at the organization of the Office of the San Mateo County Superintendent of Schools.

The governing body of the county office is the board of education and has seven members elected at large from the seven trustee areas in the county. The county superintendent of schools is an elected county official.

The services of the county office are under the direction of a deputy county superintendent and three division heads. The three service divisions of the county office are administration, education and special education. The chart on the next page shows in some detail the organization of the Special Education Division of the county office.

These programs, as indicated on the organizational chart, are operating on a 1965-1966 budget of $1,121,039. The sources of support are as follows: state apportionment based on A.D.A., $146,494; state excess cost, $206,890;

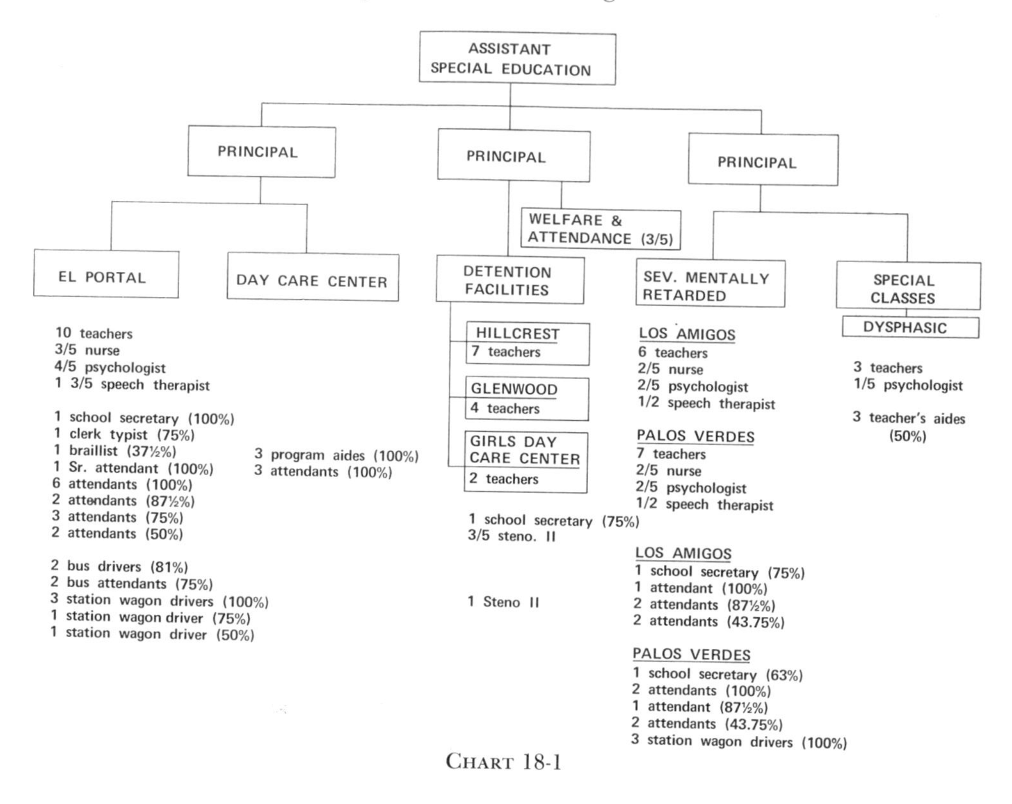

CHART 18-1

state excess cost for transportation, $121,600; district tuition charge, $187,993; county taxes, $455,162; and Federal milk subventions, $2900.

DEVELOPMENT OF SPECIAL EDUCATION WITH EMPHASIS ON COUNTY OFFICE OPERATED PROGRAMS

The preceding data indicates that programs for exceptional children in San Mateo County are conducted on a cooperative basis. It, no doubt, will be of interest to see how the "educational philosophy" existing in the county helped to shape the development of special education programs.

The oft-used but valid philosophical statement, "an equal educational opportunity for every child" is the underlying philosophy of educators in San Mateo County. This led to the development of programs designed to provide the optimum operating environment consistent with the maximum habilitation of the handicapping condition preventing a student from reaching his ultimate potential.

As a result of this, programs came into being designed to provide services in keeping with educators' opinions of the severity of the student's handicap. These programs covered the following range: hospital setting, individual instruction at home, special schools, self-contained special classes, integrated special classes, resource rooms and remedial programs.

One of the earliest special education programs established in the county was a "home and hospital teaching service for home-bound or hospitalized children suffering from illnesses or accidents and for cerebral palsied children." This program became operative during the school year 1944-1945. Shortly thereafter a special class was started for "partially seeing children" then known as a "sight-saving class." About this same time (1946) a special day class for "deaf and hard of hearing" children was also started. The "home teaching service for CP's" and the "sight-saving class" was established and operated by the San Mateo County Board of Education through the office of the county superintendent of schools. The districts requested the county board of education to provide these two services because there appeared to be very few children in either category in the county. No district felt it had enough students within its boundaries to warrant setting up either program.

The "special day class for deaf children" was established and operated by the Burlingame Elementary School District. Prior to this time the Burlingame District had been sending its deaf children to the San Francisco Unified School District. This was on the basis of an interdistrict attendance agreement with the Burlingame District paying a tuition charge to the San Francisco School District.

Following the district superintendents' recommendation, the Burlingame School Board agreed to establish a "deaf program" for Burlingame children. After the program became operative, other districts in San Mateo County asked Burlingame to accept their deaf students. It is interesting to note that, while the Burlingame Elementary School District operates eight classes with an enrollment of fifty-five, only two or 3.6 per cent of the students enrolled in the program today reside in the Burlingame District.

In 1946 California legislation provided a broad base for programs for physically handicapped children. Since the county superintendent's office was providing a "home teaching service for cerebral palsied children," the decision was made to set up a "special school for cerebral palsied children." Mrs. Ella Allan, principal of the El Portal del Sol School, a county office operated program for orthopedically handicapped minors including the cerebral palsied, has written a section on the development of the program for physically handicapped children which appears later in this chapter.

During the period 1944-1948 the number of children in special education programs increased rapidly. On July 1, 1948 a law adding new sections to the Education Code became operative in California. These new code sections had a tremendous effect on the expansion of special education programs by mandating school districts and county offices to provide programs for mentally retarded minors, ". . . who because of retarded intellectual development as determined by individual psychological examination are incapable of being educated efficiently and profitably through ordinary classroom instruction."*

The code sections originally read that any school district having fifteen or more mentally retarded minors as defined by law shall provide a program for them. The code went on to say that if any district had less than fifteen mentally retarded minors it shall be the responsibility of the county superintendent of schools to provide a program for such minors. This immediately put the responsibility for establishing programs for the mentally retarded in the hands of a large number of county superintendents in California.

This was not necessarily the intent of the legislature when they passed the law establishing mentally retarded programs. However, in 1948 California had no credentialed position as "school psychologist" and the state was very short of "clinical psychologists." As a result, many districts waiting to set up programs could not because they were unable to screen and certify the necessary fifteen mentally retarded students. Those students who were screened as eligible (less than fifteen in any one district) had to be provided for by the county superintendent of schools. This method of dividing responsibility (between district and county office) based on the number of certified children did not seem to be working very well. As a result, the law was changed the following year dividing the responsibility on the basis of average daily attendance (A.D.A.).

Mentally retarded children in districts under 901 A.D.A. were a county office responsibility. Children in districts over 901 A.D.A. were a district responsibility. The district had to provide a program, contract with another district, or contract with the county superintendent's office. At this time all districts over 901 A.D.A. asked to contract with the county office for their retarded children but it became apparent very quickly that the intermediate unit (county office) was not the proper service agency to provide the services needed for all of the educable mentally retarded children in the county.

The county superintendent, therefore, requested the districts over 901 A.D.A. to provide their own program because of the inability of the county office to obtain the necessary classroom space or personnel to adequately provide for all of the districts' retarded children. The larger districts agreed to meet this request as soon as possible. In most districts the transition from county level to district level was accomplished very quickly and smoothly. In some districts the transition took a little longer because of the various problems presented.

To complicate matters, in 1952 additional legislation was passed provid-

* Education Code, Section 6901, 1963 Ed., State of California.

ing programs for retarded children who were not eligible for existing programs for educable mentally retarded students. This program was for severely mentally retarded students and since the county office had conducted a pilot demonstration program the year before, the school districts requested the county office to again provide the program for eligible children. Mr. Joseph Marx, principal of the county operated Program for Severely Mentally Retarded Minors, has developed the history of this program which will also appear later in this chapter.

As a result of a change in the operating level for educable mentally retarded children and the development of a program for trainable mentally retarded children, the District Superintendents Association in the county was asked to appoint a committee to study the needs of exceptional children and how these needs could best be met. This committee, composed of five district superintendents and representatives from the county office, spent about six months taking a look at where special education programs were, and what the extent and future direction should be.

This Special Education Committee made its report to the District Superintendents Association, the School Boards Association, and the county superintendent and San Mateo County Board of Education. The report briefly stated that school districts should operate special education programs except where there were too few children to warrant a district or adjoining districts to provide a program, or where a program was thought to be too complicated to be easily handled at the district level.

The report went on to express the feeling of the committee that two programs would appear best handled at the county office level. One was the "program for orthopedically handicapped including the cerebral palsied" and the other one was the "program for severely mentally retarded minors." The committee felt the few children available for these programs; the multidisciplinary staffs needed; and the unique physical facilities necessary indicated the programs should be on a centralized basis. These recommendations were agreed to by the administrative bodies mentioned before. In keeping with the committee's feeling that districts should operate programs whenever practical, it was recommended that the following county operated programs be returned to district operation as soon as possible: home teaching, program for educationally blind, and the program for the partially seeing. The following year these programs were being operated on an expanded basis by the districts in the county.

The committee also recommended that the county office conduct pilot demonstration programs to help in the establishment of new programs when indicated by new legislation or modification of existing legislation. These recommendations are in effect today and have generally been responsible for the shared special education programs available in the county. These, coupled with Mr. James R. Tormey's (San Mateo County Superintendent of Schools) position that the county office is a service center and the school districts are the county office's customers led to the development of several pilot demonstration programs and the initiation of new programs involving few children in widely scattered locations.

One of the earliest "pilot demonstration" programs established in the county was the previously mentioned "home teaching service for Cerebral Palsied children." The development of this program from a home teaching service to two special schools (September 1966) for orthopedically handicapped including the cerebral palsied is fascinating and inspiring.

DEVELOPMENT OF A PROGRAM FOR PHYSICALLY HANDICAPPED CHILDREN

In 1944 physically handicapped children in San Mateo County were served by two home teachers furnished by the county superintendent's office, and the San Mateo County Society for Crippled Children and Adults (Easter Seal Society). This organized program was preceded by the pioneering efforts of some parents and civic leaders who refused to recognize, the then accepted dictum, that nothing could be done to train and educate children handicapped by cerebral palsy.

In 1946 this program was organized as a day school and housed in the carriage house on the Mills Estate in Millbrae. At that time there were two teachers, one physical therapist and one occupational therapist. There was also one cook-attendant-dishwasher-jack-of-all-trades. This program continued to be a joint operation between the San Mateo County Superintendent's Office, and the Society for Crippled Children and Adults of San Mateo County until the fall of 1949 when the county superintendent's office took over complete responsibility.

The program was maintained at the site on the Mills Estate until 1951 when a new facility was built adjoining a regular elementary school in the San Mateo City School District. At this time there were three teachers, two occupational therapists, and two physical therapists. This building was outgrown in the fall of 1958. Additional facilities were rented in a church in San Mateo and housed two additional classes with therapy available at this site.

In 1958-1959 a bond issue was presented to the voters of San Mateo County in the amount of $690,000 to build a new facility for physically handicapped children. The new school, which was planned with the help of all the staff, was completed and occupied in the fall of 1960. This facility contains eight classrooms, a physical and occupational therapy department which can accommodate eight therapists, two speech therapy rooms, and various other additional facilities. At the present time, nine classes are in operation with a double session at the nursery level.

The children who attend the El Portal del Sol School from the elementary and high school districts are of the educable level or higher. They are screened by an evaluation committee for enrollment. The staff evaluates a child's progress and goals for future placement on a once or twice yearly basis. If a child is not in need of placement at El Portal, the school district of residence is contacted and suitable placement within the district is arranged. Prior to the opening of school each year, the teaching staff sets up class divisions for the coming year. The child's age, social development, academic ability and personality are all considered in deciding the most suitable assignment.

Of the 120 children enrolled at El Portal, thirty-two are enrolled in the speech program. These children have speech from three to five times a week depending upon the need as assessed by the speech therapist. The speech, physical and occupational therapy departments work closely together to provide the best program for speech handicapped cerebral palsied children. Personnel from these departments have given demonstrations at the Annual Fall Conference for Northern Schools for Orthopedically Handicapped including Cerebral Palsied Children, and at the county speech therapists meetings. A series of demonstrations for students, particularly assigned from the Speech Department at San Francisco State College to do speech work with cerebral palsied children, have also been conducted.

Along with the regular academic program, a number of extra activities are included in the school day. A glee club, composed of thirty children from the four oldest classes is active throughout the school year. The children meet weekly and perform for the graduation program, Christmas program, and the Hootenanny in the spring. The lower grades have a "junior glee club" in training for the "senior glee club." An intramural sports program is carried on twice a week in which children divided into teams compete in team games, particularly devised by staff members for physically handicapped. These include such games as baseball and soccer. Directed sports are carried on in the lower grades twice weekly. These include team games in relay type activities. Once a week, a volunteer swim group transports children from El Portal to a local indoor swimming pool and instruction is given on an individual basis to the children. A ceramics program is much in evidence throughout the various classrooms.

The oldest group of children conduct student council meetings once a week. Representatives from each of the six upper classes attend and take notes back to their respective classes on matters discussed. The students of the council have devised rules for safety in the halls. Each year they conduct a Dream Girl Contest and elect a Dream Girl who is presented at the Spring Concert. Conducting student assemblies are a part of the function of the council, as well as presiding at these assemblies. These students have also initiated and published the first year book for El Portal School. Book covers and loose leaf folders with the El Portal emblem printed on the front are to be purchased and sold by the members of the council.

The two teachers who are teaching the double session nursery groups use the remainder of their teaching day for individual work where special emphasis with particular children is indicated. The Therapy Department is under the direct supervision of the San Mateo County Department of Public Health and Welfare and is provided consultative services from the state level. Therapy is given on a prescription basis from either the private or clinic physician. The therapists work closely with the classroom teachers regarding children needing any special handling.

Clinics are held on a weekly basis and those children eligible for Crippled Children Services are seen on a regular basis at these clinics. Scheduling of children for therapy is worked out with the classroom teachers so that it interferes as little as possible with the academic program.

The Parent-Teacher Association supports and operates activities in the program at El Portal School. The contributions in the past year have covered such things as the purchase and making of capes for the Glee Club; ponchos for outside wear for those children who are not able to manage sweaters; designing, furnishing the material and the making of metal tops for a number of the tables where cerebral palsied-blind children are in need of such equipment. A number of the parents conduct a monthly hot dog sale for the children. Ice cream is also furnished by the P.T.A. and may be purchased by the children after lunch. These two projects add to the P.T.A. treasury which furnishes a revolving fund to be used by the El Portal staff.

The establishment and maintenance of a summer camp, held for one week each summer, is another valuable service of the P.T.A. This involves the soliciting of camperships and the staffing of the camp. The camp serves thirty-five to forty children for a week's vacation in a very beautiful wooded area in San Mateo County. Each child has an individual counselor assigned to him for the week.

Due to their physical handicap, a number of cerebral palsied-deaf children cannot be accommodated in the classes for the deaf. The El Portal staff feels that these deaf children need more language training, so as a result, a teacher for the deaf will be hired next year to teach a class of cerebral palsied-deaf children.

The parents and school personnel became aware of the need for a second facility in 1964-1965. The county board of education arranged through the

San Bruno Park School District, a state aided district, to build for the county superintendent's office a second school for physically handicapped children in the northern end of the county. The completion date set for this building is the fall of 1966.

At this time, the pupil population will be divided approximately in the middle of San Mateo County which will establish two attendance areas. Children living in the northern half of the county will attend the new facility, while those in the southern half will be maintained at the present El Portal del Sol School. The El Portal del Norte School will consist of six classrooms with a maximum enrollment of ninety children. The establishment of these two attendance areas should now insure the county sufficient room to take care of any future growth for the next ten to fifteen years.

DEVELOPMENT OF A PROGRAM FOR TRAINABLE MENTALLY RETARDED CHILDREN

The second pilot demonstration program was established in the county in 1951. This led to the development of a program for "severely mentally retarded children" which today involves two special schools and 126 students.

In 1951 the parents of three severely mentally retarded children decided to try and obtain a school program for their children. The parents appealed to the San Mateo County Society for Crippled Children and Adults, and as a result, a program was established by the society in the carriage house on the Mills Estate in Millbrae (recently vacated by the El Portal School). During the school year 1951-1952 members of the Society for Crippled Children and Adults, interested school people, and members of the community appealed to the county superintendent of schools to establish a broader program. The county superintendent agreed to try to obtain funds to operate a pilot program. The California State Department of Education and the San Mateo County Board of Supervisors each agreed to appropriate $5000 to set up such a program and to determine whether or not such a program should be operated within a school setting.

The first class opened with seventeen students at the First Christian Church in Redwood City on October 1, 1952. This program was named the "Self Help School." Many of the recommendations growing out of this pilot program are still in effect today and some of the outstanding ones are as follows:

1. Entrance age of five years for school program, and eighteen years for sheltered workshop experience program.
2. Maximum class size of twelve; staff of one certificated teacher and one classified person.
3. Apportionment day of 180 minutes.
4. Regular parent conferences by members of the staff.

Today 126 students are enrolled in six classes at the Los Amigos School in San Mateo, established in 1960; and seven classes at the new Palos Verdes School in San Bruno, established in 1965. There is no waiting list. Prior to attending Los Amigos or Palos Verdes Schools, many of the children attend nursery school programs for the mentally retarded.

The curriculum activities in the primary classes begin with training in very basic skills such as dressing, washing, going to the bathroom alone. The most important goals are individual acceptance, and learning to get along with others.

The intermediate pupil is exposed to a wide variety of concrete experiences, rather than abstract knowledge. Many of the students have impaired perceptual skills which need to be developed. Members of our staff are using the special techniques and materials developed by Marianne Frostig for visual perceptual skills; while others are taking courses at the College of Notre Dame Montessori Pre-School, on scholarships provided by PARCA (Parents Association for Retarded Children and Adults).

Other staff members are working with the speech therapist in exploring better ways of developing auditory perception and stimulating language development. We are using equipment such as the "Language Master," the "Phonic Mirror," and the Peabody Experimental Language "Kit." We feel that there is a great need for further research into the effectiveness of various teaching methods used with the educationally handicapped and their application to the retarded child with perceptual handicaps.

Starting at ages of twelve to fifteen, the school day is extended to include a program in "home skills" and "work skills." The purpose of this program is to make the TMR child economically useful in a sheltered environment.

Home skills include general household cleaning, washing, ironing, sewing, food preparation and good grooming. Good grooming has developed to the point where the girls have modeled their own clothes in two fashion shows, both being very successful. The carry-over into everyday better grooming has been very evident in the girls now showing an interest in themselves and being able to keep their nails clean and shoes shined, wash and fix their hair, and present an overall neat appearance.

Work skills include animal and pet care, gardening and yard care, car washing and prevocational skills. Gardening includes planting both flower and vegetable gardens. Future plans call for a greenhouse and a lath-house, as well as constructing planter flats and preparing #10 cans to be used for potting plants. Hopefully, this will eventually result in a training level that will justify an occupational training contract with a local nursery.

Students have learned to wash a car with direction, and planning is under way to set up an occupational training contract with a private contract carrier of exceptional children to wash their passenger car type busses. Students have mastered the benchwork production of articles such as Christmas ornaments, note-pads, shoe-shine kits, and planter boxes. We now have an occupational training contract with the local sheltered workshop at the Children's Health Home in San Mateo. The goal of this program is to place TMR children between the ages of eighteen and twenty-one in sheltered employment.

We feel that the San Mateo County program has proved, beyond a doubt, that the TMR individual thrives on success, and given the proper experiences and training will become a marginally productive individual in a sheltered environment.

We must recognize that a sheltered environment goes beyond the concept of a sheltered workshop. It also means recreational and social programs; and most important for future planning is a sheltered living situation for TMR adults, no longer appropriately placed in their own home, or for whom no home is available.

DEVELOPMENT OF A PROGRAM FOR EDUCATIONALLY HANDICAPPED CHILDREN

The most recent demonstration program, and perhaps the most notable was a pilot demonstration program for neurologically handicapped children. This program was started at the request of the school districts in the county who were concerned about a small number of children who appeared "educable" but could not be maintained in a regular school environment.

These youngsters' severe management problems were the result, by-and-large, of hyperactivity and distractibility; and generally, behavior that was unpredictable and unacceptable. The county office received approval from the State Department of Education to operate a "pilot demonstration program for neurologically handicapped children" as a part of the state program for physically handicapped minors.

This program was in operation from September 1960 to June 1964 and consisted of three classes with an enrollment of twenty-four students. The age range of these children was approximately eight to twelve years. A very significant fact about this program is that about half of the children enrolled in it had been excluded from regular school by action of their governing boards. It is also important to note that these same students were able to be maintained quite adequately in the pilot demonstration classes.

This pilot program contributed much information which was used to gain support and the ultimate passage of a bill (AB464) to provide, on a statewide basis, programs for educationally handicapped minors.

Material written about this pilot program (now out of print) received national distribution. An article about this program appearing in the February 1964 issue of *Parents Magazine* did much to stimulate the development of programs for brain-injured children. As a result of the passage of AB464, the county office program had to be terminated. This was due to the wording of the bill which allowed school districts only under 901 A.D.A. to contract with a county office. Since the twenty-four students in the program for the 1963-1964 school year were all from over 901 A.D.A. school districts, the county office had to terminate the programs. This action, however, turned out to be a "blessing in disguise."

Had the program for educationally handicapped children remained at the county level, the expansion would have been very slow because of the difficulty county offices have in providing facilities for programs. Since the school districts took over the program from the county office in September 1964, the establishment of programs at the district level have been very rapid and well planned. This program has shown, without question, that children with a learning disability caused by a behavioral disorder or a neurological handicap can definitely be helped in a special program designed to meet their needs.

One of the interesting side effects of the pilot demonstration program for neurologically handicapped was the development at the county level of a program for dysphasic children.

As a follow-up of the medical diagnostic workup, a part of the pilot program screening process, some of the students were given additional examinations at available speech and hearing centers. These evaluations indicated the presence of aphasia or probable aphasia. We were concerned about these students as they did not seem to be responding to the educational environment which appeared to be very helpful for the neurologically handicapped children.

The educational placement of these dysphasic students was discussed with the school districts of residence, and as a result, the districts requested the county office to establish a program for dysphasic students. This was done and we now have three classes for dysphasic children. Two classes are located in an elementary school in San Mateo City and the third class is located in an elementary school in Hillsborough.

This program is making a slow but steady expansion and in September 1966 the fourth class was set up. This will be a secondary class and will be located in one of the high schools within the San Mateo Union High School District.

JUVENILE DETENTION FACILITY PROGRAMS

The final program to be discussed is the school programs available within juvenile detention facilities. These facilities consist of Hillcrest Juvenile Hall, Girls Day Program and the Glenwood Boys Ranch School.

The San Mateo County Board of Supervisors, by ordinance, has placed the responsibility for the operation of the school programs in these facilities in the hands of the county superintendent of schools.

Hillcrest Juvenile Hall school program consists of two elementary classes (K-8) and five secondary classes (9-12). Class enrollments are kept below a maximum of fifteen whenever possible. The schools are open all year long with the exception of a three day in-service training program in the fall, Christmas vacation and Easter vacation. Teachers in the program, however, teach on a ten-month contract. Teaching during the summer session is on a per diem basis, over and above the basic contract.

School is in session from 9 A.M. to 3:15 P.M. and consists of six, forty-five-minute periods; with a fifteen-minute break between second and third periods, and a fifty-five-minute lunch break between fourth and fifth periods. Secondary school subjects offered in Juvenile Hall are: English, mathematics, social studies, science, arts and crafts, general workshop and physical education. The elementary program offers a regular elementary curriculum with both the secondary and elementary levels stressing remediation of basic tool subject deficiencies.

The Girls Day Program is a new program that started in September 1965. It is for secondary age delinquent girls, who are in need of long term habilitative services, but on a day basis not a residential setting. This program consists of two classes of high school girls from the various high school districts in the county.

These girls receive intensive school and probation department supportive services between 8:30 A.M. and 5 P.M. as well as probation department services between 5 P.M. and 8:30 A.M. at home if needed. The school program operates between 9 A.M. and 3 P.M. on a year-round basis. The school curriculum is designed to present secondary school subjects which are oriented toward a basic domestic science home skills program.

This program is quite new and has had its share of "shake down" problems. Despite this, it appears that it is going to be a very valuable community level day program for secondary age delinquent girls.

Glenwood is a residential camp program for delinquent boys. It is a long-term facility (eight to twelve months). The school program consists of three secondary classes (9-12), and an elementary class (7-8). Here again the students go to school on a full day basis. The school is organized into six, forty-five minute periods and is in operation between 9 A.M. and 2:55 P.M.

The curriculum covers the following secondary school subjects: science, math, English, woodshop, physical education, history, geography and general business.

This program has been very successful in returning boys to their regular high school equipped with the academic skills necessary to complete a school program.

One of the most rewarding features of these detention facilities is the co-operative working relationship which exists between the county probation department and the county school department. All personnel working in these facilities are interested in one thing, "the rehabilitation of delinquent youth." In order to achieve this goal, all county departments work closely together in all phases of the rehabilitative process.

FUTURE PLANS FOR SAN MATEO COUNTY

It has been said many times that the best way to predict the future is to see what has happened in the past. However, in California with unification looming large on the horizon, the future can certainly not be predicted on the past.

A very vital concern is being shown by many people in relation to the role of the county office during and after unification. There is a possibility that unification will produce six unified school districts in San Mateo County to replace the seventeen elementary and three high school districts now in existence. This would give us unified school districts whose enrollment (based on October 1965 figures) would be as follows: 445; 1906; 11,700; 25,158; 35,765, and 40,102.

Whether this type of district organization will mean that county office functions will expand or be cut back remains to be seen. One thing can be predicted with certainty and that is "the needs of the exceptional children in San Mateo County will continue to be met whether provided by the county office or the school districts."

Chapter 19

EDUCATING THE GIFTED IN SAN DIEGO COUNTY

CLAYTON L. BENNETT

INTRODUCTION

ACADEMIC aptitude and other concepts of giftedness have been part of our educational mores for many years. Although most school programs are aimed essentially at the academically talented, in some there is recognition of excellence in other areas of performance and production. For the purposes of this chapter definitions of giftedness are left to sections of the chapter in which school district programs are described. Giftedness in children has been recognized by individual teachers for years and many have made informal provisions for their most able students within a particular classroom or subject matter. At the collegiate level honors courses and programs were in evidence and some school districts had provided organized and systematic programs long before the contemporary "bench mark" of sputnik. This latter event, however, did prompt increased emphasis and stimulate financial incentive from local, Federal and state governments.

This chapter will describe a number of school district programs in one county of one state, San Diego County, California. The treatment cannot be thorough but the range of offerings in a variety of district organizations and sizes is probably quite representative of the pattern which would be found in public schools across the country. Some programs are now almost venerable as these programs go while most have arisen from about the time of the California study project on programs for gifted children.[9] This study authorized by the legislature in 1957 directed the California Department of Education to make such a study. During the course of this three-year study some seventeen different types of programs were evaluated. These were classified in three categories:

1. Special Groupings.
2. Acceleration.
3. Enrichment in the Regular Class.

All grade levels were represented in the study, from first through twelfth, and many programs at both elementary and secondary levels were appropriate for rural as well as for urban schools. The pupils participating in the study were selected on the basic criterion of a minimum IQ of 130 on the

Stanford Binet Scale. The total number participating was 929, almost evenly divided between elementary and secondary levels. Boys and girls were also almost evenly divided within the study population.

Pupils were placed in a number of experimental programs at each grade level studied with a single control group for each grade level. The control groups consisted of pupils who had been carefully matched with those of the experimental groups on the basis of intelligence, age and socioeconomic status but for whom no special program provisions were made. Comparisons were made on a total group basis at the primary level since the experimental and control groups were highly similar. From the fifth through the twelfth grade, pairs of pupils in the experimental groups were matched for group comparisons in achievement and personal-social adjustment. A complete summary of the essential findings is inappropriate for this chapter. The reader is referred to the report.[2] It may be said, however, that all phases of the evaluation made of the programs included in the state showed conclusively that the special provisions made in these programs were beneficial. The study therefore formed the basis for the recommendations which culminated in California's legislation for mentally gifted minors. San Diego County contained a number of school districts which were participants in the state study.

The balance of this chapter will deal with descriptions of the programs for gifted children which have been developed in selected school districts of San Diego County chosen somewhat arbitrarily from those providing such services to their gifted children. Material will be cited from supporting publications produced by the several school districts.

THE GIFTED PROGRAM OF THE SAN DIEGO UNIFIED SCHOOL DISTRICT

The San Diego Unified School District more familiarly known as San Diego City Schools is the largest school district in San Diego County. This district operates a well-seasoned and carefully conceived offering for its gifted pupils. It has profited from long range planning and careful research. The research began during the 1945-46 school year. During this period efforts were directed toward learning more about the needs of gifted children and seeking better ways of meeting them. Specific measures were actually provided at first in the fall of 1949. Such measures were tentative and were regarded as "experimental" until 1958, at which time programs were evaluated. Positive findings led to the installation of programs for the gifted as a permanent part of the curriculum in June 1958. During the intervening years these programs have been modified as needs directed and as the district grew from an enrollment of about 90,000 to one in excess of 130,000 students.

Program Philosophy

The philosophy of education held in the San Diego City Schools requires that special programming be directed towards the needs of gifted children. Each child should have opportunity to develop his potential ability to its maximum. Therefore students of superior ability must have an opportunity to learn at a level commensurate with their ability to achieve. A recent brochure describing the gifted programs of San Diego City Schools states "the educational benefits and developments which are desired for gifted children are those which teachers and administrators desire for every child, that is, a curriculum flexible enough to meet the needs of the individual, methods of study that are stimulating and challenging, and an emphasis on learning that utilizes the resources in the school, the home and the community."[7]

Goals of the Program

Within a philosophical framework which directs that each child should have opportunity to develop at his maximum potential, the San Diego City Schools program for the gifted also dictates certain general and specific goals. The district is committed to an effort to locate all mentally gifted youngsters and enrich their opportunities for academic achievement. The general objectives, as these are stated in a district handbook,[6] are as follows:

1. To broaden, accelerate and individualize the educational pattern for the more able student.
2. To further the student's growth in critical thinking and to apply the scientific approach to the solution of problems.
3. To provide a learning environment with a program having a range of difficulty and interest appeal suitable to the mental abilities of each child.
4. To recognize and allow for the development of the great variety of aptitudes and individual interests of able students.
5. To encourage gifted students to search for information beyond that which is expected of regular class members.
6. To provide opportunity for roles of leadership and responsibility that will encourage the development of these capacities.
7. To provide opportunities to do work that is creative as well as that which is structured or assigned.
8. To permit the child to develop and use his own initiative.

General objectives for the secondary program in addition to those specified in the secondary curriculum guide are as follows:

1. To provide a program consistent with the basic philosophy of local, state and federal legislation adapting a program to meet the needs of the district schools.
2. To view in proper perspective a program on the elementary and college level for effective articulation of procedures and implementation of the secondary gifted program.

3. To broaden, accelerate and individualize the educational patterns for the mentally gifted and more able students.

Teacher objectives are also delineated as follows:

1. To understand the theory underlying the learning process.
2. To recognize and allow for the development of the great variety of aptitudes and individual interests of mentally gifted students.
3. To develop further the mentally gifted student's high aptitude for reasoning and conceptualization.
4. To stimulate inquiring minds to pursue intensive investigation and depth study of problems.
5. To develop a student's powers of perception for analysis, criticism and synthesis in a scientific approach to the solution of problems.
6. To develop an appreciation of the theoretical values of the sciences and the aesthetic values of the humanities.
7. To nurture creativity by social climate and educational environment which will facilitate its development and expression.
8. To provide opportunities for roles of leadership and responsibility that will encourage the development of these capacities.
9. To permit students to develop and use their own initiative.
10. To hold for these students the highest standards of performance.

Identification

Seeking the gifted student presupposes a definition and requires a planned districtwide effort. San Diego City Schools assigns the designation "gifted" to those students under eighteen years of age who score at or above two and one half standard deviations above the mean on Form L-M of the Stanford Binet administered by a certified psychologist or psychometrist approved by the Director of Guidance Services. This will be a score of about 140 or above. Occasionally students may be identified through other accepted individual tests, but such cases must receive individual consideration for eligibility. Since California's legislation in 1961 defining a "mentally gifted minor" as one who has obtained a score of 130 or higher on an individual mental examination such children may or may not be in San Diego City Schools gifted program.

There is a citywide screening program. This process utilizes standardized tests and observational procedures. The screening occurs in grades two, seven and ten. However individual tests may be given on referral of pupils from any grade. Such recommendations usually come from a classroom teacher, a principal or through an intergrade adviser or regular grade adviser. A cumulative folder may contain useful clues and the program handbooks contain other guidelines and suggestions.

Finding the gifted child sets into motion placement procedures which have been carefully prescribed. Parent notification, conferencing and cooperative planning ensue. The San Diego City Schools have modified the instructional program by grouping for enrichment, adjustment and acceleration in both elementary and secondary schools.

Placement

The principal of the elementary school center where gifted are clustered assumes responsibility for the appropriate placement of gifted children. Appropriate placement of a gifted child generally means an assignment to a cluster-grouped classroom for a program of enrichment and accelerated subject areas. However, there will be situations wherein other types of placement will be of more benefit and better suited to individual needs. Such types of placement may include the following:

1. Grade level acceleration and cluster group placement.
2. Grade level acceleration without cluster group placement.
3. Adjustment room for socially, emotionally or academically handicapped gifted.
4. Specialized adjustment room for *highly* gifted children.

The placement of children in a cluster-grouped classroom requires considerable planning and organization. In each school situation, adaptations will need to be made to suit the classroom organization most practical for the numbers of pupils enrolled for the cluster groups. Experience has shown that in organizing classes in centers, the following conditions are frequently observed:

1. Cluster-grouped classrooms may consist of approximately ten to fifteen San Diego gifted and California State identified-gifted. The balance of the class will consist of pupils who are average or above-average in achievement. If the total number of local and state gifted exceeds fifteen pupils at one grade level, it is recommended that a second classroom containing a balance of the local and state gifted be organized.
2. Pupils in the cluster groups generally move as a group each year to the next grade level.
3. Parents are frequently advised that there is no typical "group three" in this type of classroom.
4. Identified gifted pupils with social, emotional or academic problems may need to remain in a regular classroom or be placed in an adjustment class where the challenge or pressure is not so great. Referral to the class is made through the visiting teacher who discusses the situation at consulting time with the Guidance Services Department. A diagnostic study of the child may then be made upon which recommendations for school placement and further help may be determined. (Help is also available from the Pupil Study Center in the Guidance Services department for any gifted child at the request of the visiting teacher, whether the child is enrolled in a center or the adjustment rooms.)
5. Identified gifted children with very high ability may benefit from placement in specialized adjustment rooms. (The office of the coordinator for the elementary

school gifted program arranges for placement of children in these four combination grade adjustment room classes.)

6. Cluster groups are currently organized in all centers for grades 3, 4, 5 and 6.
7. Ranges of interests, abilities and achievements are often great in a cluster group. In some areas, gifted children have achieved on an adult level of comprehension.
8. Division of cluster-grouped pupils into two classrooms per grade level may occur when enrollment of state and local gifted in one classroom is high in number and when two qualified teachers are available.
9. Principals secure the "consent to participate" of all parents whose children attend a center, qualify as state gifted, and are working in an enrichment program.[6]

As the gifted child continues into the secondary schools, placement remains an important phase of the gifted program. Each secondary school has a gifted program advisor, known as an intergrade advisor, who works with the students in planning their programs, follows their progress, and advises them concerning their school activities, college requirements and scholarships. The Coordinator of the Program for Secondary Gifted Students works directly with the program advisors.

Enrichment, Adjustment and Acceleration

The San Diego City Schools have modified the instructional program by grouping for enrichment, adjustment and acceleration in both elementary and secondary schools. These terms are interpreted in the following ways in the San Diego City Schools program.

ENRICHMENT. Theoretically, enrichment takes place in all classes, if educators are interested in the needs of all individuals. In San Diego City Schools it means providing materials and study not included in the curriculum or extending the basic subject areas. The "cluster groups" in grades 3, 4, 5 and 6 at designated centers are given assignments and activities which replace routine work after the pupils have demonstrated mastery of basic material.

On the secondary level enrichment takes place in all advanced and honors classes where the gifted are programmed by providing them materials and experience to delve deeper into their special interests. Extracurricular activities in junior and senior high schools, resources in the community, summer programs, correspondence courses and tutoring further enrich the instructional program by developing potential talent and assisting personal and social adjustment.

ADJUSTMENT. Grouping also takes place in adjustment classes at designated centers in the elementary schools for students who (1) have social, emotional, or academic problems, and (2) those who are highly gifted. Both groups are identified by a school psychologist, and parents have the option of sending their children to these schools. Visiting Teacher service and clinical help are given students with emotional problems in order to study the problems that stem from their unusual ability.

ACCELERATION. Acceleration may mean one of two approved methods for advancing a student through the grades. One method is that of "enriching" basic subject areas in the curriculum to give breadth to grade-level materials. This is done by vertical upgrading of curriculum with above-grade texts and materials, a practice common to both elementary and secondary instruction. The other method of acceleration is completing academic requirements for two years in one year, a horizontal approach to enable a student to progress at a pace commensurate with his ability and his mastery of basic material.

Grouping of San Diego gifted along with the more able students in advanced and honors classes offering college-preparatory courses is the principal method of acceleration at the secondary level. In place of honors courses, a small select group of twelfth-grade students may be taking junior college courses concurrently with their high school subjects.

Acceleration is advised only after careful individual study determines it is to the best interest of the student to make more rapid progress through the grades. To facilitate the acceleration of mentally gifted students in the senior high schools, a policy has been in effect which reduces the number of credits required for high school graduation from 40 to 38 for students completing the senior high curricula in two years. In effect, this policy eliminates the requirement for the physical education credits for the year not attended and the six semesters of attendance. All other requirements must be satisfied. Mastery of required subjects needs to be established by successful results on examinations in order to have credit granted and to permit work on higher levels. The method of acceleration is left to the judgment of each school.

Administration of the Gifted Program

The administration of a special program in a large unified school district requires the elaborate planning and cooperation of many persons. Key personnel in the administration of the program include the classroom teachers and building principals in the centers where elementary gifted children are clustered, the resource teachers and the coordinators of the gifted child programs, the regional director, the director of exceptional child services and the members of the Committee for the Education of Gifted Children. The handbooks developed for the gifted child program summarize the responsibilities of these various positions. So much detail is clearly beyond the scope of this chapter, but these designations will be briefly indicated.

The director of Exceptional Child Services serves as the chief staff officer in charge of all special services for exceptional children of the San Diego

City Schools. In relation to programs for the gifted the director provides consulting services to the special education and counseling programs.

The primary function of the coordinator of the Elementary Gifted Program is to assist in the planning, development and improvement of the instructional program for gifted elementary school students. The coordinator of the Secondary Gifted Program assists the principals, intergrade advisors and teachers of the secondary schools in the district. As new junior and senior high schools are established and more intergrade advisors added and changes in assignments of teachers occur, the coordinator finds it necessary to establish guidelines for those newly appointed to work with the gifted. He also finds it necessary to assist intergrade advisors already working in the district to keep abreast of new developments in the program. Coordination is the key word. He must work with the permission of each secondary school principal to promote the educational growth of the mentally gifted and more able students.

Elementary school principals of centers for cluster group gifted are responsible for directing the program for the gifted in their own schools. To accomplish the program's purposes they enlist the assistance of the gifted program coordinator, resource teachers, the director of Exceptional Child Services, psychologists, visiting teachers, supervisors, specialists and the regional director. Gifted children are placed in the cluster group in order that they may benefit from the following:

1. The challenge of working with other children of high ability.
2. The materials, lessons and equipment of the gifted program.

He is the key person in interpreting the general policy of the program to the teachers. In addition he must exert leadership to develop internal policies for carrying on the program in his school and accept responsibility for the formulation of policies which make for the most effective education within the framework of individual enrichment.

Secondary school principals also direct the program within their own schools. They are responsible to the director of secondary schools and the assistant superintendent of secondary schools. In carrying out the procedures and recommended practices of the program principals of secondary schools may utilize the assistance of all of the other personnel with assigned responsibilities to the program. The principal interprets the general policy of the program to the teachers and exerts leadership to develop policies for carrying on the program in the school.

Much has been written about the important responsibility of teacher selection for gifted programs. San Diego City Schools program for the gifted recognizes the cruciality of this choice and offers its principals and recruiting staff careful guidelines for the selection process. In addition to the selection problem the district recognizes the need and the importance of an in-service education program which will improve the quality of the teacher's work with gifted children.

Teachers of mentally gifted secondary students will share many characteristics in common with their elementary school colleagues. It is also true that there are some qualifications more pertinent to the comprehensive junior and senior high school. In the San Diego City Schools program working in cooperation with the intergrade advisor on identification and placement is a specific responsibility.

The resource teachers for gifted children at the elementary level serve in a teaching, consultative, interpretative and advisory capacity working primarily with elementary school principals, teachers and Student Services Division personnel. Administratively they operate under the general direction of the assistant superintendent in charge of the Curriculum Services Division. Their work is done chiefly in the elementary schools and at the Education Center or Instructional Aid Center where they are engaged in collection and preparation of materials.

These resource teachers travel on a regular rotational basis to the twenty-four centers for the gifted. Their primary task is the assistance of teachers in the carrying out of the basic policies of the gifted program. On request of the principal or the teacher of a cluster group the resource teacher performs such teaching or additional duties as will contribute to the best interests of the gifted. Their assigned responsibilities are the subject of a rather extensive list contained in the *Handbook for Elementary Principals and Teachers.*[6]

The position of intergrade advisor grows out of experience showing that providing assistance to gifted students or their teachers is a time consuming task. Thus this position assists in the promotion of academic achievement and the provision of guidance for the gifted. The intergrade advisor is a teacher appointed by the principal to work with him, the gifted students, their teachers and their parents. He works in both an instructional and an advisory capacity. His concern is for helping students, teachers and parents provide the proper educational experiences, activities and materials conducive to the progress and growth of the students.

In the elementary schools division there is a regional director who serves as the chief line officer in charge of the elementary schools within a region. Here he is assigned the responsibility of assisting in the planning of programs, policies and goals for the operation of the elementary schools. In this capacity he therefore identifies and recommends teachers with high potential for work with gifted children. He assists in the selection of these teachers for assignment to the centers where vacancies occur or in new centers as they are organized. He may also review and approve exceptions to the procedure of gifted transfers.

The director of secondary schools is a line position with responsibility for schools within a region of the district. In this region he works with principals and such other personnel as may be assigned reporting directly to the assistant superintendent of secondary schools. Among the duties assumed by the director are those of directing in his region the approved program of evaluation of student progress in meeting their educational goals and conducting continuous evaluation of the operational program out of which he makes recommendations for improvement.

The visiting teachers in both the elementary and the secondary gifted program act as liaison persons between the school, the home, the guidance services department and community agencies. Students who have social and emotional problems which are interfering with their school program may be referred to them for guidance.

In the gifted program the school psychologist is enlisted to determine the ability of students, identifying them as mentally gifted or more able students. He determines their eligibility for placement in programs for enrichment, adjustment or acceleration and in the regional centers of the elementary program. He works with principals and intergrade advisors who have referred students for testing and assists in notifying parents when their children have been identified as gifted. He consults with principals, intergrade advisors and teachers on problems pertaining to the individual student.

The San Diego City Schools Committee for the Gifted operates as a permanent part of the San Diego program for the gifted. Membership of the committee consists of a cross section of personnel from the operations and services divisions including a representation of teachers, administrators, resource teachers, coordinators of gifted, psychologists, a psychiatrist and an intergrade advisor. The chairman of the committee is the assistant superintendent, Student Services Division. While the committee is not a policy making body it serves the program for the gifted by proposing research studies, conducting research studies, recommending changes to administrators, and evaluating many facets of the program.

The Program of Instruction

The program for the enrichment of education for the gifted child in the elementary division is a fundamental operation of San Diego City Schools gifted program. There is an attempt in this program to create a climate in which each child is freed from routine and needless repetition. The child is

given an opportunity to pursue his interests intensively. The program enhances the gifted child's ability to synthesize and relate knowledge to the study of topical areas which cut across subject fields.

In the San Diego City Schools program for the gifted the teacher is responsible for initiating and developing the enrichment program in the cluster group classroom. The district has provided guides to assist the classroom teacher of the gifted in her planning and preparation of a program of enrichment. The general rule is that enrichment is accomplished by means of planning supplementary assignments over and above regular class activity or replacement of basic or routine activities with more challenging assignments.

In addition to the general enrichment activities there are specific enrichment efforts directed toward several curricular areas. Enrichment in the reading program needs to be concerned not only with children who are reading above grade level but with gifted children who may need considerable help in becoming well motivated and enthusiastic pupils. In the latter case teachers are encouraged to analyze the situation through a study of the child's reading test performance and his habits and through experimentation with choices of material and methods of presentation.

Teachers who have gifted and superior students reading a year or more above grade level on a recommended reading achievement test usually begin the review period in the fall with the basic text for the particular grade. Afterward they may use a more difficult supplementary reader or go directly into accelerated readers collected from the city schools library for this purpose.

If all of the children in a top reading group score one year above grade level, teachers are entitled to a set of above grade or accelerated readers for this group. Above grade readers are available for grades 2, 3, 4, 5 and 6.

Enrichment of the reading program is further carried out by spending more time in interpretation than in simple comprehension, pursuing questions about reading which require more mature thinking, assignments involving the use of advanced reference and research skills and those that develop literary appreciation, skills of imagination and creative power. Enrichment in the language arts program deals with the fact that the language development of the gifted children tends to be varied and uneven with achievement ranging from far above average to somewhat below. This variety in achievement coupled with variety in socioeconomic background and other characteristics requires a highly variable approach to the enrichment process. Whatever the language pattern of the gifted child, however, elementary teachers have come to realize that they need to begin with a challenging, basic program. This program however must be adapted to and paced for each individual. Unlike arithmetic it has been found that more advanced language skills can be mastered with a minimum of teacher help. Since most are able to maintain perfect scores on weekly spelling tests with one or two days of study they are encouraged to use time freed in this manner to work on their own personal spelling lists or more creative types of language work.

It has been found that success in spare time work depends largely on teacher motivation, guidance and evaluation. The ultimate goal of course is to reach that point where gifted children will write spontaneously and enthusiastically on subjects of their own choosing.

Enrichment in the arithmetic program becomes especially challenging since the gap between ability level and achievement level of gifted children tends to be greater in arithmetic than in any other subject matter area. In learning a new process gifted children begin with the rest of the advanced group at concrete levels moving on to the abstract level as soon as they are ready. Sufficient practice for the development of mastery is required after which the pupil is excused from completing superfluous practice sheets or exercises unless his work indicates further need. Gifted pupils are then encouraged in the process of solving selective problems from the text or from current school or community projects.

Many teachers have found it valuable to have an arithmetic table in their room containing such things as supplementary books for extending mathematical concepts; commercial or teacher-made games to help a child develop speed and accuracy in computation; manipulating materials, for example meters and gauges of various kinds, and carpenter's tools such as a square. When and if the child has used fully all available enrichment materials provided through the gifted program and has proved by diagnostic tests that he has mastered all grade level requirements, he may on the recommendation of the teacher or principal and resource teacher be permitted to use a supplementary text at the next grade level.

Enrichment in the social studies-science program seems most amenable to creative instruction. It has been found that very capable students with careful teaching guidance plus carefully selected social studies materials and lessons produce results which prove of great value to all concerned. There are an almost limitless number of kinds of enrichment activities which may be provided in the social studies curriculum, but it is important that the teacher provide such experiences in ways that will not tend to enhance isolated study.

Scope and Sequence of the Enrichment Program

Materials for the enrichment program for elementary clustered group children include a broad selection of lesson sets, books and audio-visual equipment. Lists of gifted program enrichment lessons organized by subject level and grade level are available to the teacher of a gifted cluster from the resource teacher of the program. Instructional suggestions bulletins are also provided as supplementary and enrichment material.

SUPPLEMENTARY AND SPECIALIZED SERVICES

Teacher Assistants from Participating Colleges

One of the major problems arising in classrooms where gifted children are clustered is that of freeing the classroom teacher so that he may give more individual help to superior and gifted students in the room. One means of assisting with this problem was studied during the spring semester of 1958-59 in three of the study centers in the elementary schools. Student participants from the San Diego State College were hired as part-time paid assistants (teacher aids) to the teachers in the three schools who had the gifted in their regular classrooms. These assistants worked at the most not more than twelve hours during any one week for the teachers and in addition had their teaching assignment with their supervising teacher. Currently, teacher assistants are paid to work fifteen hours during any one week and may be enrolled at one of the participating colleges. One conclusion from the above study is that this program of teacher aids should be extended to include all centers where the gifted are grouped.

Typing Program for Centers of the Gifted

A typing program has been organized for the gifted and superior ability children in centers where the gifted are clustered. The aims of this typing program are the basics of the beginning typing course with the prospect of developing a gross stroking rate of about twenty words a minute by the end of a four-week period of daily instruction.

Saturday Art Classes for Talented Children

Classes designed to augment the art experiences pupils have within the regular instructional program in art provided by the classroom teacher are arranged on Saturday mornings in selected centers. Talented students throughout the City of San Diego are identified, recommended and selected for these classes. Enriched instruction is offered particularly in the areas of drawing and painting.

Other Resource Personnel

Should the principal and/or teacher of the gifted centers desire to extend the program of art, music and physical education beyond that of the curriculum guide, specialists in these subject areas are available to confer with them concerning an extension or enrichment of these programs.

Professional Growth Meetings

Throughout the school year in-service education or professional growth meetings are scheduled for principals and teachers who work with gifted children in the cluster centers. The basic structure of this offering is an orientation meeting before the start of the school year for teachers who are new to the instructional program for gifted children. During the fall and spring of the year demonstration lessons are given at fourth, fifth and sixth grade levels for all teachers involved in the gifted program of the elementary schools. The coordinator of the gifted program is responsible for planning the professional growth meetings in conjunction with the director of In-service Training.

Informing Parents of the San Diego Gifted Program

In addition to the initial conference held to notify parents of their child's potential, occasional meetings are held on a district or regional basis to keep parents of San Diego identified gifted children informed. In support of this procedure a brochure is also available for distribution following the initial conference. The brochure includes a brief description of the program and contains suggestions to parents to help them assist their child to make the most of his abilities.

Adjustment Classes for the Highly Gifted

Although a great majority of gifted children make a satisfactory academic and social adjustment either in regular programs or the cluster grouped program, a few require more specialized planning to assure that they will have every opportunity to reach their full potential. In the San Diego City Schools program for the gifted, adjustment classes have been developed for this purpose.

Admission to the highly gifted seminar class requires that a student has achieved an IQ score ranging in the top one-tenth of 1 per cent of all San Diego students on an individualized intelligence test, that he does not exhibit any severe adjustment problems either emotionally, socially or academically and whose individual needs cannot be met in a regular gifted cluster class. These classes with enrollment limited to fifteen are supported by a program of individual conferences with parents, counseling services, appropriate uses of resource personnel and additional in-service education conferences or meetings.

Educationally Handicapped Class for Gifted and Superior Pupils in Grades 4, 5 and 6

It has been shown that despite every possible remedial effort some gifted children in regular classes develop learning problems or problems of social and emotional nature which affect their overall functioning. Such youngsters may be accommodated within the structure of special programs for Educationally Handicapped Minors (California Education Code, Section 6750 ff).[9]

Children with some of the following characteristics may be referred for placement in this special class: low academic achievement as compared to ability, poor peer relationships, aggressive behavior, withdrawal or lack of participation, poor study habits, or extreme lack of confidence.

THE SECONDARY CURRICULUM FOR MENTALLY GIFTED AND MORE ABLE STUDENTS

Materials on curriculum, diplomas, honors and college admissions are subject to annual revision. Special note is made of this by those who are advising gifted students. Supportive materials are available in the form of "The Digest of Secondary Curriculum" which covers all subject matter areas in the secondary school curriculum and *The Handbook for Counselors* containing information on college preparation, admissions and scholarships.

Suggested Course Sequence in Major Academic Subjects

Recommendations for college preparation include the following: (1) required subjects of college preparatory English, mathematics, laboratory science, social science and foreign language; (2) electives in speech, music, art and other subjects contributing to general academic background. The aim of the program in the secondary years is to build a broad academic program which will provide a wide base for college entrance requirements. Performance of the student in all subjects will be indicated on the transcripts sent to colleges. The transcript includes explanatory notes concerning the various advanced and honors courses. Many gifted are encouraged to apply for the Advanced Placement Program.

Since the underachiever may tend to select courses with the least academic demand every effort is made to help such students see as many kinds of opportunities as possible in the curricular offerings. Notice will be made of the fact that some opportunities include higher education. Others may include vocational patterns which require a high ability but less academic work. If acceptable to the student and his parents and judged appropriate by the school, students are scheduled into advanced and honors courses in those subjects in which they have special talents.

Principals and intergrade advisors have the dual task of helping teachers in the school understand the impact of programming—the long range career or vocational goals—and simultaneously helping the gifted students make the wisest choices.

Advanced Courses

The State of California requires a report from schools on the mentally gifted minors enrolled in special programs for gifted students. On such reports it is important that the district procedure provide for a listing of the advanced courses in which students have enrolled. Courses which qualify for the designation advanced are available in art, English, foreign language, mathematics, music, science and the social studies. At the twelfth grade honors calculus and political science are part of the San Diego Junior College curriculum. College transcripts are supplied for these students.

Courses in the Curriculum of Academic Distinction

In the San Diego City Schools a "diploma with academic distinction" may be earned. Mentally gifted and more able students are usually encouraged to take the prescribed courses leading to this diploma.

The requirements for the "diploma with academic distinction" are as follows: (1) A student must attend San Diego City high schools for the entire year. (2) He must have completed fourteen semester credits in the designated courses with marks of A or B. Four of these fourteen semester credits must have been earned in the senior year. (3) He must have completed a minimum of two years credit in mathematics, science and foreign language. These requirements may be met in grades 9 through 12. Marks of A or B in these subjects are desirable but not essential.

Membership in Honor Organizations

Students have potential for membership in certain honor organizations determined by the grades which they receive in their courses. Gifted achievers and underachievers need an incentive to do the best work of which they are capable and honor societies hold for them the highest standards of performance.

In the junior high the honor organization is known as the National Junior Honor Society, a chapter affiliated with the national organization. In the senior high the honor organization is the California Scholarship Federation, a chapter of the statewide organization which is recognized throughout the country as an honor society.

Grading in Honors and Advanced Courses

Some difficulty is found in determining marks to be assigned for performance in honors and advanced courses. It is not uncommon for students and their parents to challenge the advisability of taking honors and advanced courses when the possibility exists that their grades in such courses may not be sufficiently high to meet the keen competition for college entrance grade point requirements. A student's grade point average of course is only one factor in determining college admission and it may be that undue stress is placed upon this feature in some institutions. In the San Diego City Schools program for the gifted, and for scholarship purposes especially the honors and advance courses are recommended and are providing the necessary background for college success.

In honors courses all students must receive A's or B's except in those cases where a conference has been held with the parent and the student prior to the close of the quarter. If the student's work has been less than the level of a recommending mark, a transfer from the honors course to regular class must be recommended unless the parent and the student request that the student remain in the honors course with the understanding that the teacher will award a mark on the basis of the teacher's judgment of the student's performance.

In advanced classes a similar regulation exists. In this case the recommended procedure includes the statement "with the concurrence of the teacher" as a qualification for remaining in the advanced course.

Testing Programs for College Admission and Scholarships

In the San Diego City Schools gifted program intergrade advisors may cooperate with testing advisors in helping gifted and more able students plan to attend four-year institutions. They can help students keep abreast of the college entrance and scholarship requirements and the dates on which tests are to be given. Unless a student is sure of acceptance in a college not requiring College Entrance Board Examinations or American College Tests he is advised to take them. Assistance and guidance is offered to students regarding participation in other testing programs such as the National Merit Scholarship and Scholastic Aptitude Tests.

Two programs of vital importance for San Diego's students are (1) California State Commission Scholarship Program for students of established California residency, and (2) the examination in subject "A" for University of California campuses. Appropriate guidance is offered to students so they may participate in such testing programs.

Other programs in which San Diego City Schools gifted students may participate are the National Achievement Scholarship Program for outstanding Negro students, and the College Work Study Program developed under the Economic Opportunity Act of 1964.

Enrichment Opportunities for Mentally Gifted and More Able Students

The San Diego City Schools believe that enrichment is the essence of all good education. They do not limit this offering to the gifted or those with unusual problems, but regard it as a learning concept in which experiences and methods are used to insure maximum development of the students. In particular the secondary gifted program is guided by the principle of providing gifted and more able students opportunities to delve more deeply and to range more widely than do average students in their learning experiences.

The Guidelines for Secondary Principals, Intergrade Advisors, and Teachers of Mentally Gifted and More Able Students[5] provides a substantial list of supplemental experiences and enrichment opportunities which may be made available to these students. All possible means are to be explored to nurture the growth of talent which may first be discovered in a classroom. These supplemental experiences can be used concurrently with extracurricular activities, summer school programs of schools, colleges and universities, correspondence courses, tutoring, talent programs and community resources. In addition children may have opportunity to explore various work areas as part of the general work experience program supervised by the area employment counselors of the schools. This is a school-initiated and school-controlled plan coordinated with the public agencies and the community nonprofit organizations. Further enrichment is possible through the program of seventh and eighth grade seminar class speakers utilizing eminent people from the community and seminar class field trips providing firsthand observation of many fine and stimulating community enterprises, some with worldwide significance.

THE CAJON VALLEY UNION SCHOOL DISTRICT

The Cajon Valley Union School District is an elementary school district educating children in grades kindergarten through 8. Current enrollment is approximately 11,000. The district began its program within the last decade. Its plan had been initiated somewhat prior to the California legislation for mentally gifted minors. In this program opportunities are provided for both intellectually and artistically gifted children. Changes based on continuous evaluation over the years have been made to strengthen the learning environment for these children.

Philosophy

The district assumes major responsibility for development of the potential of these children in a shared effort with the home and community. Differing kinds as well as degrees of ability are considered in the long-range plans of the district. Efforts are given to discovering and applying methods of individualizing instruction for the academically exceptional comparable to those which are applied to other unique talents.

Special recognition for outstanding use of special abilities offers stimulus to students for further growth. Since the ultimate goal is a program which will allow gifted students to realize their unusual potential, experience is offered which promotes the adoption of high personal standards of performance. Such high standards imply ability to achieve at maximum. Every sound educational means is employed to encourage the development of ideas and attitudes compatible with those high standards of performance. It is an ultimate goal also that each gifted person will acquire the inner satisfaction during school that will persist throughout life to the ultimate benefit of society in general.

The school recognizes that it is sometimes necessary to help individuals accept goals and values which may differ somewhat from those held by their peers and families. Necessary guidance must be provided to aid in the acquisition of appropriate values without the alienation of their fellow pupils or needless isolation. The Cajon Valley School District believes that programs designed to meet specialized needs of gifted students should be given at least as much priority as those given other atypical children.

Program Goals

The major objective of the gifted child program is to develop personal proficiency commensurate with pupil's intellectual capacity through the following: (1) mastery of subject matter; (2) development of effective study habits and proficient use of time; (3) development of desirable attitudes; (4) cultivation of social skills; (5) cultivation of aesthetic appreciation; (6) development of leadership responsibilities, and (7) development of physical and emotional maturity. More specifications are also considered.[1]

Definition of Gifted

The academically gifted are those meeting the criteria prescribed for mentally gifted minors in the Administrative and Education Codes of the State of California. The California standard requires a score of 130 or above on an individual test of intelligence, typically the Weschsler Intelligence Scale for Children or the revised Stanford Binet Scale Form L-M. A score at or above the 98th percentile on a group test of mental ability, and a score at or above the 98th percentile on a standardized test of reading achievement or arithmetic achievement is also required. These tests must have been administered not less than thirty-six months before identification.

Identification

Identification of the academically gifted is accomplished through prescribed procedures which are directed by the deputy superintendent for instruction through the director of guidance. Individual testing is usually done by psychometrists working under the director of guidance. Results of group and individual testing are then analyzed in the guidance office of the school district.

Artistically Gifted

The artistically gifted are defined as those pupils whose work is submitted, screened and accepted by the screening committee (assistant superintendent, curriculum; director of special programs; art coordinator, Department of Education, San Diego County; elementary principal; classroom teacher). A letter of invitation is sent from the committee to students and their parents inviting participation.

The criteria used to select students for this program include the following:

1. Persistent interest and consistent performance in art activity.
2. Ability to concentrate on art for a long period of time.
3. Awareness and sensitivity coupled with a vigorous imagination.
4. Interest in using various media and a desire to try new things.

The Art Talent Program

This program is offered on Saturday morning for pupils from fifth and sixth grades throughout the district. A continuing interest must be shown to remain in the program.

The stated objectives are as follows:

1. To identify and develop special art abilities.
2. To provide a program of additional instruction and enrichment in art, emphasizing the development of skills and techniques.
3. To stimulate an awareness of unique art abilities.
4. To provide and heighten an awareness of art.
5. To stimulate and foster a greater appreciation for the fine arts.

Program emphasis is primarily on drawing and painting, composition and design, and techniques and media.

Administrative and Personnel Procedures

This program is administered under the jurisdiction of the deputy superintendent for instruction. This is the leadership position stimulating the work of principals, the director of guidance, the director of special programs and other curriculum staff. Recommendations and reports are handled by this office and directed to the district superintendent and board of education.

The director of special programs carries districtwide responsibility for the conduct of the program. This position carries the multitude of details related to program direction. The key phrases for this position are those of assisting others in the execution of their duties, evaluation and recommendation of materials and equipment, and coordination of activities carried out in the program from grade level to grade level. Cooperation with other district staff personnel is essential and the director works closely with the guidance counseling and testing staff.

The building principal provides direct leadership to the educational program for gifted children enrolled in his school. He is responsible for implementation of the program at this level and works directly with teachers to determine their needs. He helps to evaluate program effectiveness and arranges for meetings that are directed to program improvement. There is an important responsibility in working closely with parents to explain and interpret the program for the gifted.

Teachers must provide for the best possible learning situation in their classrooms. They have a responsibility for developing positive attitudes toward individual and group competition and for understanding of gifted children and their individual needs. They also work with parents in groups and as individuals and maintain the records required on each child in accordance with the district plan.

The director of guidance is the chairman of the Admissions and Discharge Committee, calling meetings to consider children for admission and discharge from the program. His job is to provide leadership in the identification program and in the interpretation of test results. He recommends the establishment of new classes for gifted pupils and conducts research and evaluation related to the program.

Psychometrists work directly under the director of guidance in the identification process and conduct group and individual testing. District directors work directly with principals and teaching staff to upgrade the instructional program in particular areas. They may assist teachers through conference and demonstration lessons, individually and in groups, and in other ways work to improve instruction in specific areas. They encourage teachers to investigate and make use of new teaching approaches. District directors also coordinate and implement programs of instruction and are responsible for the development of teaching aids and materials. The development, implementation and evaluation of courses of study is also a director's responsibility. District Directors are also a primary source of information which they garner from attending various regional and national meetings in their specific field.

Admission and Discharge Committee

Enrollment in the program is on a voluntary basis and pupils are not assigned to a class without the written consent of parent or guardian. A child may be removed from this program and reassigned upon request from his parents. The regulation of admissions and discharges from the program, however, is a function of the Admissions and Discharge Committee composed of the deputy superintendent for instructional services, the director of guidance, the director of special programs and the principal of the school to which the classes for gifted children are assigned.

The committee considers all pertinent information available on each pupil including intelligence test scores, achievement test scores, written recommendations from teachers and principals, classroom performance and social adjustment. The committee may request a personal interview with the pupil being considered for admission to the program and with his parents if this seems advisable.

In the event a pupil does not make adequate adjustment to a gifted class, exhibits an uncooperative attitude, or fails to maintain a high level of academic performance the following steps are taken: (1) A conference including the principal, teacher and child's parents is held. As a result of this conference the pupil may be put on probationary status. If it does not appear that the problem can be remedied, the case may be referred to the Admission and Discharge Committee for evaluation and possible reassignment. (2) If a pupil is to be removed from the gifted program by the action of the Admission and Discharge Committee, the parents will be notified in writing of the reasons and the effective date. (3) The school principal keeps the director of guidance informed of the prospective or actual changes in scheduling of pupils assigned to the program.

Organization Plan for the Program

The following format is specified for the gifted program:

GRADES 3 THROUGH 8. The program for identified children in grades 3 through 8 is planned within selected schools where special classes are organized to help gifted children meet the specified objectives. In cases where parent consent has not been given for the identified gifted to enter this program the children are clustered in a fast learning group in the school of regular attendance.

GRADES KINDERGARTEN THROUGH 2. Children who have been identified as gifted at the kindergarten, first and second grade levels continue their programs at a school of regular attendance and are clustered with one teacher of each grade level.

PROGRAM OF INSTRUCTION. The curriculum of Cajon Valley gifted program is designed to be consistent with the educational program proposed by state, county and local district requirements for the elementary school. All major curriculum areas are reflected in the gifted program. In addition particular efforts are made in instruction in Spanish, creative writing, industrial arts and homemaking (at seventh and eighth grades) and typing as an elective during the summer school.

Expectancies have been outlined for each curriculum area for each grade level, kindergarten through 8, in the program. Individual progress is used to determine the skill and concept level to which the teaching effort is geared. Each child's educational development is recorded in individual progress records thus facilitating subsequent teacher's planning.

The educational program is designed to reflect the following attributes: flexibility, continuity, economy, integrated learnings, curriculum differentiation. A variety of activities, methodologies and resources are provided to insure broad experiences and foster maximal development. In addition, an analysis of special interests of individual pupils provides a means of enhancing such interests.

The district attempts to provide facilities and materials that will assist and support teachers assigned to this program. Classrooms with adequate storage facilities have been assigned within the school selected for them. These are planned to facilitate organizing total class, small group and individual activities. Library facilities are available within each school and collections provided which reflect the needs and interests of gifted children. The collections may be changed and supplemented as pupil needs dictate. Audio-visual equipment and materials of all types including film strip projectors for small group use and overhead projectors with transparencies are available to teachers at all times. Instructional supplies are maintained in sufficient quantities and provisions are made for purchasing special items. A kiln is available for ceramic work. Encyclopedias, dictionaries, atlases and other special references are also provided for each gifted class.

Pupil Evaluation

Pupil progress is measured by multiple criteria. Standardized tests are administered regularly each year. Individual case study records are maintained. A folder is kept on each child which includes all pertinent evidence found by the Admissions and Discharge Committee—information regarding personality and attitudes; achievement records; indications of creativity; descriptions of behavior and of changes in behavior; an assessment of needs and indications as to how the school might see that these needs are met; career and educational goals; family background and an assessment of the influence of the family and peer group on the child; samples of the child's work; an autobiography describing the significant events in his life and how he feels about school, college, work, his country, persons with whom he associates and himself. Judgments are also obtained through parent-teacher conferences and through informal appraisal of daily performance.

Program Evaluation

The district conducts a systematic study of those elements which can provide a means of evaluating the district's gifted program. Both academic and social progress are measured through annual comparisons of results in the standardized achievement testing program. Also employed are parent evaluation, teacher evaluation and pupil self-evaluation. The program is evaluated as well by participating teachers and principals.

CHULA VISTA CITY SCHOOLS

The Chula Vista City School District, serving a suburban population of about 50,000, has a student enrollment of about 12,000 in kindergarten through grade six. The committee organized to study methods of providing services for gifted children was created during the 1953-54 school year. During the 1957-58 school year, the district participated in the pilot program conducted by the California Department of Education. The district has continued to seek out children with ability levels prescribed in that program and to encourage their efforts to reach their potential. Specialized guidance and special materials have been developed and provided for teachers in this program.

Identification

Following the criteria of the California Mentally Gifted Minor Program, the Chula Vista Gifted Child Program carries on an identification activity throughout the year. Children are located through referral and other screening procedures and individual intelligence tests, usually the WISC or Stanford-Binet are administered by members of the special services staff of psychologists, psychometrists and counselors. Parents are notified when individual testing confirms ability in the gifted range and their permission is sought to include the child in the program. Presently about one third of the identified children are in grades kindergarten through 3 and two thirds are in grades 4 through 6. This represents about 4.3 per cent of the total district enrollment.

The Program

Three approaches are employed—enrichment in the regular classroom, special grouping for part of a day or week and acceleration. The district has adopted a clustering policy in which identified gifted children are grouped with other high achieving children in one self-contained classroom at each grade level. However, because of special problems such as year-round screening, class size and parental preference, there may be multiple clusters at a grade level.

The enrichment program for the gifted consists of curriculum modifications and special materials. Children are encouraged to develop skills needed for independent study, to master basic subjects, to be critical and creative thinkers, to be helpful members of a group and to work at a rate commensurate with their ability. Children study in greater depth and breadth the regular subjects or areas in which they have a greater interest. Special materials include reference books, library materials, tape recorders, kits and recordings. Most of these materials are ordered by teachers of the gifted from the district library. Other items are placed in each school for use by high potential children.

The auxiliary teacher, the principal, a regular teacher, or a librarian meet with special groups of gifted and high achieving children. Such groups meet daily or weekly to study subjects from science to the humanities in depth. These children are usually grouped across grade levels. Acceleration may occur at any level if a child is achieving far above grade, is mature enough to succeed at another level, and if all people concerned agree that acceleration is justified and beneficial.

Parents of gifted children are invited to have their children attend cluster groups in summer school. More than 200 students attended these sessions during the last summer session. Here they worked with new classmates transported to the center. In the summer program students work with the humanities, studying a culture in depth and extending special interests. Instrumental music, chorus and typing are offered to upper grade children. New materials are also tried during the summer and if found valuable, additional materials are purchased for use with other cluster groups. Encyclopedias, book kits, science and math materials and creative projects enter the regular program through summer school explorations.

Children with special talents are given additional opportunities for fulfillment. Those with musical gifts may participate in the All District Chorus led by the vocal music supervisor. The All District Band and Orchestra are conducted by the instrumental music director and the instrumental music teacher. The artistically talented from the Title I (Public Law 89-10) schools in the district attend special Saturday morning classes in art. Various media are offered and instructional sessions are conducted by four different teachers.

Special steps are taken to assure continuity in the program as the children move from sixth grade into the junior high schools which are operated by a separate high school district. All junior high school principals, the assistant superintendents and the directors of curriculum of both districts meet to transfer permanent records and decide programs and placements. This degree of cooperation among school district personnel is ample evidence of the commitment to gifted programs in this area.

The In-service Program

The district is sensitive to teacher needs. During September 1966 two workshops were devoted to this concern. Two committees, representing the two levels of the program, were formed to conduct additional studies on identification, characteristics of the upper and lower segments of the gifted population, special needs of gifted children and program innovations. Materials lists were examined and new lists developed to support instruction. In addition, building principals have continued in-service work on the gifted program in building meetings. A general supervisor with responsibility for the gifted program in the district works cooperatively with the director of curriculum to maintain a balance between this and other special programs in the district.

Evaluation

Anecdotal records and cumulative files are kept for each gifted child. Teachers are asked to assess progress compared to ability and effort. There has been no formal structure for evaluation of the program. Continuity has been hampered by many changes in the supervisory structure over the years. Reasonable stability has been maintained, however, by continued maintenance of good central record-keeping and the sustained interest of district teaching and administrative personnel.

PROGRAM FOR THE MORE ABLE LEARNER IN THE ESCONDIDO UNION SCHOOL DISTRICT

The Escondido Union School District occupies a coastal valley thirty miles north of the city of San Diego. Enrollment in kindergarten through grade 8 is about 6,000 pupils. Secondary students from this system attend one of three high schools operated by a separate union high school district.

This description is of the More Able Learner Program which serves the elementary school population. Development began with the appointment of a committee immediately following the passage of the California legislation for "mentally gifted minors" in 1961. This group studied current programs in California and throughout the United States and reviewed related research. The committee then met with state consultants to design a program which would be most compatible with the existing general education program of the Escondido Union School District. The most logical pattern of development followed that reflected in the district philosophy for special education. Thus a cluster program for "the more able learner" child emerged.

During 1961-62 cluster programs were initiated at the sixth and seventh grade levels as a pilot project. Other grade levels were served by enrichment in regular classrooms. Following evaluation of the pilot project in the spring of 1962 it was decided to apply the cluster group principle to all grade levels in the system. During the following school year three in-service sessions were offered for the teachers working with More Able Learner children. A More Able Learner committee was established consisting of eight More Able Learner teachers and the director of Special Services. This committee recommended educational materials and supplies for the More Able Learner Program.

The program was continued and expanded during the 1963-64 school year and in the spring a twelve session in-service program was provided. At this time the trustees of the Escondido Union School District authorized the position of coordinator of the More Able Learner Program, the position to be activated during the 1964-65 school year.

Aims and Objectives

The More Able Learner Program is seen as a logical outgrowth of the school district's philosophy of education. This direction is reflected in the following policy statements adopted by the governing board in 1959.

> We believe that there is inherent in the American belief the concept that the individual is important and that the public school system should give each individual an opportunity to develop to the maximum of his potential. We believe that the true function of the elementary school district is to nurture the intellectual growth of children—all other objectives are supplementary to this one great purpose. We believe that a school program attains excellence when it provides genuine opportunity for all and when it challenges every pupil to achieve his best.
>
> Children shall be provided learning tasks which are challenging yet within their capabilities, leading to excellence of academic performance which will develop a continuing pursuit of knowledge; insofar as their abilities permit to give each

child a sound mastery of the tools of learning such as reading, writing, arithmetic and the use of the spoken language."[4]

AIMS. The district recognizes the need for a standard by which one can measure the success of a program. It asks the question, "What type of person will this More Able Learner be as a direct result of the educational program?" The program aims toward relative success in the following designated areas. Specific behavioral objectives are listed in the guide[4]—effective thinking, basic skills, leadership, citizenship, understanding the environment, human relationships, successful family life, vocational competence, world understanding, appreciation of beauty, health and safety, use of leisure time, consumer effectiveness.

OBJECTIVES. The following program objectives are stated as means to achieve those goals:

1. Present a clear statement of objectives.
2. Reflect the acceptance of philosophy of education which is based upon the recognition of individual differences.
3. Concern itself with the development of a wide variety of talents.
4. Include a systematic program for the early discovery and identification of these more able learners.
5. Employ the most appropriate and effective methods of developing the child's potential.
6. Take advantage of a wide variety of school and community resources.
7. Attempt to increase quality of self motivation in the more able learner.
8. Provide for the selection and continuous education of teachers for the more able learner.
9. Develop desirable attitudes toward the more able learner.
10. Provide balance among intellectual, emotional, social, cultural and physical growth of the more able learner.
11. Provide for continuity of experiences.
12. Be administered by one or more trained persons who should have available those funds for supplies, learning materials and personnel necessary for success.
13. Have provisions for constant evaluation.

Demands in the More Able Learner Program

The district recognizes that these children and those who serve them are subject to many demands more or less peculiar to the condition of a high level of intelligence. The child's attitudes at school and at home are often reflective of these demands. When these demands are unrecognized or their significance neglected, negative outcomes can very well result in both the academic and social life of the child. Similarly and particularly in the case of parents and teachers there are demands which should not be ignored if the total effort on behalf of the More Able Learner is to be effective. The Guide for Teachers of More Able Learner Children[4] lists a number of these demands.

Identification

Children are identified for placement in the More Able Learner Program according to the regulations prescribed by the State Board of Education in Title V of the California Administrative Code.[8]

Program Coordination

The More Able Learner Program is administered under the direction of the deputy superintendent, Educational Services. Under his direction the coordinator of the More Able Learner Program has been assigned responsibilities in eight areas as follows:

1. *Responsibilities in the area of in-service education.* The teachers of More Able Learner children need help in understanding these children, their particular needs as well as the objectives of the program. They should also be assisted in communicating with parents, grading practices, teaching techniques and ways of adapting basic instructional programs to the needs of these children. The coordinator of the More Able Learner Program must be able to plan and conduct the substantial and continuing in-service activity for teachers in the program. Insuring the development of the appropriate curriculum experiences must be a major commitment of the coordinator.

2. *Responsibilities in the area of selection of materials.* The demands for resource materials in an enriched curriculum are usually exorbitant. The coordinator must develop lists of resources and curriculum ideas and plan with both school and public libraries for the extension of these services. To assure adequacy and appropriateness the coordinator also assists in the selection of advanced texts and materials for More Able Learner classes.

3. *Responsibilities in the area of evaluation of the program.* Program effects are judged from information obtained from parents, pupils, teachers and standardized test results. The More Able Learner Coordinator plans and coordinates this evaluation program.

4. *Responsibilities in the area of interpretation of the More Able Learner Program.* Interpreting the program to school staff, community and parent groups as well as to parents of More Able Learner children is an important task of the More Able Learner Coordinator who works closely with the staff to assure that this task is accomplished.

5. *Responsibilities in the area of parent conferences.* The More Able Learner coordinator meets with parents in both individual and group conferences regarding various problems and components such as work load and pupil adjustment.

6. *Responsibilities in the area of demonstration teaching.* The coordinator provides demonstration teaching to illustrate techniques suitable for use with More Able Learner children.

7. *Responsibilities in the area of administration of the program.* The coordinator acts as a consultant to the district administrators in the organization of the regular and the extended program for More Able Learners. He is responsible for compiling lists of outside resource personnel, supervising case histories, assisting with field trip arrangements, preparation of written materials describing the program and for providing data needed by the superintendent for the production of reports

needed by the State Department of Education. The coordinator is also responsible for the development of curriculum plans for the More Able Learner Program at all grade levels.

8. *Responsibilities in the area of identification.* Through classroom visitations and the use of information in cumulative folders the Coordinator assists in the selection of children for placement in the More Able Learner Program.

The Cluster Program

The cluster program groups children who have been identified as More Able Learners in classrooms at each grade level in each school within the district. Children who have not been classified as More Able Learners but who are functioning at or above their specific grade level may also be in these classrooms. All children functioning below grade level have been removed from the cluster classroom. Although there is no fixed limit on the number of children who will be included in a cluster the range will usually be from six to twelve children. The district feels an ideal group is about nine children.

The building principal makes the decision for placement of a child in the More Able Learner class. The decision to place, however, is arrived at cooperatively by the principal through interviews with classroom teacher, the guidance consultant and the coordinator of the More Able Learner Program. When a positive recommendation has been made this information is conveyed to the parents for their approval or rejection. One of the advantages of the cluster program is that children with special ability may place their own individual ability in perspective with that of other children in their cluster. The grouping of More Able Learner children with normal children is regarded as a positive experience for both groups.

Enrichment for the More Able Learner

Instructional support has been available for the More Able Learner Program through the development of enrichment units. These have been prepared for each grade level in various curricular areas such as science, social studies, literature, fine arts and for book length reading. The enrichment units are designed to stimulate able students to do much more reading than they would normally be asked to do. The units are designed to enrich various areas of the curriculum. For example social studies and reading units for the most part have one required book and many other related titles whereas science units and certain social studies and literature units may be composed entirely of multititled materials with no one title in quantity. It is hoped that materials will be of such high interest level that students will therefore desire to read more than the minimum requirement. Most of these high interest level books will be read silently by the children, and no restraint is placed on a child with respect to the length of time it will take to finish a given title.

Children who finish assigned reading quickly will be encouraged to read the library of related materials that are a part of the unit. These materials may cover a variety of areas. Teachers are expected to stimulate interest by book reviews and the More Able Learner Coordinator will be available to introduce books if teachers so desire.

When all children in the cluster have read a single book an oral discussion of the book is considered preferable to laborious written assignments. These discussions should be designed so that they add to the children's appreciation of the book. Discussions should not be continued beyond the point where enthusiasm has lagged.

When children in the class are not a part of the group assigned to read a particular book, they may wish to read it anyway. This is not only considered permissible but desirable. Of course the selection of the enrichment units have been made primarily with the More Able Learner child in mind. Although many of the materials will be beyond the reading abilities of the non-More Able Learner children in the same grade there is no sharp dividing line and many children with less reading skill may enjoy the content of the unit. It is also possible for teachers of the same grade level in the building to select some of these books for use with their children and this is permissible in the More Able Learner Program.

Teachers are encouraged to schedule units as far in advance as feasible. Guides for some units are available and useful to teachers in preplanning. When the unit materials arrive in the classroom it is desirable that student librarians oversee their use. All books are carded and may be checked out and taken home. Most units are scheduled into a classroom for a four-week period, but there are exceptions—a microscope unit circulates on a six-week schedule.

Improvement in units is encouraged and provided for by making a brief guide available to the More Able Learner teachers after the initial pilot use of each unit. The guides include audio-visual suggestions and may be useful in preplanning. Comments and additional suggestions arising from their use in the classroom may be incorporated in subsequent additions to the unit. In this way the More Able Learner Program is a constantly changing and improving experience for both students and teachers. The continuing preparation of units helps to assure the continuity of the program and the currency of unit materials.

During the 1966-67 school year, fifty-three enrichment units have been available for circulation on a scheduled basis and thirty new units are in the process of being made available—materials ordered, processed and organized for distribution. It is anticipated that the addition of another forty to fifty units will complete the major part of the enrichment unit program plan, which should then necessitate chiefly replacement of worn-out materials, addition of new and current materials as suitable, and creation of new units to meet the needs of teachers and changes in curriculum.

With this part of the program well underway, it is anticipated that attention may be given to pilot programs in such areas as seminar classes for highly gifted at the intermediate and junior high level, Junior Great Books groups, and similar activities carried out either during the regular school day or outside of school hours. It is also anticipated that enrichment programs other than the enrichment book units presently being used will be explored.

GROSSMONT UNION HIGH SCHOOL DISTRICT

The Grossmont Union High School District, which serves a large geographic area lying east of the City of San Diego, enrolls about 17,000 students, 9-12, on eight campuses. The programs on two of the campuses will be described—the Honors Classes of the Grossmont campus and the Honors-by-Examination program of the Monte Vista campus. A statement which reflects the support given to each school's effort by the district is found in this excerpt from the program summary:

> Back of our entire gifted and honors program is this working hypothesis: select those youth who can profit and give them ideas that are big and important. Do this and you can, with proper guidance, marshal behind them all the emotional resources and moral quality of their natures. It is our aim to generate a student's intellectual momentum by spending time finding out the abilities, interests, and needs of our students as individuals and then helping students meet their needs, exploit their abilities and develop their interests to the optimum.[11]

Participation in the financial support structure of the California Program for Mentally Gifted Minors requires that a written plan be on file. Selected statements from this plan point up the general character of the program. Its purposes are to identify students having special talents, aptitudes and abilities and to provide programs which will maximize those attributes of the identified students. They also propose to develop eagerness and commitment to learning on the part of the student as well as to develop pertinent understanding among faculty, students and community.

The general goals of the program are as follows:

1. Enabling gifted students to work at higher cognitive levels.
2. Challenging students to higher levels of excellence.
3. Enhancing the possibilities of horizontal and vertical acceleration.
4. Raising the aspiration levels of gifted.
5. Providing insights into original and creative works through "exposure to greatness."
6. Developing a specialized curriculum for the gifted.

The variety of activities developed to achieve such goals and purposes include providing special library research opportunities, seminar groupings, special individualized oral and written examinations, special field trips, independent study opportunities and special work opportunities with community sponsors. Special facilities and material, such as seminar rooms, special library facilities, language laboratories and science laboratories, have been provided. In addition, there are special classrooms, sets of books, reference materials, library books and tapes, records and other audio-visual materials.

Two approaches to programming for mentally gifted minors are illustrated by the brief descriptions following—one of the Honors Classes, the other of Honors by Examination.

Grossmont High School

The plan on the Grossmont campus is the provision of Honors Classes. These classes have been designed for eligible students in grades 9 to 12. Typically honors classes are provided in English, geometry, algebra, advanced senior math, United States and world history, civics/social problems, social studies, chemistry, physics, and freshman science. At the request of the governing board and following a study of the district's college preparation program, the Honors Program was developed as an integral part of the total program of the district.

STUDENT SELECTION. In order to assure that all eligible students will have an opportunity to participate in the program, teachers and counselors are constantly on the lookout for pupils who demonstrate superior ability in any academic area. Such students are then referred for individual study and counseling.

TEACHER SELECTION. Teachers are selected for service in this program when they demonstrate an understanding and belief in it, have had superior teaching experience, strong preparation in the subject area and ability to motivate students. They are also those who show a desire to evaluate their teaching methods and to critique program results. Teachers have been supported and encouraged through group meetings with counselors and administrators, visits to other schools, development of course outlines and special budgets.

THE PROGRAM. The curriculum follows the general pattern for college preparation. It is then strengthened either through enrichment or acceleration and through the use of specially selected methods, textbooks and instructional supplies. Grades are reported in the honors program by the same method used in other classes. However, policy requires that no student be penalized by grades as a result of having been placed in an honors section. Special effort is made in the development of the master schedule to make it possible for all gifted students to have an opportunity to participate in the student activity program. This program is considered essential to the full development of their leadership potential and is judged to be successful by the number of these students who have participated actively.

EVALUATION. The success of the program is determined by both objective and subjective evaluation procedures. The broadest possible use is made of test materials both standardized and teacher-made to determine academic progress. Subjective information is developed through other kinds of testing, student interviews and conferences with parents and teachers to evoke attitude data from those within the program as well as from others within the same school.

Monte Vista High School

The program for gifted students at Monte Vista High School functions on an Honors-by-Examination principle. Its purpose is to provide students of superior ability and achievement as much individualization of instruction as possible. Current levels of student functioning are determined and then opportunity is provided for proceeding as far as the student can go. The goal of the student is hoped to be the acceptance of the opportunity to develop his abilities and to achieve at an optimum level.

STUDENT SELECTION. Students are recommended for Honors-by-Examination from "C" level courses in five departments—social studies, English, mathematics, science and language. Ninth grade teachers check the School and College Ability Tests and Sequential Tests of Educational Progress (SCAT-STEP) stanine scores with counselors or the registrar's records. These scores and classwork form the basis for ninth grade recommendations. Teachers recommending students in the tenth through twelfth grades use the same criteria in addition to the student's past record in Honors Program participation. The basis for recommendation is a SCAT-STEP stanine score of 8 or 9 and achievement in the specific subject matter area in the top 10 per cent of the general student body.

THE PROGRAM. A committee reviews and approves the program of individual study and a reading outline for each student in specific subject matter areas. The committee is also responsible for selection and review of examinations at the end of the year which qualify students for Honors by Examination. The following information appears on an enclosure with each transcript issued on a student: "The student participated in a regular college preparatory C level class. As a result of teacher recommendation, he was judged to be in the top 10 per cent of his high school class. The C designation was changed to H (Honors) on the basis of the teacher recommendation and the passing of a comprehensive examination in the subject."

The major need of the program consists of the provision of suitable reading and study materials to challenge the student in each area of work. Suitable tests also must be selected and purchased or constucted.

Program Evaluation. Individual student results on standardized achievement tests form basic evaluative evidence. In addition, the Gifted and Honors Committee holds periodic meetings for this purpose and to study other means of program evaluation.

OCEANSIDE UNION SCHOOL DISTRICT

The Oceanside Union School District is an elementary district, grades kindergarten through 8, serving a community of about 35,000 population. Current enrollment is approximately 7,000. The city of Oceanside lies adjacent to the United States Marine Corps base, Camp Pendleton, on which the district operates a school.

Philosophy

The philosophy underlying the Oceanside Program for Mentally Gifted Minors is rooted in the American belief in the importance of the individual and his right to opportunity in the public schools for maximal development. The district holds that a school program attains excellence when it provides genuine opportunity for all and when it challenges every pupil to achieve his best.

Program Objectives

It is held that the program for mentally gifted minors should do the following:

1. Add dimension to the education program, both in depth and breadth.
2. Introduce advanced study skills that will promote research and critical thinking.
3. Assure opportunities for creative pursuits.
4. Encourage each child to use and develop his initiative.
5. Facilitate projects that further special aptitudes and interests.
6. Provide opportunities for leadership roles.
7. Foster a sense of responsibility for others.

Program Description

Enrichment, acceleration, or a combination of both are used to provide suitable programs for mentally gifted students. Remediation is also provided for those students with high intellectural ability but poor academic performance. In this district, "enrichment" means providing materials and study in areas not included in the basic curriculum, or extending the basic subject area. It is seen as an activity that further develops a particular intellectual skill or talent—for example, the ability to associate and interrelate "big ideas," to analyze critically facts and arguments, to create new ideas, or to solve complex problems. Although not every gifted child would necessarily display all of these abilities, they tend to be characteristic of the superior intellect; therefore, enrichment experiences are directed toward their enhancement.

The program not only permits each student to delve more deeply into his fields of special interest and to give creative expression to his talents, but it also guides him in the exploration of a variety of both academic and nonacademic activities. Acceleration may be in terms of the basic subject matter in the classroom. This move is made only after appropriate study and approval indicate that both intellectual ability and social maturity warrant such advancement.

Remediation is an attempt to change the teaching environment to effect a change in the learning processes of the individual. When a gifted child is not achieving satisfactorily the system moves to refer the student to the coordinator, who may then suggest a special classroom program, provide extra materials or special equipment for the teacher, enlist the aid of the guidance department or suggest other plans indicated by the specific occasion.

Administration

The district guide[3] outlines the roles and responsibilities of all personnel whose actions are necessary to insure that mentally gifted minors are identified, appropriately programmed, followed up and evaluated. Teachers are expected to assist in early identification and subsequent flexible instruction and individualized assignments. The principal attempts to control class enrollment to insure adequate grouping. He provides opportunity for in-service meetings and assumes responsibility for arranging parent conferences as needed. He is responsible for initiating case studies when deemed advisable and refers candidates for psychological interviews and testing.

The coordinator interprets the objectives of the program and provides in-service training. He also assists in the planning of the instructional program and provides materials needed for the enrichment process. He confers with teachers and principals on matters of pacing, individual problems, resource personnel and remedial activities for low achievers. The coordinator studies trends and recommends curriculum innovations. He must also initiate meetings of the Committee for the Gifted and is responsible for evaluating the effectiveness of the program in conjunction with the director of education and the principals.

The guidance department must screen all group test results and teacher referrals and administer individual tests. This department maintains a current file of test results of pupils who qualify for the state gifted program and provides needed guidance services as these are requested. Specific responsibilities are also outlined for the Committee for the Gifted, the business office, and the director of education.

Identification and Record Keeping

By October 1 each teacher lists the names of all students in his class who might benefit from an enrichment program, including those with individual IQ scores above 129 even though they are low achievers. This list is routed to the school principal, who forwards all lists from his building to the district coordinator. File cards are made and student-coordinator conferences scheduled. The guidance department forwards results of all individual tests requested to the principal and the coordinator.

A central card file on all students participating in the enrichment program is maintained in the coordinator's office. The cumulative record folder of each participating child is visibly coded. Information regarding special study activities is recorded by teachers or the coordinator on green enrichment program sheets, which remain in the cumulative folder. A complete list of enrichment materials for exclusive use of students in the program is kept in the coordinator's office. The current record of expenditures for the mentally gifted minor program is maintained in the business office.

Program Characteristics

The enrichment curriculum is calculated to avoid "more of the same." New and varied content which furnishes more intensive contacts with people, the arts and the problems demanding creative thought and critical analysis are considered the essence of the program. The program not only challenges but provides situations in which the gifted can grow.

Some specific goals which are held pertinent for gifted pupils are the following:

1. Encouragement of self-direction and teacher-pupil planning.
2. Stimulation of curiosity and eagerness to learn.
3. Broadening and deepening of children's own interests.
4. Self-evaluation.
5. Participation in group work and skill in getting along with others.
6. Standards of work in keeping with the child's ability and experience.
7. Skill in locating, gathering, organizing, presenting and using information from a variety of sources.
8. Concern for others.

The district believes that the elementary classroom can almost always be readily adapted to enrichment activities. There can be work centers for individuals and groups as well as foci for science, art, reading or other special interests. A variety of experiences for independent and individualized work can be provided through the enrichment suggestions kept in card files, folders and looseleaf notebooks. Teachers are encouragd to make collections of this sort containing ideas of both teacher and student. It is felt that a curriculum based upon large teaching units lends itself to teacher participation on various levels of difficulty. Able learners may also utilize a daily free period while other class members are engaged in strengthening basic skills already established in the gifted student.

Program Evaluation

At least once each year the Curriculum Council and the Committee for the Gifted engage in specific evaluation aiming for suggestions relating to refinement, improvement, and extension of the program. This group appraises the existing program to consider its individuality as more of a challenge and distinct from the regular classroom situation. They consider the development of more in-depth, creative and analytical learning. The practicality of the materials of instruction is examined in terms of comprehensiveness, challenge, currency and motivational aspects. The inclusion of time for creative pursuits and just "reflection" is considered as are the opportunities for leadership. They ask whether the program does stimulate the development of concern for others. They inquire whether the identification procedures are fully effective and whether communication procedures are adequate. It is necessary also to ask if the existing program is a wise expenditure of state funds and whether the effect of the mentally gifted minor program can be extended to the overall school program.

SUPERINTENDENT OF SCHOOLS, THE DEPARTMENT OF EDUCATION, SAN DIEGO COUNTY

The Office of the San Diego County Superintendent of Schools constitutes the intermediate unit in the state system of education. In this role it performs certain legal obligations to the various school districts. In addition many services are rendered to support, enhance, and supplement the educational program of the local district. In general, the nature and extent of the services rendered to schools reflect the relative size and wealth of the local school district.

It has been noted that some school districts have developed special programs for mentally gifted students. Generally they are as elaborate as the combination of state and local financial support will permit. Since the California mentally gifted minor legislation provides meager support and since school district budgets are typically fully committed to mandated programs, gifted students have not had the benefit of adequately financed programs. That such programs are nonetheless often excellent is a tribute to local motivation and educators' belief in the validity of such special programming.

Small school districts under the jurisdiction of the county superintendent of schools are served in numerous ways by the various departments of the office. Among these services are those rendered by guidance and curriculum coordinators. Following the passage of the mentally gifted minor legislation, such coordinators helped in the screening and testing of many children to determine their eligibility for inclusion in the state mentally gifted minor program. After children were identified coordinators worked with district personnel to develop instructional programs for them.

Well before the current emphasis on education of the gifted the office of the county superintendent of schools had consulted with school districts in relation to their needs. An early publication presented many suggestions for enriching various areas of the curriculum.[7] Subsequently the office prepared a work and study guide to assist school districts in developing plans of action for the gifted through the study of individual differences among pupils.[12]

Coordinators have continued to work with district personnel to develop improved instruction for the gifted. A variety of in-service activities have been offered in recognition of the vital need for continuing teacher support. Among these have been the scheduled appearances of authorities representing various disciplines to update, stimulate, and otherwise enhance the current efforts of the school districts.

Although we may expect some continued growth in programs for mentally gifted children, it is probable that such development will be quite modest until the level of state support for local school district effort has been increased. By their actions so far, school districts of San Diego County have demonstrated their belief in the value of special programs for mentally gifted minors.

BIBLIOGRAPHY

1. *Cajon Valley Gifted Program,* Cajon Valley Union School District, El Cajon, California. Revised October 1964.
2. *Educational Program for Gifted Pupils,* California State Department of Education, Sacramento. January 1961.
3. *Enrichment in the Classroom, A Guide for Teachers of Mentally Gifted Minor Children,* Oceanside Union School District, Oceanside, California. September 1966.
4. *A Guide for Teachers of More Able Learner Children,* Escondido Union School District, Escondido, California. July 1964.
5. *Guidelines for Secondary Principals, Intergrade Advisors, and Teachers of Mentally Gifted and More Able Students.* San Diego City Schools, 1965.
6. *A Handbook for Elementary Principals and Teachers of Gifted and More Able Pupils,* 3rd ed. San Diego City Schools, 1966, pp. 14, 15.

7. *Programs for the Gifted,* San Diego City Schools, 1965.
8. State of California: *Administrative Code, Title V,* Article 23.
9. State of California: *Education Code,* Section 2, Chapter 2385, Statutes of 1957; Chapter 7.1, Section 6750 ff.
10. *Suggested Enrichment Activities for the Gifted Child,* Office of the Superintendent of Schools, San Diego County. November 1954. (Out of print)
11. *Summary of the Grossmont Union High School District's Program for Mentally Gifted Minors,* Grossmont, California. 1962.
12. *What Should We Do About the Gifted?* Office of the Superintendent of Schools, San Diego County, September 1958. (Out of print)

Chapter 20

THE CONNECTICUT REGIONAL APPROACH

BERT W. SCHMICKEL

INTRODUCTION

CONNECTICUT'S planning of comprehensive statewide services for the mentally retarded rests on a firm foundation of past planning and achievement by the Office of Mental Retardation of the State Department of Health. Out of this experience has evolved a distinctive philosophy on which the present statewide program is based. The Office of Mental Retardation has always encouraged, and will continue to encourage, discussion and experimentation leading to improvement and refinement of the present program.

THE PHILOSOPHY

The Office of Mental Retardation philosophy stems from two basic concepts:

1. The problem of mental retardation is a social responsibility shared by all the elements of a society dedicated to the principles of democracy.
2. Retarded individuals are endowed by their Creator with the same rights as all other individuals. Among these rights are opportunity for self-fulfillment; personal dignity and protection of rights; opportunity to participate and contribute; attainment of happiness, and spiritual and moral development.

These concepts have been further defined as follows:

Each individual's mental health depends upon his ability to use his capacities to the best advantage in terms of vocational, social and personal success. It is our responsibility, and the responsibility of society, to furnish maximum opportunity to allow for this process of self-fulfillment. Dignity leading to enhancement of self-worth is of particular importance because retarded persons are subjected to a host of experiences which tend to degrade them and hamper the development of their abilities. Regimentation and discipline subject the individual to powers beyond his control and often lead to a loss of that most precious human feeling—self-esteem.

Happiness is a state of well being brought about not only by physical comfort (e.g., good food, pleasant surroundings, a clean body, a warm bed) but also by a sense of acceptance by others. The feeling of belonging to a group and of being loved is essential to a state of happiness. To the retardate, the security of his home and the affection of his family are perhaps even more meaningful than to the normal person, for he has less understanding and fewer other sources of affection.

The first White House Conference on Children in 1909 made the pronouncement that home care was vastly better than the best of institutional care. The child who from birth is handicapped so that he cannot compete on the same level with other children should not be further deprived of what every child needs most—the love, warmth and security of home and parent. We must not only recognize the danger that lies in the loss of community and public interest in an institution that is far removed from them, but we must take active steps toward the full utilization of all community assets in providing programs and services for our retarded children and adults.

REGIONALIZATION AND COMMUNITY-BASED SERVICES

In accordance with these principles, the Office of Mental Retardation has, from its inception in 1959, rejected the concept of expansion of existing institutional facilities or the creation of a third large residental facility. (Two large institutions have been operating in Connecticut for some time: Mansfield State Training School and Southbury Training School.) Instead, the Office of Mental Retardation has planned for the development of a network of regional centers that permit the retarded to remain close to their families. Seaside Regional Center, the first of these, has been in operation since May, 1961. A second center opened in New Haven in November, 1965 and a third opened in Hartford in September, 1966.

Since then four other centers have been established and are in various degrees of planning, construction and operation at this writing. A total of eleven are currently projected, each would serve a maximum population of 300,000 with a bed capacity of approximately 250.

In areas where regional centers do not yet exist, community services are supported by a program of grants-in-aid administered by the Office of Mental Retardation. These grants help underwrite the cost of operating day-care services, workshops and diagnostic and evaluation clinics. In addition, the Office of Mental Retardation, through its Community Services Division, assists in the planning, development and supervision of programs sponsored by private agencies and associations. These agencies and associations will play an important role in the planning of new regional centers in their respective areas as the network of centers expands.

Connecticut regional centers are designed to perform the functions both of the "area centers" and the "fixed point of information and referral" described by the President's Panel. The fixed point of referral draws upon services dispersed throughout the community or metropolitan area. Regional centers are expected to utilize every available community resource in the care, training and rehabilitation of retarded children and adults in the life of their community.

ADVANTAGES OF REGIONALIZATIONS

The regional approach offers numerous advantages over conventional institutions. Because of the proximity of regional centers and programs to population centers and because small residential units permit more permissive and more flexible visiting schedules, maintenance of close family relationships is encouraged.

The availability of many services on a day-care basis to retardates residing at home makes it possible to meet the needs of proportionately more persons than in residential institutions. Innumerable opportunities are available for utilizing specialists, services and facilities based in the same community as the regional center. For example, the cooperation of area physicians, dentists, psychologists and members of other professions as well as general hospitals, schools and social and health agencies can be enlisted in providing a full clinical service without the necessity of assembling all the components of such a service within the regional center itself.

Problems of personnel recruitment are reduced, and personnel housing needs are minimized. Volunteers in large numbers are readily available in the community to augment the work of the staff.

Community awareness of the retarded, their needs, and their potential for achievement is fostered as a result of the visibility of regional centers. The close proximity of the centers to the communities they serve enables them to stimulate new and improved services by area agencies for both residents and non-residents of the center.

Regional centers provide the same general types of services and programs as conventional institutions, but in addition are able to offer numerous community-oriented programs and activities. For example the regional centers, in cooperation with the public schools, the Bureau of Vocational Rehabilitation, the Connecticut State Employment Service and local industry, conduct programs aimed at enhancing the employability of non-resident educable retardates enrolled in public-school special classes. Among other regional center services which are closely integrated with community agencies and organizations are consultative service to physicians and public-health nursing associations in the area; assistance to area workshops in work assignments; contract procurement and liaison with industries, and consultation with area parent groups.

In addition to a wide range of day services and programs, it is expected that regional centers will stimulate the creation of, and provide supervision for, a variety of residential programs designed to meet the widely different needs of the retarded of various ability and age groupings.

PARTNERSHIP IN PROVIDING CARE

The Connecticut regional approach is based on the conviction that the needs of all the mentally retarded within a region can be met only through the cooperative and coordinated efforts of many agencies and individuals. Services to the retarded within each region are expected to be provided by the community agency best equipped to supply them. Regional centers will not duplicate services which already are being provided adequately by existing agencies, or which such agencies can be persuaded to provide.

A close partnership will be maintained between these community agencies and the regional centers as they provide, among them, the full "continuum of care" required by the retarded in the region.

An outstanding example of such partnership is the relationship between the regional center and the public schools of its service area. In each center now operating on a residential basis, educable and trainable retardates in residence attend special classes in the public schools of the town in which the center is located. The only exceptions to this policy are residents who do not meet public-school admission requirements because of emotional problems or a lack of previous training. These children are given special training at the centers aimed at overcoming obstacles to school admission. Preparation for special classes is also emphasized in the regional center program for children diagnosed as severely or profoundly retarded who show a potential for functioning at a higher level.

The partnership between regional centers and the public schools is manifested in numerous other cooperative programs. Wider opportunities for cooperation with community agencies and institutions will be available to the regional centers in the state's larger urban areas, which enjoy a broader range of community facilities and services. In New Haven, for example, the regional center has established firm relationships with the Medical School, Psychology Department, and other divisions of Yale University; Southern Connecticut State College; the Veterans Administration Hospital, and other local agencies and institutions. The Hartford Regional Center is located adjacent to the Newington Hospital for Crippled Children and has available its fine array of services and facilities.

FLEXIBILITY IN ORGANIZATON AND PROGRAMMING

The Connecticut plan provides for considerable flexibility in the organization and programming of regional centers on the basis of needs and conditions peculiar to the various regions. It is anticipated, for example, that the Putnam Regional Center located in a rural area will extend its services to a broad range of physically as well as mentally handicapped persons because no other services are currently available to them. The Bridgeport Regional Center utilizes a large facility formerly owned and operated by a parent association in that city, eliminating much of the necessity for new construction to house services other than residential and administrative.

The principle of flexibility extends to the design and construction of regional centers so as to assure their adaptability to changing needs and uses in the years ahead. This is predicated upon a steadily increasing disposition on the part of community agencies to include groups of the retarded in the services they now offer only to the normal population. Regional centers may, in years to come, conceivably be relieved of the burden of providing a number of their original services and be free to turn their attention to unmet needs of the retarded. The extent to which local agencies will assume larger roles in programming for the retarded will, of course, vary among the regions.

TRANSITIONAL PERIOD

The economics of state government dictate that the statewide network of regional centers be established over a period of years, on the basis of the relative needs of the various regions. The absence of physical facilities, however, does not foreclose the possibility of offering many of the advantages of the regional approach to all areas of the state in the reasonably near future, following the procedure set forth in the statement of specific principles. During this transitional period, the staff of each such region would be acquiring the information and experience necessary to the planning of the regional facility that would eventually be constructed. In carrying out its planning, the staff would draw on the experience of existing regional centers and the present training schools. A close working relationship would be maintained between the regional centers and programs and the training schools to enable the former to utilize the services of the larger facilities as needed and to encourage the free exchange of information, personnel and program services.

SPECIAL ROLES OF THE TRAINING SCHOOLS

In view of the broad knowledge and experience of the personnel, the quality and extent of their specialized facilities and resources and their special competence in certain areas of mental retardation, special responsibilities will be assigned to the Mansfield and Southbury Training Schools in the statewide plan of services, over and above their functions as residential centers. Among these responsibilities will be the following:

1. Special facilities and services to meet the needs of retarded persons incapable of adjusting satisfactorily or functioning happily in the community.

2. Research and investigative functions which will utilize the special competence of the research staffs, the laboratories and clinics, and the other facilities of the training schools.
3. Special training programs which will provide in-service training, state-wide summer-institute training and other types of instruction for personnel of the regional centers as well as of community facilities providing other aspects of the various regions' programs of comprehensive care.
4. Other services and counsel which the training schools are uniquely qualified to provide to the regional centers. Concomitantly, the regional centers will provide services and counsel to the training schools in areas where they are especially competent to do so.

In addition to these functions and those which, as centralized residential centers, they have traditionally discharged, the training schools will offer certain community services within the geographic areas designated for them in the overall state plan for regional service.

* * *

GENERAL PRINCIPLES

1. The mentally retarded require, throughout their lifetime and according to the degree of their mental handicap, a "continuum of care" consisting of special facilities and programs to insure the development of their maximum intellectual and adaptive potential. Many of the mentally retarded have special handicaps in addition to mental retardation, such as physical, sensory, and personality deficiencies, which require special services beyond those routinely provided.

2. The impact and value of the home upon the general development and well-being of the mentally retarded are primary factors in the consideration of adequate programming in behalf of the mentally retarded.

3. Community and general public interest in state-operated facilities for the retarded are greatly enhanced when such facilities are located close to the concentrations of population which comprise the various or metropolitan areas of the state.

4. In planning the development of new state-operated facilities for the mentally retarded, the needs of the retarded can best be met through a network of regional programs serving limited population areas and thus permitting them to remain close to their families, both geographically and in spirit, while enjoying the same quality and scope of services they would receive if they were placed in a conventional state institution.

5. According to the regional plan of operation, the state is divided into a number of regions based on population concentration and size of geo-

graphic area served. The determination of regional boundaries shall be flexible so that the number and specific functions of regional centers and programs shall be based upon the particular needs of the various regions.

6. Services to the retarded within each region shall be provided by the community agency best equipped to offer them, and regional centers shall not duplicate services which, in the judgment of the Office of Mental Retardation, are already being adequately provided by existing agencies or which existing agencies can be persuaded to provide. When such services are not otherwise available, regional centers shall make available those services necessary to assure a "continuum of care" for retardates within their region.

7. A close partnership between regional centers and services and public and private agencies within and outside each region is imperative to assure the comprehensive "continuum of care" from birth through old age which is required by retardates in each region.

8. Flexibility in the organization and development of regional programs and services is necessary to meet needs and conditions peculiar to the various regions, but programs and services shall be based upon the philosophy, general principles and specific principles set forth herein.

9. Regional facilities shall be designed and constructed on a flexible basis to assure their adaptability to changing needs and uses in the years ahead.

Specific Principles

1. Each regional center shall be responsible for the implementation on a regional basis of the duties and responsibilities of the Office of Mental Retardation which are delineated in Sec. 19-4c of General Statutes of State of Connecticut.*

2. Each regional center is intended to serve, within a specific geographical area, as a concentration point for services to the retarded; a fixed point of information and referral for services dispersed through the region or metropolitan area, and a catalytic agent in the development and coordination of services.

3. A primary purpose of the regional centers is to provide services which are easily accessible to those it is designed to serve. Regional centers shall be located close to population centers and made available to outlying districts. All mentally retarded persons living within a region as defined by the Office of Mental Retardation shall be equally eligible for all regional programs provided therein.

4. The geographic and population area served by a regional center shall

---

* See Appendix.

not be larger than that which will allow the center to maintain comprehensive programs and a wide constellation of services for all retardates within the region.

5. Each regional center shall utilize every available community resource in the care, training, and rehabilitation of the retarded, including specialists, services, facilities and volunteers located in the same region.

6. Each regional center shall strive to bring about the greatest possible integration of the mentally retarded in community life.

7. Regional centers shall encourage and promote the maintenance of close family relationships with retardates in residence, utilizing the values of close proximity of the centers to population concentrations and making the greatest possible use of small residential units with permissive and flexible visiting schedules.

8. Each regional center shall attempt to stimulate new and improved services by public and private agencies within its region, with these services to embrace both residents and non-residents of the center.

9. Each regional center shall provide a variety of opportunities for retardates in residence to participate in programs and activities based in the community.

10. Regional centers shall create and supervise a variety of residential programs designed to meet the widely differing needs of retardates of various abilities and ages, such as the following:

Hostels or halfway houses to provide residence and supervision to retardates as an intermediate step between sheltered institutional living and independent life in the community when it is determined that the retardate's own home cannot adequately meet his needs.

Community homes for independent living for adult retardates who work in the region and whose families are nonexistent or unable to accommodate them.

Foster homes for retarded children for whom such care is preferable to institutional placement, residence at a regional center, or continued residence in their own homes.

11. There shall be a close working relationship between the Mansfield and Southbury Training Schools and the regional centers in order to enable the regional centers in behalf of retarded persons and their families to utilize the services of the training schools when needed, and promote a free exchange of information, personnel, and program services.

12. The following steps shall be taken in the development of new regional services:

a. Appointment of a regional director and basic staff.
b. An inventory of existing resources and unmet needs in the region.
c. Designation of the initial regional staff to serve as a fixed point of information and referral resource.

d. Initiation of programs.
e. Stimulation by the regional staff of establishment of needed programs by local agencies.
f. Development of a plan for a regional center facility, in conjunction with the central office of the Office of Mental Retardation.

13. Regional centers shall work closely with all other divisions of the Office of Mental Retardation and with other state departments and agencies offering services in, or otherwise concerned with, the field of mental retardation.

14. Regional centers shall be responsible for conducting research, staff-development, volunteer-recruitment and training programs in conjunction with the central office of the Office of Mental Retardation.

15. Admission and disposition of persons admitted to the regional centers shall be in accordance with policies set forth by the deputy commissioner.

16. Staffing patterns of regional centers and services shall be determined by the Deputy Commissioner in conjunction with the regional directors on the basis of the particular needs of the regions they serve.

17. The superintendents of the training schools and the directors of the regional centers shall constitute an administrative council for purposes of advising the deputy commissioner regarding programs, services and policies of regional centers and other state-operated facilities which are under the jurisdiction of the Office of Mental Retardation.

APPENDIX

Statutory Provisions for the Office of Mental Retardation and Deputy Commissioner of Health for Mental Retardation

SEC. 19-4c. OFFICE OF MENTAL RETARDATION, DEPUTY COMMISSIONER. The Office of Mental Retardation, with the advice of a council on mental retardation, shall be responsible for the planning, development and administration of a complete, comprehensive and integrated statewide program for the mentally retarded. The Office of Mental Retardation shall be under the supervision of a deputy commissioner on mental retardation, who shall be appointed by the commissioner of health on recommendation of the council on mental retardation and may be removed by the commissioner after consultation with the council. The deputy commissioner shall be a person whose background, training, education and experience qualify him to administer the care, training, education, treatment and custody of mentally retarded and epileptic persons. He shall be responsible, under the general supervision of the commissioner and with the advice of the council, for planning and developing a complete, comprehensive and integrated statewide program for the mentally retarded; for the implementation of said program;

and for the coordination of the efforts of the office of mental retardation with those of other state departments and agencies, municipal governments and private agencies concerned with and providing services for the mentally retarded. He shall be responsible for the administration and operation of the state training schools and all state-operated community and residential facilities established for the diagnosis, care and training of the retarded. He shall be responsible for establishing standards, providing technical assistance and exercising the requisite supervision of all state-supported diagnostic facilities, day-care centers, habilitation centers, sheltered workshops, boarding homes and other facilities for the mentally retarded. He shall stimulate research by public and private agencies, institutions of higher learning and hospitals, in the interest of the elimination and amelioration of retardation and care and training of the retarded. He shall be responsible for the development of criteria as to the eligibility of any retarded person for residential care in any public or state-supported private institution and after considering the recommendation of a properly designated diagnostic agency, may assign such person to a public or state-supported private institution. He may transfer such persons from one such institution to another when necessary and desirable for their welfare.

Chapter 21

CALIFORNIA CONFRONTS ITS "UNDEVELOPED RESOURCE"

LEOPOLD LIPPMAN

CALIFORNIA is developing programs for the mentally retarded which are new, different and flexible. One of the most important and innovative is the statewide network of regional diagnostic, counseling and service centers. At the moment of this writing, there are only two such centers, but the plan envisions ten or more, so placed throughout California that no family will have to drive more than two hours to get service for a retarded member.

Parts of the plan are old, borrowed or remodeled from the experience of others. The total concept, however, is new. To understand the concept whole, it is necessary to look at the social and historical matrix in which it evolved.

BEGINNINGS

A generation ago, the presence of a retarded child in the family was cause for shame, guilt and often revulsion. As the public rejected the mentally retarded, so too did many of the parents themselves. This is not hard to understand as, prior to the diagnosis of retardation, each parent was in fact a member of that faceless, amorphous group, the "general public." Diagnosis of retardation stigmatized the child and shocked and saddened the family, but it did not automatically convert the parents into wise and understanding individuals. Recognizing that the retarded can be helped—that there is indeed hope for even the most handicapped to progress with training and encouragement—took years for even the most enlightened parent to learn. How much more so, then, for those neighbors and less interested citizens who had no personal concern with the problem?

With this attitude, it is not surprising that community resources were meager. There were a few classes for "slow" or "backward" children; there were even a few scattered special-education programs under professional direction. Some retarded youths and adults found sanctuary in sheltered workshops designed for the physically handicapped. Occasionally, a Sunday school teacher or a recreation director would allow a retarded youngster to sit in a group with "normal" children, though usually as a passive observer rather than as a participant. The best known and generally prescribed solution for mental retardation was commitment to an institution—isolated from the community—huge, impersonal and without hope for the future of the individual.

Through this miasma, in midcentury, there blew a fresh wind, with the organization of parents of retarded children. Some were concerned principally with improving the state institutions; others sought alternatives for their children. With the establishment of the National Association for Retarded Children, in 1950, the movement received vigorous impetus—and society began to change.

NARC, as it quickly came to be known, made an impact in several directions. It gave hope to parents of the retarded—hope, and an awareness that they were not alone. It brought the problem to the attention of magazine readers, of radio listeners, of that "general public" which had been content not to know. It focused the awareness of public officials, of school boards, of physicians and psychologists and teachers and social workers, with an insistency that would not be denied. It reached the White House, and through the President of the United States, the people of the nation.

President Eisenhower was the first to issue a proclamation calling attention to the mentally retarded and asserting that they could indeed be helped: the first, but not the last.

President Kennedy, during his first year in office, established the President's Panel on Mental Retardation. That a President could say publicly that there was a retarded person in his family took courage—but it was also a measure of how far public opinion had come in a decade.

A year after it was established, the President's Panel submitted its report, *A Proposed Program for National Action to Combat Mental Retardation.* It contained more than ninety recommendations for action, most of them to be carried out by the Federal Government. More important than any single recommendation, however, was the example the panel set of comprehensive mental retardation planning; and tucked away toward the back of the book was the suggestion that each state go and do likewise.

CALIFORNIA ACTS

Within months after the panel reported, and before Congress passed and the President signed a law to make Federal funds available for state mental retardation planning, the California legislature established a Study Commission on Mental Retardation.

The commission, a broadly representative group of public officials and knowledgeable citizens, held its first meeting in October 1963. At that session, in the State Building in San Francisco, it received its charge from Governor Edmund G. Brown:

> The mentally retarded, of whom we sometimes speak as a homogeneous group, are actually quite different from each other, with different capabilities, potentiali-

ties and needs. They range in age from infants through childhood and adulthood to the elderly. In degree of handicap, they range from the mildly to the severely retarded—and some suffer from physical or emotional handicaps as well. They vary in family circumstances and, consequently, in the services they require.

For years we have intensified our efforts to reduce the waiting lists for our state hospitals. We have given special budgetary consideration and have made every possible other effort to provide service for those waiting treatment.

Yet we also know that the answer does not lie in the building of more and more state hospitals for the mentally retarded. Service is more important than structures. Fully qualified and professional dedicated personnel are more important than facilities.

Moreover, most services are best provided in or close to the home community, rather than in large, remote institutions.

As you members of the Study Commission confront this complex problem, and begin to develop recommendations for consideration of the Legislature, I hope you will keep in mind the concept of a *continuum* of services for the mentally retarded. It is not enough to have a scattering of services in isolated areas. I ask you to develop a long-range plan and program which will insure that no mentally retarded citizen of California escapes our attention or fails to receive the assistance he needs to develop to his fullest potential, however meager that may be. It is not enough, for example, to develop good educational services *and* good rehabilitation services; they must be *interlocked* to serve the individual as a human being, so that the retarded person does not find himself defeated by bureaucratic walls.

California is a rich state, but it is not so rich that it can waste one iota of its greatest resource: its people.

With the Study Commission thus launched on a broad-gauged task, another body was also confronting the problem of mental retardation in California. For years, the legislature had been concerned about the problem of waiting lists for admission to the state hospitals for the retarded. The Assembly therefore directed its interim subcommittee on mental health services to look at the problem and to suggest a solution.

ANSWER: REGIONAL CENTERS

Although the Study Commission and the Assembly subcommittee approached the subject of mental retardation from quite different perspectives, they agreed completely on the one major program recommendation which both considered paramount: That the State of California should establish, by contract with community-based agencies, a network of regional centers which would provide authoritative, multi-disciplinary diagnosis for every person suspected of retardation, and counseling for the individual and his family.

Before it offered this recommendation, the Study Commission enunciated a series of principles on which its whole report, entitled *The Undeveloped Resource,* was founded. These principles, which set the tone of the commission's findings and recommendations and which influenced the thinking of the governor and the legislature, included the following:

> The State of California accepts a responsibility for its mentally retarded citizens. Retardation affects hundreds of thousands of children and adults directly and has an important impact on the lives of their families, neighbors and whole communities.
>
> The Study Commission believes that:
>
> 1. Mental retardation is a social problem. Every retarded person and his family are entitled to the concern and assistance of the community, expressed through public and voluntary resources.
> 2. Where necessary, the State must discharge the obligation of society.
> 3. The best hope is prevention, and it is our responsibility to develop new knowledge through research and to apply it promptly. Meanwhile, we have an obligation to the retarded who are already with us.
> 4. There is some potential for growth in every human being. For each person, society should provide the opportunity to develop to the limits of his capabilities.
> 5. Services should be planned and provided as part of a continuum, which means that the pattern of facilities and eligibility shall be so complete as to meet the needs of each retarded person, regardless of his age or degree of handicap, and at each state of his life development. It also means a continuity, including uniform eligibility standards, to insure that no retarded individual is lost in the transition from one service to another.
> 6. Because the retarded person is a human being first, and a handicapped individual secondarily, he should have access to all the general community services that he can use in common with others. Only when integrated services fail to meet his needs should there be specialized services.
> 7. Services for retarded persons should be close to their homes and families.
> 8. Provision for research, and for training of professional persons to work with the mentally retarded, should be built into service programs wherever appropriate and possible.
> 9. Retarded persons, or their families acting in their behalf, should have substantial freedom of choice among public and private services. This accords with the dignity of the individual and his right of self-determination for his own life.
> 10. The State should provide for and encourage creative flexibility in all programs operating for the mentally retarded in California.

With this vigorous opening, the commission's report proceeded to ask a series of questions, to pose a number of problems and to suggest some answers.

First, it asked: "Who are the mentally retarded? How many are there?" Many a study has foundered on the twin issues of definition and quantification. The commission coped with the first question, finally, by accepting the currently prevailing definition—that developed by the American Association on Mental Deficiency—but with heavy emphasis on social competence. This interpretation was to have significance later, as the commission defined its population and addressed itself to ameliorative and preventive measures. As to numbers, the commission rejected the prevailing estimate of 3 per cent and developed lower incidence figures of its own. These were startling enough, forecasting, as they did, some 400,000 retarded persons in California by 1970.

Then: "What is California doing now?" This was a summary of a more extensive report by the commission's committee on existing resources, functions and coverage. The committee had reviewed services already available from state agencies and in selected counties, and had found them ramified but inadequate.

Next: "The need begins before birth." Here the commission gave full due to the essential task of prevention, and to the research on which it must be based.

Finally, the Study Commission on Mental Retardation rolled up its sleeves and came to the crucial task of serving the retarded who are already with us: "Finding the retarded. Helping them toward a lifetime plan."

DIAGNOSIS AND COUNSELING

On this issue, the commission offered its analysis and recommendations along the following lines:

> Of primary importance—for the retarded child, his family and society—is early, reliable diagnosis. And with diagnosis, to make it meaningful, there must be skilled counseling.
>
> Casefinding and diagnosis may begin at birth. There are in many communities of California, a varicty of diagnostic and counseling resources. Among these are the pediatrician, the psychiatrist, the family physician, sometimes even the obstetrician. Among the professions other than medical, there are nurses, social workers, teachers, psychologists, rehabilitation specialists, clergymen. Relatives, friends, neighbors and strangers are often generous with advice.
>
> Effective diagnosis, however, is the responsibility of qualified persons, preferably working as a team. The professional disciplines should include medicine, psychology, social work, nursing, education, speech therapy, nutrition and others as needed. For comprehensive medical diagnosis, it is essential that there be available the specialized skills of pediatrics, psychiatry and neurology.
>
> Professional teams of this complexity and skill are not available in every community, and never can be. The retarded child, however, may be anywhere. It is therefore essential that basic diagnostic skills and counseling services be available to every family in California, close to their homes and readily accessible. Backstopping the first-line community services, there must be a statewide network of diagnostic and counseling teams to whom the community general practitioner can refer the family of anyone suspected of mental retardation and associated handicapping conditions.
>
> To this end, the Study Commission on Mental Retardation recommends the establishment of Regional Diagnostic and Counseling Centers throughout California.
>
> The Regional Centers can be the means for bringing to the family of every child with developmental problems the resources it needs to learn about the

handicap and to begin to make an appropriate lifetime plan. Each center would have the staff and facilities required to establish definitive diagnosis. It would also offer professional counseling to the family immediately after diagnosis and on a continuing basis as needed; it would provide the link between the family and the community's resources, including the Departments of Education, Mental Hygiene, Public Health, Rehabilitation and Social Welfare; it would help the family select the appropriate service for the retarded person and assist in making the arrangements, including financial; it would be a continuing resource for the retarded individual and his family; it would maintain a registry; it would establish relationships with teaching institutions and residential facilities; and it would stimulate opportunities for applied research and for professional training.

In short, the Regional Diagnostic and Counseling Center will provide one door—the "fixed point of referral and information" recommended by the President's Panel—through which the retarded person and his family can enter to obtain the help they need. (This does not mean, however, that the Regional Center need necessarily be a single building or a group of physical structures. Rather, it is to be a group of *services,* all available to the individuals and families that need them.)

Diagnosis acquires meaning only as it is interpreted to the parents through skilled counseling. All members of the diagnostic team may have a positive role in the first interpretation of the diagnosis. Thereafter, continued counseling may be best provided by the social worker, the public health nurse or other qualified professional, depending on the degree of the child's handicap and the parents' level of understanding.

It is the hope of the Study Commission that by 1970, if not sooner, the family of each retarded person may have a variety of choices as to the type of care he should receive, within a broad range of suitability determined by skilled and informed professional people. For such a choice to be meaningful, there must obviously be a variety of services in existence; equally important, the family of the retarded individual must have sound counseling. The presentation of appropriate alternatives, and the provision of counseling, will be major responsibilities of the Regional Center staff.

In addition, the Regional Center staff will gather information about the resources of the retarded person and his family, will determine eligibility for public and private services, and will assist in assembling funds for use of the retarded individual in purchasing services.

For the community, each Regional Center will become the hub around which existing resources can be arranged, and through which new services may be established. It will also serve as an arm in the State in defining and interpreting standards of community care for the mentally retarded.

The Study Commission recommends that the Legislature place responsibility for establishing the Regional Centers on the Department of Public Health. Each Regional Center may be operated under a variety of sponsorships depending on the resources available in a particular locale.

Each Regional Center should have a core professional staff, augmented by consultants representing additional fields and specialties. A typical staff organization pattern might follow these lines:

A. Professional
   Physician—Board eligible or certified by an appropriate American Specialty Board
   Social Worker—With a master's degree

Psychologist—Certified by the State of California—with a Ph.D. degree
Public Health Nursing Supervisor—Preferably with a master's degree in public health
Educator

B. Non-professional
Secretary
Nurse's Aide

C. Consultants—part time—Fee for service basis
Dentist
Hearing and Speech Consultant
Metabolic Consultant
Neurologist
Nutritionist
Ophthalmologist
Orthopedist
Pediatrician (if not on staff)
Psychiatrist (if not on staff)

The services of a Regional Diagnostic and Counseling Center should be available within reasonable distance of every California family which may have a retarded child. Insofar as possible, "reasonable" shall be interpreted to mean within two hours' driving distance. When it is difficult for a family to get to the Center, transportation should be provided.

The Centers should be located close to population centers where they are most needed, and wherever possible in proximity to institutions of higher education and research. In some areas of the State, two or more counties would constitute a single region, because of the level of community resources and the number of families to be served. Elsewhere, one county might constitute a region. In the Los Angeles area, several Regional Centers may be needed to give the coverage necessary.

In sparsely settled areas, it is not always practical to provide a fully-staffed Regional Center within reasonable distance of every family. In such cases, the Study Commission recommends that the Regional Center organize traveling diagnostic teams, bringing mobile clinics to the rural areas. On their periodic visits to remote communities, the traveling teams would also stimulate the development of local services and help to train local professional workers in the skills necessary to diagnose mental retardation and to counsel the families.

The Study Commission wishes to emphasize that diagnosis and evaluation is not a one-time task. It calls for periodic review and revision. The Regional Center can arrange for systematic follow-up on children in their preschool and later years. As the retarded child progresses through the school years, evaluation becomes a useful tool in designing appropriate prevocational training and, ultimately, proper placement of the retarded adult.

When there is evidence or suspicion of a hereditary aspect to retardation, the Regional Center will have a special responsibility to investigate the genetic aspects. Adequate sources of known genetic information should be available to all families who seek it, with special emphasis on those known to harbor recessive genes that may cause mental retardation.

DIAGNOSIS AND COUNSELING . . . AND SERVICE

Such was the concept of the Study Commission for a network of regional centers throughout California. To this the Assembly Interim Subcommittee on Mental Health Services added one dimension: that the regional centers seek out for the retarded, *and help the families obtain,* alternative services, close to home, rather than institutionalization in a state hospital.

The legislative committee, in a mail questionnaire of thousands of families of retarded persons on the waiting lists for admission to state hospitals, found that many parents would prefer alternative services closer to home, if such services were available. In its report, *A Redefinition of State Responsibility for California's Mentally Retarded,* the committee therefore said: "We propose that the State shift its responsibility from the time when the child enters the state hospital to the time when expert diagnosis establishes the fact that special care is needed that the family cannot provide."

Agreeing with the Study Commission that regional centers should be established by contract between the State Department of Public Health and appropriate community agencies, the legislative committee further proposed that the regional centers be authorized to disburse state funds on behalf of those families whose children were found to be eligible.

A bill to effectuate the recommendations of the Study Commission and the Assembly subcommittee was offered to the legislature at its regular session in the spring of 1965. As enacted, Assembly Bill 691 contained these provisions:

1. That a network of regional diagnostic, counseling and service centers, easily accessible to every family, should be established throughout California.
2. That the centers should provide diagnosis, and counseling on a continuing basis. The law was explicit that the centers were not to charge for either of these services.
3. That the centers should use state funds to pay for services to the retarded, "when failure to provide such services would result in state hospitalization." In cases where state hospital care is necessary, however, the law directed the regional centers to assist in hospital placement.

The measure also carried an appropriation of $1,500,000. The legislature enacted the law on the final day of its regular session; the governor signed it shortly afterward; it became effective September 17, 1965; and by early 1966 there were two regional centers in operation.

OTHER LEGISLATION ON MENTAL RETARDATION

Assembly Bill 691, important as it was, came as one of a series of new and imaginative enactments of the 1965 legislative session. Some fifteen measures were introduced, enacted and signed, carrying forward the principles enunciated by the Study Commission and reflecting the interest and concern of the people of California for more effective service to the mentally retarded. Several of the other bills have an impact on the work of the regional centers, and a brief summary is therefore appropriate.

Essential to the successful operation of the regional centers is the setting and enforcing of standards of care. If the centers were to purchase services for the retarded from nongovernmental agencics, in lieu of placement in a state hospital, it was essential that these services be of appropriately high quality. Throughout the work of the Study Commission and the Assembly subcommittee, it was understood that the parents would have the right to participate in every decision affecting the welfare of their retarded children; and it was obvious that if the alternative, community-based services were inferior in quality, many families would prefer care in a state hospital, and the regional center program would fail.

By enactment of Assembly Bill 769, therefore, the legislature placed on the administrator of the Health and Welfare Agency the responsibility for setting and enforcing standards, for setting rates to be paid, and for providing a list of approved vendors from whom the regional centers might purchase services for the retarded. The Health and Welfare Agency, in California, is an administrative body which embraces the departments of Mental Hygiene, Public Health, Rehabilitation and Social Welfare.

Because the agency itself had a very small staff, the administrator was directed to name a coordinator of mental retardation programs and such other staff as he might require to execute his new responsibilities. Assembly Bill 769 also provided for the establishment of the Mental Retardation Program and Standards Advisory Board, to bring the viewpoints of consumers, providers of care, local government and the general public to bear on the decisions the Agency now had to make.

The legislature also did the following:

1. Made permanent what had previously been known as pilot child care centers for the mentally retarded. Renaming them Development Centers for Handicapped Minors, Senate Bill 499 also extended the age range, so that the centers might serve youngsters between three and twenty-one; provided more adequate financing; and raised the limit to eight centers. (Under a further amendment, enacted by the 1967 Legislature, the law now sets no limit on the number of Development Centers.) The development centers provide an educational and training program for children so handicapped that they cannot meet the admission requirements of even the special classes in local public schools. Operated under the auspices of a local school district or county superintendent of schools, the development center is financed largely with state funds, through the State Department of Education.
2. Made mandatory the testing of infants for phenylketonuria (PKU) and other preventable, heritable disorders. Assembly Bill 12 specified that tests and regulations are to be designed by the State Department of Public Health.
3. Directed the State Department of Mental Hygiene to move 500 retarded persons into Agnews State Hospital, which formerly had served only the mentally ill. This action, taken by amendment to the budget act, seemed to some a regres-

sive step, but it was used by the responsible authorities as an opportunity for creative innovation. The departments of Mental Hygiene and Rehabilitation developed an agreement whereby the program for the retarded at Agnews would be the responsibility of the Rehabilitation Department, so that it might would be the responsibility of the Rehabilitation Department.

HOW IT IS WORKING

Within a few months after the effective date of the law, there were two regional centers in operation, one in Los Angeles and one in San Francisco. Purposefully, the Department of Public Health sought out different administrative auspices for the first two centers, so that alternative routes might be explored.

The regional center in Los Angeles came into existence by contract with an already established diagnostic center, the Child Development Clinic at Childrens Hospital of Los Angeles. Directed by Richard Koch, M.D., this center had been in operation more than a decade and was nationally recognized for the excellence of its diagnostic and counseling services, its training of professional personnel and its research activities. In recent years the clinic has also been carrying its multi-disciplinary team activities to other communities beyond Los Angeles County, partly to serve retarded children and their families in the remote communities but also to help stimulate professional interest. The traveling-clinic concept will eventually be an integral part of the regional centers, making them even more accessible to families who live far from the metropolitan centers.

The regional center in San Francisco was established by contract with Aid Retarded Children, Incorporated, the local association of parents and friends of the mentally retarded. Medical director of the center is Peter Cohen, M.D., professor of pediatrics at the University of California Medical Center. The Golden Gate Regional Center serves five counties: San Francisco, San Mateo, Marin, Alameda and Contra Costa. One of the first steps taken by San Francisco ARC, in launching the regional center, was to establish working relationships with the coordinating councils on mental retardation and other community service organizations in all five counties.

It will not be possible to assess the full impact of the regional centers on the problem of mental retardation until the whole network has been in operation for some time. Today there are only two centers, and it will be some time before the ten recommended by the Study Commission are in operation. Nevertheless, it is already clear that the centers are having an effect on community planning and coordination of services for the mentally retarded, on the availability of services and on the quality of those services. Most poignant and symbolic is the following excerpt from a letter sent to

Governor Brown when the first retarded child was served by the Golden Gate Regional Center:

> The first family to be served in the Golden Gate Regional Center is a young couple and their severely mentally retarded two-year-old child. The mother is expected to deliver their second child within a week or two.
>
> This couple epitomizes the first premise on which the regional center is based: namely, that the family is the primary resource for a handicapped individual. This family with meagre financial resources, gave loving care to a very retarded child until the day arrived when care at home was no longer in the best interest of everyone concerned. They now are accepting with dignity, and in love for their child, the assistance from society which is their privilege and which benefits the entire community.

As the Health and Welfare Agency confronted its responsibility to establish standards and rates for the purchase of services by the regional centers, it found that it too was having an impact on other programs. The state hospitals had been placing retarded persons in private institutions and family-care homes for years. County welfare departments, too, had been making placements and paying for the care of retarded persons in foster homes and other community residential facilities. It quickly became apparent that the rates paid by the various governmental units would have to become consistent with one another and, at least equally important, that all services would eventually come up to the standards being established for the regional centers.

There have, of course, been problems in the establishment of a program so new, so ramified and so challenging to the old ways of doing things. The speed with which the regional centers were launched made for some oversights and some flaws, which are being corrected as they are discovered. The creation of the centers, moreover, has not automatically and instantly created the hoped-for services. The services which do exist are of uneven quality, and it was in some measure necessary to compromise with what is ultimately desirable in the setting of standards.

And there have been other problems. The rates set at the outset did not fully satisfy the vendors. Families, too, have been impatient, and some have been disappointed that the miracle of new services did not come about immediately. Regional centers, by definition, serve regions, and two cannot accomplish what a full network of ten can do.

The regional center program is not the perfect, complete answer to the needs of the mentally retarded and their families. It is, after all, not itself a goal, but only a road to the goal, which is more effective services.

Nevertheless, the regional center approach *is* the beginning of something new and hopeful. Beyond what it does for the retarded persons it serves directly, each regional center is a catalyst, a stimulant to community action toward the improvement of other services. It suggests new approaches to old problems—a new pattern of administrative organization which is closer to the people and their needs. It is a creative expression of the flexibility of programming called for by the Study Commission.

The Mental Retardation Program and Standards Advisory Board, likewise, is a new mechanism for the solution of old problems. It focuses the concern of diverse officials and interested citizens, and gives them tools with which to work. In the first months of its existence, the board participated actively in crucial decisions and began to provide meaningful leadership. It is significant that the board created its first committee to solve a problem which deeply troubles the parents of every retarded child: "What will happen to my child when I can no longer care for him?" The Advisory Board's Committee on Guardianship hopes to find an answer, fitting yet another important piece into the unsolved puzzle of mental retardation.

BIBLIOGRAPHY

President's Panel on Mental Retardation: *A Proposed Program for National Action to Combat Mental Retardation.* Washington, D.C., 1962.

State of California, Study Commission on Mental Retardation: *The Undeveloped Resource: A Plan for the Mentally Retarded of California.* Sacramento, 1965.

California Legislature, Assembly Interim Committee on Ways and Means, Subcommittee on Mental Health Services: *A Redefinition of State Responsibility for California's Mentally Retarded.* Sacramento, 1965.

Lippman, Leopold: A state plans for its mentally retarded. *Children, 12*:171-177, September-October 1965.

Dybwad, Gunnar: A critique of California's report on mental retardation. *Children, 12*:177-178, September-October 1965.

Lippman, Leopold: New focus on the fate of the retarded. This World, *San Francisco Chronicle,* 34-35, December 13, 1964. Also, 1965 can be historic for the retarded. This World, *Chronicle,* 20-21, December 20, 1964.

Chapter 22

PERKINS SCHOOL FOR THE BLIND

EDWARD J. WATERHOUSE

IN 1966 all but nine of the fifty United States of America have well-established residential schools for blind children.* Most of these are state-operated; the three outstanding exceptions being The Overbrook School for the Blind in Philadelphia, The New York Institute for the Education of the Blind in New York and Perkins School for the Blind in Watertown, Massachusetts, a suburb of Boston. All these three opened their doors to blind children during the same year, 1832.

While no one person can be said to have been the sole founder of Perkins, the first man known to have recognized the need for a school for blind children in New England was Dr. John D. Fisher who, as a medical student in Paris, had visited *L'Institution National des Jeunes Aveugles* (The National Institution for Blind Youth). This was, and is, the parent of all schools for the blind on earth. It was founded in 1784, five years before the outbreak of the French Revolution by Valentin Hauy, the pioneer in whose footsteps walk all those who teach blind girls and boys.

In 1826 Dr. Fisher returned to his native Boston to become a medical practitioner. He shared his thoughts about educating blind children with a small group of his friends who met on an icy day in February 1829 at the Exchange Coffee House. He aroused their interest and they immediately applied to the Massachusetts Legislature for a charter. On March 2, 1829 the New England Asylum for the Blind was incorporated "to educate sightless persons."

The charter named thirty-nine prominent Bostonians as incorporators. These are indeed historically the founding fathers. Among them was John Fisher, himself, and the blind historian, William H. Prescott. Also included was a wealthy merchant, Thomas Handasyd Perkins, whose name the school was soon to bear. Included also were members of two Boston families who have provided the school with a succession of trustees. These were Thorndike and Lowell.

In 1830 the corporation elected its first officers and twelve trustees, one of

* States without schools are Alaska, Delaware, Maine, Nevada, New Hampshire, New Jersey, Rhode Island, Vermont, Wyoming. Children from these areas are accepted into schools elsewhere. Several states have more than one school.

whom was Horace Mann. Their first task was to find a man who would set their ideas to work.

Meanwhile another Boston physician, Samuel Gridley Howe, had come home from fighting and doctoring in the Greek War of Independence. On Boylston Street one day Howe met by chance with Fisher and some of his fellow trustees. "Here is Howe! The very man we have been looking for all the time!" said Fisher. The response was immediate: A "meeting of flint with steel," as Howe's daughter Laura described it some years later. Without realizing it, the founding fathers had made an historic decision.

The Howe Regime 1831-1876

The years which began with the accidental encounter between Fisher and Howe on Boylston Street in Boston were indeed important ones for blind children in all the years that followed. Decisions made then and standards then established still have their effect today not only in Boston but in distant corners of the globe.

Lessons from Europe

The story begins with Howe visiting European schools for the blind at the request of the trustees. On his return he wrote an extensive report which in many ways can still serve as a basis for educational programs for blind youth. He reported, "I visited all the principal institutions for the blind in Europe, and found in all much to admire and to copy, but much also to avoid." He was distressed by the inadequacy of programs as a whole. In France hc found, "There are only one in three hundred of their blind who receive an education."

With universal free education a burning issue in the United States at that time, it is not surprising that Dr. Howe, who was to become the close friend and collaborator of Horace Mann, should be dissatisfied with this situation and determined to provide a program which would be available to all blind persons who could profit from an education.

He found there was a grievous shortage of embossed books and other equipment, and much of this he felt was of poor design. He was particularly disappointed to find that most of the boys and girls on leaving school were ill prepared for adult life and that only a very few of them were able to support themselves. He was delighted, however, with the oustanding successes of a few, and recognized the great importance of these successes as examples for others. On the whole he decided that the European schools were "beacons to warn rather than lights to guide."

The happiest of his recollections was of boys from the school in Paris playing in a park where "they run away among the trees, and frolic and play together with all the zest and enjoyment of seeing children. They know every tree and shrub, they career it up one alley and down another, they chase, catch, overthrow and knock each other about, exactly like seeing boys; and to judge by their laughing faces, their wild and unrestrained gestures, and their loud and hearty shouts, they partake equally the delightful excitement of boyish play." Perhaps as a result of this observation, thousands of Perkins boys and girls were provided with such experiences.

He wanted to avoid anything which would restrict the normal growth of blind children. "We should depend entirely neither upon physical or intellectual education, nor should we lay down any general rule to be observed toward all pupils. One ought to be even more observant of the bent of a blind boy's mind, and the direction of his talent, than he is in the education of seeing children." This might serve as the charter of our guidance programs today.

He also recognized that blind persons must be encouraged to behave as normally as possible if they were to live satisfying lives in their own communities. "I would observe that sufficient attention is not paid to the personal demeanor of the blind, either by their parents, or in the public institutions, they contract disagreeable habits, whether in posture or in movement. . . . All of this can be corrected by pursuing the same means as used with seeing children and by accustoming them to society."*

The First Classes

The name under which the school was chartered indicates the attitude of Boston society to the blind at that time. While the word "asylum" did not have the same association with mental sickness that it acquired later, it indicated a refuge. Howe had no intention of providing anything of the sort. He proposed to offer a well-balanced education of academics, crafts, games and music, and when he referred to the school he usually called it the New England Institution for the Education of the Blind. He wanted his pupils to live lives as closely akin to those of their seeing brothers and sisters as possible.

While in Europe Dr. Howe recognized the advantages of having some blind teachers on his staff. He knew that it was not only the disinterested public and the over-concerned parents of the pupils who had to be shown that blind children could learn and that blind adults could support themselves. Blind children themselves needed encouragement, and the example of competent blind instructors was invaluable. When he returned from Europe Dr. Howe brought with him two blind men—M. Emile Trencheri from Paris to teach academic subjects, and Mr. John Pringle from Edinburgh to give instruction in crafts.

---

* These quotations are from Annual Reports of Perkins School for the Blind.

In July 1832, with two little girls as pupils—Sophia Carter, eight, and her six-year-old sister Abbey—Howe began teaching in his father's house at 140 Pleasant Street, Boston. By August the enrollment had increased to six, ranging in age from six to twenty years.

The Move to Pearl Street

The school soon outgrew the Howe family home. Thomas Handasyd Perkins, who was one of the trustees and vice-president, was a wealthy Boston merchant. In April 1833 he offered his home on Pearl Street for the use of the school, provided that during the month of May a fund of fifty thousand dollars be raised by wealthy persons for its support. This was done, for Boston society was already learning of Dr. Howe's school and giving it support as it has done most generously ever since. Support from a wider group of Bostonians came also in these very early years and a bazaar was held for it in Faneuil Hall.

Public Demonstrations

Although Dr. Howe had felt that European schools gave too much attention to public exhibitions, he soon recognized their importance. The school needed not only the financial support, but the understanding of the public, if his boys and girls were ever to be employed on completing their education. Every Saturday the school was thrown open and the pupils read aloud from their scanty supply of embossed books; wrote painstakingly, but in a legible script; performed arithmetical calculations; located geographical features on raised maps, and played musical instruments. Most of the visitors were deeply impressed, but some skeptics believed the children could actually see, and to counter this suspicion, Dr. Howe had the children wear strips of cloth over their eyes.

Demonstrations were also given in many public places, some of which were of great importance. Interest was aroused amongst legislators in the New England States, and several schools for the blind—including some in the Middle West—owe their origins to demonstrations by the Perkins' pupils in their state capitals.

Early Books and Equipment

When Dr. Howe returned from Europe he brought with him three embossed books acquired in France and England, which now form a part of the historical collection in the Perkins library. He soon recognized that education could not proceed without many good books. He also recognized that the cost of such books if they were made for the school alone would be prohibitive. Consequently, he set out to raise money by his own efforts to establish a printing department whose publications could be sold to institutions for the blind throughout the world, or could be used in exchange for books made by other presses, notably those in Scotland. His pioneering nature expressed itself in the design of a new font of type which became known as Boston Line Type. This is still used by the Howe Press at Perkins on the title pages of its braille books. Unfortunately, decades of controversy between proponents of different designs of type now began, and "the war of the types," which later involved several forms of braille, was not satisfactorily concluded until the 1920's.

Dr. Howe also recognized the need for maps and designed many himself. At his request, the school printer, Mr. S. P. Ruggles, designed and manufactured a giant embossed globe which nowadays has an honored place in the entrance to the Howe Building in Watertown.

Dr. Howe never solved the problem of embossed textbooks to his own satisfaction. He made efforts to establish a national library for the blind without avail, though his agitation no doubt paved the way for the founding in 1858 of The American Printing House for the Blind in Louisville, Kentucky. The printing department which he established in 1836 was the forerunner of the Howe Memorial Press established in his memory by his successors.

Music

The rules and regulations which the trustees drew up when the school opened required that "the pupils will be taught reading, writing, arithmetic, algebra, geography, history, physiology and such other subjects that are taught in the best common schools; beside vocal and instrumental music."

The school actually opened with a staff of five, including Dr. Howe and a matron. We have already mentioned M. Trencheri and Mr. Pringle. The third instructor was Mr. Lowell Mason, professor of music. Among the earliest appeals for funds by Dr. Howe was a request for two thousand dollars for pianofortes, organs and other instruments. Soon the school had thirteen pianos, and it was reported that they were kept in almost continual action from six o'clock in the morning until nine in the evening. Vocal music was much cultivated and with great success, the pupils giving public concerts which afforded "entire satisfaction to the audiences." Some of the pupils were prepared to become church organists. The curriculum for the day was "in general terms, the pupils devote four hours daily to intellectual labor; four hours to vocal and instrumental music; four to recreation and eating; four hours to manual labor and eight to sleep."

It is notable that even as early as the 1837 report Dr. Howe states that "we would also ask for our pupils a share of public patronage in the business of tuning pianofortes. Some of them can tune in the best style. Pianofortes will be kept in order by the year at a reasonable rate and the work warranted to give satisfaction to competent judges."

It should be noted also that in 1837 ten pupils had been discharged and "we are happy to add that all of them left under circumstances creditable to themselves and much benefited by the instruction they had received. One of them—A. W. Penniman—was employed by the trustees of the new institution in the State of Ohio to commence and direct their school, and he is now thus employed both respectably and profitably to himself. Charles Morrill, one of the earliest pupils, has become such a proficient in the science of vocal music that he readily found employment as a teacher and is now so employed in the Academy at Derry, N. H. He has large classes of seeing children under his charge and succeeds well. His knowledge of the organ and tuning pianofortes afford him additional means of obtaining a livelihood. Three of the others who had attended chiefly to mechanical employments have commenced work in their native towns and with the capacity and prospect of being able by industry and perseverance to obtain their own livelihood."

1837—A Memorable Year

An important event took place in 1837. Among the pupils admitted that year was Laura Bridgman, a seven-year-old child from New Hampshire. Laura, the first deaf-blind child ever to be successfully educated, was Dr. Howe's own personal pupil.

In this year, also, Dr. Howe opened a workshop. He did this reluctantly for he had hoped by including crafts in the school program and by giving a normal education to his boys and girls he could demonstrate satisfactorily to the wealthy manufacturers and merchants of Boston that blind men and women were desirable employees. While he never seemed to have much trouble in persuading his rich friends to open their pocketbooks, he found that they were extremely reluctant to add blind persons to their payrolls.

Consequently, he decided he would have a demonstration shop where blind men and women could obtain specific training in usable skills. He desired strongly to avoid patterns which he had observed in Europe in which the majority of the adult blind were employed permanently in sheltered workshops.

However, even with this demonstration shop, Howe was never able to place all of his pupils in satisfactory employ, and the workshop which opened in 1837 was to continue until 1952, the longest span of years of any American Workshop for the Blind to date.

> The main object of all these instrumentalities is to give to the pupils a store of useful knowledge; to develop in them the aesthetic sense; to train them up in vir-

tuous and industrious habits; to cultivate and strengthen their mental and bodily powers by systematic and constant exercise; and, lastly, to make them hardy and self-reliant, so that they may go out into the world, not to eat the bread of charity, but to earn a livelihood by honest work.

The Move to South Boston

In 1839 the school enrollment had grown to sixty-five and the Perkins residence on Pearl Street was no longer adequate. At this time the large hotel, known as the Mount Washington House at South Boston, came on the market. To provide funds for the purchase of this property, Mr. Perkins allowed his Pearl Street estate to be sold. This generous act was recognized by the corporation changing the name of the school to Perkins Institution and Massachusetts Asylum for the Blind.

Ten years after Dr. Howe met Dr. Fisher, he could look back on a remarkable achievement. The school had been founded and its finances, while strictly limited, were adequate for the moment. Certain principles and standards had been established which had already proved beneficial to the pupils in the school and which were to benefit many more as the years went by.

For another thirty-four years Howe directed the school, enlarging and improving the buildings. In 1870 he introduced, on a small scale, the cottage system of student living which is such an important feature of the school today. To the end of his life he emphasized always the desirability of training blind children for adult careers in which they would share to the fullest the lives of their families and participate in community life. Dr. Howe died in 1876 at the age of seventy-four.

The Anagnos Years

It was appropriate that Dr. Howe's successor, Michael Anagnos, should be a Greek. Howe had fought for the political independence of Greek citizens before he began laboring for the social and economic independence of blind men and women in America.

In 1867 Howe was back in Greece distributing relief supplies to the Cretans who were rebelling against the Turks. There he met Michael Anagnos who followed him back to Boston where he not only became his son-in-law, but served as his right-hand man during the last years of his life.

The international outlook which Howe brought to the school was maintained by Anagnos, and one of the first acts of his directorship was to cooperate with a school for the blind in Vienna in building up a Blindiana Library and Museum. In later years this library was to prove invaluable in our teacher-training programs.

Michael Anagnos had been a newspaper editor in Athens. His early struggles for an education made him sympathetic to the desire for learning wherever he found it, and this desire was strong among many blind boys and girls at Perkins. In his efforts to raise the standard of instruction to a higher level, he soon encountered the same shortage of embossed books which had plagued Dr. Howe. In spite of all Dr. Howe's efforts, the school printing press was small and inadequately financed. As a tribute to his predecessor, Michael Anagnos in 1881 established the Howe Memorial Press and appealed successfully to the public for funds for its endowment.

First Kindergarten for the Blind

Anagnos is best remembered for the "kindergarten for the blind" which he established in Jamaica Plain, a section of Boston, in 1887. Up until this time pupils were not usually accepted at Perkins below the age of eight or nine. In the new kindergarten they started as early as five. This school unit, which included not only a kindergarten year, but the first six grades, was generously financed by the people of Boston under the persistent and skillful urging of the school's second director.

Anne Sullivan and Helen Keller

Probably the incident in Michael Anagnos' career which is the best known throughout the world was his choice of Anne Sullivan, a recent graduate from Perkins, to go down to Alabama to work with the infant Helen Keller. Using only the reports which Dr. Howe had compiled of his work with Laura Bridgman, Anne Sullivan proved equal to the task of teaching language to Helen Keller. The two of them spent the years 1889 to 1893 at Perkins as the guests of Michael Anagnos whose encouragement was a major factor in the success of these two remarkable women.

Faculty Growth

Perhaps the real measure of Michael Anagnos' directorship was the spectacular increase in the number of teachers. When he became director in 1876 there were eleven teachers for 147 pupils, or one teacher to each thirteen children. Moreover, no fewer than five of these eleven were music teachers. For academic instruction there was one teacher for every twenty-nine pupils.

At the time of his death, which took place in Romania in 1906 in his seventieth year, there were two separate schools, the Lower School in Jamaica Plain, and the Upper School in South Boston. In the former, eighteen teachers (five of them for music) taught 118 children, a ratio of one to six and a half. Teachers of academic subjects were one to nine.

In the Upper School in South Boston forty-six teachers taught 171 pupils, a ratio of one to four. In academic subjects the ratio was one to nine, the same as in Jamaica Plain. This unique high ratio of teacher to pupils has been a characteristic feature of Perkins ever since.

Edward E. Allen, Educator

Dr. Howe was a physician, and Michael Anagnos, while a scholar, was primarily an editor. The school's third director, who succeeded Michael Anagnos on his death in 1907, was an educator. After graduating from Harvard he had taught for several years in the Royal Normal School for the Blind in London—a school whose first director was Francis Campbell, a former music teacher at Perkins. From London Dr. Allen returned to Boston where he taught at Perkins for several years. He was then appointed superintendent of the School for Blind in Philadelphia where he remained for sixteen years.

In 1906 he was called back to Boston on the death of Michael Anagnos, and almost immediately began a campaign to move the school from South Boston to some site where there would be space for greater physical activity. Quoting the philosophy of Francis Campbell, whom he greatly admired, he made a plea for facilities where the blind boys and girls could be brought up in a much more active manner than was possible within the narrow confines at South Boston. In 1910 he had found the spot he was looking for on the Stickney estate in Watertown, and during the next two years both the school in South Boston and the kindergarten in Jamaica Plain were moved to the present site.

Dr. Edward E. Allen is responsible for many firsts in the education of the blind. His strong interest in physical activity for youth led him to appoint the first trained physiotherapist in any school for the blind in 1908.

The Watertown plant carried to fruition the cottage family plan inaugurated by Dr. Howe, but Dr. Allen immediately recognized that for the plan to succeed as he hoped, it was necessary that a much closer contact between the Perkins Cottage Family and the pupils' own families was desirable. In 1916 he appointed a home visitor, the first ever to serve a school for the blind on a full-time basis. A year or two later, together with the Overbrook School for the Blind, Dr. Allen engaged the services of Dr. Samuel P. Hayes, head of the Psychology Department at Mt. Holyoke College, to prepare the first psychological tests for blind children. These tests—known as the Hayes-Binet Tests—successfully demonstrated for the first time that the population of blind people does not differ in intelligence from the population of the seeing. There is approximately the same percentage of superior, normal and inferior blind as you find among seeing boys and girls.

In 1920 Dr. Allen took the first steps towards placing the education of blind children on a professional level comparable to the best public and private schools in the country. In this year, the first graduate-level teacher-training program for teachers of the blind was established at Perkins in cooperation with Harvard University. In 1924 Dr. Allen appointed the first speech therapist as a full-time employee in a school for the blind.

By the end of the first century of the school's history when Dr. Allen retired, the shape of Perkins as we know it today, its ideals and its standards were firmly established.

The three directors who headed the school throughout this century were all mindful of the fact that the population of blind people is a relatively small one. The blind would always be a minority group, and consequently, if blind men and women were to take their place among the seeing majority, they must make a greater effort to exceed in whatever they set out to accomplish.

In a larger sense, however, it was not so much the efforts of these three men that made the school what it is today, but the fact that throughout ten decades the challenges which these directors and their staffs hurled at their pupils were picked up and eagerly accepted, and in many cases exceeded. All that the Perkins faculty could do was to offer opportunities to their boys and girls. It was the good use to which these young people put these opportunities that made Perkins a great success. The history of the school was written rather in the efforts of Sophie Carter, the first blind child to come to Perkins, and her many successors: such as Laura Bridgman, A. W. Penniman, Stephen Blaisdell, Anne Sullivan and Helen Keller.

Second Century

On the retirement of Dr. Edward E. Allen and the appointment of Dr. Gabriel Farrell to succeed him, the school started on its second century. Dr. Farrell, who was an Episcopalian minister of varied experience, brought to the school a vigor and organizing ability that led to immediate improvements.

One of his first tasks was to organize the work for the deaf-blind into a special department under the leadership of Miss Inez B. Hall, a pioneer in the use of the vibration technique of teaching deaf-blind children to speak.

In Dr. Farrell's early years also many improvements in the business of the institution took place, and a notable event was the creation of the office of bursar to handle business affairs. In these years, too, the school which had virtually been three schools, Lower School, Boys Upper School and Girls Upper School, combined into a single unit with the educational program under the control of a single principal.

The Perkins Lantern

Dr. Farrell was an experienced journalist and it was natural that as a result he should inaugurate a magazine to acquaint friends of Perkins with the affairs of the school. This magazine, *The Lantern,* which is issued quarterly in print and braille form, was established in 1931. It has done much to acquaint workers in this field with the school's endeavors and to bring it many friends among the general public. It also serves to keep former students more closely in touch with their school.

The years of World War II were difficult ones for the school and a number of the older boys left earlier than they would have otherwise to obtain employment. However, the changing situation in the labor market since World War II has brought about many new opportunities for employment among the blind. The goal which Dr. Howe sought of finding unsheltered employment for all the boys and girls of the school finally became a reality in the closing years of Dr. Farrell's directorship which ended in 1951.

The Fifth Director

As a result of this changing economic situation, one of the first acts of the fifth director, Dr. Edward J. Waterhouse, who succeeded Dr. Farrell in 1951, was the closing of the workshop which Dr. Howe established in 1837. This workshop was partly rendered superfluous by the establishment in recent years of state workshops. For over a decade no Perkins pupil had sought employment in the Perkins shop. It was only a matter of time before the plant would close down of its own volition. It seemed wiser to bring about a more orderly demise, and the workshop was officially closed in June 1952.

While the last decade is too close to the present for evaluation, certain events may be recorded. The work of Dr. Hayes, encouraged by both Dr. Allen and Dr. Farrell, led in turn to the establishment of a guidance department employing several clinical psychologists. Dr. Allen had added a psychometrist to the staff, a practice which Dr. Farrell had continued. In the 1950's guidance counseling became an important part of the school program.

The Retrolental-fibroplasia Wave

The first child to be admitted to Perkins whose blindness was caused by retrolental-fibroplasia was enrolled in 1946. This disease which resulted from excessive exposure of prematurely born infants to oxygen was soon to add thousands of girls and boys to schools and classes for the blind in the 1950's. Fortunately this disease was rapidly brought under control and it is a rare event for a child to lose his sight for this reason nowadays. At Perkins, where the enrollment has been steadily declining, an immediate increase was experienced. Between 1946 and 1951, while the Upper School population decreased by twenty-eight the Lower School increased by thirty-two. Soon the total school population, which had declined to 234 in 1943 was in excess of 300.

This increase would have been far greater had it not been for the rapid increase at this time of classes for blind children in the public schools throughout the United States. This was largely the result of the retrolental-fibroplasia wave and the desire of parents to keep their children at home. In a few years more than half the blind children in America were being educated in this way. Had it not been for this program in New England, Perkins would have been forced to increase its capacity considerably.

The Deaf-Blind Department

The Deaf-Blind Department which had flourished since its organization in 1931 until the outbreak of World War II was in serious danger of collapse in the years which followed the war. There was an acute national shortage of trained teachers of the deaf—the source upon which Perkins has mainly drawn for its teachers for its deaf-blind children. It became necessary for Perkins to establish its own program for training teachers of the deaf-blind which was worked out in cooperation with Boston University in 1955. A program of research was also established in the Deaf-Blind Department at this time. The department grew from five pupils in 1953 to forty pupils in 1964, making it by far the largest in the world. It included over one third of all deaf-blind pupils in special programs in the United States.

Education of the Public

Ever since Dr. Howe's days, it has been recognized at Perkins that one of the important responsibilities of a school for the blind is to educate the public wherever possible concerning the abilities of blind persons. The demonstrations which Dr. Howe inaugurated are still carried out, though nowadays they are held annually instead of weekly. Modern methods of mass education are now used, and during recent years, two professional motion picture films—one entitled *The Perkins Story* and the other dealing with the Deaf-Blind Department and entitled *Children of the Silent Night,* have been produced for the school. Over a hundred copies of these two films are in constant use throughout the world and have had a remarkable effect upon the school's program. Incoming mail shows a great increase in interest in what the school is doing and an increased request for assistance in all forms, sometimes coming from distant parts of the world.

Overseas Interests

Probably the first example of the influence of Perkins and its ideas overseas was the choice by Dr. Armitage in London of Francis Campbell from the Perkins staff to head the Royal Normal School for the Blind. Here the debt which Dr. Howe acknowledged from the lessons he learned from visiting schools in Europe was in some measure repaid.

As has been mentioned, Michael Anagnos worked out a cooperative arrangement with schools in Europe for the exchange of equipment and literature. However, it was with the establishment of a teacher-training program at Harvard in the 1920's that opportunities for serving blind children overseas really began. Ever since this course started applications were received from candidates from other countries and by 1960 there were graduates of the two teacher-training programs teaching blind children in between forty and forty-five foreign lands.

Partly as a result of this Perkins has enrolled a number of blind pupils from overseas. Perkins graduates are found today in many lands, some of them engaged in the education of the blind and others leading successful lives in various fields.

Unchanging Pupils

Were Dr. Howe to return to the school he would find that many of his dreams had been fulfilled. He would wholeheartedly endorse the spirit of determination of the blind and deaf-blind boys and girls of today to overcome their handicap of blindness in the same way that they did in the school's early years. He would be particularly gratified to find that virtually all pupils leaving the school have become economically and socially independent.

Postscript

PROMISES TO KEEP AND MILES TO GO

ERNEST P. WILLENBERG

THE topic of my presentation is a line from Robert Frost which contains the words: ". . . promises to keep and miles to go. . . " This title seems especially appropriate to those of us in special education who feel a deep commitment to children with special needs and the enormity of the task which lies ahead.

You may recall the past National Convention theme of The Council for Exceptional Children in Portland was: *New Frontiers in Special Education.* The program for the International Convention in Toronto had as its major subject: *Exceptional Children: Strategies for Educational Progress.*

In preparation for my meeting with you this afternoon, I have gone through the Toronto program in search for key words or phrases on which to hitch a few ideas or thoughts. The search was fruitful for it did yield the structure upon which the "promises to keep and miles to go" in special education are validated in the contemporary concerns of more than 4600 program participants. Let us look at some of these themes in an hierarchial arrangement and assess the current status of each.

PHILOSOPHY

Among the words in common usage in special education is the term *philosophy*. Philosophy is defined as knowledge of general principles—elements, powers, or causes and laws—as explaining facts and existences. Philosophy deals with the general laws that furnish the rational explanation of everything. It is a study of the origin, nature and ultimate destiny of man. It is the substance from which man derives power and obtains direction for the expenditure of energy. It provides the scope for the sequence of his existence.

One of the fallacies extant is the idea that there is a philosophy of special education. One might even go so far as to challenge the notion that such a thing as a "philosophy of education" exists. If any of you in the audience teach or have taken a course on philosophy of education, please bear with me, for it is not my purpose to devaluate the offerings that may be provided under the aegis of such a course title. My point is to merely suggest that what we call a philosophy of special education may be more appropriately entitled something else. Probably a theory of special education is the title we are searching for. Let us consider this point for a moment.

THEORY

(The Perfectibility of Man)

In 1835 Alexis De Toqueville stated that "The Americans have all a lively faith in the perfectibility of man. They judge that the diffusion of knowledge must necessarily be advantageous, and the consequences of ignorance fatal. They all consider society as a body in a state of improvement, humanity as a changing scene, in which nothing is, or ought to be permanent. And they admit that what appears to them today to be good, may be superseded by something better tomorrow."

Although this statement was made more than 130 years ago, it would be my contention that if the foregoing were to be proposed today as the theoretical basis for public education in the United States, it would be overwhelmingly supported. Such a theory implies a plan or scheme existing in the minds of man based upon principles verifiable by experiment or observation.

The "lively faith in the perfectibility of man" of which De Toqueville spoke, has its modern interpretation in the Pledge to Children of the Midcentury White House Conference on Children and Youth. The pledge affirms the following:

> We will provide you with rewarding educational opportunities, so that you may develop your talents and contribute to a better world.
>
> We will protect you against exploitation and undue hazards and help you grow in health and strength.
>
> So may you grow in joy, in faith in God and in men, and in those qualities of vision and of the spirit that will sustain us all and give us new hope for the future.

At the very core of a theory of special education, then, is the ideal of the *perfectibility* of exceptional children—faith in them and in their ability to achieve higher levels of wisdom and accomplishment. At this time in history it is imperative that man have faith in man and in his own institutions. Or, as Voltaire so aptly expressed it, "He who has not the spirit of his age, has all the miseries of it." But theory alone is not enough. There is the next step which involves the *transformation of theory into practice*.

RATIONALE

(The Concept of Ecology)

What is the benefit for special education? The rationale for public education is that society has collective *responsibility* for the protection and general welfare of all of its members. Included in the concept of general welfare is the provision of tax supported public education ($10 billion Federal funds) which has been liberalized to include programs for increasing varieties and numbers of divergent children and youth and, furthermore, extended offerings for adults and higher education. Never before has the world been so sensitive to the imperatives of education in the general scheme of social and political life. Not only is public education provided in accordance with the principles established many years ago, but new principles are being enunciated by recent enactment of Federal legislation. No longer is it sufficient to say that society is responsible for providing a common education for all its members. Society provides for its defense through the *National Defense Education Act,* for the eradication of poverty and dependency through the *Economic Opportunity Act.* By means of state and Federal enactments as well as local actions, the public school is coming to be regarded as an instrument to *facilitate rapid social change.* Such is the climate in which we live that never before has it been so clearly visible that schools are responsible for more than the perpetuation of the national culture. Hardly have the schools recovered from the public reaction against the methods of the professional strategists when there is thrust upon the professional strategists of this generation such responsibilities that progressive educators of a previous generation would never have dared to assume. Such are the vicissitudes of our times and our trade.

Let me now propose for your consideration a tentative rationale for special education by drawing upon the language of biology using the term *ecology* to denote the relationship between the organism and its environment. More specifically, as used here, ecology has to do with the relationship between the internal and external environment of the individual. By definition, the internal environment is deemed to be the organic substance and ability of the individual to establish a reciprocal relation with the external environment in the evolvement of modification of growth and development, cultural characteristics and in the adaptation of behavior followed upon and induced by and as a result of experiences leading to the establishment of new patterns of response to external stimuli. Thus the external environment is the force from *without,* whereas the internal environment is the force from *within.*

Often have we heard posed the question, "What is special about special education?" I would submit to you that the *rationale for special education* submits very readily to an exposition of those principles that form the logical basis for an optimal relationship between the internal and external by means of the many mediating resources available to the exceptional child.

Starting with some of the common examples in everyday experience, let us then work up to the specific cases in point that illustrate what we mean.

Take the case of the ordinary plant. Other things being equal, the plant will grow and thrive in the land in which it is indigenous. But now change one *variable*—the variable of light—and what happens? The plant withers and dies. It is not because the internal environment (organic ability) has failed to do its job; it is because the external condition was modified in such a way (the light was changed) as to be beyond the means of the internal resources of the plant to cope with the change in relationship. In some instances plants possess the internal resources to send out long tentacles until the proper relationship can be established. In this latter instance the modification the external condition of light resulted in a reciprocal change in the internal structure of the plant to cope with the problem of its survival. But enough of plant life: let us deal with the ecology of people—more particularly exceptional children.

What is the ecological problem of the individual who suffers intellectual deficit? What are the means by which the best possible ecological balance may be achieved?

What about the crippled child? The child with sensory deprivation? The child whose emotional behavior is disordered? The environmentally deprived child? And others?

If we are able to accept the principles of ecology as applied to special education, then let us move on to the next step in the hierarchical arrangement of themes in our consideration of the "promises to keep and miles to go" in special education.

DESIGN

(Taxonomy Involving the Structure for Scope and Sequence in Learning Opportunity)

We now have a logical basis upon which to assess the special educational needs of exceptional pupils. The rationale for special education is to help the individual child restore or achieve the best possible ecological balance between his internal resources and his external environment. The next step is to *design* the kind of program that combines the best of our scientific knowledge with the art and skill essential to the task at hand. The creative program designer is a rare creature; he is the visionary, the theorist, the idealist, the realist, the scientist, the technician and the artist rolled into one.

The program designer has an awful tradition to circumvent. Somehow or other he has to move around the obstacle of our firmly entrenched diagnostic categories and come up with the more appropriate educational classifications applicable to the tasks in special education. It is not enough to cate-

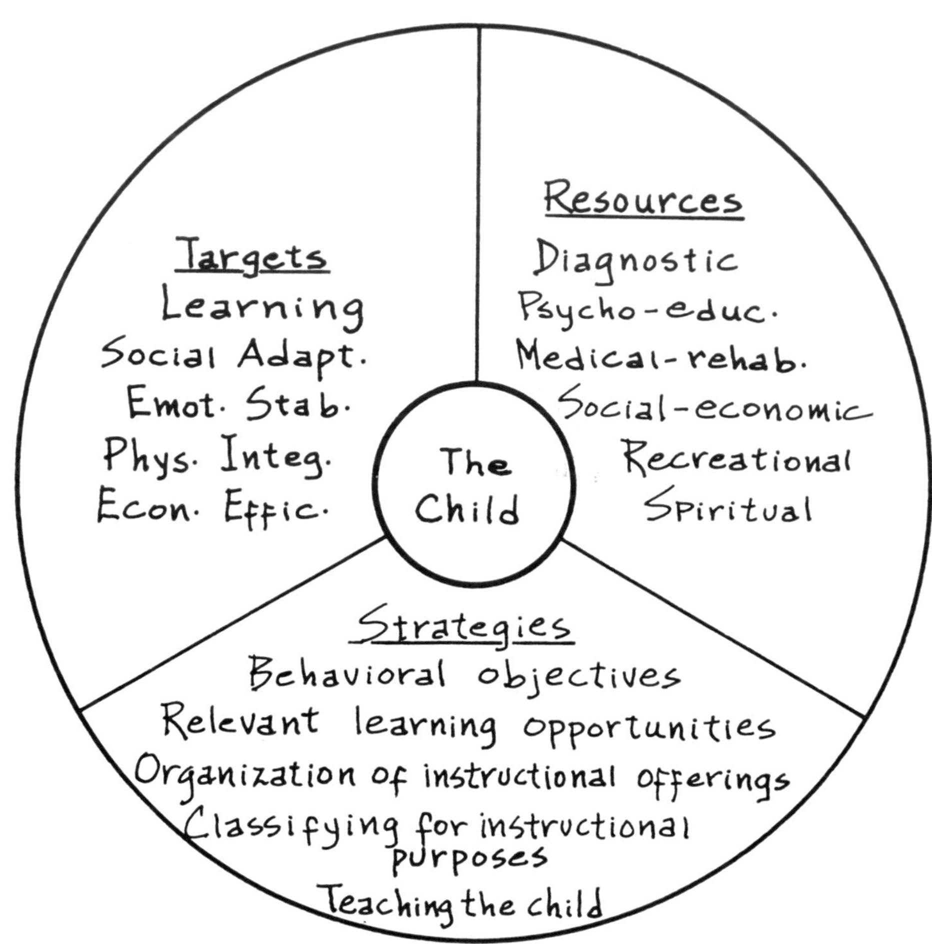

gorize a child as mentally retarded, as emotionally disturbed, as having a learning disorder, etc. Our design for a special education program must take into consideration *what* the program is going to *do* in order to help the exceptional pupil achieve that ecological balance we seek. And in many instances, that program design for special education must take into consideration the kinds of modifications in the external environment essential to effective reciprocal relations. It is not appropriate or possible for me to suggest to you a tentative *model* for program design based upon that department of knowledge that embodies the laws and principles of classification. I have reference to a *taxonomy* for special education which would give us a systematic arrangement of the internal and external imbalances shown in relationship to modifications or actions needed in juxtaposition with the resources essential to a comprehensive special education and rehabilitation program.

STRATEGY AND TACTICS

Leadership

The final step in this hierarchical arrangement brings us to the subject of educational strategy—the generalship or skill in management involving the science and art of leadership. The strategy is usually concerned with long range objectives. Whereas tactics are for the more immediate objectives and involve any maneuvering or adroit management to affect the objectives.

There are some who say there is no such thing as a special curriculum for exceptional children—but there are special strategies and tactics. I would like to employ the concept of strategy in the sense of differentiating between *administration* and *leadership.*

There is a science and an art of leadership. Administration may differ from leadership. Administration may provide an umbrella of orderliness. Administration may be interested in the maintenance of the status quo and public relations. Administration may be most interested in avoiding dissension or dispute.

Leadership may be diametrically opposed to this. It may be concerned with throwing things off balance. Leadership is interested in foraging into the unknown, acting in the forefront.

It is a rare quality in an administrator that he be a leader. Important transitions are being made. We are beginning to conceptualize what special education is all about.

CONCLUSION

In conclusion, let me affirm that the main task of special education is the same as that of education in general—to teach children to learn and to keep on learning. We are in the business of modifying behavior and development of the cognitive processes involving the acquisition of knowledge and skills and values. We have made progress, but there remains much progress to be made. Goethe has observed that "Progress has not followed a straight ascending line, but a spiral with rhythms of progress and retrogression, of evolution and dissolution." It is as if Goethe had in mind the history of education and of special education in particular. There has been time barely to intimate only a part of the opportunities in the contemporary mood of progress and evolution in our work with exceptional children. Although change is not synonymous with progress, in the words of Robert Browning, "Progress is the law of life." For those who fear the future and resist change there is a verse by Frank L. Stanton called "Keep A-goin'," which may express just the right kind of sentiment:

If you strike a thorn or rose,
Keep a-goin'!
If it hails or if it snows,
Keep a-goin'!
'Taint no use to sit and whine
'Cause the fish ain't on your line;
Bait your hook and
Keep on trying!
Keep a-goin'!

It is not easy to talk about the distance we have come without relating it to the journey we are traveling and distance yet to go. Each one of us embarked upon some kind of mission the very moment we entered the field of special education. I have the notion there is a way that each of you can affirm the relevance of these lines from Robert Frost:

The woods are lovely, dark and deep.
But I have promises to keep
And miles to go before I sleep,
And miles to go before I sleep.

INDEX

D

E

F

J

K

L

M

N